Lebanon

the Bradt Travel Guide

Paul Doyle

edition
I

www.bradtguides.com

Bradt Travel Guides Ltd, UK
The Globe Pequot Press Inc, USA

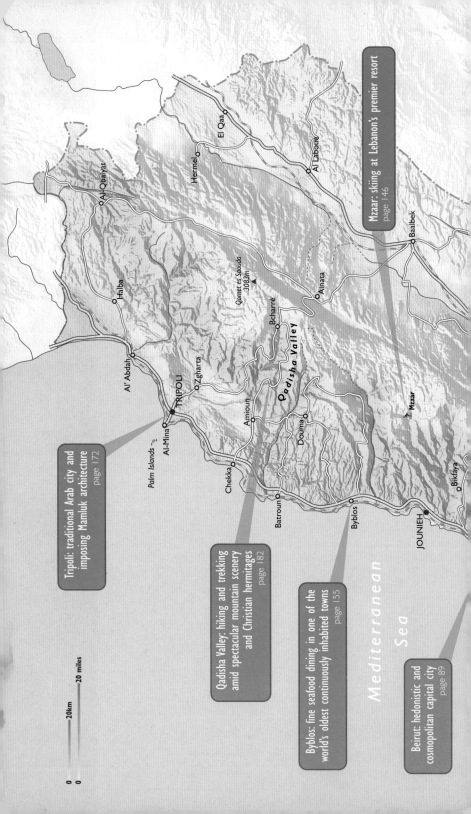

Tripoli: traditional Arab city and imposing Mamluk architecture
page 172

Qadisha Valley: hiking and trekking amid spectacular mountain scenery and Christian hermitages
page 182

Byblos: fine seafood dining in one of the world's oldest continuously inhabited towns
page 155

Beirut: hedonistic and cosmopolitan capital city
page 89

Mzaar: skiing at Lebanon's premier resort
page 146

20km
20 miles
0
0

Al-Qbaiyat

El Qaa

Hermel

Al Laboué

Baalbek

Halba

Qornet es Saouda
3083m

Ainata

Zgharta

Bcharré

Al' Abdah

TRIPOLI

Amioun

Qadisha Valley

Al-Mina

Palm Islands

Chekka

Douma

Mzaar

Batroun

Byblos

Bikfaya

JOUNIEH

Mediterranean Sea

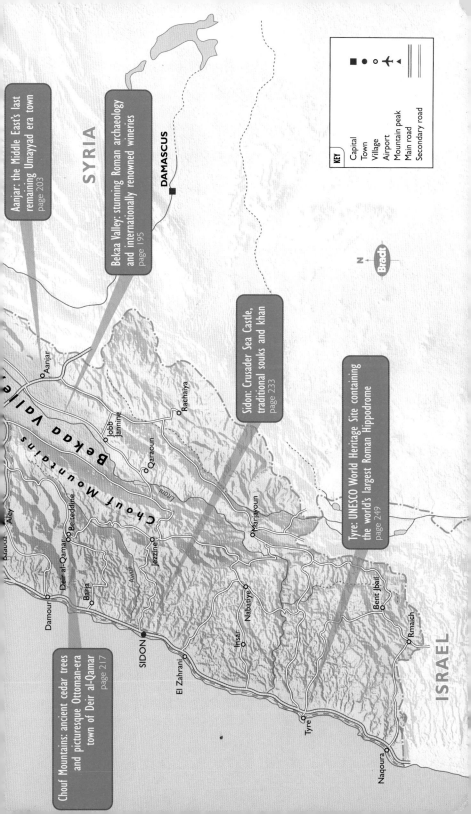

SYRIA

Aanjar: the Middle East's last remaining Umayyad era town
page 203

Bekaa Valley: stunning Roman archaeology and internationally renowned wineries
page 195

DAMASCUS

Chouf Mountains: ancient cedar trees and picturesque Ottoman-era town of Deir al-Qamar
page 217

Sidon: Crusader Sea Castle, traditional souks and khan
page 233

Tyre: UNESCO World Heritage Site containing the world's largest Roman Hippodrome
page 249

ISRAEL

N
Bradt

Chouf Mountains

Bekaa Valley

Daouud
Aley
Aanjar
Bdadoun
Damour
Deir al-Qamar
Beiteddine
Baria
Jobb Jannine
Qaraoun
Rachaiya
Awali
Jezzine
SIDON
El Zahrani
Insar
Nabatiye
Litani
Marjayoun
Bent Jbail
Rmaich
Tyre
Naqoura

Lebanon
Don't
miss...

Byblos
The town of Byblos has
been in existence for
7,000 years, making it a
contender for the world's
oldest continuously
inhabited town
(PD) page 155

Baalbek
The Baalbek complex contains some
of the largest and most impressive
Roman remains in the world
(PD) page 210

Jeita Grotto
This karstic limestone landscape, fashioned by geology, time and water, has resulted in a stunning array of stalactite and stalagmite rock formations
(PD) page 149

Beiteddine Palace
The home of Lebanon's final ruling prince, Beiteddine Palace was built over a 30-year period using Italian architects and highly skilled artisans from Damascus
(PD) page 225

National Museum, Beirut
Lebanon's premier museum is arguably the first sight to visit in the country, in order to gain an overview of the history and peoples that have helped to shape its development
(SS) page 130

above left Traditional building, Beirut; the city once boasted the nickname of the 'Paris of the Middle East' (SS) page 89

above The ornate interior of Beirut's iconic Muhammad Al-Amine Mosque (SS) page 126

left Cafés at night, Nejmeh Place; with an ever increasing number of bars, cafés, discos and nightclubs, Beirut's nightlife has something for everyone (SS) page 110

below A stroll along the Corniche is a ritual that should be undertaken by every visitor to Beirut (PD) page 125

above The Ottoman Clock Tower in Downtown Beirut was built in 1897 in honour of the tenth anniversary of the coronation of Sultan Abdel Hamid (PD) page 126

right A monument to the 1975–90 civil war, the *Hope for Peace* at Yarze is one of the world's largest modern sculptures (PD) page 134

below Beirut's 60m-high Pigeon Rocks are relics from one of the numerous earthquakes that have afflicted the city (SS) page 125

REASON 207

REASON 205

REASON 206

روتانا
R∘tana

More reasons to book your next vacation at Rotana

There are 365 different reasons for you to book
with Rotana.
Enjoy the superior comfort and services of our
hotels, with three locations near major shopping
centers, business districts, downtown and
its vibrant nightlife.

To learn more about our offers please call:
Gefinor Rotana on 00961 1371888,
Hazmieh Rotana on 00961 5458000
and Raouché Arjaan by Rotana on 00961 1781111
or email us on marketing.lebanon@rotana.com

Gefinor
R∘tana
Beirut

Hazmieh
R∘tana
Beirut

Raouché
Arjaan
by Rotana
Beirut

rotana.com

AUTHOR

Paul Doyle was born and brought up in Hampshire, England, where his youthful excursions around the county helped sow the seeds for his enduring interest in travel. Following a few years working in the aviation industry, a new departure eventually beckoned and he decided to pursue a career as a freelance photographer. He began to work for a variety of public-sector clients, with travel to Arab lands such as Jordan, Lebanon, Libya and Syria fitted into his schedule. His travel photography has subsequently appeared widely in in-flight magazines, books and travel guides both in the UK and overseas. His interest in travel
writing developed out of his part-time photography degree, where his earlier social science education had been instrumental in inspiring him to undertake a final year photojournalistic project documenting the reconstruction of post-war Beirut. Following more than 20 years residing in west London, Paul has now decamped back to Hampshire where he hopes that the ongoing reconstruction at his beloved football club, Portsmouth, will lead to a similar change in the club's fortunes, and that alternate Saturdays spent at Fratton Park may once again become tear free.

For further information visit www.pauldoylefoto.co.uk.

AUTHOR'S STORY

When I decided to embark on a photojournalistic study of Beirut's post-war reconstruction for my degree project in photography, Lebanon seemed to fit the bill perfectly as a destination that had been off the tourist radar for many years but was familiar to the world through the reports and images of its devastating 15-year long civil war. I wanted to learn more about this tiny but significant country which had entered the public consciousness in an overtly negative manner. I recall one evening sitting in a bar quenching my thirst on the local brew *almaza*, listening to the sound of the 1970s Bee Gees' hit *Stayin' Alive*, when it occurred to me that Beirut and Lebanon were doing much more than that. Stained by the blood of war Lebanon may have been but the friendliness and hospitality of the Lebanese never ceased to amaze me, nor their desire to move forward and rebuild their shattered country. Lebanon without doubt represents the pinnacle of my forays to Arab countries. Despite its civil war, the country offers so much variety in cultural, historical and political terms when compared to Jordan, Syria and its other neighbours, and provides probably the best introduction to any visitor wanting to appreciate and gain a greater understanding of the Middle East. Even beyond its familiar and strategic importance in the region, another aspect of Lebanon's draw are those moments spent just walking around the capital and chatting to someone in the street or in a bar or café; you might find yourself striking up a conversation with someone on a bus or with a farmer in the Bekaa Valley leading his flock across the road. Moments like these enhance the travel experience in Lebanon and change any lingering stereotypical preconceptions. Furthermore, they come on top of other wonderful experiences the country has to offer, such as the soaring Roman temples at Baalbek or nature's remarkable handywork at Jeita Grotto.

Lebanon offers geographical proof of the maxim 'size doesn't matter' – a tiny country that can nevertheless cater to the interests of a wide variety of tourists, from dedicated clubbers to history buffs. It has witnessed much violence, of course, but in recent years the renaissance of Beirut has been much lauded, and Lebanon has enjoyed a significant growth in tourist traffic. This is a forward-looking nation with arguably the greatest commitment of any in the Middle East to the civil rights and freedoms of its people. It was notable by its absence on the Bradt list; I'm so pleased that Paul Doyle has rectified that with a book that's filled with a deep knowledge of, and passion for, this pint-sized country.

First published January 2012
Bradt Travel Guides Ltd
IDC House, The Vale, Chalfont St Peter, Bucks SL9 9RZ, England
www.bradtguides.com
Published in the USA by The Globe Pequot Press Inc,
PO Box 480, Guilford, Connecticut 06437-0480

Text copyright © 2012 Paul Doyle
Maps copyright © 2012 Bradt Travel Guides Ltd
Photographs copyright © 2012 Individual photographers (see below)
Project Manager: Elspeth Beidas

ISBN: 978 1 84162 370 2

British Library Cataloguing in Publication Data
A catalogue record for this book is available from the British Library

Photographs Paul Doyle (PD), Keith Erskine/Alamy (KE/A), Edward Karaa/Dreamstime. com (EK/D), SuperStock (SS)
Front cover Carving at Baalbek (SS)
Back cover Lebanese coffee (KE/A), Tripoli (SS)
Title page Cedar tree (PD), Druze man (SS), Traditional building, Beirut (SS)
Maps David McCutcheon (regional maps in this guide based on ITM map *Lebanon*, Beirut maps in this guide based on ITM map *Beirut* and *Zawarib Beirut & Beyond*)
Colour map Relief map base by Nick Rowland FRGS

Typeset from the author's disc by D & N Publishing, Baydon, Wiltshire
Production managed by Jellyfish Print Solutions; printed in India

Acknowledgements

Paul Doyle would like to thank the following people who have all proved extremely helpful during the production of this guide with their information and assistance in one form or another. A couple of big 'shukran's go to Nada Sardouk, Director General of Lebanon's Ministry of Tourism, and Joumana Nakhlé at Lebanon's Ministry of Culture for their invaluable assistance and information. Thank you to Louise Rutherford at BMI for kindly putting an Airbus at my disposal for my visits to Lebanon. To the staff at Rotana Hotels in Beirut and the Grand Hotel Kadri in Zahlé for their assistance with accommodation and for ensuring my stays were memorable ones. To Rami Hasan at the Mleeta Resistance Tourist Landmark for his knowledge and hospitality. A big thank you also to Lilian Button, Kay Johnson and my father John for their support and advice. For her expertise and invaluable help with language and translation, a huge 'shukran jazeelan' to Magda Gholam. To the many travellers I have met during my Lebanese journey who have chipped in with useful advice and information about their experiences. In particular, thank you to Mariko Sato and Martin Bader and Diane and Gaëlle. The many Lebanese I have met along the way who have always been courteous and friendly and provided valuable local knowledge about their country and who help make Lebanon such a welcoming and fascinating destination for travellers, serving to deepen my affection for this wonderful little nation. Thanks also to Nicolas Succarieh and Sarah al-Sarraf at the Lebanese Commuting Company (LCC) for their time and help with bus transport information. And last but not least, a debt of gratitude to Assadour Andekian at the Aanjar archaeological site for his encyclopaedic knowledge and assistance with mapping.

And, finally, a special thanks to all the friendly staff at Bradt for their assistance and support during this project and for continuing to commission guides to less mainstream, yet totally rewarding, destinations. In particular, I would like to thank Adrian Phillips, Publishing Director at Bradt, for commissioning this guide in the first place, and to Elspeth Beidas and Emma Thomson for their expertise with editing and valuable comments.

DEDICATION

To my grandparents, with love.

UPDATES WEBSITE AND FEEDBACK REQUEST

As with all travel guides, things change. This is especially true of a country such as Lebanon, an emerging and dynamic nation whose facilities and services for visitors are constantly developing as quickly as its politics. New hotels, restaurants, bars and services are constantly opening (and closing), and prices go up (and even down!); keeping abreast of developments is a perennial work in progress. The author and Bradt would be delighted to hear from travellers about their experiences – good and bad – so as to make future editions even more relevant to the next generation of travellers. Please contact Bradt on ✆ 01753 893444 or e info@bradtguides.com. Alternatively you can add a review of the book to www.bradtguides.com or Amazon. You can also email the author direct at info@pauldoylefoto.co.uk.

Periodically our authors post travel updates and reader feedback on the Bradt website. Check www.bradtguides.com/guidebook-updates for any news.

Contents

NOTE ABOUT MAPS

Several maps use grid lines to allow easy location of sites. Map grid references are listed in square brackets after listings in the text, with page number followed by grid number, eg: [104 C3].

LIST OF MAPS

Introduction

Lebanon is unique in comparison to its Arab neighbours: there is no desert, it is the most religiously diverse country in the region, alcohol is freely available almost everywhere and it is the most heavily wooded country in the Middle East. Yet nothing has demonstrated Lebanon's distinctive character more than its involvement – or lack thereof – in the recent wave of turmoil that has engulfed the region from Tunisia to Bahrain and, latterly, Syria. It is perhaps indicative of Lebanon's unique and pluralistic history and culture that the country has been insulated from the tumultuous events of the Arab Spring, whose effects have been so significant elsewhere. Yet Lebanon's peculiar history has not left it without its own issues and problems, some of which have spawned their own tensions and conflicts over the years, often fuelled by foreign interference. Despite these problems, the mixture of history, cultures and religions found within Lebanon make the country a fascinating introduction to the broader Middle East region, an area of equally variable climate and terrain.

Lebanon is a pint-sized country accounting for around 2% of the size of the landmass of its former colonial ruler, France. It may be small on a global map, but, like the tardis in the *Dr Who* TV series, appearances can be deceptive, and Lebanon manages to pack a lot in within its diminutive borders. Visitors can indulge in a *mezze* of pursuits and attractions, from the hedonistic nightlife of cities such as Beirut and Jounieh to more sedate activities such as walking the Lebanon Mountain Trail or hiking in the Qadisha Valley and exploring some of the country's least visited areas. Adrenalin junkies can take to the slopes of Lebanon's many ski resorts or paraglide around mountain vistas while culture and history buffs can delight in perambulating the UNESCO World Heritage Sites at Baalbek, Byblos and Tyre to gain an appreciation of the legacy of the country's 7,000 years of history, left by wave after wave of civilisations including the likes of the Phoenicians, Romans and various Arab dynasties.

Of course, not everything in the Lebanese garden is rosy and the country, like the region as a whole, faces many challenges. The sectarian divide remains intact, as does the confessional-based system of power politics. Tensions still exist between Israel and Hezbollah along Lebanon's southern border, and it remains to be seen what, if any, are the ramifications of the issuing of indictments against suspects for the 2005 killing of former prime minister Rafiq Hariri. In economic terms, Lebanon has weathered the global downturn much better than the majority of countries around the world, but major infrastructure projects such as improvements to the country's roads and electricity supply need ongoing development.

Despite the many problems that Lebanon faces – and will no doubt overcome if its history is anything to go by – the country is an inherently safe place for tourists and other visitors. It is also one of the easiest to visit in the Middle East, with none of the bureaucratic red tape which characterises other Arab countries such as Iran and Libya. Although the media and marketing departments, both in Lebanon and overseas, continue to wax lyrical about the renaissance of Beirut as the born again 'Paris' and party centre of the Middle East, you shouldn't hesitate to travel beyond the capital and explore the host of other natural and manmade attractions that the country offers. If you have not previously been to the Middle East or perhaps have only visited places such as Dubai, Lebanon will certainly come as something of a culture shock. However, its infinite variety is one of the best introductions to the Middle East you can find. I hope that you will find this guide a helpful companion on your Lebanese journey and that you leave, like I have, with an enduring fascination and love for the country and the Arab world.

Part One

GENERAL INFORMATION

Full name Republic of Lebanon (Al-Jumhuriyah al-Lubnaniyah in Arabic, République Libanaise in French)

Location West Asia at the eastern end of the Mediterranean Sea: 33°50' N, 35°50' E. Borders Syria in the north and east, and Israel in the south.

Size 10,452km²

Climate Mediterranean with hot dry summers and mild wet winters. Heavy winter snow in the mountains.

Status Republic, independent from France since 1943. President and prime minister with legislative power residing with the 128 members of the National Assembly elected through universal suffrage.

Population 4,143,101 (July 2011 estimate)

Life expectancy Men 73.48 years, women 76.62 years (2011 estimate)

Capital Beirut (*Bayroot* in Arabic, *Beyrouth* in French): 33°52' N, 35°30' E; population 1,909,000 (2009 estimate)

Other main towns Byblos, Sidon, Tripoli, Tyre, Zahlé

Economy Overwhelmingly based on service sectors such as banking and tourism, which accounts for around 79% of GDP. Agriculture accounts for 5.1% and industry 15.9% of GDP (2010 estimates).

Natural resources Iron ore, limestone, salt, arable land and water

GDP per head US$14,400 (2010 estimate)

Languages Official language is Arabic; French, English and Armenian also spoken

Adult literacy rate Male 93.1%, female 82.2%; one of the highest in the Middle East

Religion 18 officially recognised sects including Shi'ite and Sunni Muslim, Christian Maronite, Druze

Currency Lebanese lira (LL), widely known as the Lebanese pound (LBP)

Exchange rate £1 = LBP2,443.13, US$1 = LBP1,507.32, €1 = LBP2,148.96 (September 2011)

National airline Middle East Airlines – Air Liban (MEA)

International airport Beirut Rafiq Hariri International Airport (airport code: BEY)

International telephone code + 961

Time GMT + 2 in winter (October–March); GMT + 3 in summer (April–September)

Electrical voltage 220 volts AC, 50Hz – European style round two-pin plugs

Weights and measures Metric

Flag Two horizontal bands of red (top and bottom), white band in the middle containing a green cedar tree, the country's national emblem

National anthem *Kulluna lil-watan* (All of us! For our Country!). Adopted 12 July 1927 by Presidential decree; words by Rachid Nakhlé (1873–1939).

Main public holidays Fixed-date holidays: 1 January (New Year's Day), 9 February (Feast of Maroun, Patron Saint of Christian Maronites), 18 April (Qana Day), 1 May (Labour Day), 6 May (Martyrs' Day), 22 November (Independence Day), 25 December (Christmas Day). Muslim holiday dates vary according to the lunar calendar which moves back about 11 days each year. Notable holidays are: Eid al-Adha, Ras as-Sana, Ashura, Mouloud.

1

Background Information

GEOGRAPHY

Lebanon is a tiny country (ranked 170 in the world out of 250 nations according to Central Intelligence Agency (CIA) country comparison figures), making it easy to visit in a short space of time. Traffic permitting, it is perfectly feasible to travel from the extreme north to the far south of Lebanon in three to four hours. Yet despite its extremely compact size – about 2% the size of the landmass of France – Lebanon possesses a remarkable diversity of topography ranging from rocky coastal landscapes, snow-capped mountains, fertile plains, lush valleys, rivers and waterfalls, all packed into a mere 10,452km². Roughly rectangular in shape, Lebanon runs approximately 225km from Nahr al-Kabr (the Great River) on the northern border with Syria to Naqoura near the Israeli border in the south and averages only 50km from east to west. Its northeastern border with Syria extends for some 375km whilst the southern border with Israel stretches for 79km. Together with Israel and the Occupied Palestinian Territories, Jordan, Syria and Turkey, Lebanon forms part of the Levant – the 'land of the rising sun' – at the eastern end of the Mediterranean Sea and lies within the Fertile Crescent, a band of rich agricultural land extending from Egypt to Iraq.

Lebanon can be divided into four main regions with an approximate north–south configuration. The mainly narrow and broken maritime plain on the country's Mediterranean coast reaches its widest point of only 6.5km at the northern city of Tripoli. This region is home to the capital Beirut, together with the country's other main centres of population such as Byblos, Sidon and Tyre which have their origins in ancient port settlements. Innumerable rivers such as the Musa, Ibrahim, Kalb and Awali make their exit here into the Mediterranean Sea from the mountains. Inland from the coast the western Mount Lebanon range of mountains ('Jebel Lubnan' in Arabic) runs almost the entire length of the country and accounts for over a third of Lebanon's landmass. Like most of the country, this is composed of limestone rock from the Jurassic and Cretaceous periods and reaches its and Lebanon's zenith at Qornet es Saouda (3,083m) in the northern section of the range northeast of Bcharré which remains blanketed with snow for much of the year. The section southeast of Beirut contains the picturesque and lush green relief of the Chouf Mountains where unique and favourable geological conditions have enabled cultivation and human settlement to flourish at higher altitudes of up to 1,500m. The Chouf is also the main location for Lebanon's national emblem, the ancient cedar tree (*Cedrus libani*); evergreen coniferous trees attaining heights of over 40m. Progressive deforestation by man since biblical times has severely depleted the number of trees but an active regeneration programme is currently in progress.

Forming a natural geological boundary with neighbouring Syria, eastern Lebanon is composed of the Anti-Lebanon range of mountains (*Lubnan ash-Sharqi* in Arabic).

3

Lower in height than the Mount Lebanon range, geologists believe that at one time the two formed a single structure. This eastern range of mountains is considerably more arid than those to the west and many peaks retain a carpet of snow for much of the year – it is from this that Lebanon derives its name (*Lubnan* in Arabic, meaning 'white'). The highest point of the Anti-Lebanon range is reached at Mount Hermon (2,814m) in the southeastern part of the country straddling the Lebanese–Syrian border. Southwest of Mount Hermon is possibly one of the geographically smallest territorial disputed areas in the Middle East: that of the 22km² Shebaa Farms. This small portion of land, occupied by Israel along with the Syrian Golan Heights captured during the 1967 Six Day War between the two countries, is claimed by Lebanon as sovereign territory but disputed by Israel who claim the area falls wholly within Syria's borders.

Sandwiched between the Mount Lebanon and Anti-Lebanon mountains is Lebanon's agricultural and wine-producing heartland, the Bekaa Valley, ancient Rome's breadbasket and only 30km east of Beirut. The valley extends some 125km from north to south and varies in width from around 8km to 16km. A plateau, the Bekaa can nevertheless still attain a height of over 1,000m above sea level in parts. It comprises the northern extremity of the Great Rift Valley, which runs from the Jordan Valley in Syria to Mozambique in east Africa. The Bekaa accounts for more than 40% of Lebanon's arable farmland and the country's two main rivers have their source in the region: the Orontes or Rebel River, due to the unusual direction of flow northwards into Syria and Turkey, and the Litani which flows south from near Baalbek before finally meandering west and emptying into the Mediterranean Sea some 10km north of the southern city of Tyre. As the flow of the Litani nears the Chouf Mountains, the artificial 11km² Lake Qaraoun was created in 1959 for the purposes of irrigation and hydro-electric power generation. Extending for some 140km in length, the Litani is Lebanon's largest river and the only major river in the Near East not crossing an international boundary.

CLIMATE

Unlike the overwhelming aridity of neighbouring Arab states in the region, Lebanon's climate is as diverse as its terrain. Temperatures and precipitation differ markedly from region to region, with the country's climate and weather systems broadly coinciding with its topographical zones. Nevertheless, Lebanon as a whole enjoys around 300 days of sunshine annually, making the country a year-round destination for visitors.

THE COAST The coastal areas of the country experience a typical Mediterranean climate system, similar to that enjoyed by other areas sharing similar latitudes such as Los Angeles in California. Summer (June–September) on the coast is characterised by hot, dry and humid conditions, especially in July and August, though they are often modified slightly by sea breezes. Beirut, for example, has average summer temperatures which range from 28°C to 35°C and from June to September rain is virtually unheard of. The winter months (December–February) see temperatures drop to more palatable levels of between 11°C and 18°C (though Beirut has recorded a January temperature of 25°C), but the flip side to this is that these months can see the heaviest and most concentrated periods of precipitation, and even a sprinkling of snow is possible, as occurred most recently in March 2011. Beirut, for instance, receives more rainfall than the city of Manchester in the UK, seeing over seven inches of rain in both December and January, but has only half the number of rainy days. This plentiful supply of precipitation together with an absence of frost has helped to ensure that the coastal districts are an important agricultural region with many citrus fruits and vegetables cultivated. Springtime (March–May) in the coastal districts is pleasantly warm with temperatures between 15°C and 25°C and as the winter rains have receded the whole country begins to blossom with an assortment of vegetation and wildflowers. However, in late spring and early summer the coastal areas can witness the onset of a hot, dust-laden and oppressive wind from the Sahara Desert, the *khamsin*. This wind has reputedly endured for up to 50 days (*khamsin* translates as 50 in Arabic) but for the most part is far more short-lived, lasting a week or so at most. Autumn (October–December) on the coast is also characterised by nice weather with lower temperatures than in summer, less humidity and minimal rainfall.

INLAND Inland from the coast, the higher altitudes of the Lebanon and Anti-Lebanon mountain ranges considerably modify the country's basic Mediterranean climatic pattern. During summer, the mountains have a pleasantly cool and alpine feel providing locals and visitors alike with a welcome respite from the more sultry conditions on the coast. Whilst daytime temperatures can often approximate those on the coast, the mountain air is much drier with a consequent decrease in humidity and by nightfall temperatures have dropped much lower. In winter the dominant polar air masses prevail and combined with the effects of altitude this season is much cooler than on the coast with most precipitation falling as snow from December onwards. This heralds the start of Lebanon's ski season which can run until April or even May with some peaks, such as Mount Hermon, remaining snow covered for the majority of the year. If you want to live the cliché and ski in the morning and take a dip in the Mediterranean in the afternoon then this is the time to do it. Autumn and spring both bring very pleasant weather with temperatures varying from 0°C to 20°C and are the ideal times for hiking, trekking and exploring Lebanon's natural beauty.

Lying between the two mountain ranges, the Bekaa Valley is characterised by a more continental climate with extremely hot and dry summers. The town of Ksara near Zahlé, for example, has an average July temperature of 31°C, comparable to Beirut on the coast, but minus the humidity due to the rain shadow effect produced by the Mount Lebanon range which blocks the moisture-laden winds arriving from the sea. Night-time temperatures fall dramatically, however, and can be quite cool like the mountains. The winter months in the Bekaa can also be very severe and are characterised by cold, windy and wet conditions with frequent snowfall. Ksara, for instance, has a recorded minimum temperature of 3°C in December, some 10°C lower than in the capital.

NATURAL HISTORY AND CONSERVATION

Whilst Lebanon may lack the predominantly dry conditions of neighbouring states in the region the country more than makes up for this by being the most heavily wooded country in the Middle East. The marked variations in topography, varying between upland, lowland and plateau together with equally diverse meteorological conditions and a large water resource in an otherwise severely depleted region has given rise to a range of animal and plant life. Species range from sub-tropical to alpine. Combine this with a government and a variety of NGOs actively conserving and promoting the country's natural beauty and the importance of the environment and sustainability issues, and Lebanon has all the ingredients needed for those interested in an ecotourism adventure.

FLORA The coastal areas of Lebanon are particularly lush and an important agricultural region. Among the vegetation which grows and is cultivated are orange, lemon, banana, palm and olive trees. In the mountains pine, juniper, oak, fir, beech and cypress trees are plentiful. Lebanon's most famous flora, and the country's national symbol, is the cedar tree (*Cedrus libani*), which are found in the environs of Bcharré in northern Lebanon and the Chouf Mountains southeast of Beirut. Progressive deforestation since biblical times, which saw the ancient Egyptians use the resin from the tree to embalm their pharaohs and the Phoenicians use the wood to build their ships, has severely depleted their numbers but around 400 still remain and some are estimated to be over 2,000 years old. The much drier Bekaa Valley lacks any significant tree population and the flora here is mainly characterised by fields of vegetation and vineyards. Springtime throughout the country sees smaller vegetative types such as poppies, anemones (a type of buttercup), narcissus, clematis, cyclamen, wild herbs, shrubs and the vibrant Lebanon violet carpeting the Lebanese landscape.

FAUNA The mountain landscapes provide a haven for a range of animal life such as deer, wild cats, porcupines, badgers, foxes, squirrels, hedgehogs, hares, wolves, wild boar, goats and gazelles. Of the marine life in Lebanon, the country's plentiful rivers are well stocked with eels, bass and mullet and a variety of turtles such as the endangered green sea turtle (*Chelonia mydas*) and the loggerhead turtle (*Caretta caretta*) lay their eggs on the Palm Islands Nature Reserve off the coast of Tripoli and in southern coastal regions, whilst the Mediterranean monk seal also frequents the coastal areas. In terms of the reptile kingdom a number of snake species have been identified such as the Lebanon viper and the green whip snake, as well as varieties of lizard. Snakes are particularly prevalent during the warmer summer months and the usual advice about wearing shoes or boots in areas where they are known to reside, and not to poke around in crevices with your hand, obviously applies. A most unusual mammal found in Lebanon is the hyrax (*Procavia capensis*). This small, rodent-like creature, similar in size to a domestic cat, has brown fur and its hoof-like toes can be likened to a horse. Despite its small size, modern DNA techniques have revealed that the elephant is the hyrax's nearest relative.

For ornithological enthusiasts, Lebanon offers a wealth of habitats and sightings and the country has a number of areas which BirdLife International have designated Important Bird Areas (IBAs). Around 135 different species of birds have been spotted around the coastline of Lebanon whilst at the Palm Islands Nature Reserve bird observations have detected more than 300 varieties, with many such as finches, ospreys, broad-billed sandpipers, mistle thrush and tern choosing to build their

NATIONAL PARKS AND PROTECTED AREAS

- Aammiq Wetlands (see pages 206–7)
- Bentael Nature Reserve (see page 163)
- Chouf Cedar Reserve (see pages 230–2)
- Horsh Ehden Forest Nature Reserve (see page 189)
- Jebel Moussa Biosphere Reserve (see page 164)
- Palm Islands Nature Reserve (see page 181)
- Tannourine Cedars Forest Nature Reserve (see page 187)
- Tyre Coast Nature Reserve (see page 256)
- The Orange House Project (see page 253)

nests on the islands. Cuckoos, kites, falcons and woodpeckers are present in the mountains. In the marshlands of the Bekaa Valley, ducks, flamingoes, herons, storks, buzzards, hoopoes, kestrels and golden eagles all use the area as stop-off points on their annual migratory routes in spring and autumn.

ENVIRONMENTAL ISSUES AND CONCERNS Unlike in many other Arab nations an awareness of the impact of man's activities on the environment is at a more advanced stage in Lebanon. The country's Ministry of Environment (*www.moe. gov.lb*), the government agency responsible for raising awareness of and protecting the country's natural world, has implemented over 30 Protected Areas. The department's mission statement on its website reads: 'Let's all work together for the environment towards a better quality of life...' and in this respect has made good progress, often working alongside the many NGOs and voluntary organisations in the country. In 2001, the government allocated substantial funds to undertake the ongoing National Reforestation Plan (NRP) which aims to increase Lebanon's forested areas from its then 13.3% to 20% by 2030, replacing those trees and other flora lost or damaged through persistent deforestation, fires, wars, climate change, etc. Lebanon is also a party to a number of international agreements concerning the environment such as biodiversity, climate change (Kyoto Protocol), hazardous wastes, law of the sea, ozone layer protection, ship pollution, environmental modification and marine conservation.

However, despite the environmental strides accomplished, Lebanon still has some way to go in preserving its environment. Recycling facilities and services, for example, are nowhere near what they are in western Europe or North America and domestic and industrial waste continues to be disposed of into rivers and valleys with no thought as to the environmental impact. Along the coastline you will see dumped bottles and plastic bags and other refuse which could all be easily recycled given the necessary infrastructure. In Beirut, air pollution from high-density car use and industry is a particular concern and in the hot summer months the air can be quite thick. Continued hunting and pesticide use are also ongoing issues which need to be addressed. The prognosis for Lebanon's environmental future was addressed at an October 2010 conference, the first in the country to highlight both the prevailing issues and possible solutions, and drew attention to the worldwide problem of global warming, which in Lebanon's case could lead to the disappearance of five species of plant together with the economic impact of a much shorter winter ski season owing to significant reductions in annual snowfall. On a local level, the conference drew attention to the high levels of pollution in the cities, the need for improved water purification systems, the ongoing need to protect the country's green spaces and the task of reducing Lebanon's 700+ rubbish tips which pose a serious threat to both the environment and human health.

The most recent major damaging event to affect Lebanon's environment, however, came not from climate change or environmental mismanagement, but from the July 2006 34-day conflict between Israel and Hezbollah. Over a period of two days, the Israeli air force bombed the 40,000m² thermal power plant at Jiyeh, 30km south of Beirut, resulting in around 15,000–20,000 tonnes of oil being spilled into the Mediterranean Sea creating a slick 10km wide and extending 150km along the Lebanese and Syrian coasts, and which threatened at one point to engulf Turkey and Cyprus. The result was that scores of fish were killed along with disruption to other marine life such as the already endangered green sea turtle. The one 'plus' point was that the type of oil released was of the heavy variety which meant it sunk quite quickly to the seabed before it could spread more widely to the beaches.

FACTS ABOUT LEBANON

- Hollywood actor Keanu Reeves was born in Beirut on 2 September 1964
- Lebanon is mentioned over 70 times in the Bible
- Lebanon holds the Guinness World Record for making the biggest wine glass, measuring 2.40m high and 1.65m wide, and which can hold 1,577 litres
- Lebanon holds the Guinness World Record for producing the largest pile of hummus at 10,452kg, equal to the country's total land area
- Lebanon receives an annual rainfall quota of 860mm per annum
- There are some 10–15 million more Lebanese people living outside the country than in Lebanon itself

Nonetheless, with a clean-up operation running into hundreds of millions of dollars it is estimated that it will take around ten years to completely clean up the most devastating environmental disaster the eastern Mediterranean has ever seen.

HISTORY

Lebanon as an independent state is a recent creation of history but its shores have been occupied since the dawn of time, with the country's history telling the story of wave after wave of mostly foreign conquest and occupation. Lebanon's location within the Fertile Crescent also assures it of a place among the Cradles of Civilisation, for it was in this region that one of the oldest civilisations on earth has been recorded, that of the Sumerian people from Mesopotamia in modern-day Iraq c5000BC. This early non-Semitic tribe are credited with the invention of the wheel, the measurement of time and its division into hours and minutes together with the oldest known form of writing, a wedge-like cuneiform script inscribed on clay tablets to aid business transactions. The Sumerians also used slaves to cut down and export Lebanese cedarwood. The history of the Middle East has also seen the dawn of the world's three great religions and civilisations with Christianity, Judaism and Islam. The history of Lebanon can be seen in terms of the architectural and cultural achievements left by a succession of foreign invaders and rulers. Over 400 years of Turkish rule has left an indelible footprint of Ottoman-style architecture in Beirut and the Chouf Mountains. The ancient Phoenician ramparts are less conspicuous but the Temple of Echmoun in Sidon and the Temple of Baalat Gebal in Byblos remain the most visible reminders of this once innovative civilisation. The relatively short-lived Roman occupation has bequeathed some of the most awe-inspiring architecture you will ever see in the Middle East at Baalbek. The onset of Muslim rule in the 7th century has left a unique and delicate archaeological legacy at Aanjar in the Bekaa Valley in the form of an Umayyad trading town, courtesy of the first of the Arab dynasties. Two centuries of Crusader presence in Lebanon has left imposing monuments in Sidon and Tripoli whilst the French colonial era has left a range of Parisian-style architecture in the capital. With such a rich and varied history, Lebanon is an ideal destination for aficionados of archaeology and culture in one of the region's smallest, yet most fascinatingly diverse countries.

PHOENICIAN SETTLEMENT Although archaeological evidence unearthed in the coastal town of Byblos testifies to the existence of Neolithic dwellings dating back more than 7,000 years, it wasn't until c3000BC that anything like permanent city-states were established on Lebanon's shores. Descendants of the Semitic Canaanites who inhabited the land of Canaan – broadly comprising modern-day Israel and the Levant, the seafaring Phoenicians are widely considered to be the first settlers in Lebanon and established maritime trading colonies at Tyre, Sidon, Beirut and Byblos. For centuries they traded with Egypt exporting Lebanese cedarwood, used to build King Solomon's Temple, in exchange for gold and other precious metals from the Nile Valley.

A quasi-autonomous people, the ancient Phoenicians lacked an overall sense of political unity with their cities being overseen by hereditary kings and dominated by an economic elite. Although the least despotic of Lebanon's succession of invaders and occupiers over the years, their autonomy was frequently interrupted by more omnipotent civilisations wanting access to the flourishing Levantine sea trade. In c1600BC, tribal warriors from central Asia, the Hyksos, conquered and ruled both Egypt and Phoenicia for a century before Egypt regained control. The Hittites, from Anatolia in modern-day Turkey, who are credited with instigating the Iron Age, conquered the region in c1200BC before Egyptian rule was once again restored. Out of the turmoil which engulfed the eastern Mediterranean around this time came the destruction of the Hittite Empire by the elusive Sea Peoples, probably from north Africa, and the decline of Mycenaean or late Bronze-Age Greek civilisation, which heralded the start of a golden era of stability and prosperity for the Phoenicians. This innovative and enterprising race expanded its maritime trading activities by sailing all over the Mediterranean, founding colonies on the islands of Cyprus and Malta, Tarshish in Spain and by c814BC had founded ancient Rome's nemesis, Carthage in present-day Tunisia. Phoenician ships, with their uniquely designed hulls, were able to cope with the rigours of long and often arduous sea journeys. They were also the first people to utilise the Pole Star for celestial or night-time navigation.

Revered as superb artisans and craftsmen using a variety of indigenous and imported materials to manufacture a range of luxury and utilitarian goods, the Phoenicians forged trading partnerships with peoples as diverse as the Israelites, the Euboens and Nuragic peoples from Sardinia. Ivory was imported from Africa, India and Syria and fashioned into ornate items of furniture. Glass making, metalwork and wine production were also important aspects of the Phoenician economy. But perhaps the most important aesthetic and economic product which they produced was the purple dye which was applied to clothing, producing eye-catching garments coveted by the rich and royalty alike. It was from the Greek word for purple, *phoinikes*, which gave the Phoenicians their name. The dye was extracted from the hypobranchial glands of the murex mollusc which was caught in nets off the Lebanese coast. Once the shells of the trapped mollusc had been smashed they were allowed to dry out before salt water was added to produce the colour purple. Owing to the small amount of dye procured from each shell, production was necessarily on a huge scale. At the southern city of Sidon, a mound of waste murex shells more than 40m high has been discovered. The whole process was also a very pungent one and the famous Greek geographer, Strabo, offered the following observation on his visit to Tyre: 'The great number of dyeworks renders the city unpleasant as a place of residence, but the superior skill of the people in the practice of this art is the source of its wealth.' Perhaps the greatest legacy of the Phoenicians today, however, is their invention of a 22-letter phonetic alphabet which they devised to aid record keeping and communication in business transactions. Though not the first people to assign spoken words to written form, the system they devised was the forerunner to all later alphabets, including our modern Roman one.

An important part of Phoenician life was their worship of a range of gods such as Melqart (God of the City), Astarte (God of Fertility), Echmoun (God of Healing)

CHRONOLOGY OF HISTORY AND KEY EVENTS IN LEBANON

The following is provided as a useful crib sheet and quick reference of principal invaders, occupiers and events from antiquity to the present day.

c3000BC	Settlement of the Semitic Canaanite peoples in modern-day Lebanon
c2500BC	Phoenicians establish colonies at Tyre, Sidon, Byblos and Beirut and develop enduring trade relations with Egypt
c1550BC	Egypt expands its empire and assumes control of Phoenicia
c1200–842BC	Phoenician independence returns and they invent a 22-letter alphabet
842BC	Assyrians, under King Ashurnasirpal II, conquer Phoenicia
c814BC	Phoenicians found Carthage in modern-day Tunisia
538–332BC	Persian Empire conquers and rules Phoenicia
332BC	The Greek general, Alexander the Great, defeats Persians at the Battle of Issus and Lebanon comes under Greek rule
64BC	Pompey the Great conquers Phoenicia and Lebanon becomes part of the Roman province of Syria, ushering in a *Pax Romana*
AD395	Roman Empire divides into two parts and Lebanon comes under the control of the eastern or Byzantine Empire with its capital in Constantinople (modern-day Istanbul)
AD551	Earthquake and tsunami destroy Beirut resulting in 30,000 deaths in the city
AD570	Birth of the Prophet Muhammad in Mecca, Saudi Arabia
AD610	Prophet Muhammad founds Islam on the Arabian Peninsula
AD632	Death of the Prophet Muhammad
AD636	Battle of Yarmouk marks the first wave of Arab conquests following the death of the Prophet Muhammad. Caliphate of Rashidun defeats the Byzantine armies in a six-day war and ends Byzantine rule in Anatolia (present-day Turkey).
AD652 (up to 1517)	A succession of Arab armies and dynasties sweep across the Middle East and beyond in a combination of conquest and peaceful conversion to the new faith of Islam
1098–1291	Crusaders (Franks) from western Europe embark on a series of conquests to liberate the Holy Land from Islamic rule. In Lebanon, they capture Tripoli, Beirut, Sidon and Tyre.
1260–1516	Mamluk dynasty of former slaves
1516–1918	Ottoman Empire rules over Lebanon
1918	Germany's defeat in World War I also signals the end of its ally, the Ottoman Empire
1920	Lebanon is placed under French Mandate rule
1926	Lebanon becomes an independent republic and drafts its first constitution
1943	Lebanon gains full independence from France
1945	Lebanon becomes a founding member of the United Nations and the Arab League
1948	The State of Israel is formed and following the first Arab–Israeli war over 100,000 Palestinians flee to Lebanon, which signals the origin of the Palestinian refugee issue
1958	At the request of President Camille Chamoun, US Marines

	land in Beirut to suppress a Muslim uprising
1967	5–10 June. Arab–Israeli Six Day War. Further intake of Palestinian refugees to Lebanon and surrounding states.
1970	Black September. Palestine Liberation Organisation (PLO) expelled from Jordan and sets up new headquarters in Beirut.
1975	13 April. Start of 15-year Lebanese civil war.
1976	October. Syrian troops enter Lebanon heralding the start of Syria's long history of involvement in Lebanese affairs.
1978	Israel launches Operation Litani to destroy PLO infrastructure south of the Litani River
1982	4 June. Israel invades Lebanon in Operation Peace for Galilee, in an attempt to eliminate the PLO from Lebanon. September. Massacre of Palestinian civilians by Christian Phalangist militia allies of Israel in refugee camps in Beirut.
1983	23 October. 241 US Marines and 56 French paratroopers are killed in co-ordinated suicide bomb attacks in Beirut.
1989	October. Taif Accord equalises power between Muslims and Christians and ends civil war in Lebanon.
1991	May. Lebanon and Syria sign the Brotherhood, Cooperation and Coordination Agreement.
1991	September. Lebanon and Syria sign a Common Defence and Security Agreement.
1992	October. Rafiq Hariri becomes Lebanon's prime minister.
1993	July. Israel launches Operation Accountability in Lebanon against Hezbollah; Rafiq Hariri launches Horizon 2000, the blueprint for Lebanon's post-war reconstruction.
1996	11–26 April. Israel begins Operation Grapes of Wrath against Hezbollah; 106 civilians killed in an attack on a UN base in Qana.
2000	May. Israel withdraws its occupying forces from the south. Its proxy militia, the South Lebanon Army (SLA), collapses.
2005	14 February. Former prime minister Rafiq Hariri is killed, along with 21 other people, by a car bomb in Beirut. Syria is blamed, which prompts Cedar Revolution calling for all Syrian military and intelligence presence in Lebanon to end. April. Syria withdraws the last of its military and security personnel from Lebanon.
2006	Israel launches attacks against Hezbollah forces in southern Lebanon following the abduction and killing of Israeli soldiers
2007	Special Tribunal for Lebanon (STL) begins its work of identifying and bringing to justice those responsible for the 2005 murder of former prime minister Rafiq Hariri and others
2009	June. Peaceful parliamentary elections result in Saad Hariri being elected as prime minister who forms a government of national unity in November.
2010	Lebanon wins the alternative – hummus – war against Israel
2011	January. Collapse of unity government following resignation of 8 March Alliance members over the STL. June. STL announce indictments against members of Hezbollah for the murder of Rafiq Hariri.

and Baal (Storm God) among their range of deities. Despite these, however, this interlude of innovation and considerable economic and cultural achievements, the Phoenicians' mastery of the sea and their independence once again came under threat from the Assyrians from modern-day northern Iraq, who had succeeded the Sumerians c3000BC. At its zenith the Assyrian Empire embraced Iraq, Iran, Arabia, Turkey, Syria, Lebanon, Egypt and Cyprus. The Assyrians, eager to gain access to the sea trade like earlier powers, and expand their influence from a basically landlocked empire, under the Great King of Assyria, Ashurnasirpal II burdened the Phoenician states with heavy tributes of silver, gold, tin, bronze and ivory to their powerful invaders. From c612–538BC the Babylonians from southern Iraq broke the stranglehold of the Assyrians on Phoenicia and imposed another round of tributes on the Phoenicians. The arrival of the Persians in 539BC, under Cyrus the Great, was initially a cathartic experience for the Phoenicians from Babylonian domination and they supported the Persians during the Greco-Persian Wars (490–49BC), supplying their navy with ships and manpower. However, revolts and rebellions ensued against the empire as heavier and heavier tributes began to be imposed which continued until the arrival of the Greeks on Lebanon's coast.

GREEK AND ROMAN CONQUEST Despite his forces being outnumbered by two to one the Macedonian general, Alexander the Great, dealt a crushing blow to the Persian Empire under Darius III at the Battle of Issus in 333BC. Shortly afterwards, Alexander took the Phoenician city-states of Byblos and Sidon with ease but the southernmost port of Tyre chose to staunchly resist the iconic leader. Tyre's reaction to the forces of Alexander was initially one of acquiescence but when he declared his intention to offer a sacrifice to their god Melqart this fell on deaf ears with the city's citizens. In Alexander's eyes, Tyre was too important a city to leave untouched; as a stronghold of the Persian navy, if left undefeated it would leave his forces vulnerable to a rearguard attack whilst *en route* to his conquest of Egypt. Negotiations with the Tyrians having failed, a seven-month-long siege of the city ensued; the longest and most protracted of Alexander's short but illustrious military career. Although many of Tyre's women and children were evacuated to Carthage, the remaining 40,000 or so Tyrian citizens stayed in the city but with Alexander's overwhelming military might of over 200 ships, the general proceeded to massacre around 8,000 people and consigned the remainder to a life of slavery.

Phoenician identity and independence was now on the wane and soon replaced by Greek cultural influences. Alexander's untimely death in 332BC at the age of 33 meant that his Hellenistic empire was split up between his three generals – Antigonous, Ptolemy and Seleucus. Seleucus gained control of Phoenicia and the Hellenistic Seleucid Empire held sway over the region, interrupted by frequent power struggles with the Ptolemies until 64BC when the emerging power of Rome under the general Pompey incorporated Lebanon together with Palestine in the south into the Roman province of Syria. The onset of Roman rule ushered in the period known as the Pax Romana, characterised by an increase in population and an era of peace and prosperity as the Phoenician people were given Roman citizenship and their economic and artisanal activities were permitted to flourish once again. This more sanguine period of colonisation also saw the Roman Empire establish a School of Law in Beirut which was revered throughout the empire. This period was also characterised by the building of huge and lavish temples of which those at Baalbek testify to the optimism and ambition of Rome. The year AD395, however, marks an important stage in Lebanon's history at which the Roman Empire finally split into a western region (with its capital remaining in Rome), and an eastern portion known as the Byzantine Empire with its capital in Constantinople (modern-day Istanbul). One of the most salient points in this period of Roman rule was the widespread diffusion of Christianity, formerly a much-persecuted faith, both within Lebanon and throughout the wider empire, under the emperor Constantine who formally endorsed the 'new' religion in the Edict of Rome in AD312. By AD381, Christianity had become the Roman Empire's official religion. However, during the 5th century, fierce ecumenical discussions and schisms ensued including those relating to Christ's true nature and will.

From these theological conflicts arose a splinter group from the orthodox Christian Church, the Maronites, who take their name from a hermit called Saint Maroun. Because of the strict orthodox Christianity imposed by the Byzantine rulers, the Maronites came into conflict with the emperor Justinian II and were forced to take refuge in Lebanon's mountainous regions, which remain to this day a place of sanctuary and pilgrimage. A weakened Byzantine Empire, a result of both internal religious disharmony and repeated incursions from eastern invaders, heralded the start of a new chapter in Lebanese, and Middle Eastern history; one that would usher in both a new language and a new religion.

ARAB CONQUEST AND RULE The transition to Arab rule and the consequent Islamisation of Lebanon was a remarkably peaceful event when compared with many earlier periods of Lebanese history. Founded in AD610 by the Prophet Muhammad following a series of visitations from Jibril (Archangel Gabriel to Christians and Jews) who had revealed the final and true word of God to him and which were eventually written down in a series of verses known as the Koran (see page 31). Muhammad began the process of unifying the people and pantheistic faiths of Arabia who had hitherto worshipped some 360 different deities. After a period of struggle and conversion, Islam eventually became the third great monotheistic faith after Christianity and Judaism and the new religion spread like wildfire from the desert regions of the Arabian Peninsula. The seeds of Islam were planted in Lebanon some four years after the death of the Prophet Muhammad (in AD632) at the Battle of Yarmuk in AD636, the present-day border between Jordan and Syria. This early six-day war between the expanding Muslim forces and those of the Byzantine Empire saw the Arab armies emerge victorious and led to the decline of a Byzantine Empire already weakened by its long wars with the Persians, paving the way for the march west of the Muslim conquerors.

The first Arab dynasty, the Umayyad Caliphate, was established in Lebanon by AD661 and ruled from their capital in Damascus. Theirs was an empire which extended from India to central Asia and incorporated north Africa, Spain and Portugal. In AD732, the Umayyads were engaged in the Battle of Tours in France where their advance was only halted by the Christian ruler Charles Martel. Some scholars have suggested that if Martel had lost this battle western Europe itself may well have come under the banner of Islam. Nonetheless, despite less than a century of Umayyad rule they made Arabic the formal language, introduced an Islamic currency and overhauled the tax system. Following a coup in AD750, the Umayyads status quo fell to the Abbasid Caliphate who ruled from Baghdad, and Islam continued to expand throughout Lebanon and the wider Middle East. This period of Arab rule is often referred to as the Golden Age of Islam for it heralded great advances in literature, philosophy and the natural sciences, especially chemistry, mathematics and medicine. Economic activity also blossomed, especially in the port cities of Tyre and Tripoli. The onset of the Fatimid Caliphate in AD973, with their capital in Cairo was, like the Umayyad dynasty, a short one lasting only around a century but which left an enduring legacy in the form of the Ismaili sect who eventually established the enigmatic Druze religion (see pages 32–3). As the Fatimid dynasty eventually fragmented and weakened they were succeeded by the Seljuks in 1058, originally a group of Turkish chieftains who invaded Syria and Mesopotamia (modern-day Iraq) and ruled from their capital at Isfahan in Iran. As in previous Arab eras, the Seljuks made great headway in the arts and technology, and the economy prospered.

CRUSADER CONQUESTS The Middle Ages were a time of great turmoil and change in Lebanon. The Golden Age of Islam had receded and the great Islamic empires of the Fatimids and the Seljuks were weak and in decline. Yet the initial impetus for the Christian Crusaders (or Franks as they were also known) from western Europe – mainly Britain and France – can be traced back to 1009 and the destruction of the Church of the Holy Sepulchre in Jerusalem at the behest of the Fatimid Caliph Al-Hakim. This epochal event, together with the power vacuum which existed within the Islamic empires, provided the Franks with an ideal opportunity to exploit the situation. Finally, in 1095, Pope Urban II galvanised the European knights into action, culminating in a series of eight Crusades to reclaim 'Jerusalem the Golden' and the Holy Land from the Seljuk Turks. Following three years of struggle the city of Jerusalem was captured by Godfrey of Bouillon in 1099. The knights were undiscriminating and ruthless in their military quest for spiritual and territorial gains, killing Muslims, Jews and Christians in their wake. Turning their sights towards Lebanon the Franks captured Tripoli in 1109 followed by Beirut and Sidon a year later and, after a long siege, Tyre capitulated in 1124. During the 200-year period of Crusader presence in Lebanon they formed enduring alliances with Rome, who saw the Crusaders as a liberating force from Muslim rule. Despite their relatively short stay the Crusaders left eclectic architectural footprints in Sidon, Byblos and Tripoli. Other more mortal legacies include the present-day Christian families with names such as Franjeh (Frankish), Duahi (Douai) or Bardawi (Baldwin), who claim descent from the medieval knights.

MAMLUK DYNASTY Ruling from their capital in Cairo for over 250 years, the elite class of soldiers and warriors who comprised the Mamluk Sultanate were not Arabs but former Turkish and Circassian slaves (Mamluk variously means 'slave', 'possessed' or 'owned' in Arabic) from the Christian lands of central Asia and the Caucasus. As young boys they were captured and brought to Cairo. Here, they were schooled in Islam and trained to the very highest standards in combat and warfare and owing total devotion to their masters. Eventually overpowering their owners they succeeded the Ayyubid dynasty and became both a repressive and revered fighting force. Their CV of military achievements was impressive, having beaten the French Crusader army of King Louis IX in 1249, beaten back the Mongol army in 1260 at the Battle of Ayn Jalut, and by 1291 ousted the remaining Crusader knights from Islamic soil. At its height Mamluk power and influence embraced Egypt, Syria and Arabia. In Lebanon, economic and cultural prosperity continued apace and the country's second city of Tripoli shows the most striking reminders of this sultanate's legacy with an abundance of mosques and other architecture. By the early 16th century, however, the Mamluks' hold on power was broken by the expansionist ideology of an empire which was to change the face of Lebanon and the Middle East for the next four centuries and beyond: the Ottoman Empire.

OTTOMAN LEBANON The Ottoman Empire had become established by the end of the 13th century under Osman I, from whom the name Ottoman derives, fighting the Christian Byzantine Empire in northern Anatolia in modern-day Turkey with its capital initially at Bursa and later at Constantinople in present-day Istanbul. The history of Ottoman rule following that period was characterised by progressive expansion and consolidation of its powers. On 24 August 1516, a 20,000-strong Mamluk army, led by its 49th sultan, al-Ashraf Qansuh al-Ghawri, confronted some 60,000 soldiers commanded by Selim I 'the Grim', the 9th Ottoman sultan, at Marj Dabiq 40km north of the city of Aleppo in northwest Syria. The Mamluks, although courageous and highly skilled warriors, were not only outnumbered but also outgunned as the Ottoman forces had, in addition to a skilled and disciplined army, modern firepower in the form of rifles. It wasn't long before numerical supremacy and the tools of modern warfare comprehensively cut down the Mamluk ranks whose crushing defeat paved the way for Ottoman dominance over Syrian and Arab lands for over 400 years. Ottoman rule over Lebanon, as in many of its extensive territories which stretched from Asia Minor to southeast Europe, has been described as one of 'benign neglect' with existing power structures in lands under its authority permitted to retain a degree of autonomy as long as local rulers deferred to the power of the Sublime Porte (government) and sultan, and paid their taxes in full and on time.

In Lebanon the Ottomans allowed the existing feudal rule of the Druze Maan family to continue to oversee the Mount Lebanon region on their behalf. The Maans' most famous member was the Emir Fakhreddine II (see box, page 223), who proved a good choice as proxy leader for a time until his expansionist and territorial ambitions posed a threat to Ottoman power, which led to his execution in Istanbul in 1635 after 45 years of rule. Following a period of struggle, rule passed to Fakhreddine's nephew for the next two decades after which his grandson, Ahmad Maan (1658–97) took the helm and sought to perpetuate his grandfather's quest for independence for Lebanon from the Ottoman yoke. After his death without a male heir the Maan dynasty declined and power was delegated to the related Sunni Shihab family. The pinnacle of their power was reached in 1788 with the ascent of Bashir Shihab II. Dubbed the 'Red Emir' for his omnipotent and often brutal suppression of his opponents including cutting their throats, the Shihabs had adopted Christianity by the end of the 18th century and forged an alliance with Egypt's rebel pasha Muhammad Ali to expel the Ottomans from Lebanese soil in 1831. The shift of power to the Shihabs and the harshness of their rule led to sectarian conflict between the Christians and the increasingly alienated Druze. To counter the threat to their economic interests the Ottomans, aided by Britain and Austria, banished Bashir Shihab from Lebanon and he went into exile to Malta, which signalled the demise of emirate rule in Lebanon. In order to fill the power vacuum the Ottomans decided to divide up Mount Lebanon into Christian north and Druze south administrative and political districts (qa'im maqamiya) in 1842, but this served merely to accentuate sectarian divisions and regular conflict as both areas possessed majority Christian populations. This paved the way for the 'events of 1860' which saw unprecedented ethnic cleansing between Christians and Druze which cost 5,000 lives, the destruction of 200 villages and the displacement of 100,000 people in the Mount Lebanon region alone.

In 1861, the Ottomans, assisted by France who sent their forces to Beirut to support the Christians, once again reorganised Mount Lebanon into a singular unit or *mutasarrifiya* under a Christian governor, and assisted by a council consisting of 12 members numerically representative of the country's sectarian communities implemented with European guarantees. Until the instability created by the outbreak of World War I, this new arrangement worked and this period saw a return to peace and economic prosperity, particularly in the capital that witnessed the growth of its silk and publishing industries as well as a revered seat of learning which opened its doors in 1866 as the Syrian Protestant College, later renamed the American University of Beirut (AUB). The Ottomans sided with the Central Powers during World War I, but following the defeat of Germany in 1918, Ottoman rule ended, to be replaced by another foreign power which would also impose its hegemony on Lebanon.

FRENCH MANDATE The instruments for more than two decades of French rule in Lebanon were drawn up even before World War I had ended. In anticipation of an Allied victory, Britain and France held a series of meetings between 1915 and 1916, to discuss how they might divide up the former Ottoman lands between them following Germany's defeat. The end agreement of negotiations between Britain's Sir Mark Sykes and France's François Georges-Picot resulted in the Sykes–Picot Agreement of 1916, where it was agreed that Lebanon along with Syria would be mandated to France and the UK would get Palestine and Iraq. For France, who had long cherished an expansion of its existing colonial presence in Arab lands, notably Algeria, Morocco and Tunisia, it also offered the opportunity to further strengthen its ties with the Christian Maronites. At the San Remo Conference in April 1920, which was expressed by the Treaty of Sèvres, France was finally granted Lebanon and Syria and it could now realise its ambitions to impose its hegemony over the new State of Greater Lebanon (État du Grand Liban) with the initial avowed aim of supporting the Maronites', and Lebanon's, goal of achieving complete independence.

The passage of time, however, saw France begin to impose its own agenda on Lebanon. In line with Maronite wishes at the 1919 Paris Peace Conference, France extended Lebanon's borders beyond the Mount Lebanon area to encompass its 'natural boundaries' including Beirut, the eastern Bekaa Valley to the Anti-Lebanon Mountains, Sidon, Tyre and Tripoli, thereby sowing the seeds of discontent from the numerically superior Pan-Arab Muslims who had no inclination to be part of a Christian-dominated order. Opposition from Muslims reached fever pitch in the summer of 1925 which saw violent conflicts between the Druze, who felt betrayed after French promises of autonomous rule failed to materialise, and the French, who harshly suppressed the Druze resistance. From hereon, France began to export its own culture and politics, with the flag becoming the French tricolour; new infrastructure emerged such as roads, healthcare, agricultural methods, a rise in the standard of living, and adoption of the French penal code, and the French language became compulsory in schools. But perhaps the most important aspect of French rule took place in 1926 when it initiated the still-current 'confessional' based political system whereby power was apportioned along religious or sectarian lines heavily biased in favour of the Maronite population and the country became the Lebanese Republic.

Although the 1936 Franco-Lebanese Treaty guaranteeing Lebanon's future independence was signed in both Beirut and Damascus, its ratification was blocked by Paris. With the advent of World War II in 1939 and the invasion of France in May 1940 by German forces, France, along with Lebanon, experienced a period of Vichy rule until the Free French forces under General Charles de Gaulle and Britain reclaimed Lebanon in June 1941 who promised the country complete independence. This was music to the ears of Lebanese nationalists who now took matters into their own hands and began to prepare the road to an independent Lebanon, free of French influence and control.

INDEPENDENT LEBANON In the aftermath of the Allied powers' victory over Vichy forces, Lebanon remained, in practice, under French rule but in 1943 nationalist politicians held elections which voted in Bishara al-Khoury as the country's first president who in turn selected Riad al-Solh to become the first prime minister. In their quest to gain absolute autonomy from France the constitution was redrafted to exclude the French mandate. Arabic was now made the official language and the Lebanese flag was redrawn into its current red and white stripes with a cedar tree in its centre. French anger at the changes prompted the speedy arrest of the president and prime minister by French forces; they were later released from detention in the Bekaa Valley town of Rashaya but only after much internal dissent and British pressure on the French. Independence was formally declared on 22 November 1943, but it would be another three years before the French military and security services departed Lebanon. Yet the changes and reforms to the constitution brought about by the new country enshrined the basic principles which had already been drawn up in 1926. The new unwritten National Pact of 1943 established in the new country the same confessional principles that had been drawn up under the French. It was agreed that the president would be a Maronite Christian, a Sunni Muslim would have the post of prime minister and the parliamentary speaker would be a Shi'ite Muslim, with the Druze also allocated cabinet posts. Such a system, something of a white elephant in Middle Eastern politics dominated by more authoritarian regimes, proved a remarkably stable system for a time and with the end of World War II in 1945, Lebanon became a founding member of both the newly formed United Nations (UN) and the 22-member Arab League in the same year. Economic prosperity and political stability was a hallmark of this early period of independence and not even the creation of the state of Israel in 1948 after the first Arab–Israeli war, which saw the initial influx of more than 100,000 Palestinians from their former homeland, was sufficient to yet upset the economic and political applecart, though even at this early stage the Lebanese government refused the refugees citizenship of Lebanon.

BACKGROUND TO CIVIL WAR The long, protracted Lebanese civil war continues to cast an equally long and dark shadow over the country. Images and stories of wanton death and destruction, hostage taking, and the murder and displacement of innocent people are horrors difficult to convey in words. With the country in the throes of recovery, traversing the heavily restored and pristine Downtown area of Beirut, once the epicentre of the conflict, it is difficult to imagine the horrors once perpetrated there. Moreover, to this day there is still ongoing debate in political and scholarly circles as to what caused the war in the first place with the different factions all having their own versions to tell. The following therefore is a timeline of the 'events' which started off with violence born of internal schisms in the country but which eventually embroiled a number of countries from Europe and the region.

Since independence in 1943, Lebanon's demographic balance had begun to shift dramatically. Through a combination of high Christian emigration and higher birth rates amongst Muslims, the latter were widely believed to be numerically superior to their Christian counterparts thus reversing the findings of the 1932 census. Christian concern that this posed a potential threat to their dominance was exacerbated by the presence of some 127,600 Palestinian refugees by 1950. During this period the Pan-Arab stance of Egypt's president Gamal Abdel Nasser, which sought to unify Arab nations whose ideology was successful in ousting the pro-Western government in Iraq in 1958, also found favour amongst Lebanese Muslims which brought them into conflict with their own pro-Western economy and government dominated by

Camille Chamoun. Sectarian conflict resulted in street battles and in 1958, Chamoun became the first leader to evoke the Eisenhower Doctrine, inviting US forces into the country to quell the Muslim rebellion which quickly suppressed the uprising but did little to ameliorate the growing schisms within Lebanese society which would be flagged up to more devastating effect within two decades.

The 1960s and 1970s witnessed, by and large, an age characterised by relative stability and prosperity and Lebanon emerged as the Middle East's financial centre. Economic prosperity and tourism ushered in a golden era, and Beirut was often referred to as the 'Paris' of the Middle East for its affluence and style. Though Lebanon took no part in the 1967 Six Day War with Israel, the country saw a further influx of Palestinian refugees whose increasing radicalisation manifested itself in cross-border attacks on northern Israel from its bases in southern Lebanon, and the Palestinians found an ally in the Muslim faction the Lebanese National Movement (LNM) led by Kamal Jumblatt. No such alliance took place with the Christians, who feared for the Muslim and Palestinian threats to their dominance in the country, and fighting erupted between the groups once again in 1969. This was only halted following Nasser's intervention which brokered the Cairo Accord in November permitting the Palestine Liberation Organisation (PLO) to launch attacks against Israel from Lebanese territory, much to the chagrin of the Maronite Christians. This volatile mix was added to again in 1970, following the PLO's exodus from Jordan during Black September in which some 3,000 Palestinians had died in clashes with Jordanian forces who had no intention of allowing a militant Palestinian group to operate from its soil. By 1975, the total Palestinian presence in Lebanon numbered some 350,000 and with their new headquarters established in Beirut continued to launch attacks and raids into northern Israel which continued with the onset of the 1973 October (Yom Kippur) War, though Lebanese forces took no part in that conflict. By March 1975, unofficial estimates made the Muslim population a majority over the Christians.

CIVIL WAR By March 1975, the demographic realities of the country had been translated into yet another conflict in which the Christian controlled army violently suppressed a strike by fishermen in the southern port city of Sidon, which served to exacerbate an already tense situation. Less than four weeks later, on Sunday 13 April 1975, Muslim militiamen launched an attack on the Maronite leader Pierre Gemayel which he survived but which killed his personal bodyguard, among others, and is widely held to be the straw that broke the camel's back and ignited the flames of conflict in Lebanon. In reprisal, Christian Phalangist gunmen laid siege to a bus carrying Palestinians through the Christian neighbourhood of Ain al-Rummaneh in Beirut, killing all its 28 occupants. From this point on this first stage of the war was characterised by a plethora of tit-for-tat killings which would claim the lives of some 30,000 people with over 70,000 wounded until the first ceasefire, of which there were many, in October 1976. People were killed purely on the basis of their religious affiliation. On Black Friday Beirut saw ten Christians massacred which was followed by the even more horrific Black Saturday in December following which Christian militiamen, in retaliation for the death of four of their fighters, proceeded to kill over 300 Muslims with the latter responding by killing a similar number of Christians. The carnage continued almost unabated and in January 1976, Christians entered the Muslim enclave of Qarantina in Beirut, killing hundreds of Palestinians and razing the town to the ground. This was followed by Palestinians entering the town of Damour south of Beirut, killing 500 of this town's Christian inhabitants. In June, Christian forces entered the Tal al-Za'tar Palestinian refugee camp in east Beirut, killing some 3,000 of its 30,000 population during a two-month siege of the area. Eventually whole swathes of the capital were engulfed in the conflict with few areas spared. The city became partitioned into a Muslim west and Christian eastern sector with the no-man's-land in between dubbed the 'Green Line'.

FOREIGN INTERVENTION Towards the end of 1976, Lebanon had degenerated into a totally anarchic and chaotic state, with the Christian-dominated economic and political elite increasingly concerned at their inability to oust the Palestinians from Lebanon. The war entered a new phase in October with the entry of Syrian forces, initially in support of the Christians to prevent Israeli involvement in the event of a Muslim victory, and to secure its own hegemony over the country which would come to endure for nearly 30 more years. Some 26,500 Syrian troops entered the country along with an additional 3,500 committed by other Arab League states as part of the League's peacekeeping force, but to no avail. With no end in sight to continued Palestinian attacks from Lebanon on northern Israel, its southern neighbour entered the fray for the first time in March 1978. In an operation code-named Operation Litani, Israeli forces crossed the border into southern Lebanon in response to a Palestinian guerrilla attack on an Israeli bus travelling on the Haifa–Tel Aviv road which killed 37 Israelis. The avowed aim of the military action was to destroy PLO infrastructure south of the Litani River and set up a security zone to protect its northern border. Given the escalating situation Israel, under pressure from the United Nations to withdraw its forces, did so, leaving its self-imposed 'security zone' in the hands of its Christian proxy militia, the South Lebanon Army (SLA), to assist in protecting its northern border areas. A United Nations peacekeeping force, the United Nations Interim Force in Lebanon (UNIFIL) was also established following UN Resolution 425, to maintain some semblance of order and peace with the 'interim' period remaining to this day. North of the Litani the fighting raged on with innumerable ceasefires coming and going. Syria became more and more drawn into the conflict as its relationship with the Phalange became strained resulting in conflict between the two as well as Israel.

With the strengthening of the relationship between Israel and the Christians between 1977 and 1980, their alliance saw an opportunity to despatch the Palestinians, and Syria, from Lebanon once and for all. The momentum for this was the reshuffling of the Israeli cabinet in 1981 which saw the hard-line Yitzhak Shamir become foreign minister and Ariel Sharon granted the post of defence minister, both of whom saw the elimination of the PLO and Syria as a necessary step to eventual peace with Lebanon and the installation of a favourable Christian order, which resulted in the most intense period of fighting yet in the conflict. Although Israel's second 1982 invasion of the country had been in the planning stage for some months between Sharon and Gemayel, its stimulus was the assassination attempt on the life of Israel's ambassador to London, Shlomo Argov, near London's Dorchester Hotel on 3 June by the Palestinian splinter group of Abu Nidal. Three days later Operation Peace for Galilee was put into effect, a much more wide-ranging and intense invasion than its 1978 effort. According to United Nations figures, 17,000 Lebanese and Palestinians were killed and a further 30,000 wounded during the ten-week Israeli operation which dealt a heavy and decisive blow to the major cities in the south. As the PLO fighters retreated, they were pursued north to Beirut by the Israeli army and its 1,200 tanks where they laid siege to the capital, shelling PLO areas and cutting off food, fuel, water and other utility supplies. Following an international outcry over the operation, US intervention brought about a ceasefire and Yasser Arafat, the Palestinian leader, and his PLO were allowed to leave Beirut under the protection and supervision of a multi-national force comprising US,

French and Italian troops to other Arab states which included Algeria, Iraq, Sudan, Yemen and Tunisia (where the PLO set up its new headquarters). In all, around 11,000 Palestinians left the country which signalled the death knell for Arafat's longtime and passionate quest for a state and a homeland for the Palestinian people. The multi-national force left soon after the PLO's evacuation and Bashir Gemayel was elected president on 23 August 1982, only to be assassinated at his Kataib Party headquarters three weeks later, sparking outrage and calls for revenge and leading to Israel's return to the capital. Retribution duly arrived in horrific fashion only two days later when some 150 Christian militiamen entered the Palestinian refugee camps at Sabra and Shatila, where, over the course of just three days, they perpetrated an orgy of torture and killing against innocents which shocked the world and claimed up to 2,000 lives, many of those women and children. In its aftermath, eyewitness accounts and international investigations seemed to confirm that this macabre act and a war crime had at the very least tacit Israeli approval; in Tel Aviv alone, half a million Israelis demonstrated at the role of the Israeli Defence Force (IDF) in the massacre, which resulted in Sharon stepping down from his post, but with no-one brought to justice for the crimes. The killing spree also led to the return of a 6,000-strong multi-national peacekeeping force in an attempt to broker a peace deal between the warring militias a week after Amin Gemayel had succeeded his brother Bashir as the new president. Obliged to enter into the 17 May Agreement of 1983 by the US to guarantee the security of Israel's border in the north, the agreement was opposed by Muslims and Syria who soon attacked Christian neighbourhoods in Beirut. Meanwhile, fighting took place between Christian and Druze militias in the Chouf Mountains and despite its hitherto claims to be an honest broker in the war, the USS battleship *New Jersey* used its colossal 16-inch guns to batter Druze positions in the Chouf from the Mediterranean, which served to further Muslim hostility towards the US and its perceived support of Israel.

Although not the first suicide bombing on Lebanese soil during the civil war, it was a tactic and weapon which was to increase in frequency and severity by groups hostile to US interests. In April 1983, a suicide bomber killed 63 people, a death toll that included all the leading CIA agents in the region and destroyed the US embassy in Beirut. This was followed on 23 October by simultaneous suicide attacks on the US marine barracks near Beirut airport which killed 241 US servicemen. A truck laden with explosives was also driven into the headquarters of the French military, killing 58 French paratroopers. These attacks were deemed to be the work of the hitherto shadowy groups of Islamic Jihad and Hezbollah (see box, page 25), Lebanese Shi'ite organisations influenced by the Iranian Revolution and progressively radicalised by the Israeli presence in south Lebanon. During 1984, the Multi-National Force (MNF) departed Lebanon and the Israelis vacated the security zone in the south. Fighting continued between militias throughout the rest of the 1980s, with vestiges of the PLO in conflict with the Shi'ites and the Syrians increasing their stranglehold on the country. The Christians, despite their own internal conflicts, fought both. Some of the most intense fighting during this period was in the so-called 1985–87 'War of the Camps', which pitted the Shi'ite Amal militia against the Palestinians in west Beirut and the south of the country. Amal (Movement of the Dispossessed or Harakat al-Mahrumin in Arabic) had been founded back in 1975 by a theologian of Iranian origin called Mussa al-Sadr as offering 'Hope' to the impoverished Shi'ites by staving off Palestinian influence and thus the return of Israeli reprisals. Over the course of two years, in which the more secular Amal was also engaged in heavy fighting with the Druze and Hezbollah, it is estimated that the camp battles cost the lives of some 3,000 people.

With Amin Gemayel's tenure as president coming to an end in 1988, additional chaos and crisis ensued with Gemayel's appointment of the vehemently anti-Syrian general Michel Aoun as the new prime minister. Aoun embarked on a 'War of Liberation' with military assistance from Iraq who sought retribution for Syrian support for Iran during the 1980–88 conflict against the Syrian presence, in an attempt to unite the nation, but to no avail. In the absence of agreement across the sectarian divide the Muslims set up their own counter government in west Beirut, led by Prime Minister Salim al-Hoss, and intense fighting not seen since Israel's 1982 invasion once again arose between the militias across the Green Line. Following a ceasefire in September 1989, the Arab League initiated talks with the Lebanese politicians in the Saudi Arabian town of Taif to help resolve the conflict and pave the way for national reconciliation. The 23-day conference culminated in the Taif Accord which preserved Lebanon's confessional-based political system but led to a more equitable distribution of parliamentary seats from the previous 6:5 ratio in favour of the Christians. The accord also stipulated that all militias must lay down their weapons – except Hezbollah who were permitted to carry on their *jihad* of liberation against the Israeli occupation of south Lebanon. On 5 November, the accord was ratified by the Lebanese parliament. René Moawad was elected as the new president but assassinated a mere 17 days after taking office. Though Aoun was one of many other suspects, no-one has ever been charged with the killing of Moawad. Within 48 hours, Elias Hrawi replaced him, whose pro-Syrian stance brought him onto a collision course with the anti-Syrian Aoun who was finally forced to go into exile to Paris following heavy Syrian bombardments and internal schisms with the Lebanese Forces (LF) commander Samir Geagea. With the civil war formally ending on 13 October 1990, the death toll was deemed to have cost somewhere between 100,000 and 200,000 lives, with as many more wounded and displaced from their homes.

POST-WAR DEVELOPMENTS With an end to general hostilities a semblance of normality began to return to the country not witnessed for a decade and a half. It was a tenuous peace, however, and sporadic outbursts of fighting continued. The various militias began the process of disarmament, in accordance with the Taif Accord, except for Hezbollah who were permitted to retain their arms to continue their struggle against Israel, and the south of Lebanon remained a volatile area. By the summer of 1992, the remaining Western hostages were released from their captivity and plans began in earnest to rebuild the devastated country and economy.

Following the first elections since the war, in 1992, the new billionaire prime minister Rafiq Hariri initiated Solidere, a joint stock company charged with rebuilding Beirut's Downtown district with the aim of rejuvenating the capital which, it was hoped, would percolate through to drive economic growth and prosperity. It has proved controversial, amid rumblings about corruption and kickbacks, but it has undoubtedly transformed the aesthetics and the fortunes of Downtown Beirut. Meanwhile, Syria cemented its continuing presence in the country and in May 1991 signed the Brotherhood, Cooperation and Coordination Agreement which was supplemented in September 1991 with a military treaty called the Common Defence and Security Agreement. In the south, fighting between Israel, its proxy the South Lebanon Army (SLA) and Hezbollah continued with major incursions by Israel in 1993 and 1996; the latter provoking worldwide condemnation for its killing of 106 innocent civilians sheltering at a United Nations base in Qana.

In May 2000, following public concern in Israel at its high military losses in Lebanon, its forces withdrew from the south of the country, which also saw the collapse and surrender of the SLA to Hezbollah. Israel remains in control of the

The Special Tribunal for Lebanon (STL) is a UN-backed International Criminal Court (ICC), founded in June 2007 following a request from the Lebanese government in December 2005 with a mandate to: '…prosecute persons responsible for the attack of 14 February 2005 resulting in the death of former prime minister Rafiq Hariri and in the death or injury of other persons.' The STL officially began its work in March 2009 with no firm deadline set for completion, its hybrid character drawing on the Lebanese penal code – but excluding the death penalty – and international law, with any future trial taking place near The Hague in the Netherlands. Any person(s) convicted will serve their sentence in a country to be designated by the STL president from a list of countries who have said they would be willing to accept the convicted person(s).

The STL's budget for 2011 is US$65.7 million with the Lebanese government meeting 49% of the costs and the remainder from voluntary contributions from other countries which have included the UK and other EU nations, and the US. There is also provision for the scope of the STL to be broadened to include investigations into attacks on Lebanese soil between 1 October 2004 and 12 October 2005 if evidence becomes available that they are related to Hariri's murder. The STL is the first ICC to investigate a 'terrorist' act against a specific individual. But what, prima facie, seems merely a quest for justice, has polarised Lebanon's delicate sectarian political scene with the STL's procedures and possible verdict a highly controversial issue and seen by many as a catalyst for potential renewed civil strife in the country and the region.

Following a series of demonstrations and rallies in March 2005 in the wake of the Hariri killing, culminating in the Cedar Revolution which called for the withdrawal of Syrian military personnel and political interference, the domestic political scene became polarised into a pro-Western and anti-Syrian March 14 alliance and a Pan-Arab and pro-Syrian March 8 coalition. Whilst the March 14 group, led by Saad Hariri, the son of the former prime minister, has an 'unswerving commitment to international legitimacy' and the STL, the opposing March 8 faction, dominated by Hezbollah, totally rejects the legitimacy of the STL, which they designate an 'Israeli project' which serves Western interests designed to 'guillotine the resistance.' They point as well to the 'false witnesses', which implicated Syria in the 2005 attack whose illegitimate claims March 14 refuse to investigate.

In 2010, talk of the STL indicting rogue members of Hezbollah for the Hariri assassination led to further schisms between the groups culminating in March 8 cabinet members leaving the unity government, leading to its collapse in January 2011. Later the same month, the March 8 group nominated a new prime minister, Najib Mikati, and the president has appointed him as the new prime minister and following five months of political impasse finally formed his cabinet in June 2011. Later the same month the STL formally announced indictments against a number of members of Hezbollah with the STL's work continuing and the ramifications for Lebanon and the wider region uncertain at the time of writing. For further details and to keep abreast of current developments, visit the STL's official website at www.stl-tsl.org.

small enclave known as the Shebaa Farms, which remains a source of conflict and justification for Hezbollah's continued military action against Israel. Meanwhile, although dissent at another continuing occupying force, namely Syria, had been simmering away since the end of the civil war, when Damascus sanctioned extending the pro-Syrian Emile Lahoud's term as president, the UN Security Council's Resolution 1559 calling for all foreign presence to cease in Lebanon, Rafiq Hariri resigned from office in opposition to Syria's ongoing presence. Just five months later, on Valentine's Day 2005, a one-tonne bomb killed the former leader along with 21 other people close to Beirut's Saint George's Yacht Motor Club in Ain al-Mreisse, setting in motion a chain of events which at the time of writing remain unresolved. One month to the day later, a million Lebanese citizens took to the streets in Martyrs' Square in Downtown Beirut to protest at alleged Syrian involvement in the assassination and demanded that the totality of Syrian presence in the country end. This mass wave of demonstrations and protests came to be dubbed the Cedar Revolution and engendered the political group known as the March 14 Alliance, a pro-Western grouping, led by Saad Hariri, the son of the murdered ex-premier, the Druze leader Walid Jumblatt, and Samir Geagea, committed to terminating Syria's occupation and meddling in Lebanese affairs. Following continued internal and foreign outcry Syria finally succumbed to the pressure and withdrew its 14,000 military and security personnel from Lebanon on 26 April 2005, following a 29-year occupation which also saw the return of the banished Aoun to Lebanon.

2006 LEBANON WAR

Popularly known as the July War by the Lebanese, this 34-day conflict between Israel and the resistance force of Hezbollah was the most recent large-scale battle between these implacable foes. The start of the war on 12 July was precipitated by the Shi'ite militias' abduction and killing of members of the Israeli Defence Force (IDF) inside Israeli territory. Israeli reprisals were severe with large-scale air strikes and land assaults with Hezbollah launching over 4,000 Katyusha rockets into northern Israel. By the end of the war some 1,191, mainly Lebanese, civilians were killed and some 160 Israelis, mainly IDF members, with 4,405 Lebanese and 4,262 Israelis wounded. Lebanon's infrastructure was decimated with many of the country's roads and over 100 bridges destroyed. Almost one million Lebanese had been displaced and 30,000 homes were destroyed. The intense Israeli air bombardment on Lebanon's main power plant at Jiyeh has resulted in an environmental catastrophe unprecedented in the eastern Mediterranean (see pages 7–8). In south Lebanon a large amount of unexploded cluster bombs continue to pose a threat to locals and visitors alike. Although an Israeli naval blockade remained in place until 8 September, United Nations Security Council Resolution 1701 on 11 August led to a final ceasefire three days later. Despite both sides claiming victory, Israel's avowed aim of destroying Hezbollah had not been achieved, nor had the UN call for the disarmament of all militias in Lebanon. The end result was for a more intense United Nations peacekeeping force in the south of the country and, for the first time in many years, the deployment of Lebanese forces around the country. Meanwhile, both Israel and Hezbollah have been busily replenishing their arsenals with the latter now estimated to possess around 40,000–50,000 longer range and more powerful rockets whilst Israel's continued receipt of military aid from the US carries on apace…

However, the peaceful Cedar Revolution did not usher in an equally peaceful new era for Lebanon free of foreign control. Following the departure of Syrian forces the country was once again subjected to a number of assassinations and bombings which targeted journalists and prominent political figures, which is still being investigated by the UN-backed Special Tribunal for Lebanon (see box, page 22). Following elections in 2005, the country was governed by the March 14 Alliance with Prime Minister Fouad Siniora at the helm and which also saw Hezbollah gain 14 parliamentary seats and in the summer of 2006, took part in renewed hostilities with Israel which became known as the July War (see box, page 23). Further internal discord resulted following the resignation of politicians from Hezbollah, and the political vacuum which this created following the end of Emile Lahoud's term as president was only filled in May 2008, when the Doha Accord ended months of political crisis which has seen once again a veneer of stability return to the country. It remains to be seen at the time of writing what effects the STL's findings will have on Lebanon's, and the region's, immediate and future stability. It is perhaps indicative and not a little ironic that Lebanon's unique history and sectarianism has left the country hitherto untouched by the 'Arab Spring' and recent waves of activism which have engulfed other Arab nations such as Algeria, Bahrain, Egypt, Libya, Tunisia and, latterly Syria, that the country has remained 'outside' these attempts to challenge years of autocratic rule. With developments in Syria still uncertain at the time of writing it is possible, however, that given the geographic and historical ties between the two countries any regime change could yet impact on Lebanon and beyond.

GOVERNMENT AND POLITICS

Lebanon's modern political constitution dates back to 1926 when the country was under French colonial rule (see page 16), which gave birth to the nation's confessional basis of politics which proportions political power amongst the various religious groupings. Following independence in 1943, the National Pact extended and reinforced Lebanon's sectarian system of power sharing whilst the Taif Accord in 1989, the agreement reached in the Saudi Arabian town which ended the 1975–90 civil war, further amended the country's constitutional powers.

Lebanon is a republic and parliamentary democracy with a centralised system of government. Under the terms of the country's confessional-based system, the president must be a Christian Maronite, the prime minister a Sunni Muslim and the parliamentary speaker a Shi'ite Muslim. These three posts comprise the troika of Lebanese politics. The power to implement legislation resides with the 128-member National Assembly (parliament) whose seats are shared equally between Christians and Muslims. Elections are held every four years and all Lebanese over the age of 21 years are eligible to vote. In turn the parliament appoints a president for a six-year term but the president is not permitted to stand for consecutive terms of office. In addition to being the head of state and a 'symbol of the nation's unity', the president is also commander-in-chief of the country's armed forces. The president, in consultation with the National Assembly, appoints the prime minister and his deputy. The 30-member cabinet is then chosen by the prime minister after consulting with the president and parliament.

The judicial branch of government, whose personnel are also apportioned along sectarian lines, is heavily influenced by former French rule and incorporates the Napoleonic Code together with a mix of Ottoman, civil and canon law. Lebanon's four-court system includes three courts for civil and commercial cases and one for

HEZBOLLAH

Designated a 'foreign terrorist organisation' by the US and others and often compared to groups such as Al-Qaeda and the Taliban, the Party of God continues to be one of the most enduring and high-profile aspects of modern Lebanese history and politics with which most Westerners are familiar. This Shi'ite organisation founded in 1982 traces its origins back to the Iranian Revolution in 1979 which overthrew the country's shah and ushered in the fundamentalist Islamic Republic of Iran. Lebanon's Shi'ites, long the most impoverished, powerless and poorly educated of Lebanon's religious mosaic, saw the Iranian Islamic success story as hope for a greater voice and participation in their country's affairs which they had hitherto lacked. This realm of ideas was given the catalyst to be translated into practice following Israel's 1982 invasion of Lebanon. The overwhelming firepower and the long and destructive siege of Beirut only served to galvanise an already dispossessed and radical Shi'ite population who had long suffered from Israeli reprisals following the cross-border conflict between Israel and the Palestinians. The fertile Bekaa Valley provided, in the strategic town of Baalbek, an equally fertile educational, theological and military training ground for Iranian Revolutionary Guards to support their Shi'ite compatriots in expelling Israel from Lebanon and fighting what Hezbollah saw as its expansionist aims in the Middle East in general.

The organisation from its inception implemented a back-to-basics Islamic ideology with their role model the 'martyr' Imam Hussein, killed at the Battle of Karbala in AD680 and held up as the example of sacrifice against injustice and the struggle against Israel akin to that between Islam and the Crusaders during the Middle Ages. Whilst Hezbollah's resistance to Israeli occupation and US support involved suicide bombings, hijackings and the kidnap of Westerners during the civil war, it has consistently denied involvement with the 1983 suicide attacks on the US and French military barracks in Beirut. Yet ever since the organisation first went public in 1985 declaring itself the Islamic Resistance (*al-moqawama al-Islamiyah*; www.moqawama. org), Hezbollah has always been about much more than armed struggle, including the establishment of an Islamic state in Lebanon, and insists on its consensual nature: 'we do not seek to impose Islam on anyone... and we do not want Islam to reign in Lebanon by force... But we confirm that we are convinced by Islam as an ideology and a system.' Following the end of the civil war Hezbollah has increasingly been at the centre of Lebanese political life and whilst its ideology is not universally shared, its resistance operations against Israel have widespread backing, even by many Christians. In the 1992 elections, Hezbollah gained eight seats in parliament, increasing this to 14 in 2005, and they were only narrowly defeated by the pro-Western government in the last elections of 2009. In addition to its political influence the organisation operates a number of schools and hospitals, provides low-cost housing and broadcasts from its own TV station, Al-Manar ('the beacon').

criminal proceedings. There are no jury trials and a Supreme Council presides over matters against the president and prime minister as required.

At a local level, Lebanon is divided into six separate governorates or *muhafazat*, not unlike the county system in the UK and these, with their capitals in brackets, are: Beirut (Beirut), Bekaa (Zahlé), Mount Lebanon (Baabda), North Lebanon (Tripoli), South Lebanon (Sidon) and Nabatiyye (Nabatiye). These regions are further sub-divided into 25 districts or *cazas* with further divisions into numerous smaller municipalities containing locally elected leaders and officials.

The last elections were held in June 2009, and the turnout was estimated at over 50%, the highest in Lebanese electoral history. The election was won by Saad Hariri, the son of Rafiq Hariri, the former prime minister who was assassinated on Valentine's Day 2005 by a lorry bomb. His pro-Western March 14 Alliance narrowly defeated the Shi'ite party Hezbollah, winning 71 of the 128 parliamentary seats. First and foremost a businessman, Saad Hariri was an unlikely politician, thrust onto the political stage following the death of his father who did much to help reunite the country and revitalise the economy following 15 years of civil strife, and following a period of political uncertainty, Hariri managed to form a government of national unity in November 2009. In January 2011, however, Hariri's coalition collapsed following the resignation of the opposition March 8 group composed principally of members of Hezbollah and their allies and their rejection of the UN-backed Special Tribunal for Lebanon (see box, page 22) which was widely held, and subsequently confirmed in June, to be about to indict Hezbollah members for their alleged involvement in the killing of Rafiq Hariri in 2005. At the time of writing concern that the indictments could spark off a new round of sectarian conflict has not materialised but it remains the current political hot potato for the country.

ECONOMY

As the majority of the world's economies floundered in the wake of a global economic downturn not witnessed for a generation, Lebanon was one of only seven countries to record economic growth in 2008. Although the International Monetary Fund (IMF) forecast a slowdown in growth to around 6% in 2009, the Fund estimated GDP growth to rise to 8% by the end of 2010, the fourth highest in the world and second only to oil-rich Qatar in the Middle East region. Unlike many of its Arab neighbours, who derive their revenues and wealth from huge oil and natural gas deposits, Lebanon's economic success derives from its unique geography, history and the resourcefulness of its people, as it has for thousands of years. With a long-standing *laissez-faire* economic tradition, the future for Lebanon's economy seems well placed to meet past and present challenges to regional and political instability.

The mainstay of the Lebanese economy is the service sector with banking, finance and tourism predominating, accounting for around three-quarters of the country's GDP. Lebanon's banking system offers many advantages to investors including no restrictions on foreign investment or movement of capital, a strict banking code guaranteeing secrecy and a country free of any international trade sanctions. A vitally important revenue stream is the remittances which the country receives from the estimated ten–15 million Lebanese diaspora, many of whom fled Lebanon during the civil war to eke out a better life in Europe, the Americas and Australia. The money these expatriates send home to family members in Lebanon is immense and in 2009 reached US$7 billion, representing some 22% of the country's GDP, one positive aspect of Lebanon's 'brain drain', which has seen such foreign capital inflows benefiting both the real estate and banking sectors. Tourism, employing around half a million people or 38% of the workforce, has long been a salient part of the Lebanese economy and, although the industry receded following the 2006 summer conflict between Israel and Hezbollah, this sector has shown remarkable resilience and in 2009 the United Nations World Tourism Organisation (UNWTO) ranked Lebanon in first place for world tourism growth. According to figures from the Lebanese Ministry of Tourism revenues from tourism reached US$8 billion in 2010, an increase from US$7.2 billion in 2009, and visitor numbers exceeded two million in 2010, an increase of 10% on 2009.

Lebanon's industrial sector accounts for some 15% of GDP, centred on food processing, jewellery manufacture, cement, textiles, metal fabrication, mineral and chemical products together with wood and furniture. The country's main trading partners for exports in descending order of size are: Syria, United Arab Emirates, Saudi Arabia and Switzerland. For imports they include France, the US, Syria, Italy, China, Germany, Ukraine and Turkey. Agriculture, whilst accounting for just over 5% of GDP, remains an important source of income with well over a third of Lebanon's land area given over to this sector, though less so than previously. Lebanon's location within the Fertile Crescent, with its well-watered soils and favourable climate, has given the country the highest proportion of land given over to agriculture in the Arab world. Consequently, a wide variety of crops are grown including citrus fruits, grapes, apples, vegetables, potatoes, olives, and tobacco together with livestock in the more mountainous areas. It is viticulture, however, which is probably Lebanon's best-known agricultural product, with the wineries in the Bekaa Valley such as Ksara, Kefraya and Musar having well-established local and international reputations.

Despite Lebanon's efficient banking system and once again burgeoning tourist industry, the country continues to suffer from an economic hangover from the civil war years of 1975–90. Not surprisingly, this 15-year conflict had a high economic as well as human cost, cutting national output by half, destroying the majority of the nation's infrastructure and severely devaluing the Lebanese currency from a pre-war LBP2.50 to US$1 to the current rate of LBP1,500 to US$1. To meet these challenges the government has had to borrow heavily and tap into its foreign exchange reserves to fund major reconstruction projects such as those in the Downtown area of Beirut, the area most heavily damaged during the civil war (see pages 17–21 and *Chapter 3*, page 125). The result is that public debt remains high and in June 2010 was US$51 billion, some 147% of GDP, the fourth highest in the world.

Intermittent and regional instability has also served to hamper continued economic progress. The assassination of former prime minister Rafiq Hariri in 2005 led to the peaceful Cedar Revolution which saw thousands of protesters nationwide successfully demonstrate for the withdrawal of Syrian troops and security personnel from the country and which brought some degree of stability to the country. But a 34-day conflict in the summer of 2006 between Israel and Hezbollah (see box, page 23) set Lebanon back markedly and the economic cost of this war was estimated at US$3.6 billion worth of infrastructure damage following the decimation of 80% of the country's main roads. Since then there have been pledges of aid; the Doha Accord of 2008, which brought an end to political infighting, together with peaceful parliamentary elections in 2009, which ushered in a government of national unity, has put much confidence back into the country as a whole. The Economist Intelligence Unit (EIU) has forecast real GDP growth of 5.5% in 2011. The future of Lebanon's economy, however, whilst heavily pegged to the wider Middle East peace process, is also dependent upon the country's ability to alleviate its national debt together with ongoing economic reforms such as privatisation.

PEOPLE

In Lebanon, the issue of the sectarian balance of the population is a highly sensitive one and no official population census has been undertaken since 1932. According to the latest 2011 estimates, however, the population stands at 4,143,101, with some 87% of people residing in urban areas and nearly half resident in the capital, Beirut. There is a roughly 50/50 split between males and females and the population, in common with most Arab countries, is predominantly a youthful one, with 68% of Lebanese aged between 15 and 64 years. In 2011, Lebanon's population growth rate was estimated at 0.244%, one of the lowest in the world. According to United Nations figures Lebanon has 404 people per km^2, making the country one of the most densely populated in the world (25th out of 239 countries surveyed). An astonishing figure is the additional 10–15 million Lebanese, or those of Lebanese descent, living outside the country. Many of these have fled the country over the years; a mass migration which began in the 19th century, to escape wars, unemployment, political and sectarian repression and who have settled in North and South America, Australia and Europe. A large number of these diaspora continue to retain close ties with their country by frequent visits and remitting significant sums of money 'home' to family members.

ARABS Ethnically, Arabs – an eclectic name for equally diverse religious and ethnic groups – comprise some 95% of Lebanon's total population. Out of this total some 60% are Muslim, spread across the different denominations such as Sunni, Shi'ite and Druze, with the remainder composed of a plethora of Christian sects such as Maronite, Greek Orthodox, Roman Catholic or Protestant. Many Christians, however, often eschew the word 'Arab' in favour of being identified with their ancient Phoenician roots while the Druze, an offshoot from Islam comprising some 5% of the population and concentrated mainly in the Chouf and Metn mountains, are considered by many to be so far removed from Islam's basic tenets so as to constitute an entirely separate religion (see pages 32–3). There are also differences between the Sunni and Shi'ite sects and this variety adds to the cosmopolitan mix, rendering Lebanon a fascinating place for visitors, evident in its contrasting architectural styles such as churches, mosques, temples and costumes together with a variety of celebrations and festivals.

ARMENIANS The Armenian diaspora constitute 4% of the country's ethnic makeup and are mostly concentrated around the Bourj Hammoud district in east Beirut, with smaller numbers resident around the cities of Aanjar in the Bekaa Valley, Byblos and Tripoli. The Armenians fled to Lebanon in great numbers in 1915 due to the genocide in Ottoman Turkey in which it is estimated that well over a million people were killed. They now have a thriving community which is fully integrated into Lebanese society with full citizenship rights and representation in parliament. The Armenian university in Beirut continues to teach their language and culture, and shop and street signs still bear the Armenian script.

PALESTINIANS Not so fortunate as the Armenians are the 425,640 United Nations Relief Works Agency (UNRWA) registered Palestinian refugees – about 10% of the country's population – of which 226,553 eke out a miserable existence in Lebanon's 12 refugee camps scattered across the country. Many of these are those who fled what is now Israel in 1948 with later influxes from the 1967 Yom Kippur War with Israel and the expulsion of Palestinians from Jordan during Black September in 1970. In contrast to the Armenians the Palestinians are unwanted in Lebanon and possess no civil or political rights, no access to social services, and they are forbidden by law from engaging in over 70 occupations. They are almost entirely dependent on handouts from UNRWA, with Lebanon having the highest percentage of refugees in the region living in abject poverty and registered with UNRWA's Special Hardship programme. In June 2010, thousands of refugees took to the streets of Beirut to protest their plight and demand a degree of integration and civil rights they have hitherto lacked. It remains to be seen whether the momentum generated by activism will be translated into a future change in government policy.

MIGRANT WORKERS In addition to the large number of Syrian workers in the country, especially on construction sites in the cities and undertaking agricultural labour in the Bekaa Valley, it is estimated that there are around 200,000 additional foreign workers in Lebanon. These are mostly from countries such as Ethiopia, Nepal, the Philippines and Sri Lanka, a small proportion of the millions of mainly women workers who have journeyed from Africa and Asia in search of employment and a better life. They generally work as domestic servants in private households and businesses, work which is often seen as demeaning and degrading by Lebanese. Some live in with their employer, whilst others rent accommodation elsewhere. You can often see them around the streets of Hamra in west Beirut dog walking or pushing a pram in their trademark pink uniforms and on their day off strolling the city. According to Human Rights Watch, however, their plight is not always a happier one with many forced to work up to 18 hours a day and denied any time off, whilst others experience psychological, physical and even sexual abuse at the hands of their employer which has led to an alarming suicide rate amongst this vulnerable group of imported labour.

LANGUAGE

Fortunately for the first-time visitor to Lebanon, the country doesn't have quite as many languages to get to grips with as it does ethnic and religious groups, though in ancient times there were a variety of Semitic languages spoken such as Canaanite, Phoenician, Aramaic and Arabic. During the period of French colonial rule, French became the dominant language and was compulsory in schools. Since Lebanon's independence in 1943, however, the lingua franca of the country is Arabic, the largest of the Semitic language family and the native language spoken by more than 300 million people, mainly in north Africa and the Middle East. The specific type of Arabic spoken in Lebanon by Muslims, Christians and Druze is called Levantine Arabic, which is also the common language spoken in Jordan, Syria and by the Palestinians in the Occupied Territories and beyond. In Lebanon's schools, Arabic is a compulsory part of the school curriculum for children up until the age of 12 years.

After Arabic, French is the second most spoken language and is particularly prevalent among the Christian Maronite community in east Beirut where you can often encounter people with French-sounding first names such as Antoinne, Michel or Pierre as well as many road and shop signs in French. As the international language of business, English has had a high profile for many years amongst the entrepreneurial Lebanese. It is also the main language of instruction at two of the country's top universities – the American University of Beirut (AUB) and the Lebanese American University (LAU). A common linguistic trait of the Lebanese, especially the younger generation, is to skilfully mix and match Arabic, French and English during the course of a conversation and even within a single sentence. Thus, the greeting '*Hi, Habibi, ça va?*' combines the English greeting 'hi' with the Arabic 'baby'/'darling' and the French 'how are you?'. Such versatility in the use of language has caused concern in some circles that the younger generation are losing contact with their linguistic roots, preferring English and French, to the detriment of their Arab and national identity.

Despite its veneer of Western cosmopolitanism, openness and tolerance, couples from different faiths are still not permitted to marry in Lebanon because marriage is controlled and regulated by the religious authorities. Unless one partner converts – impossible in the Druze religion which forbids conversion from outside sects – or the ceremony takes place overseas, only religious weddings are permitted under current Lebanese law. For those couples sharing the same faith, impending nuptials may also come at a price. The death of a Sunni husband, for instance, results in his widow permitted only to receive 50% of her dead husband's estate whilst the Maronite sect prohibits divorce. Opponents of the system have long campaigned to see the back of what they view as an archaic, morally unjust system, which serves merely to perpetuate already deep sectarian divisions in society. Some progress was made in 2009, when the Lebanese government announced people would have the choice as to whether they declare their religious affiliation on their national ID cards. But for the time being at least, in the absence of civil marriages in the country, star-crossed lovers will have to continue to pop over to places like nearby Cyprus where, for under US$2,000, they can tie the knot and be back in Lebanon in time for the wedding breakfast.

Although comprising a small part of the total population, the Armenian diaspora in the Bourj Hammoud district of east Beirut, Byblos and Aanjar in the Bekaa Valley continue to honour their linguistic roots by speaking Western Armenian, an Indo-European language which is identical to that spoken in the Republic of Armenia and the disputed south Caucasus region of Nagorno-Karabakh. Educational institutions such as the Haigazian University in Beirut continue to teach the Armenian language and the script is also visible on many banks, shops and road signs in their community heartlands.

LEARNING AND USING ARABIC One of the problems for non-native speakers of the language is understanding the dichotomy between Classical Arabic and its descendant, Modern Standard Arabic, which are two quite different linguistic animals. The latter is the written form of the language and closely resembles its predecessor, the language of the Koran and early Arabic literature, especially poetry. It is uniform throughout the Arab world and used in books, magazines and newspapers, and is one of the six official languages of the United Nations. Thus a daily Lebanese Arabic newspaper such as *An-Nahar* is perfectly intelligible to an Arab reader in Libya or Iraq and vice versa.

It is essentially the spoken form of Arabic which varies from country to country and even from region to region. The enigmatic Druze community, for instance, have what amounts to their own distinctive dialect. Happily, despite some small differences, spoken Levantine Arabic is very similar to Modern Standard Arabic and learning a few words and phrases can only serve to enhance your cultural and travel experience. For more practical details on the everyday use of the Arabic language, see *Appendix 1*.

RELIGION

Lebanon has the most religiously diverse population in the entire Middle East with 18 different officially recognised sects in the country: Muslim (Shi'ite, Sunni,

Druze, Ismaili and Alawite), Christian (Maronite, Catholic, Greek Orthodox, Melkite Catholic, Armenian Orthodox, Syrian Catholic, Armenian Catholic, Syrian Orthodox, Roman Catholic, Chaldean, Assyrian, Copt, Protestant), and Judaism. As the last – and only – official census was held way back in 1932 it is a tricky business to ascertain the exact numerical proportions of each sect. Although the census showed a slight majority in favour of the Christian Maronites, it is now generally recognised that owing to differences in birth rates and the high rates of emigration amongst Christians, Muslims comprise the majority of the country's religious groups. According to the latest estimates, Christians number some 39% of the population whilst Muslims make up 59.7% of the population.

One of the defining characteristics of Lebanon has been the history of co-existence between such diverse faiths over the years characterised by periods of harmony, often for pragmatic reasons, and discord most recently witnessed during Lebanon's long 15-year civil war. Whilst the post-war era has seen a time of remarkable stability compared with the smouldering resentment of that period, the importance of religion in both daily and political life remains as entrenched as ever for most Lebanese. The country remains governed along 'confessional' lines, as it has since 1926, meaning that politics and religion remain inseparable. The social fabric of life is also touched by faith and couples of different sects are not permitted to marry outside their own religion (see box opposite). In order to understand Lebanon and its people better a general awareness and understanding of Islam and the basic tenets of each sect is useful.

ISLAM With some 1.6 billion practising Muslims, Islam, the third of the great monotheistic faiths after Christianity and Judaism, is the second-largest religion in the world after Christianity and also the world's fastest growing faith. The founder of Islam was the merchant Arab, the Prophet Muhammad, who was born in the city of Mecca in modern-day Saudi Arabia around AD570. Prone to seeking solace and spiritual contemplation in nearby Mount Hira, Muhammad received a series of visitations over a period of more than two decades from Jibril (known as the Archangel Gabriel to Christians and Jews) who revealed to him the final and true word of God (Allah). Although God's word had been received by earlier prophets such as Adam, Abraham, Jacob, Jesus and Moses, his words had been corrupted and distorted over time and Muhammad thus represents the last and true final prophet. Eventually, Muhammad and his followers wrote down these words of God to form the Koran, the holy book of Islam. In AD622, following a period of persecution and struggle in which the Prophet and his initially small band of believers fought against sceptics and unbelievers, Muhammad and his entourage embarked on the Hejira or migration from Mecca to Medina (City of the Prophet). This epochal event marks the beginning of the burgeoning Islamic community or *umma*, and the birth of the Islamic calendar. According to the verses laid down in the Koran, the word of God, the devout Muslim must follow an Islamic way of life, which is enshrined in the Five Pillars of Islam. The first and most fundamental principle is the *shahadatayn* or 'Two Testimonies' in which the true Muslim asserts that 'there is no God but God and Muhammad is His messenger'. The remaining duties of every true Muslim, in order to lead a moral and virtuous life are: *salat*, to pray five times a day (dawn, midday, mid afternoon, sunset and nightfall), alone or in a mosque; *zakat*, or almsgiving to the poor or to those less fortunate; *sawm*, to fast during the holy lunar month of Ramadan; the *hajj*, or annual pilgrimage to Mecca, should be undertaken at least once by those physically and materially able. Muhammad died in AD632 but within a few years of his death the new religion experienced a major rupture centred on the future leadership of the Islamic community which endures to this day and which resulted in the division into the Sunni and Shi'ite religious sects.

SUNNI MUSLIMS For Sunnis, who comprise some 90% of Muslims around the world, and are numerous around the main coastal cities of west Beirut, the western Bekaa Valley, Sidon and Tripoli, successive leaders, or caliphs, should be chosen among the most virtuous of Muslims who will uphold the customs or *sunna* of the Prophet Muhammad, expressed through the *hadith* or words and deeds of the Prophet. Lacking any discernible heirs, the caliphate was succeeded by Muhammad's ally and friend Abu Bakr who in turn were followed by Umar and then Uthman. Upon the latter's death in AD656, the Sunni–Shi'ite split took on a new and more violent dimension. Unlike the Shi'ites, Sunnis have traditionally been the more affluent and educated of the two sects.

SHI'ITE MUSLIMS Fundamentally, the Shi'ites, representing around 8% of the world's Muslims, reject the legitimacy of the first three caliphs under Abu Bakr, Umar and Uthman. In their eyes, only direct familial descendants of the Prophet Muhammad could become leaders. When Ali ibn Abu Talib, Muhammad's cousin and son-in-law, was named fourth caliph after the murder of Uthman, he too was killed by his opponents in AD661. This Muslim faction has since come to be known as the 'Partisans of Ali' or 'Shi'ite Ali'. Ali's son and the Prophet's grandson, Hussein', revolted but was slain at the Battle of Karbala on the banks of the Euphrates in modern-day Iraq in AD680. These two events rank amongst the most important in the Shi'ite calendar with the deaths of both Ali and Hussein seen as examples of martyrdom. In Lebanon, the annual Shi'ite festival of Ashura at Nabattiye in south Lebanon (see page 256) is celebrated in memory of the slaying of Hussein and is a moving and remarkable visual and vocal spectacle of faith with young boys and men flagellating themselves whilst mourning his passing. The Shi'ites in Lebanon, comprising perhaps 40% of the total population, number the largest of the Muslim sects and are concentrated mainly around the southern suburbs of Beirut, Baalbek in the Bekaa Valley, and in many towns and villages in the south of the country.

DRUZE This enigmatic but highly influential sect, numbering some 200,000 or 5% of Lebanon's total population, was founded in Cairo in the 11th century as a splinter group from the Shi'ite Ismaili faith following the 6th-century Fatimid caliph, al-Hakim, proclaiming himself to be God's incarnation on earth and thus the final imam. Prior to his death in 1021, Hakim despatched two envoys, Hamza ibn Ali and Muhammad ibn Darazzi (from whom the name Druze derives) to spread his ideology in Syria, which included modern-day Lebanon and converted many Ismailis, setting in motion a theology and practice considered by many Sunni Muslims to be so far removed from the *umma* or customs of Islam so as to constitute an entirely separate religion. Widely seen as a highly secretive sect, even amongst themselves, Druze are divided into an elite 10% who are entrusted to haemorrhage knowledge of the faith only to chosen family members. It is known that they retain an Islamic identity but reject its Five Pillars and believe in reincarnation. Conversion from other faiths is not permitted and you can only be Druze by birth with intermarriage between sects also prohibited. For Druze the main holy day is not Friday as in mainstream Islam, but Thursday evening when they will pray secretly, not in mosques, but in inconspicuous places like halls, known as *khalwats*.

Concentrated mainly in the Chouf and Metn mountain areas, the Druze are probably the most easily identifiable sect with men dressed in trademark baggy trousers called Sarawak, sporting eccentric moustaches and beards and white caps, and women wearing white veils and long, flowing black dresses. Despite a long history of persecution the Druze has nonetheless been a significant part of Lebanon's religious mosaic. During Ottoman rule they found a voice and a national hero in the form of Fakhreddine Maan and they continue to play an active role in modern-day politics under their current leader Walid Jumblatt. Jumblatt has been quoted as saying that Druze 'is not a secretive religion, that is apart from the Secret Books...You could say our faith is inspired by Neo-Platonism, and that in some respects it reflects the teachings of Socrates and Plato...' The worldwide Druze population comprises around one million people, with concentrations of over 100,000 in the Galilee and Golan Heights in Israel, more than 400,000 in Syria, and there are smaller communities in Jordan, North and South America, Australia, Africa and Europe.

CHRISTIANS Of the numerous Christian denominations in the country the Maronites are the largest group, with large communities in east Beirut, Byblos and throughout the Mount Lebanon region. As an eastern branch of the Roman Catholic Church, the Maronites trace their roots back to the 4th-century hermit called St Maroun who lived along the Orontes River in Syria. As their ecclesiastical views on the nature of Christ's divine and human will brought them into conflict with mainstream Christian orthodoxy, they retreated to Mount Lebanon around the period of the Arab invasions in the 7th century to continue to practise their doctrines free from persecution. Although they reunited with the mainstream Roman Catholic Church in the 11th century, important differences remain including their retention of the liturgy in the Syriac language and no requirement to take a vow of celibacy for non-ordained priests. The Maronites are an important religious group in Lebanon, and as enshrined in the 1943 National Pact the president must be a Maronite Christian.

EDUCATION

Lebanon has a long and established history as a centre of educational excellence throughout the Arab world. During Roman rule, Beirut's School of Law was one of the most prestigious in the entire Roman Empire. In 1866, a Protestant missionary founded the modern-day American University of Beirut (AUB), which to this day is widely recognised as one of the finest educational institutions in the country, if not the region. Also highly respected is the francophone St Joseph University (USJ), founded by Jesuit Fathers in 1875, with a wide range of faculties teaching classes in Arabic and English in addition to French as the main language of instruction. The Lebanese American University (LAU), whose origins date back to Ottoman times, is modelled on the US education system with classes taught in English and is a highly valued institution both within and outside the country. This tradition continues where education is a highly prized asset. Considerable investment and restructuring of the system is ongoing and this is reflected in a combined literacy rate approaching 90% for adults over the age of 15 years, the highest in the Middle East. Under Lebanon's constitution, schooling is free for all Lebanese children up to the age of 12 years, regardless of ethnicity and religious affiliation. This provision is not extended to the Palestinian diaspora in the country who are totally dependent upon the educational services and facilities provided by UNRWA.

SCHOOLING While there are around 2,000 state-run primary schools and around 1,400 secondary schools in the country, private schools far outnumber these on account of the latter's higher-quality facilities and their philosophy of encouraging more independent and analytical thinking than state schools. Around three-quarters of pupils and students are educated in the private sector. All pupils must attend six years of primary school education (ages 6–12), followed by three years at intermediate school (ages 12–15), at the end of which students sit and must pass the Brevet or intermediate test prior to entering secondary school (ages 15–18). At the end of a student's secondary school years, they take the Lebanese Baccalaureate exam, which is modelled on the French educational system. Unsurprisingly, there are marked variations in educational attainment across the country with much lower literacy rates and school attainment in poorer regions such as the Bekaa Valley, and north and south Lebanon when compared with Beirut and the Mount Lebanon areas.

UNIVERSITY AND HIGHER EDUCATION Successful completion of the Baccalaureate is a prerequisite for university entry and students wishing to embark on higher education may also have to sit an additional university entrance exam. Lebanon has over 40 higher education institutions, including universities and a host of more vocational seats of learning, but only one of these is state-run – the Lebanese State University, founded in 1967, in Beirut. One area of concern is that many of these fee-paying establishments are mainly pegged to a political or religious group, which serves to fuel sectarianism and hinders opportunities for national solidarity and integration. An additional and perennial issue for Lebanon is the way the country haemorrhages many of its most highly qualified and skilled personnel. Owing to low wages and a lack of career progression, many well-educated Lebanese leave the country to take up more rewarding and better-paid positions overseas, especially in Europe and the Gulf.

CULTURE

Cultural life in Lebanon is infused with confusions and contradictions, making this small country a fascinating mosaic of cultural mores for visitors. For a country which has been to hell and back many times throughout its history, a perhaps surprising aspect of cultural life is the overwhelming sense of friendliness, hospitality and openness of its people, evidenced from the warm and smiling 'Welcome to Lebanon' to an offer of a drink or meal, a trait you can find from Tripoli to Tyre and across the religious spectrum. Greetings too can perhaps be more gregarious than you might expect in an Arab country with three kisses on the cheek and a hug a common welcome to friends and family, though a normal handshake is customary for an initial welcome. Lebanon's culture has been described as akin to *fattoush*, a *mezze* dish containing a variety of contrasting ingredients borne of the country's many influences over the millennia. You have the overwhelming Arab influence of course most apparent in the use of language together with the numerous mosques and churches of differing styles reflecting the various Christian sects. Alongside this is the French influence from the colonial era, where the language and street names are still apparent in Beirut neighbourhoods as is the cuisine.

Whilst Beirut basks in its renewed status as the party capital of the Middle East where alcohol is freely available, the southern city of Sidon has a more conservative and reserved café culture where alcohol is available at only one establishment. The family remains the bedrock of Lebanese society across all regions and religious groups creating a sense of community within and outside the home where even in the capital people will often have an extended family living in close proximity. Sons and daughters generally live at home until they marry, with the expectation that they will do so within their own sect (see box, page 30), and the importance of family life is extended to visitors as Lebanese adore children and your offspring will be made a fuss of. Lebanese women espouse a beauty and a glamour that can seem to belie their Arab traditions and they are less constrained by religion than many of their Arab sisters. A visit to the Gemmayze or Achrafieh districts in east Beirut, for instance, where there are immaculately manicured and stylishly dressed young women in short skirts, evokes Lebanon's cosmopolitanism. It is not unusual to see a woman sitting alone in a bar or café and there is no stigma or taboo attached to this as perhaps you might find in Western culture. Though women, as in many cultures, are still constrained by their gender into defined roles such as homemaker, many Lebanese women hold down careers in media, government departments and the scientific professions but again, as in other countries, the top echelons of business and politics remain a primarily male preserve.

Lebanon remains a male-dominated society, as are most Arab countries, and one area where this is most noticeable, or more accurately absent, is the issue of homosexuality. As it is deemed to be an act against nature according to Lebanese law and punishable by prison you will not see any gay cruising on the streets of the capital or elsewhere in the country, but obviously it still occurs and Beirut has a handful of venues which are gay-friendly and there are organisations and information websites increasingly available offering advice and support. As a gay visitor, however, discretion is advised and public displays of affection should be avoided.

VISUAL AND PERFORMING ARTS For aficionados of archaeology and architecture Lebanon is an open-air museum. The country's long history of invasion and occupation has left a rich historical legacy of fine castles, churches, mosques, palaces and temples all over the country. The Crusader castles at Byblos and Tripoli, the Phoenician Temple of Echmoun in Sidon, the soaring Roman temples at Baalbek and the world's largest Hippodrome in the southern city of Tyre are just a few highlights testifying to Lebanon's cultural past. A visit to the Umayyad-era town of Aanjar in the Bekaa Valley affords a beautiful and rare insight into the early years of Arab rule. Supplementing these *in-situ* remains are those in Lebanon's variety of museums, particularly the National Museum in Beirut which houses an eclectic array of finds from the Phoenician to the Mamluk periods.

In Downtown Beirut restored Ottoman-era architecture is apparent along with Roman-era baths overlooked by modernity. Lebanon's most contemporary famous architect is Bernard al-Khoury who divides his time between Beirut and New York. He has been involved with many rebuilding projects since the end of the civil war with perhaps his most famous creation, the BO18 dance club in the capital, constructed on a wartime site and using coffin-like seating together with a fully retractable roof. One of the reasons for Beirut once being dubbed the 'Paris of the Middle East' was its flourishing art scene which is certainly seeing a revival. There are many art galleries, mainly in Beirut, which showcase both national and international talent with the relatively new and largest of these being the Beirut Arts Centre which has multi-media shows across a range of genres attracting worldwide press attention. There is an equally lively film and theatre scene catering for both mainstream and independent audiences. Though the Lebanese film industry is nowhere near as prolific as Bollywood or Hollywood there are a number of independent production companies making experimental and independent movies. The work of director Ziad Doueiri (*West Beirut*, 1998) and actress-turned-director Nadine Labaki (*Caramel*, 2007) is well worth seeing for their contrasting themes and issues of civil war and social issues respectively. Beirut also hosts two annual film festivals attracting Lebanese as well as international filmmakers.

In 2010, Lebanese cinematographer Muriel Aboulrouss picked up the Bayard d'Or for Best Cinematography for her work on the film *Stray Bullet* at the Festival International du Film Francophone de Namour in Belgium and it was also screened at the British Film Institutes (BFI) London Film Festival in the same year. The songs of Fairuz (see box below), Lebanon's and the Arab world's best-loved singer, continue to delight audiences but numerically speaking there can't be many who can touch the achievements of the other Lebanese diva, Sabah. Although well into her eighties her musical career dates from 1943, and she has released more than 50 albums, appeared in nearly 100 films and reputedly has a repertoire of

FAIRUZ

> *To Beirut – peace to Beirut with all my heart*
> *And kisses – to the sea and clouds,*
> *To the rock of a city that looks like an old sailor's face.*
> *From the soul of her people she makes wine,*
> *From their sweat, she makes bread and jasmine.*
> *So how did it come to taste of smoke and fire?*

Born on 21 November 1935 in Beirut, the Lebanese singer Fairuz – the name is Arabic for 'turquoise' and was given to her by an early musical mentor for the precious quality of her haunting and silky voice – was christened Nouhad Haddad, the elder of two children who has become Lebanon's and the Arab world's best-known and loved diva. Winner of a string of musical accolades, Fairuz was born into a working-class family: her father was a typesetter for a local print shop and her mother a full-time housewife. By all accounts Fairuz was a shy child with a love for singing from an early age. By the age of ten she was regularly performing at school concerts, and by 14 was discovered by a scout from the Lebanese conservatory and soon became a vocalist in the chorus at a radio station. It was her long-time collaboration with the well-known musical Rahbani Brothers, Assi and Mansour, whom she met there that helped to propel her onto the national and international stage. She married Assi in 1954, with whom she had four children. They composed many of her songs over the years which Fairuz performed at many of the world's most famous venues including New York's Carnegie Hall, the London Palladium and the Royal Albert Hall in the UK. Her soprano repertoire ranged from folk and jazz to religious songs characterised by a non-partisan message but always linked to hope, peace and unification. Almost from its inception Fairuz was a regular artist at the Baalbeck Festival as well as performing at the Beiteddine Festival. Exiled in Paris during the civil war she famously performed in front of some 40,000 adoring fans upon her return in 1994, something she said would only happen once the fighting had stopped. Since the death of her husband in 1986, her musical compositions have been produced by her eldest son Ziad, an accomplished composer and musician in his own right who fuses jazz and oriental music styles. Today, well into her seventies, Fairuz continues to perform her velvety lyrics championing the causes of justice, liberty and love.

3,500 songs to her name. Oh, and she's been married ten times! The colourful and internationally renowned Caracalla Dance Company (*www.caracalladance.com*) are prolific performers all over the world and are well worth seeing, whilst the *dabke*, a group dance often performed at weddings or other family gatherings and occasions, is Lebanon's national folk dance.

LITERATURE Lebanon has a literary tradition as old as the Lebanese themselves with Lebanon's forays into the written word dating back to the ancient Phoenicians, whose 22 letter alphabet formed the basis for our modern alphabet. As a seat of scholarly learning since Roman times and Beirut a hub of printing and publishing in the 19th century, it is a tradition that lives on. Of course, mention must be made of the Koran, the great work of Islamic literature which remains an important source of motivation in life for many Muslims in Lebanon. The Lebanese are quite avid readers of newspapers, magazines and books as the number of bookshops in Beirut can testify, with stores selling works in the three main languages of Arabic, English and French. Lebanon's most famous and iconic writer, Khalil Gibran (see box, page 192), spent much of his life out of the country but captured the hearts and minds of the Lebanese with his almost mystical and heartfelt prose which dealt with universal human themes such as love, pain and relationships. His works have been translated into numerous languages and inspired other cultural mores. Another contemporary writer worth checking out is Hanan al-Shaykh (b1945) whose novels, short stories and playwriting deal with an eclectic array of women's lives and issues.

SPORT AND ADVENTURE Lebanon's varied geography and climate has helped to endow the country with a wonderful array of possibilities for outdoor pursuits, for both participant and spectator, and is an activity the Lebanese indulge with a passion. During the winter months the country's six mountain ski resorts cater to the beginner as well as more seasoned skiers with well-developed après-ski facilities, and have a popular following. Boating, canoeing and kayaking, scuba diving, golf and weekly horse-race meetings in Beirut are also avidly followed as is soccer and basketball, the latter a sport at which Lebanon most excels, most notably winning the FIBA Asia Stankovic Cup in 2010, beating Japan 97–59 in the final. The increasing awareness and concern for the environment has led to a marked increase in a culture of conservation and sustainability with many NGOs and smaller groups springing up to champion the cause of the great and healthy outdoors and run walks, hikes and treks the length and breadth of the country.

2

Practical Information

WHEN TO VISIT

Lebanon really is a 'go anytime' destination and deciding on which season to go depends almost entirely upon your own interests and priorities. In terms of temperatures, the dry **summer** months (June–September) can be extremely hot and humid on the coast with temperatures in Beirut often well in excess of 30°C, which is fine if you just want to while away the days by the pool or on the beach and catch some Mediterranean rays, but it can be uncomfortable and a retreat to the mountains for the cooler alpine air affords a range of activities such as hiking, rafting, trekking and mountain biking. Summer, however, is also the main season for Lebanon's slew of annual artistic and cultural festivals such as those at Baalbek, Beiteddine, Broummana, Byblos, and Tyre.

Winter (November–February) on the Mediterranean coast sees temperatures plummet to milder, more palatable levels than in summer but this season is often accompanied by the heaviest rainfall, though this tends to be in short bursts rather than the prolonged periods which often characterise many countries in northwest Europe. The winter months also herald the start of the main ski season and the country has a range of well-equipped resorts, the best of these at Mzaar, with snow often remaining on the highest peaks until April and even May. This is also the season where you can ski in the morning and swim in the Mediterranean in the afternoon.

Autumn (September–October) sees cool temperatures in the mountains (5–20°C) and warm weather (18–28°C) on the coast though with the increased risk of some rainy days. This period is also outside the main summer and winter tourist seasons and often accompanied by a reduction in the price of hotel accommodation. It is also wine-tasting time in the Bekaa Valley and the annual olive harvest.

Without doubt **spring** (March–May) is an ideal time to visit Lebanon as the country is carpeted with beautiful and varied flora, the stifling summer heat has yet to arrive, and the winter rains have disappeared. Temperatures in coastal areas range from 12°C to 26°C whilst more mountainous regions experience temperatures ranging from 0°C to 15°C. Snow remains on some of the mountain peaks, which make an extremely picturesque backdrop when visiting some of the country's ancient sites. Spring also presents a wealth of possibilities for outdoor enthusiasts and is a great time for visiting the Chouf Cedar Reserve, with hiking in the UNESCO World Heritage Site Qadisha Valley among the adventurous activities together with alfresco dining all over the country.

The onset of the holy month of Ramadan in Lebanon, while not a time to be avoided as in other Arab countries, nevertheless requires visitors to be sensitive to fasting Muslims. It would be polite to avoid drinking, eating or smoking during daylight hours in more devout Muslim neighbourhoods. Also be aware that some stores shut for a few hours during the daytime, but reopen later in the day.

You didn't decide to visit Lebanon to marvel at picturesque and undulating rocky desert landscapes or ride a camel, which is just as well, because Lebanon is the only country in the Middle East which is entirely without a desert. However, with an annual sunshine quota of around 300 days, a liveable cliché of skiing in the morning and swimming in the Mediterranean in the afternoon, world-class archaeological sites, breathtaking natural scenery and a diverse and cultured people, the absence of an oasis of sand and palm trees isn't going to spoil your visit too much. As the initial point of entry to Lebanon for the vast majority of visitors, Beirut warrants a few days of exploration by any visitor in order to appreciate the country's turbulent past and its optimism for the future. Nowhere is this hope more apparent than in the restored Downtown district of the city. The capital also makes an excellent base for organising daytrip excursions to other areas of the country if time is precious.

The following are my pick of the highlights to visit in Lebanon:

BAALBEK Step back in time and admire soaring Roman columns and well-preserved temples, which are amongst the finest in the world.

BYBLOS This ancient and charming Phoenician port with Crusader castle, fine fish restaurants and souks is enchanting at any time, but particularly at sunset.

SIDON This traditional port city has busy, traditional souks, and a photogenic sea castle.

JEITA GROTTO Majestic and stunning stalactites and stalagmites, and currently a finalist for one of the 'New 7 Wonders of Nature'.

TYRE A UNESCO World Heritage Site containing the world's largest Roman Hippodrome.

QADISHA VALLEY Picturesque mountain scenery in this UNESCO World Heritage Site containing churches, grottos, hermitages, villages and waterfalls.

JEBEL SANNINE The location for some of Lebanon's best winter ski resorts.

CHOUF MOUNTAINS A beautiful, scenic region and the location for ancient cedar trees, the lovely old Ottoman-era town of Deir al-Qamar and the opulent Beiteddine Palace, home to some of the world's finest Byzantine mosaics.

TRIPOLI Lebanon's second city has history aplenty with labyrinthine and anachronistic souks, imposing Crusader castle, travellers' inns or *khans*, *madrasas* and mosques.

AANJAR This unique 8th-century Islamic trading town in the Bekaa Valley is the last remaining Umayyad-era site in the entire Middle East.

BEKAA VALLEY VINEYARDS As one of the oldest places in the world for wine production, a visit to at least the Ksara or Kefraya vineyards affords an important insight into this still flourishing aspect of Lebanese culture.

The suggestions below are just that: suggestions. Lebanon is so small, around half the size of the landmass of Wales, that it is easy to mix and match these attractions as you are never more than about three hours away from even the most remote areas, traffic permitting.

LONG WEEKEND/SHORT CITY BREAK With its compact size, a little over four hours flying time from London and a negligible timezone impact on European visitors, Lebanon is ideally suited to a short citybreak destination. Explore the Downtown area of Beirut, the restored Ottoman-era architecture and the Al-Omari Mosque; stroll the treelined Corniche and go (window?) shopping in upmarket Verdun and explore the excellent Beirut National Museum. For a change of pace, take a 45 minute drive up the coast to Byblos, stopping off *en route* to visit the natural marvel of Jeita Grotto, to experience this quiet, picturesque port, with fine fish restaurants before heading back to Beirut after dinner to experience the pulsating nightlife in Gemmayze. An alternative to Byblos could be a day trip to Baalbek, visiting the wineries and Roman temples.

ONE WEEK A week-long itinerary would allow you to see all of Lebanon's main sites (and sights) and could include the following: two nights in Beirut; one night in Byblos including a stop on the way to see the Jeita Grotto; two nights in Tripoli; one night in Baalbek, and return to Beirut via a day trip to the Chouf Mountains to see the quaint little village of Deir al-Qamar and the Beiteddine Palace.

TWO WEEKS This is the ideal timescale to see and fully appreciate everything that Lebanon has to offer at a more leisurely pace. A comprehensive circular tour in spring or summer could commence in Beirut before travelling north up the coast to the port of Byblos, stopping off at Jeita Grotto, before continuing up to Tripoli to see the Crusader castle, souks and Old City. From Tripoli head southeast towards Bcharré to visit the Horsh Eden Forest Nature Reserve, Qadisha Valley and the legendary cedar trees. Continue the journey southeast to visit the Roman temples at Baalbek before heading towards Zahlé to visit the wineries and the unique Umayyad town of Aanjar. Head back to Beirut at the start of the second week and from there travel south to the coastal towns of Sidon and Tyre for their ancient ruins and ports. On the way back up to Beirut stop off to admire the Chouf Mountains, Chouf Cedar Reserve and the beautiful Ottoman-era Beiteddine Palace and picturesque town of Deir al-Qamar before returning to Beirut.

ONE MONTH If you are fortunate enough to have four weeks to spare in Lebanon, then this will give you enough time to explore in depth the country's cocktail of natural and manmade attractions, and also experience many of the places off the beaten tourist track. Such a time frame will also afford you maximum flexibility to swap and change your schedule at will and perhaps stay longer than anticipated in areas that particularly interest you. The following itinerary can be used as a starting point for your own Lebanese forays:

Beirut (seven nights): Not only is a week plenty of time for exploring beyond the capital, it also gives a great opportunity to experience this revitalised city with its varied shopping districts, pulsating nightlife venues, fine dining, art galleries and an active and flourishing theatrical scene. The world-class National Museum demands a few hours of any visitor's schedule and could be combined with a trip to the

Lebanese Museum of Prehistory. If arriving in summer there are plenty of festivals to keep you occupied in Beirut and a few within easy reach beyond the capital.

Byblos (two–three nights): To experience the culinary delights of this delightful and romantic little town which is easily combined with a visit to the nearby natural limestone wonder of Jeita Grotto and the Téléférique cable car ride from Jounieh to Harissa.

Sidon and Tyre (four nights): A few days in the less visited south of the country offers a great contrast to cosmopolitan Beirut and here you will gain a much more authentic Middle Eastern flavour of the country.

Bekaa Valley (five nights): Perhaps using Zahlé as your base, with day and half-day trips to Aanjar, Baalbek and the many wineries. Self-drive car hire or car with driver is an ideal way to explore this region though minivans and taxis are available.

Chouf Mountains (three nights): To savour a still feudal region with breathtaking scenery and a slew of beautiful sites. A great place to relax if you have hitherto overindulged in the hedonistic capital.

Tripoli (four nights): For exploring the atmospheric souks, citadel and perhaps a trip to the offshore Palm Islands Nature Reserve.

Qadisha Valley (three–four days): For hiking in the Qadisha Valley during spring. An alternative itinerary during the winter ski season would be taking to the slopes at the Mzaar and/or the Cedar resorts.

LEBANON MOUNTAIN TRAIL (LMT) A recent initiative, the LMT is divided into 26 sections of hiking and walking routes which pass through over 70 rural villages from the extreme north of the country down the backbone of Lebanon to the far south. Each designated route can be undertaken in around a day and offers an alternative and fascinating glimpse into less visited rural communities and with opportunities to stay in less mainstream lodgings such as guesthouses, family homes and monasteries at prices to suit most budgets. For outdoor types, travellers wishing to gain an alternative insight into the country and those wishing to give something back by helping rural economies this itinerary, the trail could prove a very rewarding journey, taking in some of Lebanon's most beautiful and least visited areas. For more details on the LMT, see box, page 181.

TOUR OPERATORS

Lebanon is not new to tourism and has a well-established tourist infrastructure in place. Tour companies have an equally long history of serving the country. Although the 34-day conflict between Israel and Hezbollah in 2006 scared many operators away, the years since have seen a burgeoning number of companies offering tours including returnees. For details of local tour operators, see pages 100–2.

UK

Abercrombie & Kent St Georges Hse, Ambrose St, Cheltenham, Gloucestershire GL50 3LG; ☎ 0845 618 2203; e info@abercrombiekent.co. uk; www.abercrombiekent.co.uk. Offers a 7-night Cedars of Lebanon itinerary which takes in many of the country's highlights including Baalbek, Beiteddine, Byblos, Sidon, Tyre & the Ksara winery in the Bekaa Valley. Prices from £1,995 including luxury hotel & return flights.

Ace Cultural Tours Babraham, Cambridge CB22 3AP; ☎ 01223 835055; e ace@aceculturaltours. co.uk; www.aceculturaltours.co.uk. Runs 16-day tours to Syria which include 'av excursion to the Roman temples at Baalbek & the Ksara winery with departures from London in Apr & Sep. Prices from £2,490 including flights & accommodation.

Andante Travels The Old Barn, Old Rd, Alderbury, Salisbury, Wiltshire SP5 3AR; ☎ 01722 713800; e tours@andantetravels.co.uk; www. andantetravels.co.uk. Specialist company offering archaeological tours of the ancient world. Their 8-day tour of Lebanon's ancient past costs £2,150 including flights & hotel (£1,715 excluding flights).

Audley Travel New Mill, New Mill Lane, Witney, Oxfordshire OX29 9SX; ☎ 01993 838400; e arabia@audleytravel.com; www.audleytravel. com. They offer tailor-made itineraries & also offer a 6-day Lebanon Uncovered itinerary which visits Aanjar, Baalbek & the wineries, Jeita Grotto & Byblos. Prices from £1,740 including hotel & return flights. Their 13-day Highlights of Lebanon & Syria package (£3,600 including flights & hotel) covers the main sites in both countries.

Black Tomato 40–42 Scrutton St, London EC2A 4PP; ☎ 020 7426 9888; e info@blacktomato. co.uk; www.blacktomato.co.uk. Bespoke & upmarket operator providing long-weekend 4-night tours to Beirut from £2,250 including flights, 5-star hotel, driver & guide. Also specialises in ski itineraries from £3,000 including flights & hotel.

Corinthian Travel 63 Foley Rd, Claygate, Esher, Surrey KT10 0LY; ☎ 01372 469300; e info@ corinthiantravel.co.uk; www.corinthiantravel. co.uk. Specialises in 'excelling in luxury private journeys' to the Middle East with the emphasis on the gastronomy, culture & history of Lebanon. Not cheap with their 4 night 'Beirut Sojourn' costing £1,450 including hotel but excluding return flights.

Cox & Kings 6th Fl, 30 Millbank, London SW1P 4EE; ☎ 020 7873 5000; e sales@coxandkings. co.uk; www.coxandkings.co.uk. The world's longest-established travel tour company celebrated its 250th anniversary in 2008. Specialises in historical & cultural tours offering a short 4-night break in Beirut from £1,195 & a 6-night Lebanon: Land of the Phoenicians tour visiting Byblos, Sidon, Beirut & the Roman temples at Baalbek from £995 on a group tour & £1,675 as a private tour including flights & hotel. Their 5-night Jewel of the Levant itinerary from £1,245 including flights & hotel visits many of the country's highlights.

Elegant Resorts The Old Palace, Chester CH1 1RB; ☎ 01244 897111; e enquiries@

elegantresorts.co.uk; www.elegantresorts.co.uk. As their name suggests, this company operates at the luxury end of the tour market with a 7-night stay in Beirut costing from £1,555 including flights & accommodation at the Le Gray Hotel in Downtown Beirut.

Exodus Grange Mills, Weir Rd, London SW12 0NE; ☎ 020 8772 3936; e sales@exodus.co.uk; www.exodus.co.uk. Offers a 5-day Lebanon Long Weekend with departures in Apr, May, Sept, Oct & Nov visiting Beirut, the Bekaa Valley & the vineyards, Jeita Grotto from £989 including flights.

Explore! Nelson Hse, 55 Victoria Rd, Farnborough, Hampshire GU14 7PA; ☎ 0845 868 6351; e res@explore.co.uk; www.explore.co.uk. Emphasis on small group adventurous travel with plenty of different tour options. A 15-day Exploring the Old Levant in conjunction with Syria is £1,598, or £1,179 excluding flights; Grand Tour of the Middle East is a 22-day adventure holiday trekking in Jordan, Syria & Lebanon for £2,361 including flights or £1,745 excluding flights; the Lure of Lebanon is a 9-day adventure in Lebanon at £1,022 including flights, £1,190 excluding flights. Between Jan & Feb, they also offer a 5-day snowshoeing tour in the Chouf Cedar Reserve with visits to Bcharré & the Qadisha Valley & Beirut for £1,017 including flights, £549 excluding flights.

Greentours Leigh Cottage, Gauledge Lane, Longnor, Buxton, Derbyshire SK17 0PA; ☎ 01298 83563; e enquiries@greentours.co.uk; www. greentours.co.uk. A specialist natural history operator offering small group tours for between 5 & 15 people. Their April 2012 14-day Aphrodite's Tears itinerary takes in the flora & fauna of the Chouf Mountains, Bekaa Valley, Adonis Valley, Bcharré & environs together with the Roman temples at Baalbek. £2,795 including return flights & hotel.

Indus Tours & Travel Ltd KBC Harrow Exchange, 2 Gayton Rd, Harrow, Middlesex HA1 2XU; ☎ 020 8901 7320; e holidays@industours. co.uk; www.industours.co.uk. Runs a few different tours ranging in duration from 4 to 8 days with prices from £685 to £970 including flights & accommodation with daily excursions visiting many of the country's main highlights.

Kirker Travel Limited 4 Waterloo Court, 10 Theed St, London SE1 8ST; ☎ 020 7593 1899; e travel@kirkerholidays.co.uk; www.

kirkerholidays.com. Offers a 7-night tour (£1,858 including flights & hotel) visiting Beirut's National Museum, Byblos, Harissa, Tripoli, the Cedars, Bcharré & the Chouf Mountains.

Martin Randall Travel Voysey Hse, Barley Mow Passage, London W4 4GF; ☏ 020 8742 3355; e info@martinrandall.co.uk; www.martinrandall. com. Specialist & upmarket tour operator with a twice-yearly (in Apr & May) 10-day visit to Lebanon's archaeological sites. The price of £3,280 is fully inclusive of flights, hotel & admission fees & has a maximum group size of 22 with specialist lecturer.

Middle East Journeys 3rd Fl, Hamilton Hse, Mabledon Pl, London WC1H 9BB; ☏ 020 7935 5677, 0800 028 0826; e info@mejourneys.com; www.mejourneys.com. A good & relatively new company established in 2010 offering a number of tours taking in Lebanon's main attractions, ranging from 3–7 nights, catering for those interested in a short city break, honeymooning couples, cultural & history buffs together with visitors interested in less mainstream off-the-beaten track homestay accommodation & sites. Prices range from £380–£1,750, excluding flights.

Neilson Adventures Locksview, Brighton Marina, Brighton BN2 5HA; ☏ 01273 668982; e sales@neilsonadventures.com, customerservices@neilson.com; www. neilsonadventures.com. This award-winning & activity-based company run a number of tours ranging from 5 to 13 days. At the time of going to press they stopped running tours to Lebanon for the forseeable future, but it is worth keeping an eye on their website in case the situation changes.

Original Travel 1b The Village, 101 Amies St, London SW11 2JW; ☏ 020 7978 7333; e ask@ originaltravel.co.uk; www.originaltravel.co.uk. Offers bespoke itineraries which range from £1,000 to £2,000 excluding flights.

Pax Travel 152–156 Kentish Town Rd, London NW1 9QB; ☏ 020 7485 3003; e info@paxtravel. co.uk; www.paxtravel.co.uk. A specialist tour operator offering Christian pilgrimages to a variety of destinations worldwide. At the time of writing the company were not offering tours to Lebanon but the country is on their 'wish list' for visits over the next few years so it may be worth periodically checking their website for updates.

Peregrine Adventures 1 Betts Av, Martlesham Heath, Ipswich IP5 3RH; ☏ 0845 004 0673; e uksales@peregrineadventures.com; www. peregrineadventures.com. This company's small group tours offer a 17-day Crusader Trails itinerary (combined with Jordan & Syria) & visits Beirut, Byblos, Bekaa Valley, wineries & Jeita Grotto from £2,450 excluding flights. An 11-day Syria & Lebanon Discovery tour from £1,595 excluding flights, takes in Beirut, Byblos, Baalbek & Aanjar, Jeita Grotto, Sidon & Beiteddine.

Quintessentially Travel 29 Portland Pl, London W1B 1QB; ☏ 0845 269 1152; e info@quintessentiallytravel.com; www. quintessentially.com. A bespoke, specialist luxury tour operator offering tailor-made journeys for the upmarket traveller. As a rough guide, a 4-night stay at a 5-star hotel in Downtown Beirut, including return flights, breakfast & airport transfer will cost around £1,300.

Red Spokes 29 Northfield Rd, Stamford Hill, London N16 5RL; ☏ 020 7502 7252; e office@ redspokes.co.uk; www.redspokes.co.uk. A specialist adventure tour operator offering 16-day cycling holidays, combined with Syria, of moderate difficulty covering over 50 miles per day & visiting Baalbek, the Chouf, Bcharré & Tripoli. You can bring your own bike or hire from the company for £130. Tours cost from £1,375 including accommodation, but excluding flights.

Responsible Travel Pavilion Hse, 6 Old Steine, Brighton, East Sussex BN1 1EJ; ☏ 01273 600030; e amelia@responsibletravel. com; www.responsibletravel.com. Specialising in a range of cultural tours which aim to offer a 'lived' Lebanon experience. Their 9-day small group tour (16–20 people) costs from £1,072 including flights & accommodation. An 8-day tailor-made itinerary from £1,860 including flights & hotel taking in many of Lebanon's highlights. They also offer a combined 17-day tour with Syria from £1,584 including flights.

Robert Broad Travel 2 Boley Park Shopping Centre, Ryknild St, Lichfield, Staffordshire WS14 9XU; ☏ 01543 258631; e dave@robertbroadtravel.co.uk; www. robertbroadtravel.co.uk. Offers a 4-night Beirut city-break for £1,095 including flights; a 7-day Land of the Phoenicians tour (£1,025 including flights) & a 7-night Lebanon Contrasts Tour (from

£1,858 including flights) & will also tailor-make itineraries.

Silk Road & Beyond Unit 6, Hurlingham Business Park, 55 Sullivan Rd, London SW6 3DU; ☎ 020 7371 3131; e sales@silkroadandbeyond. co.uk; www.silkroadandbeyond.co.uk. Their 8-day Best of Lebanon tour, from £1,860 including flights & accommodation, visits the country's key sites. Also offers bespoke itineraries on request.

Simoon Travel Limited 177 Ferndale Rd, London SW9 8BA; ☎ 020 7737 2664; e info@ simoontravel.com; www.simoontravel.com. Offers an 8-day cultural Classical Lebanon tour from £1,885 including flights & hotel which visits the main archaeological sites & Qadisha Valley. Also offers an 11-day Highlights of Syria & Lebanon itinerary from £2,230.

Steppes Travel Travel Hse, 51 Castle St, Cirencester, Gloucestershire GL7 1QD; ☎ 01285 880 980; f 01285 885 888; e enquiry@ steppestravel.co.uk; www.steppestravel.co.uk. They have a 9-day Classic Lebanon tour from £2,495 including flights & hotel but also happy to tailor-make itineraries upon request.

The Traveller & Palanquin 10 Bury Pl, London WC1A 2JL; ☎ 020 7436 9343, 020 7269 2770; e info@the-traveller.co.uk; www.the-traveller. co.uk. Specialist archaeological, historical & cultural operator with tours led by respected experts in their field. This company's 9-day Landscapes of Lebanon tour costs from £1,795 including flights & accommodation with an emphasis on Lebanon's principal archaeological sites at Aanjar, Baalbek, Sidon & Tyre.

Travel the Unknown Hyde Park Hse, 5 Manfred Rd, Putney, London SW15 2RS; ☎ 020 8823 0705; e info@traveltheunknown.com; www. traveltheunknown.com. Environmentally conscious & cultural operator which has a 6-day Crusaders & Caves tour visiting Baalbek, Jeita Grotto, Byblos, Qadisha Valley & the Ksara winery from £1,250 including flights & accommodation. For the more adventurous traveller, a 6-day trip hiking in the Qadisha Valley for £1,145 including flights & accommodation, staying in monasteries & homestays, offers a more authentic & offbeat experience.

Voyages Jules Verne 21 Dorset Sq, London NW1 6QE; ☎ 0845 166 7003; e sales@vjv.co.uk; www.vjv.com. At the time of going to press Voyages Jules Verne stopped running tours to Lebanon for the forseeable future, but it is worth keeping an eye on their website in case this changes.

World Discovery 32 Rothes Rd, Dorking, Surrey RH4 1LD; ☎ 01306 888799; e enquiries@ worlddiscovery.co.uk; www.worlddiscovery. co.uk. Runs a 5-day Beirut Holiday from £552 excluding flights together with a 6-day Treasures of Lebanon tour which takes in Beirut, Byblos, Beiteddine Palace, Aanjar & the Ksara winery in the Bekaa Valley & Sidon from £995 excluding return flights. For lovers of the great outdoors they also offer a 7-day Nature & History holiday, from £1,295 excluding flights, which takes in the Qadisha Valley, Bcharré, Chouf Cedar Reserve & Ehden together with Baalbek, Byblos & Sidon.

REPUBLIC OF IRELAND

Citiescapes Suite 30, The Hyde Bldg, The Park, Carrickmines, Dublin 18, Ireland; ☎ +353 1 294 1000; e book@citiescapes.ie; www.citiescapes.ie. Offers a 9-night tour of Lebanon (with Syria) visiting Beirut, Byblos, the Chouf Mountains, & Baalbek from €2,199 including flights from Cork & Shannon via London (Heathrow) & accommodation. Also offer a Greece, Cyprus & Lebanon cruise (€999 pp including

return flights from Dublin to Milan), which includes a day in Beirut.

The Irish Lebanese Cultural Foundation 79 The Paddocks, Kells Rd, Kilkenny, Ireland; ☎ +353 56 775 6700; e irishlebanese@hotmail. com; www.irishlebanese.com. This active organisation run a couple of tours each year, usually in Mar & Oct.

USA AND CANADA

Bestway Tours & Safaris Suite 206, 8678 Greenall Av, Burnaby, British Columbia, Canada V5J 3M6; ☎ +1 604 264 7378, +1 800 663 0844 toll free within USA & Canada; e bestway@

bestway.com; www.bestway.com. A cultural tour operator who offer an 8-day Lebanon: Pre-Biblical to Modern itinerary, a wide-ranging tour of most of the country's main sites for US$1,995 excluding flights but inclusive of accommodation. They also offer a 9-day From Palmyra to Baalbek tour which takes in Syria & Lebanon from US$2,795 excluding flights & a 14-day From Petra to Baalbek tour combined with Jordan for US$4,660 excluding flights.

iExplore Suite 500, 833 W Jackson, Chicago, IL 60607; ☎ +1 312 492 9443, +1 800 439 7567 toll free within USA; www.iexplore.com. Has a 5-day Lebanon Long Weekend from US$810 excluding flights & a couple of 11- & 17-day tours starting from US$2,490 excluding flights, which combine Lebanon with Jordan & Syria.

Travel in Style 459 Fulton St 108, San Francisco, CA 94102; ☎ +1 415 440 1124; e info@travelinstyle.com; www.travelinstyle.com. Provides a couple of private luxury 6- & 8-day tours taking in Lebanon's main highlights including Beirut, Sidon, Beiteddine, Bekaa Valley, Byblos, etc. Prices from US$1,890 excluding flights but including accommodation in Beirut.

TOURIST INFORMATION

Lebanon's official **Ministry of Tourism** office (*550 Central Bank St, Hamra, Beirut; ☎ 01 340 940/1/2/3/4; Tourist hotline, dial 1735 within Lebanon; f 01 340 945; e mot@destinationlebanon.gov.lb; www.destinationlebanon.gov.lb; ⏰ 08.30–17.00 Mon–Thu, 08.30–14.00 Fri, 08.30–15.00 Sat*) is an excellent and friendly resource when in the country and you can obtain a range of free brochures, maps, including those showing Beirut bus maps and routes (ask for *kharita*), hotel, entertainment and restaurant information for all areas of Lebanon in a variety of languages (Arabic, English, French, German, Italian and Spanish). If you are planning on an extensive tour of Lebanon the Hamra office is the place to go to collect most of your material as stocks of brochures and maps etc are not normally as plentiful in the regional offices and at the archaeological sites themselves. The Ministry of Tourism also maintains an office at Beirut airport which is situated to your left as you emerge into the arrivals hall (see page 94). Additionally, there is a regional network of tourist information offices at Baalbek, Batroun, Bhamdoun, Byblos, Jeita Grotto, Sidon, Tripoli and Zahlé in the Bekaa Valley. In common with other government departments, the officially stated opening times for all tourist information offices around the country, in both summer and winter, are from 08.00–14.00 Monday to Thursday, from 08.00–11.00 Friday and from 08.00–13.00 Saturday. All tourist offices are closed on Sunday. However, in practice, these times seem to be subject to some flexibility and in the regional chapters which follow the opening and closing times given are those which the author experienced with the times stated in the listings confirmed by local staff members in those offices.

In addition to the above, the Lebanese Ministry of Tourism maintains two overseas offices, in Cairo and Paris, and their addresses, dialling codes and numbers from the UK are as follows:

Cairo Lebanon Tourist Office, 22 El Mansour Muhammad Street, Zamalek, Cairo, Egypt; ☎ +20 2 738 2823/4/5/7; f +20 2 738 2818, 735 9591.

Paris Office du Tourisme du Liban, 124 Rue du Faubourg St Honoré, 75008 Paris, France; ☎ +33 1 4359 1036; e libanot@aol.com; www.destinationliban.com

RED TAPE

ARRIVING BY AIR Citizens of all countries require a visa to enter Lebanon. Nationals of Bahrain, Kuwait, Oman, Qatar, Saudi Arabia and the United Arab Emirates (Gulf Co-operation Council States) and Jordan are issued with a three-month visa, free of charge, upon arrival at Beirut international airport. Nationals of the following countries are currently issued with a free, single-entry, one-month visa, upon arrival at Beirut international airport which is renewable for up to three months, upon production of a valid passport valid for at least six months: Andorra, Antigua and Barbuda, Argentina, Armenia, Australia, Austria, Azerbaijan, Bahamas, Barbados, Belarus, Belgium, Belize, Bhutan, Brazil, Bulgaria, Canada, Chile, China, Czech Republic, Costa Rica, Croatia, Cyprus, Denmark, Dominican Republic, Estonia, Finland, France, Great Britain, Georgia, Germany, Greece, Hong Kong, Hungary, Iceland, Ireland, Italy, Japan, Kazakhstan, Kyrgyzstan, Latvia, Lithuania, Liechtenstein, Luxembourg, Macedonia, Macau, Malaysia, Malta, Mexico, Moldova, Monaco, Montenegro, Netherlands, New Zealand, Norway, Palau, Panama, Peru, Poland, Portugal, Russia, Romania, Saint Kitts and Nevis, Samoa, San Marino, Serbia, Singapore, Slovakia, Slovenia, South Korea, Spain, Sweden, Switzerland, Tajikistan, Turkmenistan, Ukraine, USA, Uzbekistan, Venezuela.

At the time of writing, a single-entry Lebanese visa entitles the holder to cross the border to visit neighbouring Syria, provided they return within five days. This policy could change at any time, especially with the current wave of unrest which is affecting Lebanon's neighbour, and if you are intending to travel to Syria from Lebanon see the additional visa information below, which recommends that you purchase your visa in advance of travel. It is also possible to obtain a Lebanese visa in advance from the Lebanese embassy or consulate in your own country (see *Embassies and consulates*, pages 117–18). It is essential to note, however, that if your passport contains evidence of a visit to Israel (including entry/exit stamps from the land border crossings between Egypt and Israel or Jordan and Israel), permission to enter Lebanon *will* be refused. The information in this section can change at any time and it is a good idea to check with the Lebanese embassy in your own country or your own embassy or consulate for the most up-to-date regulations prior to finalising your travel arrangements. In the UK the Foreign and Commonwealth Office website (*www.fco.gov.uk*) is an especially good source of ever-changing country-specific officialdom. In the US the Department of State operates a couple of informative websites (*www.state.gov & www.travel.state.gov*) which contain country specific information and travel advice for US citizens.

ARRIVING BY ROAD If arriving from Syria by bus or taxi, a Lebanese visa can be obtained at the Lebanese border which may or may not be issued free of charge and seems to depend upon your nationality. For European Union (EU) passport holders and those from the USA and Canada a one-month visa is usually issued free of charge but for some passport holders, for example those from the African continent and Asia, the following charges may be applicable: 15-day visa (LBP25,000); one-three-month visa (LBP50,000). Also bear in mind that the Lebanese authorities will only accept any due visa payments in Lebanese currency. A 48-hour transit visa for passport holders of all countries is issued free of charge.

VISA EXTENSIONS In practice, at the time of research, your one-month tourist visa is actually valid for two-months! So, unless you are planning to stay in the country longer than this, the following details will not apply to you. To extend your original one-month visa to a three-month visa you will need to visit the **General Directorate of General Security** (*Bldg 1, 2nd Fl, Bd Sami El-Solh (near the Palace of Justice), Beirut;* \ *01 425 610; www.general-security.gov.lb;* ◷ *08.00–14.00 Mon– Thu, 08.00–11.00 Fri, 08.00–13.00 Sat*). You will need to produce your passport, passport-sized photo, photocopies of your passport ID page and the original visa entry stamp page a few days prior to the expiry of your original one-month visa.

2

The current cost of a three-month visa is LBP50,000. Once again, official policy is subject to change and a quick check on the above website or telephone call to the Directorate could prove invaluable.

VISAS FOR ONWARD TRAVEL TO SYRIA As many visitors to Lebanon often combine their visit with a cross-border trip to neighbouring Syria it is worth noting that at the time of writing a Lebanese visa issued at the airport does entitle you to cross the border into Syria. However as this concession can change it is highly recommended that you obtain your Syrian visa from the Syrian embassy or consulate in your own country before you travel. Although there have been reports of some travellers being granted a Syrian visa at the border posts you should not rely on this and to avoid the risk of being turned away at the border it is best to adhere to official policy and *obtain a visa in advance of travel* from the Syrian Embassy (*8 Belgrave Sq, London SW1X 8PH;* ℡ *020 7245 9012;* f *020 7235 4621; www.syremb.com*) which has a downloadable visa application form together with visa entry requirements on their website. At the time of writing the cost of a single-entry Syrian visa for holders of British passports was £30 valid for three-months and £50 for a multiple-entry visa valid for six months. As with entry into Lebanon, a visa and entry to Syria *will* be refused if your passport shows any evidence of a visit to Israel. Currently, nationals of the following countries do not need to be in possession of a visa to enter Syria: Algeria, Bahrain, Egypt, Jordan, Kuwait, Lebanon, Libya, Mauritania, Morocco, Oman, Qatar, Saudi Arabia, Sudan, Tunisia, UAE or Yemen. At the time of writing a Syrian exit tax of SYP500 (cUS$10) was payable upon your departure from Syria.

CUSTOMS AND DUTY-FREE Personal items such as photographic still and video cameras, laptop computers and the like, are excluded from any form of customs duty. The current duty-free allowances for the most common types of goods being taken **into Lebanon**, whether arriving in the country via air, land or sea, are as follows: two bottles of spirits or four litres of any other alcoholic beverage, 800 cigarettes or 50 cigars or 1,000g of tobacco. These allowances can change from time to time and current allowances are displayed on the Lebanese customs website (*www.customs.gov.lb*). From **Lebanon to the UK**, and other European Union (EU) countries, the duty-free allowances are currently 200 cigarettes or 50 cigars or 250g of tobacco, one litre of spirits or two litres of wine. To keep up-to-date with periodic changes to UK customs and duty-free regulations, visit *www.hmrc.gov.uk*.

LEBANESE EMBASSIES AND CONSULATES ABROAD

Lebanon has a wide network of diplomatic representation in overseas countries and most foreign nationals will have no problem obtaining a visa for travel to Lebanon. At the present time, as entry visas for many countries are issued free of charge at Beirut airport, there seems little need to obtain one in advance of your visit though this can change at any time and it would be a good idea to check before you travel. A comprehensive listing of Lebanese embassies and consulates around the globe can be found by visiting www.embassy.goabroad.com/embassies-of/lebanon. For a list of embassies and consulates in Beirut see pages 117–18.

Australia 27 Endeavour St, Red Hill, Canberra, ACT 2603; ℡ +61 02 6295 7378; f +61 02 6239 7024; e lebanemb@tpg.com.au; www.lebanemb.org.au

Austria 6/1/3 Oppolzergasse, A-1010 Vienna; ℡ 01 533 8821; f 01 533 4984; e ambassade. liban@vienne.telecom.at

Belgium Rue Guillaume Stocq 2, Brussels;
☎ 32 2 645 7765; f 32 2 645 7769;
e ambassade.liban@brutele.be
Canada 640 Lyon St, Ottawa, Ontario K1S 3Z5;
☎ +1 613 236 5825; f +1 613 232 1609;
e info@lebanonembassy.can; www.
lebanonembassy.ca
France 3 Villa Copernic, Paris 75116;
☎ +33 1 40 67 75 75; f +33 1 40 67 16 42;
e na@amb-liban.fr
Germany 127 Berlinerstrasse, 13187 Berlin;
☎ +49 30 474 9860; f +49 30 4748 7858;
e lubnan@t-online.de; www.libanesische-
botschaft.info
Italy (embassy) 38 Via Giacomo Carissimi, Rome
00198; ☎ +39 06 853 7211; f +39 06 841 1794;
e liban@tiscalinet.it; (consulate) 26 Via Larga,
Milan 20122; ☎ +39 02 806 1341; f +39 02 720
0468; e consolatolibano@libero.it; www.
conslibano.org

Netherlands Frederikstraat 2, 2514 LK, The
Hague; ☎ +31 703 658 906/7; f +31 703 620
779; e info@lebanonembassy.nl, consular@
lebanonembassy.nl; www.lebanonembassy.nl
Spain 178 Paseo de la Castellana, Madrid
28046; ☎ +34 913 451 368/9; f +34 913 455
631; e leeme@teleline.es
Switzerland Thunstrasse 10, Berne; ☎ 31 950
6565; f 31 950 6566; e ambalibch@hotmail.com
UK (embassy) 21 Palace Garden Mews, London
W8 4RA; ☎ 020 7229 7265 ; f 020 7243 1699;
e info@lebaneseembassy.org.uk; (consulate) 15
Palace Garden Mews, London W8 4RB; ☎ 020
7229 7275, 020 7792 7856; e consular@
lebaneseembassy.org.uk; www.
lebaneseembassy.org.uk
US 2560 28th St, NW Washington DC, 20008;
☎ +1 202 939 6300; f +1 202 939 6324;
e info@lebanonembassyus.org;
www.lebanonembassyus.org

GETTING THERE AND AWAY

BY AIR Beirut's only commercial international airport is Rafiq Hariri International Airport (airport code: BEY) (☎ *01 628 000, dial 150 within Lebanon; www. beirutairport.gov.lb*) which is served by more than 40 international airlines and this is the way the vast majority of visitors will arrive. From the UK there are daily non-stop flights leaving from London (Heathrow) airport and the flying time is a little over four hours. The national carrier Middle East Airlines (MEA) flies from Terminal 3 whilst the UK airline, British Midland International (BMI), uses Terminal 1. From continental Europe Beirut is around six hours from Paris, four hours from Frankfurt and five hours from Rome. There are currently no direct flights to Lebanon from the USA or Canada which means a stopover in one of the main European capitals such as London or Paris will be required in order to complete your onward journey via a connecting flight.

Beirut airport adopted its present name in honour of the country's assassinated former prime minister. Its bright, airy and modern interior is the culmination of a ten-year reconstruction plan which has totally transformed the former drab and outdated building into a major regional hub and in the first five months of 2010, the airport handled 1,931,213 passengers, an increase of nearly 19% on 2009. Although the airport still feels a little spartan, it nonetheless has a good range of facilities to offer the traveller including airport lounges, banking and foreign exchange facilities, a post office, disabled access (elevators, ramps, airline wheelchairs and on request ground assistance) and a full range of duty-free shopping (*www. beirutdutyfree.com*), which is on a par with most European and North American airports. There are also prayer rooms for both Christians and Muslims above the duty-free area in the departures level. The airport also boasts a range of car-hire companies together with cafés and restaurants in both the arrivals and departure halls. In general, customs, health and visa procedures are courteous, efficient and hassle-free. The airport's excellent website also provides live departure and arrival flight information which is updated every three minutes.

2

When departing Lebanon you will need to complete a short pink country exit form available all over the departures hall and official advice is to be at the airport about three hours before your flight departs. The journey time to the airport by taxi from Beirut's Downtown area is approximately 20 minutes and the fare should cost no more than US$20.

The following major international airlines all have daily direct flights to Beirut:

Air France (airline code: AF) www.airfrance. com. The French national carrier flies direct to Beirut daily from Paris Charles de Gaulle Airport (airport code: CDG).

Alitalia (AZ) www.alitalia.com. Italy's national airline has direct daily flights to Beirut from Rome's Leonardo da Vinci International Airport (Fiumicino) (airport code: FCO).

British Midland International (BD) Donington Hall, Castle Donington, Derby DE74 2SB, UK; ☏ 01332 854 000 (switchboard), 0844 848 4888 (reservations inside the UK), +44 (0)1332 854854 (reservations outside the UK); www.flybmi.com. BMI, a member of the Star Alliance, is Heathrow's second-largest airline & operates a modern fleet of Airbus aircraft offering excellent business & economy-class service, & is the only British carrier with daily direct flights to Beirut from Terminal 1.

Lufthansa German Airlines (LH) www.lufthansa.com. Germany's national airline has daily direct flights to Beirut departing from Frankfurt Main International Airport (airport code: FRA).

Middle East Airlines (ME) ☏ 020 7467 8000 (within the UK), 01 628 888 (within Beirut); e lontome@mea.aero; www.mea.com.lb. The national carrier operates a modern fleet of Airbus A330's, A321's & A320 aircraft & flies direct every day, departing & arriving at respectable times from Terminal 3 at Heathrow. The airline also has an excellent network of routes across the Middle East, Africa, North & South America, connecting many of the world's major cities via its code-share agreements with partner airlines.

In addition to those airlines listed above the following carriers all fly regularly into Beirut: Aeroflot, Air Algerie, Air Arabia, Air Baltic, Air Germania, Air Maroc, Armavia, Bahrain Air, Belavia, Bulgaria Air, Cyprus Airways, Czech Airlines, EgyptAir, Emirates, Ethiopian Airlines, Etihad Airways, FlyDubai, Gulf Air, Iran Air, Iraqi Airways, Kuwait Airways, Malev Hungarian Airlines, Olympic Airways, Oman Air, Qatar Airways, Royal Jordanian Airlines, Saudi Arabian Airlines, Syrian Arab Airlines, Tarom, Tunis Air, Turkish Airlines and Yemen Airways.

BY ROAD After flying, overland travel is the most popular and accessible way for visitors to arrive in Lebanon. Although Lebanon shares a 79km land border with its southern neighbour Israel the two countries remain in a state of war and despite the Israeli's withdrawing the majority of their military presence from Lebanese soil in May 2000 it is still not possible to enter Lebanon from Israel, a state of affairs highly unlikely to change any time soon. The result is that entry to Lebanon by road is only possible via its northeastern neighbour, Syria. At the time of writing, a Syrian exit tax of SYP£500 (cUS$10) is payable on departure from Syria.

From Syria From the Syrian Arab Republic there are four main roads and border crossing points for entry into Lebanon and buses and taxis depart regularly from the main Syrian cities of Aleppo, the capital Damascus, Hama, Homs and Lattakia. The first and most popular of the border crossing points and routes is at Masnaa a few kilometres from Aanjar in the Bekaa Valley along the main Damascus–Beirut road which sees plenty of bus and taxi traffic into and out of Beirut's Charles Helou station. Bus fares from Damascus to Beirut cost around US$8–12 with a service taxi costing about US$16–18. The journey time can take anywhere between four to six hours depending upon traffic and bureaucracy at the border. Southeast of Hermel in the northern Bekaa Valley the border crossing at Al-Qaa is a popular point for entry into Lebanon from the Syrian cities of Homs and Lattakia invariably arriving at Lebanon's second city of Tripoli. The coastal border post at Aarida is on the bus and taxi route from Aleppo and Lattakia to Tripoli whilst the fourth and northern most border control point is at Abboudiye used for the route from Homs to Tripoli. If travelling from the northern city of Aleppo the journey time is approximately seven hours and the bus fare is around SYP700 (cUS$15) to Beirut which also stops at Tripoli en route to the capital.

From Jordan Overland travel from the Jordanian capital Amman is possible only by service taxi or taxi at the time of writing with no direct bus services operating at the present time. Expect to pay around US$40–50 for a taxi from Amman to Beirut's Charles Helou station.

From Turkey There are regular bus services to Lebanon from the Turkish cities of Antakia and Istanbul which ply the route to and from Beirut and at the time of writing cost around US$33 and US$80 respectively to the capital's Charles Helou bus station.

BY SEA Lebanon's principal ports of entry for commercial sea-going traffic are Beirut and Tripoli, but the country is not presently overly well served by boat. Nevertheless, there are a few options if you would like to visit part of the country this way, perhaps combining Lebanon with other countries in the Levant, but choices are fairly limited at present. As companies offering cruise itineraries which include Lebanon may well increase in the future it could be worth keeping an eye on the following two websites for developments: www.discovercruises.co.uk (Passenger Shipping Association Consumer website), and www.noblewhite.co.uk (Choosing Cruising).

The following companies all offer cruise itineraries which include a short stopover in Lebanon:

MSC Cruises Queen's Hse, 55–56 Lincoln's Inn Fields, London WC2A 3LJ; ☎ 0844 561 7412; e info@msccruises.co.uk; www.msccruises.co.uk. During the months of Apr, Jul, Sep & Oct this company run a 11-night Mediterranean cruise departing from the Italian port of Genoa which includes a full-day in Beirut before the ship continues on to Egypt, Greece & back to Genoa. Optional half- & full-day shore excursions to Jeita Grotto, Byblos & Baalbek are available. Cruise prices £899–1,099 excluding flights.

Noble Caledonia 2 Chester Close, Belgravia, London SW1X 7BE; ☎ 020 7752 0000; e info@ noble-caledonia.co.uk; www.noble-caledonia. co.uk. This company offer a number of 10–14-night cruises around the Levant region, all of which include 1 or 2 days in Beirut with shore excursions to Baalbek, Byblos & Tripoli. Prices start from around £2,295 for a 14-night

cruise including return flights from London to the seaport of departure.

Page & Moy Compass Hse, Rockingham Rd, Market Harborough, Leicestershire LE16 7QD; ☎ 0844 567 6633; www.pageandmoy.co.uk. This company operates an 8-day Turkey & the Middle East cruise which includes a day in Beirut. Prices from £895 including return flight from London to Larnaca & transfer to the port of Larnaca for the cruise.

Swan Hellenic Lynnem Hse, 1 Victoria Way, Burgess Hill, West Sussex RH15 9NF; ☎ 0844 871 4603; e info@swanhellenic.com, reservations@ swanhellenic.com; www.swanhellenic.com. A stylish cruise company offering a 15-day Aegean & Levant itinerary starting from £2,275 pp, including return flights from the UK, & includes a full day ashore in Beirut & Tripoli. The company's 14-day Castles in the Sand cruise starts from £1,595 including return flights from the UK & includes full-day stopovers in Beirut & Tripoli.

Voyages to Antiquity 8 South Parade, Summertown, Oxford OX2 7JL; ✎ 01865 302550 (enquiries), 01865 302557 (request a brochure), 0845 437 9737 (reservations); e reservations@voyagestoantiquity.com; www.voyagestoantiquity.com. A new Mediterranean specialist cruise company offering a 15-day Limassol to Cairo itinerary which includes a 2-day/1-night stopover in Beirut with a whole-day shore excursion to Baalbek & a half-day tour of Byblos & Beirut. Prices from £2,295 including return flights from London.

HEALTH

Generally speaking, Lebanon is a healthy country with life expectancy and infant mortality rate levels much better than other countries in the region and you are no more likely to fall ill or contract an infectious disease than anywhere else in the Mediterranean region. The standards of health care are high with many medical personnel having been educated overseas, many in Europe, and several also speak English and French in addition to their native Arabic. Lebanon has 33 doctors and 34 hospital beds per 10,000 of the population; above average figures for the MENA (Middle East and North Africa) region. Emergency and routine medical treatment is available to overseas visitors but as Lebanon does not have any reciprocal health agreements with either North America or Europe payment for any medical care received will be required at the time you are treated. It is therefore essential to have comprehensive medical insurance in place prior to visiting Lebanon.

TRAVEL PREPARATION Prior to your departure it would be advisable to be up to date with your vaccinations against tetanus, polio and diphtheria, which are now available as an all-in-one vaccine, Revaxis, which is valid for ten years. It is also a good idea to be up-to-date with hepatitis A and typhoid vaccines. If travelling for more than two months a hepatitis B vaccine is recommended which is given as a course of three injections over a minimum of three weeks and can be administered as a combined dose with hepatitis A. These schedules are restricted for those aged 16 and above. Longer hepatitis B schedules over a minimum of eight weeks are needed for younger people. Vaccination against rabies (see below) is recommended if you are planning to visit remote rural areas of Lebanon and envisage coming into contact with animals and will be more than 24 hours away from medical assistance. A certificate or other proof of vaccination against yellow fever is the only vaccination requirement for entry to Lebanon for those aged over one year old, if arriving from a yellow fever endemic zone, such as parts of sub-Saharan Africa and South America, or if you are travelling on passports from those countries.

MALARIA Lebanon is not in a malaria zone, so there is no risk of contracting the condition in the country. Nevertheless there may be other mosquito-borne disease present, such as dengue fever, so it is worth having an insect repellent to hand.

RABIES Rabies is carried by all mammals (beware the village dogs that are used to being fed in the parks) and is passed on to humans through a bite, scratch or lick over an open wound. You must always assume any animal is rabid, and seek medical help as soon as possible. Meanwhile scrub the wound with soap under a running tap or while pouring water from a jug. Find a reasonably clear-looking source of water (but at this stage the quality of the water is not important), then pour on a strong iodine or alcohol solution of gin, whisky or rum. This helps stop the rabies

Any prolonged immobility, including travel by land or air, can result in deep-vein thrombosis (DVT) with the risk of embolus to the lungs. Certain factors can increase the risk and these include:

- A previous clot or a close relative with a history
- People over 40, with increased risk to the over 80s
- Recent major operation or varicose-veins surgery
- Cancer
- Stroke
- Heart disease
- Obesity
- Pregnancy
- Hormone therapy
- Heavy smokers
- Severe varicose veins
- People who are very tall (over 6ft/1.8m) or short (under 5ft/1.5m)

A DVT causes painful swelling and redness of the calf or sometimes the thigh. It is only dangerous if a clot travels to the lungs (pulmonary embolus). Symptoms of a pulmonary embolus (PE) include chest pains, shortness of breath, and sometimes coughing up small amounts of blood. Anyone who thinks that they might have a DVT needs to see a doctor immediately.

PREVENTION OF DVT
- Keep mobile before and during the flight; move around every couple of hours
- Drink plenty of fluids during the flight
- Avoid taking sleeping pills and excessive tea, coffee and alcohol
- Consider wearing flight socks or support stockings (see *www.legshealth.com*)

If you think you are at increased risk of a clot, ask your doctor if it is safe to travel.

virus entering the body and will guard against wound infections, including tetanus.

Pre-exposure vaccinations for rabies is ideally advised for everyone, but is particularly important if you intend to have contact with animals and/or are likely to be more than 24 hours away from medical help. Ideally three doses should be taken over a minimum of 21 days, though even taking one or two doses of vaccine may be better than none at all in some circumstances. Contrary to popular belief these vaccinations are relatively painless.

If you are bitten, scratched or licked over an open wound by a sick animal, then post-exposure prophylaxis should be given as soon as possible, though it is never too late to seek help, as the incubation period for rabies can be very long. Those who have not been immunised will need a full course of injections as well as rabies immunoglobulin (RIG), but this product is expensive (around US$800) and may be hard to come by – another reason why pre-exposure vaccination should be encouraged. If you have had the full three doses of pre-exposure vaccine then you will not need the RIG, but

A basic kit could contain the following:

- A good drying antiseptic, eg: iodine or potassium permanganate (don't take antiseptic cream)
- A few small dressings (Band-Aids)
- Suncream
- Insect repellent; impregnated bednet or permethrin spray
- Aspirin or paracetamol
- Antifungal cream (eg Canesten)
- Ciprofloxacin or norfloxacin, for severe diarrhoea
- Antibiotic eye drops, for sore, 'gritty', stuck-together eyes (conjunctivitis)
- A pair of fine-pointed tweezers (to remove hairy caterpillar hairs, thorns, splinters and such like)
- Alcohol-based hand rub or bar of soap in a plastic box
- Condoms or femidoms

just two further doses of vaccine three days apart. It is important to tell the doctor if you have had pre-exposure vaccine. And remember that, if you do contract rabies, mortality is 100% and death from rabies is probably one of the worst ways to go.

LEISHMANIASIS Leishmaniasis is spread through the bite of an infected sandfly. It can cause a slowly growing skin lump or ulcer (the cutaneous form) and sometimes a serious life-threatening fever with anaemia and weight loss (Kala-azar). Infected dogs are carriers of the infection. Sandfly bites should be avoided whenever possible. The female sandflies or 'no-see-ums' (as they are called) are usually more of a problem at night and when the wind dies down on the beach. The first line of defence is to apply insect repellents containing 50–55% DEET to exposed skin. Wear long-sleeved shirts, long trousers, and socks in the evenings.

PROTECTION FROM THE SUN During the height of summer temperatures can soar to 30–35°C or even higher, especially on the coast, and for those unused to these temperatures or from more temperate climates, the intensity of the heat could be a real problem. It would be sensible to pack some suncream and to keep out of the sun during the middle of the day if possible, but if you must expose yourself to the sun, build up gradually from 20 minutes per day and wear a T-shirt and apply suncream (at least SPF25, but preferably 30) and use waterproof suncream if swimming. Exposure to the sun can age the skin, making people permanently wrinkly; and increases the risk of skin cancer. Cover up where possible and wear long, loose-fitting clothes and a hat. Prickly heat or heat rash is a related problem identified by a fine pimply rash on the trunk; cool showers, dabbing dry, and talc will all help. Treat the problem by slowing down to a more relaxed schedule, wearing only loose, baggy, 100% cotton clothes and sleeping naked under a fan; if it's bad you may need to check into an air-conditioned hotel room for a while.

DRINKING WATER Tap water is not generally drinkable so stick with bottled mineral water which is plentiful, cheap and available in hotels, restaurants, supermarkets and corner shops all over the country and often from Lebanon's own mountain springs such as Mount Sannine.

SMOKING Smoking is widespread in Lebanon, as in most Arab countries, with nearly 60% of adults and almost a third of women regular smokers, and a 2010 World Health Organisation (WHO) study ranking Lebanon as the world's most prolific nation for smoking. Consequently you will find many people lighting up in bars, cafes, restaurants, hotels and internet cafés, so passive smoking can be an issue in all these establishments. Many Lebanese smoke well-known American brands such as Kent, Marlboro and Winston. In August 2011, however, Lebanon followed the example of Syria and the United Arab Emirates by becoming the Arab world's third country to pass a law banning smoking in public places, legislation which includes an advertising and sponsorship ban on tobacco companies. The new legislation is due to come into force in 2012, imposing substantial fines on both establishment owners (LBP1–3 million) and individuals (LBP100,000) who flout the ban, but many people seem to think that the rules won't be enforced and people will ignore them anyway.

STOMACH UPSETS Although hygiene standards in Lebanon's cafés, hotels and restaurants are generally excellent, a change in climate, diet and routine can all upset the normal digestive pattern and, apart from being caught short, you are unlikely in Lebanon to experience anything more serious beyond having a short bout of diarrhoea. If you do experience diarrhoea, the best advice is to drink plenty of fluids such as coke, orange squash or water to help stave off the worst effects of dehydration and to stick to plain foods such as biscuits until the condition passes.

HIV/AIDS The incidence of this life-threatening condition in Lebanon is extremely low. A 2010 UNAIDS/WHO Working Group report stated that there were some 3,400 adults over the age of 15 living with HIV in Lebanon, around 0.1% of the total population, giving Lebanon a world ranking of 119th out of 170 surveyed countries. As having unprotected sex with an infected person exposes you to risk of catching the disease, the only sure way to be safe is to abstain from any sexual contact. If you must indulge, use condoms or femidoms, which help to reduce the risk of transmission. If you notice any genital ulcers or discharge, get treatment promptly since these increase the risk of acquiring HIV. If you do have unprotected sex, visit a clinic as soon as possible; this should be within 24 hours, or no later than 72 hours, for post-exposure prophylaxis. The chances of contracting HIV through infected needles or by blood transfusion is practically zero in Lebanon.

JELLYFISH In the height of summer, during July and August, jellyfish can be a nuisance for swimmers as the creatures embark on their annual migration northwards along the Mediterranean coastline. Although not generally life threatening their stings can be extremely painful and medical assistance should be sought at the earliest opportunity. An antiseptic cream is usually sufficient to treat more minor stings.

SNAKEBITE Lebanon has several poisonous species of snake which often inhabit archaeological sites, rocky and rural terrain, though no variety is of the highly venomous type. Snakes rarely attack unless provoked, and bites in travellers are unusual. To prevent bites wear stout shoes and long trousers when you are in areas where snakes are known to be present. Most snakes are harmless and even venomous species will dispense venom in only about half of their bites. If bitten, then, you are unlikely to have received venom; keeping this fact in mind may help you to stay calm. Many so-called first-aid techniques do more harm than good: tourniquets are dangerous; suction and electrical inactivation devices do not work. The only treatment is antivenom. In case of a bite that you fear may have been from a venomous snake:

2

- Try to keep calm – it is likely that no venom has been dispensed
- Prevent movement of the bitten limb by applying a splint
- Keep the bitten limb BELOW heart height to slow the spread of any venom
- If you have a crêpe bandage, wrap it around the whole limb (eg: all the way from the toes to the thigh), as tight as you would for a sprained ankle or a muscle pull
- Evacuate to a hospital

And remember:

- NEVER give aspirin; you may take paracetamol, which is safe
- NEVER cut or suck the wound
- DO NOT apply ice packs
- DO NOT apply potassium permanganate

If the offending snake can be captured without risk of someone else being bitten, take this to show the doctor – but beware since even a decapitated head is able to bite.

MEDICAL FACILITIES IN LEBANON In the capital, the **American University of Beirut Medical Centre** (☎ 01 374 374, 01 350 000; www.aubmc.org) in the Hamra district is a highly respected teaching hospital throughout the region with a full range of medical departments, including 24/7 emergency admissions. The nearby **Clemenceau Medical Centre** (☎ 01 372 888; www.cmc.com.lb), affiliated with John Hopkins International, is another facility providing cutting-edge medical technology and well-qualified staff and in 2010, was recognised as one of the top-ten World's Best Hospitals for Medical Tourism by the Medical Travel and Health Tourism Quality Alliance (MTQUA). In the Achrafieh district of east Beirut **Hôtel-Dieu de France** (☎ 01 615 300, 01 615 400; www.hdf.usj.edu.lb) offers similar facilities. In addition to these hospitals, private doctors and dentists abound, working in both general and more specialised fields, and you will see their plaques advertising their services on buildings around the country. The website of the British embassy in Beirut (☎ 01 960 800; www.ukinlebanon.fco.gov.uk) has a comprehensive list of nationwide hospitals, with telephone numbers, which you can download from their site. They can also help you with locating a doctor should you require one. The website of the United States embassy in Beirut (☎ 04 542 600, 04 543 600; www.lebanon.usembassy.gov) also has a comprehensive listing of nationwide hospitals together with a list of those doctors and dentists working in more specialised fields of medicine.

Well-stocked pharmacies are also ubiquitous, with many remaining open until late in the evening and a few even open 24/7. There are an increasing number of pharmacies who can also undertake minor medical procedures for less serious complaints. Contraceptives, tampons and sanitary towels are widely available in most pharmacies and supermarkets around the country.

TRAVEL CLINICS AND HEALTH INFORMATION A full list of current travel clinic websites worldwide is available on www.istm.org/. For other journey preparation information, consult www.nathnac.org/ds/map_world.aspx. Information about various medications may be found on www.netdoctor.co.uk/travel.

UK

Berkeley Travel Clinic 32 Berkeley St, London W1J 8EL (near Green Park tube station); ☎ 020 7629 6233; ⏰ 10.00–18.00 Mon–Fri, 10.00–15.00 Sat

The Travel Clinic Ltd, Cambridge
41 Hills Rd, Cambridge CB2 1NT; ☎ 01223 367362; e enquiries@travelclinic.ltd.uk; www.travelcliniccambridge.co.uk; ⏰ 10.00–16.00 Mon, Tue & Sat, 12.00–19.00 Wed & Thu, 11.00–18.00 Fri

The Travel Clinic Ltd, Ipswich
Gilmour Piper, 10 Fonnereau Rd, Ipswich IP1 3JP; ☎ 01223 367362; ⏰ 09.00–19.00 Wed, 09.00–13.00 Sat

Edinburgh Travel Health Clinic
14 East Preston St, Newington, Edinburgh EH8 9QA; ☎ 0131 667 1030; www.edinburghtravelhealthclinic.co.uk; ⏰ 09.00–19.00 Mon–Wed, 09.00–18.00 Thu & Fri. Travel vaccinations & advice on all aspects of malaria prevention. All current UK prescribed anti-malaria tablets in stock.

Fleet Street Travel Clinic
29 Fleet St, London EC4Y 1AA; ☎ 020 7353 5678; e info@fleetstreetclinic.com; www.fleetstreetclinic.com; ⏰ 08.45–17.30 Mon–Fri. Injections, travel products & latest advice.

Hospital for Tropical Diseases Travel Clinic
Mortimer Market Bldg, Capper St (off Tottenham Ct Rd), London WC1E 6AU; ☎ 020 7387 4411; www.thehtd.org; ⏰ 13.00–17.00 Wed & 09.00–13.00 Fri. Consultations are by appointment only & are only offered to those with more complex problems. Check the website for inclusions. Runs a Travellers' Healthline Advisory Service (☎ 020 7950 7799) for country-specific information & health hazards. Also stocks nets, water purification equipment & personal protection measures. Travellers who have returned from the tropics & are unwell, with fever or bloody diarrhoea, can attend the walk-in emergency clinic at the hospital without an appointment.

InterHealth Travel Clinic
111 Westminster Bridge Rd, London SE1 7HR; ☎ 020 7902 9000; e info@interhealth.org.uk; www.interhealth.org.uk; ⏰ 08.30–17.30 Mon–Fri. Competitively priced, one-stop travel health service by appointment only.

MASTA
(Medical Advisory Service for Travellers Abroad) At the London School of Hygiene & Tropical Medicine, Keppel St, London WC1E 7HT; ☎ 09068 224100 (premium-line number, charged at 60p/minute); e enquiries@masta.org ; www.masta-travel-health.com. For a fee, they will provide an individually tailored health brief, with up-to-date information on how to stay healthy, inoculations & what to take.

MASTA pre-travel clinics
☎ 01276 685040; www.masta-travel-health.com/travel-clinic.aspx. Call or check the website for the nearest; there are currently 50 in Britain. They also sell malaria prophylaxis, memory cards, treatment kits, bednets, net treatment kits, etc.

NHS travel websites
www.fitfortravel.nhs.uk or www.fitfortravel.scot.nhs.uk. Provide country-by-country advice on immunisation & malaria prevention, plus details of recent developments, & a list of relevant health organisations.

Nomad Travel Clinics
Flagship store: 3–4 Wellington Terrace, Turnpike Lane, London N8 0PX; ☎ 020 8889 7014; e turnpike@nomadtravel.co.uk; www.nomadtravel.co.uk; walk in or appointments ⏰ 09.15–17.00 daily, late night Thu. See website for clinics in west & central London, Bristol, Southampton & Manchester. As well as dispensing health advice, Nomad stocks mosquito nets & other anti-bug devices, & an excellent range of adventure travel gear. Runs a Travel Health Advice line on ☎ 0906 863 3414.

Trailfinders Immunisation Centre
194 Kensington High St, London W8 7RG; ☎ 020 7938 3999; www.trailfinders.com/travelessentials/travelclinic.htm; ⏰ 09.00–17.00 Mon, Tue, Wed & Fri, 09.00–18.00 Thu, 10.00–17.15 Sat. No appointment necessary.

Travelpharm
www.travelpharm.com. The Travelpharm website offers up-to-date guidance on travel-related health & has a range of medications available through their online mini-pharmacy.

Irish Republic
Tropical Medical Bureau
54 Grafton St, Dublin 2; ☎ 01 2715200; e graftonstreet@tmb.ie; www.tmb.ie; ⏰ until 20.00 Mon–Fri & Sat mornings.

For other clinic locations, & useful information specific to tropical destinations, check their website.

USA

Centers for Disease Control 1600 Clifton Rd, Atlanta, GA 30333; ☎ 800 232 4636 or (800) 232 6348; e cdcinfo@cdc.gov; www.cdc.gov/travel. The central source of travel information in the USA. Each summer they publish the invaluable *Health Information for International Travel.*

IAMAT (International Association for Medical Assistance to Travelers) 1623 Military Rd #279, Niagara Falls, NY 14304-1745; ☎ 716 754 4883; e info@iamat.org; www.iamat.org. A non-profit organisation with free membership that provides lists of English-speaking doctors abroad.

Canada

IAMAT Suite 10, 1287 St Clair Street West, Toronto, Ontario M6E 1B8; ☎ 416 652 0137; www.iamat.org

TMVC Suite 314, 1030 W Georgia St, Vancouver, BC V6E 2Y3; ☎ 604 681 5656; e vancouver@tmvc. com; www.tmvc.com. One-stop medical clinic for all your international travel health & vaccination needs.

Australia and New Zealand

TMVC (Travel Doctors Group) ☎ 1300 65 88 44; www.tmvc.com.au. 30 clinics in Australia & New Zealand, including: Auckland Canterbury Arcade, 174 Queen St, Auckland 1010, New Zealand; ☎ (64) 9 373 3531; e auckland@traveldoctor. co.nz; Brisbane 75a Astor Terrace, Spring Hill, Brisbane, QLD 4000, Australia; ☎ 07 3815 6900; e brisbane@traveldoctor.com.au; Melbourne

393 Little Bourke St, Melbourne, Vic 3000, Australia; ☎ (03) 9935 8100; e melbourne@traveldoctor.com.au; Sydney 428 George St, Sydney, NSW 2000, Australia; ☎ (2) 9221 7133; e sydney@traveldoctor.com.au
IAMAT 206 Papanui Rd, Christchurch 5, New Zealand; www.iamat.org

South Africa

SAA-Netcare Travel Clinics ☎ 011 802 0059; e travelinfo@netcare.co.za; www.travelclinic. co.za. 11 clinics throughout South Africa.

TMVC NHC Health Centre, cnr Beyers Naude & Waugh Northcliff; ☎ 0861 300 911; e info@ traveldoctor.co.za; www.traveldoctor.co.za. Consult the website for clinic locations.

SAFETY

The very words 'Beirut' and 'Lebanon' continue to resonate with images and reports of danger, terrorism and war more than two decades after the end of the 1975–90 civil hostilities. Memories still linger in the minds of hostages such as John McCarthy, Terry Waite and a host of other individuals who had their freedom taken away during a period of utter chaos and hatred in Lebanon's history. Thankfully, these events are firmly in the past and, although it cannot be said that the country's internal problems and wider issues have been completely solved, the fact remains that foreign tourists and visitors are not targets for abductions or violence. The occupation of parts of the country by Syria ended in 2005 and the Israelis withdrew the vast majority of their forces from south Lebanon in May 2000. With the exception of a tiny parcel of land called the Shebaa Farms (see pages 4 and 23) at which Israel maintains a military presence, the only 'occupying' force in Lebanon now is the United Nations Interim Force in Lebanon (UNIFIL) who are located in a Security Zone in south Lebanon monitoring the security situation between Israel and Hezbollah. In Beirut you will no doubt come across soldiers, armoured vehicles and checkpoints which, while it can be a little unnerving initially, is nothing to be worried about. You will find the Lebanese army courteous towards visitors, though you should always carry your passport (or a photocopy) in case you are asked for your ID. Current UK Foreign and Commonwealth Office advice is to refrain from visiting any Palestinian refugee camps and to avoid, unless essential, all travel to south of the Litani River. The author visited both these areas and encountered absolutely no hostilities or problems. The US Department of State travel advice, whilst it has dropped its blanket ban on US citizens travelling to the country, now advises against all travel to Lebanon. The main area of concern in the south, however, is the amount of unexploded ordnance rather than any tangible threats to visitors (see page 236). As regards crime against the person, Lebanon is probably one of the safest countries in the world with a very low crime rate compared with countries such as the UK and US. There have been recent reports of occasional bag snatching and a spate of robberies in taxis in Beirut, but these are rare exceptions to the general conclusion that Lebanon remains an inherently safe country for visitors, but like anywhere in the world it pays to be vigilant.

DRIVING There is a high accident rate on Lebanon's roads and in 2008 car accidents accounted for the number one cause of death in the country. Whilst road signs, traffic lights and speed cameras are becoming more widespread, these are often ignored by drivers. The Lebanese are not known for following rules and when you factor in a lack of anticipation of other road users, speaking on a mobile phone whilst driving, not wearing a seat belt (assuming one is fitted) and a tendency towards road rage, the mix becomes potentially even more dangerous. Although the police will often stop and enforce the road laws, the following general advice should be followed by anyone travelling by taxi or hire car with a driver in Lebanon.

- If possible sit in the back of the car but if you must sit in the front, wear a seat belt if there is one.
- Travel by day, not by night. Street and road lighting is often inadequate, especially in more remote mountain and rural areas.
- Avoid drivers who have been drinking.

There are positive signs of things changing, however, and there are now a couple of well-established charities and pressure groups which have emerged to campaign for improved standards of driving on Lebanon's sometimes hazardous roads:

Kunhadi 1st Fl, Feghali Bldg, Damascus Rd, Hazmieh, Beirut; ↘ 05 450 516; m 71 264 415; f 05 959 412; e kunhadi@kunhadi.org; www. kunhadi.org. Founded in 2006 this campaigning charity is highly regarded for its many publicity initiatives in raising awareness amongst young drivers of a variety of road safety issues such as drink driving, improved roads, new & improved traffic laws, new speed limits, the use of radar to track speeding drivers & visits to schools & universities to educate potential & younger drivers in safe road use.
Youth Association for Social Awareness (YASA) 2nd Fl, Akl Bldg, St Rock St, Hazmieh,

Beirut; ↘ 05 452 587; f 05 952 587; m 03 601 972; e yasa@yasa.org; www.yasa.org. Part of the international NGO network, YASA Lebanon was set up in 1996 to combat 'reckless driving' & focuses on campaigns designed to foster improved child & pedestrian safety, the education of drivers in following the rules of the road, the perils of drink driving & safe vehicle operation & maintenance. For visitors considering a self-drive tour of Lebanon the YASA website, like Kunhadi above, provides some very useful background information on what to expect from 'going it alone' on Lebanon's roads

POLICE AND MILITARY You will find that the police mostly keep a low profile and are not as visible a presence on the streets as in many western countries. You will most likely see them on some street intersections directing and controlling the flow

2

of traffic and they are hospitable and helpful to foreigners. More conspicuous is the presence of the army, armoured vehicles and numerous checkpoints around the country. Although this might initially be a little intimidating to the first time visitor it is perfectly normal in this part of the world, and apart from the occasional checks at checkpoints their presence will have minimal impact on your visit. Like the police, the Lebanese Army are generally courteous and helpful to foreigners.

DISABLED TRAVELLERS

Lebanon will not currently win any awards for being the most disabled-friendly nation in the world. Facilities are still a little thin on the ground for those with special needs though Beirut airport, the National Museum and the AUB Museum, together with the rebuilt Downtown district of Beirut all have a range of facilities such as wheelchair and lift access to assist the disabled visitor. Many of the luxury hotels have lifts and even a few of those at the budget end of the market offer this facility but I have yet to find a hotel with comprehensive and specially adapted facilities for those with physical disabilities. Negotiating the streets of Beirut as well as other areas of the country would make for a challenging experience at best for the disabled traveller – pot-holes, the lack of street lighting, uneven road surfaces, chaotic traffic and no buses or taxis with adapted facilities, would in all probability detract from what would otherwise be an enjoyable visit. Sadly, for the time being at least, solo disabled travel to Lebanon cannot be recommended. If as a disabled person you do decide to travel to Lebanon take a look at the following websites: www.disabledtravelersguide.com for some generic information for disabled travellers including a free downloadable visitors' guide covering a wide range of practical topics of use in many countries and www.able-travel.com which also has some useful information and tips for disabled travellers intending to embark on adventurous and challenging holidays and/or business trips.

WOMEN TRAVELLERS

Whether travelling solo or as part of a group tour, female travellers will find Lebanon a breath of fresh air compared with some other Arab countries where the fairer sex is often given less than fair treatment. In a country justly famed for its cosmopolitanism and hospitality, female travellers constantly state that they have encountered an easy-going and safe place to visit without the constant pestering and hassles which they have experienced in countries like Morocco. In terms of dress, pretty much anything goes in Beirut, and at times with the revealing and fashionable clothing worn by many young women you would hardly know you are in an Arabic country. That said, a short, skimpy top or skirt would be totally inappropriate attire in a mosque or in more conservative towns such as Baalbek, Sidon or Tripoli though even here you can still see fashion-conscious and sexily dressed local women. Though Lebanon has a certain machismo, bars are by no means a male domain and as a lone woman you should not expect any more unsolicited attention than you would get back in your own country. With a vibrant café culture in the capital you often see many lone Lebanese females passing time over a beer or cappuccino in a relaxed manner.

GAY TRAVELLERS

Homosexuality is illegal under Lebanese law for being a 'sexual act against nature' and the country does not have an overtly 'gay scene' where 'outed' homosexuals can freely mingle. Public displays of affection are taboo, and could cost you your liberty, with up to one year in prison. Whilst there are a couple of what might be termed 'gay friendly' establishments in Beirut (see page 110), discretion is the order of the day for both Lebanese and visitors alike and discrimination and raids by police on known and suspected gay haunts do occur. The following organisations and websites are well worth a look, with a cornucopia of gay and general human rights information on Lebanon and the wider Arab world.

Bint el Nas (Arabic for 'Daughter of the People') www.bintelnas.org. For LBTQ (Lesbian, Bisexual, Transgender & Queer) women in Lebanon.
GME www.gaymiddleeast.com

Helem (Arabic acronym for Lebanese Protection for Lesbians, Gays, Bisexuals & Transgenders) 1st Fl, Zico Hse, Yamout Bldg, 174 Spears St, Beirut; 01 745 092 (12.00–20.00); m 70 123 687 (24/7 helpline); e lgbtq-centre@helem.net; www.helem.net

WHAT TO TAKE

Lebanon has a plentiful supply of shopping malls, supermarkets, stores and pharmacies, especially in Beirut, and you can find almost anything you will need for your visit, including items such as condoms or tampons. If you are currently taking any form of prescribed medication it may be better to bring with you an extra supply as not all pharmacies will dispense additional supplies should you run out. As you cannot buy Lebanese currency overseas it would be a good idea to bring US dollars in cash as these are easily exchanged and readily accepted in 99.9% of places.

It would be a good idea to be sensitive to the time of year you are visiting and to bring sufficient clothing appropriate to the season, with summer and winter being the main considerations, though you will have no problem obtaining any items you forgot to bring. In summer do not underestimate both the heat and humidity especially in Beirut and along other parts of the Mediterranean coast. A hat and suncream would be essential items to bring with you together with loose-fitting and light-coloured cotton garments to help offset the worst effects of the sun's intensity. A strong pair of sandals would also be beneficial. Inland and mountainous areas can be decidedly cooler in the evenings and even in the height of summer a thin jumper may be required. The winter months with their consequent drop in temperature and advent of often heavy rainfall means a waterproof jacket and/or umbrella will also be essential. For light sleepers, a pair of earplugs could prove useful if staying near a mosque and you want to sleep through the dawn call to prayer, or at hotels where your room is overlooking the street with noisy traffic or late-night revellers. If you are planning on skiing in season then bring appropriate clothing, though equipment can be rented.

Whatever time of year you decide to visit a good pair of walking boots or at least a sturdy pair of training shoes or such like will make your progress around Beirut's often pot-holed streets and the country's mountainous and historical sites a much more comfortable experience. If you are planning to undertake some formal dining out in restaurants or perhaps a visit to one of the capital's numerous nightclubs, more formal attire such as trousers, jacket and even tie may be required at some of the more upmarket establishments. These places often insist on smart or at least casual dress, much like in cities such as London, New York or Paris. Similarly, more customised clothing, especially for women, is the order of the day when visiting sensitive or religious sites such as mosques. For women, a headscarf

2

will often be required and it would be sensible to 'dress down' at these places in more conservative attire. As power cuts and electricity rationing occur regularly throughout the country a useful accessory to bring would be a small torch, perhaps of the Maglite variety, for help in negotiating the sometimes dark streets of the capital as well as in more remote areas of the country.

For those visitors who are taking their mobile phone, laptop, video or still camera (or any other electronic device) to Lebanon a power adaptor plug will be an essential item to include in your luggage. Lebanon's power supply works on the European-style round two-pin plug system and once again adaptor plugs are readily available almost everywhere in the country should you forget to bring your own. Lebanon is an extremely beautiful country, with a stunning range of natural scenery as well as an array of manmade architecture, which can make for a very photogenic experience – therefore bringing a camera is almost as essential as packing your passport (see also pages 75–6). Bring an SLR (Single Lens Reflex) camera, either digital or film, together with a plentiful supply of memory cards or slide/negative film. In Beirut especially, memory cards, slide, colour and black-and-white film can be obtained in shops and photo labs often offer a full range of processing services for film as well as the option of 'burning' your memory cards to CD/DVD.

MAPS A Lebanon map is produced by **GEOprojects** (*8 Southern Court, South St, Reading RG1 4QS;* \ *0118 939 3567;* e *enquiries@geoprojects.net; www.geoprojects. net; Barakat Bldg, Jeanne d'Arc St, Beirut;* \ *01 344 236;* e *geoproj@cyberia.net.lb*), which is part of their Arab World Map Library series, and their latest 2008 edition (scale 1:200,000) is available in Arabic, English and French. It has a very detailed main map of Lebanon with the reverse side containing a decent city map of Beirut and the Downtown area together with useful overview information on the country. They also publish a separate and equally good Beirut city map (scale 1:10,000). At the time of writing the future of the company's UK map operations was uncertain and the aforementioned maps may only be available in Beirut bookshops while stocks last.

International Travel Maps and Books Ltd (ITMB) (*12300 Bridgeport Rd, Richmond, BC, Canada V6V 1J5;* \ *604 273 1400;* e *map@itmb.com; www.itmb. com*) produce an excellent 2011 Lebanon country map on one side (scale 1:190,000) and containing an equally excellent city map of Beirut (scale 1:8,000) on the reverse side and which has been used to produce some of the maps used in this guide. The map is available from the publishers themselves (US$12.95; €8.95) via mail or online order. In the UK, **Stanfords** bookshop (*12–14 Long Acre, London WC2E 9LP;* \ *020 7836 1321;* e *sales@stanfords.co.uk; www.stanfords.co.uk*) is also a stockist and offers online ordering.

In addition to the above, the Ministry of Tourism has a range of free maps which you can pick up at their desk in the arrivals hall at Beirut airport or at their main office in the Hamra district of west Beirut (see page 99). Bookshops such as the excellent Librairie Antoine on Beirut's Hamra Street also stock a range of maps (see page 117).

Explorer Publishing (*PO Box 34275, Dubai, UAE;* \ *+971 (0) 4 340 8805;* f *+971 (0) 4 340 8806;* e *info@explorerpublishing.com; www.explorerpublishing.com*) have also produced a 2011 Lebanon Road Map which is useful for those touring the country by the self drive method. The map should be available from Waterstones or Stanfords bookshops in the UK and from the publishers themselves by international mail order (€13.95 / US$16.95).

MONEY

The Lebanese currency is known as the Lebanese lira (LL), but commonly referred to as the Lebanese pound (LBP). For some years the exchange rate has been pegged to the US dollar, simmering at a relatively stable LBP1,500 to US$1. In September 2011, the exchange rate for the euro, sterling and the US dollar were as follows: €1 = LBP2,148.96; £1 = LBP2,443.13; US$1 = LBP1,507.32. Lebanese currency is issued as banknotes in denominations of LBP1,000, LBP5,000, LBP10,000, LBP20,000, LBP50,000 and LBP100,000, and there are also coins to the value of LBP50, LBP100, LBP250 and LBP500. The LBP50 and LBP100 coins will rarely, if ever, be encountered except perhaps when given as change in supermarkets or the like. If paying for goods or services in US dollars you will usually receive any change in LBP. It is currently not possible to pre-order Lebanese currency outside the country. However, US dollars are universally accepted throughout Lebanon at restaurants, hotels and stores and the two currencies are virtually interchangeable for all practical purposes. It is a good idea to keep a supply of small-denomination notes and coins – US or Lebanese – for tipping, bus and taxi fares.

CHANGING MONEY Banks are plentiful throughout all the major towns and cities. Opening hours can vary slightly between banks but are generally from 08.00 to 15.00 Monday to Friday and 08.00 to 13.00 Saturday, with Sundays closed. The banks will exchange the major foreign currencies such as the US dollar, sterling and euros. ATMs are also ubiquitous, and at some of the luxury hotels, and you can withdraw cash in both Lebanese currency and US dollars 24/7 in most areas. The current official bank at Beirut airport is BankMed (\ *01 628 622/3/4, 01 628 828; www.bankmed.com.lb*), which has a number of 24/7 ATMs for cash withdrawals in the arrivals and departure halls and also a foreign exchange service. An alternative to ATMs and the banks is the many private moneychangers, operating especially in the Hamra district of west Beirut, who will exchange currency for variable commission rates. It is not advisable to bring travellers' cheques with you to Lebanon as most banks seem reluctant to change them (unless, in some cases, you have an account with the bank) and at the time of research there were only a couple of places in Beirut who were willing to swap travellers' cheques for hard currency (see page 120).

CREDIT CARDS All the major credit-card companies such as American Express, Diners Club, MasterCard and Visa are accepted everywhere, except at perhaps the smallest hotel or store.

INTERNATIONAL MONEY TRANSFER Sending and receiving money internationally can be done through Western Union Money Transfer (*www.westernunion.com*), whose main agent in Lebanon is Online Money Transfer or OMT (\ *01 391 000; www.omt.com.lb*), easily recognised by their large yellow signs. They have hundreds of offices all over the country at banks, shops, post offices and other retail outlets.

BUDGETING

For the first-time visitor to Lebanon the price of hotels and restaurants, the largest costs usually incurred by tourists, can come as a bit of a surprise compared with some other countries in the region, with accommodation costs generally on a par with those in western Europe or North America. That said, there is an increasing supply of budget accommodation, especially in the capital, where a double room can be obtained for as little as US$25 per night, though don't expect frills. At the luxury end of the hotel scale a double room in high season can easily cost you anywhere between US$200 and US$450. Mid-range establishments probably offer the best value accommodation options as they tend to offer a decent standard of comfort for around US$100 for a double room in high season. Outside the main summer tourist season prices can fall substantially, as they can for those planning an extended stay, and it is always worth asking about discounted room rates, whatever your budget. In all cases check whether the obligatory 10% government tax is included in the room rates you have been quoted.

If you are on a self-catering visit, there is a plentiful supply of supermarkets and stores throughout the country. The plethora of nationwide shopping malls and Lebanese chains such as Spinneys, TSC and Goodies all stock a wide range of food, cosmetics, clothing and general household items, pretty much like the chain stores in western Europe and North America, with prices generally comparable. Eating out can cost as little or as much you like. A tasty and filling street snack in Beirut can cost around US$2–3, but restaurants will obviously cost more. A main course for two people in a decent eatery will cost around US$20–25, whilst in more expensive eating establishments you could easily pay double that. The Western fast-food chains such as Burger King, Domino's Pizza, KFC and McDonald's are ubiquitous in Lebanon, and once again prices are on a par with what you would pay back home. Alcohol is not particularly cheap in Lebanon and a small bottle of local almaza beer can cost you anywhere between US$2–5, in many bars but will be cheaper if bought in a supermarket. The national drink, *arak*, an aniseed-flavour beverage often served with *mezze*, can vary widely in price from US$3 to US$8 for a glass, with a bottle costing from US$12 to US$30. Wine is a popular drink, especially those from the vineyards of Ksara, Kefraya and Musar in the Bekaa Valley and is served in most establishments. A bottle from one of these labels can cost around US$16–20.

Transportation around the country is both plentiful and cheap, with the public buses and taxis the principal options available to the visitor. The buses cover most areas of the country and are great value. Within Beirut the fare to any area should not exceed US$1 and you can travel by bus to Byblos, Jounieh and surrounding areas of Mount Lebanon for the same price, though the journey will obviously take longer than by taxi. A bus to Baalbek in the Bekaa Valley from Beirut is around US$3 whilst a non-stop, air-conditioned bus to the southern city of Sidon from the capital costs less than US$2. Taxi fares are subject to some negotiation but generally speaking a shared (*servees*) taxi within the central Beirut area is around US$2 but will cost a lot more if used as a taxi. Car-hire costs also vary according to season. In general, expect to pay somewhere around US$30–35 in low season and US$40–45 in high season for a small three-door Renault or Kia Picanto. If you are after renting a vehicle with more bells and whistles such as a Mercedes, Porsche or Range Rover, expect to pay around US$300+ in low season, US$400–450 in high season. There are plenty of companies and thus plenty of competition so it pays to shop around for the best deal. A car with driver will add a minimum of US$30 to the cost of car hire.

Admission fees to Lebanon's plethora of archaeological, touristic sites, museums and natural wonders represent excellent value for money. A number of these are free and the current maximum charge for entry is LBP18,150 to see the world-class stalactites and stalagmites at Jeita Grotto.

TIPPING Tipping, or *baksheesh*, is as prevalent in Lebanon as it is in many other countries of the world. Although the amount you should leave for services rendered is by no means an exact science, invariably depending on the quality of service you have received, gratuities to airport and hotel porters are normally around US$1–2 per item of luggage. In restaurants, where an additional service charge (usually 10–15%) has not already been added, a tip of around 10% of the total bill is usual practice. There is no expectation or requirement to tip bus or taxi drivers.

SOME AVERAGE DAY-TO-DAY COSTS

Bottle of water	LBP1,000	Bus fare from Beirut to Sidon	LBP1,500
Bottle of beer	LBP4,000	Bus fare within Beirut	from LBP1,000
Can of coke	LBP1,000	*Servees* taxi in Beirut	from LBP2,000
Cup of coffee	LBP4,000	Basic hotel (double room)	LBP30,000
Loaf of bread	LBP3,000	Mid-range hotel (double room)	LBP150,000
Mars bar	LBP1,000	Luxury hotel (double room)	LBP300,000+
Snack	LBP3,000	Museum entry	LBP5,000
T-shirt	LBP8,000	2GB memory card	LBP16,500
Camera film	LBP7,000	Aspirin (pack of 30)	LBP1,500
Litre of petrol	LBP1,600	Burning memory card to CD	LBP7,000
Litre of diesel	LBP1,000	Pack of 4 AA batteries	LBP3,000
Newspaper	LBP2,000	Postcard	LBP1,000
Internet café access	LBP3,000p/h		

GETTING AROUND

Lebanon is a very small nation and its 7,200km of paved roads, though often pot-holed and narrow with hairpin mountain bends, are going to be your principal means of travelling around the country by whatever mode of transport you choose. Driving is on the right-hand side of the road, though this can change at any time depending on the whim of the driver. Traffic lights, signs and speed limits have increased in recent years, but generally have the status of ornamental features rather than any real practical use. Traffic conditions, especially in Beirut, are also overwhelmingly characterised by congestion and chaos, not to mention the environmental impact of not so environmentally friendly cars, which account for around 40% of CO_2 emissions in the capital. That said, public transport is plentiful and cheap in most areas of the country and you will not have to wait long to depart to your chosen destination. One private-sector initiative designed to provide 'a partial solution' to ease the pressure and congestion on the capital's roads and along the coastal highways is the proposed introduction of boat services between Beirut, Byblos, Jounieh, Sidon and Tyre. Although not yet operational, if it becomes a reality it will be great for the local commuter and a real bonus for visitors who will be able to see Lebanon from the sea for the first time in many years. Keep an eye on www.beirutwatertaxi.com for developments, as it could well be, *inshallah*, up and running by the time you read this.

BY AIR There are no internal air services within Lebanon.

BY BUS Whilst travelling by bus may be one of the slowest means of getting around, the flip side is that it is also one of the cheapest, with fares ranging from LBP1,000 within Beirut to a maximum of around LBP6,000 to almost any destination outside the capital. Bus stations are scattered all around the country and buses link the vast majority of sites and towns of most interest to the visitor. The capital obviously has the most comprehensive network of bus routes and the main provider of these is the privately owned **Lebanese Commuting Company (LCC)** whose fares range from LBP1,000 for short journeys to LBP1,500 for those further afield. At the time of writing the state-run bus company, **OCFTC (Office des Chemins de Fer et du Transport en Commun)**, has suspended its formerly comprehensive route network due to a lack of government funding.

Complementing the LCC is a range of private buses and minivans which ply their trade around Beirut and nationwide. The downside is that there is a distinct lack of clear timetable information. Beirut has three main bus stations within an easy walk or a short taxi ride of most areas in the city and these tend to be set up to serve specific destinations within Lebanon as well as neighbouring Syria and countries beyond (see pages 96–7). They are not particularly salubrious venues so don't expect ultra-comfy waiting rooms and restaurants, but are adequate enough for the purpose. Most signs on the buses are in Arabic and usually it is best to just ask where and when the next bus leaves for your destination. Standards range from modern air-conditioned Pullman coaches to antiquated, non air-conditioned rust buckets belching out their less than ecofriendly choking fumes. Although it is possible to obtain route maps for the LCC buses, timetables do not exist, and like many places in the region buses other than those run by LCC tend to depart the station only when full.

BY CAR Hiring a car in Lebanon is both straightforward and a distinct advantage if you are planning on doing a lot of touring and want the freedom to just up and go at your leisure rather than being tied to public transport. It is also an excellent choice if you want to visit more out-of-the-way places which are less accessible by public transport or taxi, and to areas such as the Chouf Mountains where transport is virtually non-existent after dark. All the major car-hire companies such as Avis, Europcar, Hertz, and Thrifty are well represented with offices at the airport and in Beirut itself. Supplementing these is the plethora of local companies all vying for your custom. Rates for self-drive hire range from around US$30 per day upwards for a small car such as a Renault or Ford Ka to anything from US$300–400 for a 4x4 or BMW vehicle. Discounts are often available and offered in low season and also for more than a few consecutive hire days. You normally need to be over 21 years old (sometimes 23) and be in possession of a full driving licence issued in your own country. Car hire with a driver will obviously be more expensive and as a rough guide you should factor in at least an extra US$30 per day (plus tip and a meal for the driver) to the cost of hiring the car.

BY FOOT Walking has the obvious benefits of being both free and the most environmentally friendly method of getting from place to place. But given Lebanon's varied size and terrain it can also be one of the most pleasurable ways to see many parts of the country. Beirut's compact size means that its main sites and points of interest are easily reached on foot and there are now guided walks available which are highly recommended and comprehensive, though walking around the city in the height of summer can be a demanding experience given the often-experienced extremes of heat and humidity. The major towns of Byblos, Sidon, Tripoli and Tyre are also eminently walkable and provide the best way to see their respective areas of interest. Away from the towns and cities, the country's upland and lowland regions such as the Chouf Mountains and Chouf Cedar Reserve, the Qadisha and Bekaa valleys also lend themselves to walking tours in order to fully appreciate and experience the beauty of the landscape. There are now many organisations who offer rural hikes and treks, including the Lebanon Mountain Trail (see page 181) and the Chouf Cedar Reserve, which can also arrange walks of varying length and difficulty. A local NGO, Greenline (*3rd Fl, Yamout Bldg, 174 Spears St, Sanayeh, Beirut;* \ *01 746 215;* e *greenline@greenline.org.lb; www.greenline.org.lb*) committed to the preservation and sustainable development of the natural world, organises campaigns and projects throughout the country including ecofriendly walks.

BY RAIL You will not be able to travel by train within Lebanon; nor are there any rail links with neighbouring Syria or Israel. Although Lebanon was the first Middle Eastern country to establish rail travel in 1895 during the Ottoman era, when services commenced from Beirut to Rayak some 20km south of Baalbek in the Bekaa Valley, the civil war together with the 2006 Israeli–Hezbollah conflict derailed the entire system which is now rendered totally unusable: the last service was in 1997. Although there has been intermittent talk and feasibility studies undertaken for reinstating travel by train, the logistics and cost of doing so means that rail travel in Lebanon remains a distant prospect at best.

For rail enthusiasts, a Lebanese NGO, Train/Train (m *03 212 885;* e *contact@ rayakrailway.org; www.rayakrailway.org*) is a committed group of volunteers attempting to transform the rusting rolling stock, ticket office, buildings and hotel at the Bekaa Valley's famous old station into a museum. Their ambitions extend to at least a partial renaissance of Lebanon's once-extensive domestic and international rail network.

BY TAXI Taxis are the most ubiquitous form of transport for getting around in Lebanon. Usually ageing Mercedes with red number plates distinguishing them from other cars, they cruise the streets of Beirut and all the other main cities and towns nationwide; they congregate at bus stations and can also be pre-booked by phone or in person from any of the taxi firms which exist throughout the country. Taxis are quicker than using the bus but will cost roughly double the bus fare. In order to avoid overpaying for your taxi journey, it is essential to learn the 'language' of taxi travel as this directly impacts on the price you will pay the driver. The more expensive option is to hail (or phone) a taxi to take you to your destination in which you will have the vehicle to yourself at a fixed and agreed price. The more common scenario is to flag down a taxi and ask for *service* (pronounced '*servees*') and tell the driver where you want to go. For most short journeys the fare is fixed at LBP2,000 though you may be charged a *serviceain* or twice the normal service fare (LBP4,000) to more remote areas. With both *service* and *serviceain* the driver is at liberty to pick up and put down other passengers *en route* to your destination so you can sometimes find yourself sharing the car with other people and taking a little longer to reach your destination.

TOURS There are a burgeoning number of tour operators all over the country offering itineraries to suit all budgets and interests ranging from luxury city tours to those taking in areas off the beaten track with a more adventurous slant. These can be a good way of structuring your visit if time is precious, and leaves someone else take care of the traffic problems. For a list of local tour operators, see page 100.

 ## ACCOMMODATION

Aside from your airline ticket the cost of accommodation, pretty much like anywhere else in the world, is likely to be your largest single financial outlay during your visit. Fortunately, with Lebanon's ever-burgeoning number of visitors and tourists there continues to be an ever-increasing range of hotels, currently over 300 and growing according to the latest figures from the Ministry of Tourism, to choose from. Not surprisingly, the widest choice is in the capital, Beirut. Here, the ongoing trend is for visitor accommodation aimed firmly at the middle- and high-income-bracket traveller as the city attempts to once again provide the chic and luxurious offerings which helped to engender Beirut's pre-war label of 'the Paris of the Middle East'. The big international chains such as Intercontinental, Mövenpick, Ramada and Four Seasons are all represented in the capital and a double room in any of these, with all the usual refinements and facilities you would expect to find in their Western equivalents, can easily cost upwards of US$150 a night. Many include the obligatory 10% tax or service charge levied on rooms but it is still a good idea to check at the time of booking. All the major credit cards are universally accepted at these establishments but payment can also be made in US dollars or Lebanese pounds (LBP). In the high season of summer and over some public and religious holidays hotel prices can rocket, sometimes by as much as 50% and often doubling in price, but outside these times it is worth enquiring about room discounts, especially if you are planning on staying longer than a few nights.

Less common in Beirut are hotels catering for the more price conscious visitor. Accommodation in the mid-range and budget categories, whilst much better than a few years ago, is still a little thin on the ground. Many of these proliferate around the Hamra area in west Beirut and generally are clean and functional, albeit without the five-star bells and whistles of jacuzzi, swimming pools, health spas, etc. Mid-range establishments vary in price from around US$100–150 a night for a double room, whilst budget accommodation can be obtained for around US$20 for a double. As with the five-star options, it is still a good strategy to enquire about discounted rates for extended stays.

Away from the capital your choices of accommodation become more limited but on the plus side prices drop considerably even in main towns like Tripoli, Tyre, Sidon and Byblos, which generally are home to smaller and more atmospheric establishments. The chains are mostly conspicuous by their absence though the Intercontinental Group has a well-located five-star offering in the ski-resort town of Faraya, whilst the Eddé Sands Wellness Resort and Hotel recreates the hedonistic pursuits of 1960s Byblos. The budget traveller is well catered for as a growing number of hostels provide an affordable alternative to the hotels. The Lebanese Youth Hostel Federation (*www.lyhf.org*) runs a growing number of hostels throughout the country at rock-bottom prices, though at present none are located in Beirut. Similarly, camping, formerly quite alien to most Lebanese, is also growing in popularity as people become more environmentally aware with both a concern for protection of the environment and a desire to experience the wonders of the natural world. La Reserve (*www.lareserve.com.lb*) near Afqa Grotto and Camping Amchit Les Colombes near Byblos are two organisations championing the cause of the great outdoors. If you are interested in less mainstream accommodation off the beaten track where your stay will also be supporting less prosperous rural communities the excellent DHIAFEE Program (*www.dhiafeeprogram*) has an extensive countrywide network of campsites, guesthouses, ecolodges, hostels and monasteries outside the capital at prices catering for most budgets. You can book online via their website, which also has useful information and links to a range of outdoor pursuits in Lebanon.

For those contemplating an extended stay in Lebanon, perhaps a month or more, there is the further accommodation option of renting an apartment for the duration of your visit. The availability of apartments is quite plentiful, especially in Beirut and also along the coast and in the mountain areas. Prices per week or month can

ACCOMMODATION PRICE CODES

Based on a double room per night in high season:

Luxury	**$$$$$**	LBP300,000+
Upmarket	**$$$$**	LBP225,000–300,000
Mid range	**$$$**	LBP150,000–225,000
Budget	**$$**	LBP75,000–150,000
Shoestring	**$**	LBP30,000–75,000

be comparable to what you would pay in many Western cities and countries so don't necessarily expect bargain-basement prices. A good place to start your search is the classified advertising section in Lebanon's English-language newspaper *The Daily Star* and by perusing the notice board at the American University of Beirut (AUB) and at the Saifi Urban Gardens Hotel. A company which comes highly recommended by many visitors is Beirut Flats (*Ain al-Mreisse;* ☎ *01 363 200/1, 01 369 210;* f *01 363 222;* e *info@beirutflats.com; www.beirutflats.com*) who are in a nice location overlooking the sea and within easy walking distance for the Hamra and Downtown districts of the capital. They offer a good range of furnished and utility-equipped apartments with all modern conveniences including laundry facilities and internet access. Also take a look at Ahlein (e *feedback@ahlein.net; www.ahlein.net*) which has an extensive range of properties for both rent and sale throughout Lebanon.

EATING AND DRINKING

FOOD Few people depart Lebanon with anything other than positive experiences of Lebanese cuisine. As with many other aspects of Lebanese culture its eating and drinking options are incredibly diverse, mirroring the Arab, Turkish and, more recently, French presence on its shores. When you factor in the country's own favourable geographic and climatic conditions which help to nurture a range of tasty and healthy ingredients such as cheese, chicken, lamb, wheat and a host of fresh fruit and vegetables, Lebanon's gastronomy is quite justifiably renowned throughout the Middle East and beyond. Like the French, the Lebanese take their food very seriously and lunch or dinner can be a lengthy and sociable occasion. The favourite and main meal of the day is the eclectic *mezze*, a wide array of small savoury dishes, served hot or cold. These typically consist of salad-based plates such as *fattoush* and *tabbouleh*, the well-known *hummus* dip, grilled aubergine known as *moutabel*, olives and the creamy cheese-based *labneh*. The most popular meat dishes are chicken and lamb which often accompany a *mezze*. The national dish is known as *kibbeh*, minced lamb and onions fried into conical-shape mortars which are served hot or cold and even raw. A main course may also consist of a fish dish, fried or grilled, with the coastal regions of Byblos and Tyre serving locally produced fresh fish in extremely picturesque settings. At Aanjar in the Bekaa Valley trout is farmed and is a speciality of the area. Desserts often pander to the Arabic sweet tooth and a popular option is *baklava*, a very sweet and syrupy pastry with pistachio nuts. The *knafeh* is another favoured dessert consisting of pastry with cheese and a drizzling of syrup which is also sometimes eaten for breakfast. Assorted fresh fruit is also a popular dessert. Patisseries abound around the country serving a variety of cakes and sweets, with many towns having their own local delicacy such as the sweets of Tripoli and the crumbly and sugary biscuit *sanioura* of Sidon. A common

RESTAURANT PRICE CODES

Based on the average price of a main course for two people (no drinks):

Expensive	$$$$$	LBP60,000+
Above average	$$$$	LBP45,000–60,000
Mid range	$$$	LBP30,000–45,000
Cheap & cheerful	$$	LBP15,000–30,000
Rock bottom	$	LBP7,500–15,000

and filling breakfast will often be *man'oushe*, a type of pizza topped with cheese or herbs such as thyme. Other popular snacks, perhaps already familiar to many people, are *Shish Tawouk* and *shawarma*.

Lebanon is an ideal country for alfresco dining and great for lingering over a meal amid fantastic natural and manmade settings, whether it is in Downtown Beirut amongst the restored Ottoman-era façades, admiring the sunset from the capital's Corniche, whilst the Mediterranean waves lap at the coastline next to you, or eating fine fish overlooking the ancient ports of Byblos or Tyre. Supplementing these authentic culinary experiences are a range of more international eating options, with the fast-food chains of KFC, McDonald's and Burger King ubiquitous. More formal dining is also plentiful, ranging from Armenian, French, Italian, Chinese and Japanese restaurants, offering a more home-from-home experience. Enjoying a street snack is another popular option and one indulged by many Lebanese throughout the country. When in Beirut do check out Barbar in Hamra for its wide range of sandwiches and snacks.

Vegetarians Following a meat-free diet and lifestyle will in no way preclude you from enjoying the wide range of excellent Lebanese cuisine. The country's geography and climate, coupled with its agricultural output of an abundance of fruit and vegetables ensures that vegetarians are well catered for in Lebanon. Many *mezze* dishes are in any case vegetable based such as *hummus, fattoush, moutabel* and *tabbouleh*, the latter being an extremely popular dish, and you will have little problem avoiding meat dishes in most Lebanese restaurants though restaurants catering solely for vegetarians are not widespread. In Beirut the weekly Souk al-Tayeb and Earth Markets (see *Chapter 3*, page 115) are both good sources of fresh fruit and vegetables and other meat-free products from farmers around the country and great places to shop for a picnic or if you are on a self-catering visit. In common with many Mediterranean countries, olive oil is a widely used ingredient and is drizzled over dishes such as *labneh* which is delicious when scooped up with bread. An absolutely fantastic website and blog to have a look at is Mama's Lebanese Kitchen (*www.mamaslebanesekitchen.com*) which features Lebanese recipes from Lebanese mum Esperance who hails from the north of the country near Bcharré, and who shares her foody passion with a whole host of vegetarian (and meat) recipes and cooking methods, including a vegetarian potato *kibbeh*.

DRINK Unlike many of its Muslim neighbours, Lebanon is far from being a 'dry' country with bars, cafés and restaurants serving a wide choice of alcoholic beverages, though in more conservative towns, such as Sidon in the south, the availability of beer, spirits or wine is limited to just one venue. The national drink is *arak*, a high alcohol and potent aniseed-flavoured beverage resembling Greek *ouzo* or French anise, which is often drunk as an accompaniment to a *mezze* meal due in part to its palate-cleansing properties between dishes. Beer is predominantly *almaza*, a refreshing local canned, bottled and draught lager which comes in both alcoholic and non-alcoholic versions and is available in bars everywhere, though brands such as Heineken and Mexican beer are also available. As one of the oldest countries in the world for wine production, Lebanon produces some excellent-quality brands with labels such as Kefraya, Ksara and Musar perhaps already familiar to some international visitors for their availability overseas; these too are widely available in bars and restaurants all over Lebanon. On the non-alcoholic front, soft fizzy drinks such as Coca-Cola are ubiquitous as are a range of freshly squeezed lemon and orange juices. Among the hot drinks, traditional Arabic or Turkish coffee, drunk very strong with copious amounts of sugar in small cups or glasses, is very popular with the Arab sweet tooth. Western-style coffee such as Nescafé is also widely available though often whitened with powdered rather than 'real' milk. The coffee chains such as Costa Coffee and Starbucks, together with Dunkin' Donuts are the places to go if you need your latte, americano or cappuccino fix. Tea is also widely drunk without milk and like coffee is served in small glasses, often with the addition of mint. A vibrant and diverse café culture is alive and flourishing in Lebanon, a hangover from French colonial days. This ranges from the youth patronising the Western-style chains as a meeting place to socialise and while away a few hours checking emails, to the independent cafés in Beirut offering a range of both alcoholic and non-alcoholic drinks with meals and cakes, served in more intellectual surroundings often accompanied by independent film showings and live music. In more traditional cities such as Sidon or Tripoli, for instance, cafés fill up with the older generation playing cards and backgammon whilst drinking tea. An integral part of this cultural scene is also indulging the great Arabic tradition of smoking the *nargileh* pipe (aka hubbly bubbly, water pipe or *sheesha*), with its aromatic range of flavours hanging heavy in the air. In Beirut, the Gemmayze Café just east of Downtown is a great venue to visit, with its excellent retro feel and the accompaniment of live music.

PUBLIC HOLIDAYS AND ANNUAL FESTIVALS

FIXED DATE HOLIDAYS

1 January	New Year's Day
9 February	Feast of Saint Maroun – patron saint of Christian Maronites
18 April	Qana Day
1 May	Labour Day
6 May	Martyrs' Day
15 August	Assumption Day
1 November	All Saints' Day
22 November	Independence Day
25 December	Christmas Day

ISLAMIC HOLIDAYS WITH MOVEABLE DATES There are also a number of annual Islamic public holidays, which follow the Muslim lunar or Hejira calendar, as opposed to the Gregorian calendar, and these move back about 11 days each year. Notable Islamic holidays with their upcoming dates are:

Eid al-Fitr	The end of Ramadan, marked by three or more days of feasting and the giving of gifts (19 August 2012)

Eid al-Adha	The Feast of Sacrifice which marks the end of Hajj (expected to be around 26 October 2012)
Ras as-Sana	Islamic New Year (26 November 2011)
Ashura	The tenth day of the Islamic New Year commemorating the assassination of the Prophet Muhammad's grandson, Imam Hussein expected to be around 5 December in 2011 (see *Chapter 8*, page 256 for details)
Mouloud	Prophet Muhammad's birthday (5 February 2012)

FESTIVALS In addition to the main public and Muslim holidays above, which for the visitor mostly have the practical impact of shortening shop opening hours and inflating hotel prices, the Lebanese love a festival and their zest for enjoying life can be seen in the extensive cocktail of annual arts, cultural and sporty festivals all over the country, many of which have attracted celebrities and stars of international repute. Some of these utilise Lebanon's array of archaeological sites, such as those at Baalbek, Beiteddine, Byblos and Tyre, for a dramatic and atmospheric backdrop to the events. Not surprisingly many of these festivals take place during the summer months and the listings below are some of the main ones, all of which are covered in detail in the relevant chapters together with those additional festivals which have a more local character and flavour.

January–March
Al Bustan International Festival of Music and the Arts (*www.albustanfestival. com*) see *Chapter 4*, pages 142–3
Beirut Fashion Week (*www.beirutfashionweek.com*) see *Chapter 3*, page 132
Mzaar Winter Festival (*www.skimzaar.com*) see *Chapter 4*, page 147

April–June
Beirut International Platform of Dance (*www.maqamat.org*) see *Chapter 3*, page 132
Beirut International Tango Festival (*www.tangolebanon.com*) see *Chapter 3*, pages 132–3
The Garden Show and Spring Festival (*www.the-gardenshow.com*) see *Chapter 3*, page 133

July–September
Baalbeck International Festival (*www.baalbeck.org.lb*) see *Chapter 6*, pages 213–14
Batroun International Festival (*www.batrounfestival.org*) see *Chapter 5*, page 172
Beiteddine Art Festival (*www.beiteddine.org*) see *Chapter 7*, page 228
Broummana Summer Festival (*www.brummana.org.lb*) see *Chapter 4*, page 143
Byblos International Festival (*www.byblosfestival.org*) see *Chapter 4*, page 163
Deir al-Qamar Festival (*www.deirelqamarfestival.org*) see *Chapter 7*, pages 224–5
Ehdeniyat (*www.ehdeniyat.com*) see *Chapter 5*, page 189
Tyre and South Festival (*www.tyrefestival.com*) see *Chapter 8*, page 256
Zouk Mikael International Festival (*www.zoukmikaelfestival.com*) see *Chapter 4*, page 72

October–December
Beirut International Film Festival (*www.beirutfilmfoundation.org*) see *Chapter 3*, page 132
Docudays (Beirut International Documentary Festival) (*www.docudays.com*) see *Chapter 3*, page 133

Beirut International Marathon (*www.beirutmarathon.org*) see *Chapter 3*, page 132
Vinifest (*www.vinifestlebanon.com*) see *Chapter 3*, page 133

SHOPPING

Lebanon offers a diverse and comprehensive shopping experience catering to the mainstream as well as the less commercial consumer, but don't expect bargain-basement prices as costs are on a par with those in Europe and North America. Opening hours are similar to Europe and can vary enormously but generally speaking the large shopping malls open from 10.00 to 22.00 daily, though some will close at 19.00–20.00 outside Beirut. Many general stores and bookshops open 09.00 to 19.00 Monday to Saturday. Corner shops and supermarkets often have more variable trading times and you will generally be able to find a supermarket open until midnight and some even stay open 24/7 offering free delivery. Pharmacies, especially in Beirut, are usually open from 08.00 to midnight and a few stay open 24/7. The capital obviously has the widest and most concentrated selection of shopping. The ABC Group, the large Middle Eastern retail chain, has a big presence in Beirut with a selection of malls selling all manner of international designer brands and labels. In the Downtown district Virgin's flagship Megastore offers its usual range of entertainment products – books, magazines, music CDs and films – and is also the venue to buy tickets to many of Lebanon's festivals and sometimes to performances at some of Beirut's theatres.

The Achrafieh and Verdun districts are the places to visit for upmarket clothes and jewellery shopping along with the many outlets in the Downtown area such as the Beirut Souks, which opened to great fanfare in late 2010 and unashamedly catering for the larger wallet. The pristinely restored Saifi Village (Le Quartier des Arts) on the outskirts of Downtown houses art galleries, antique shops, boutiques and craft stores within its perfectly manicured environs. For those in search of more traditional items in the form of glassware, old postcards, *nargileh* pipes, mosaics and tablecloths, etc, head for the L'Artisan D'Orient in Ain al-Mreisseh or the L'Artisan du Liban in Achrafieh, the latter able to deliver purchases worldwide. A little further afield, Beirut's Armenian Bourj Hammoud district has a range of traditional goods at more competitive prices. The capital also hosts a number of weekly markets selling everything from CDs to organic farm produce. The main ones to look out for include Souk el Ahad in east Beirut, Souk el Tayeb in Downtown and the Tuesday Earth Market in the Hamra district (see *Chapter 3*, pages 114–15 for more details). Beirut is home to some marvellous bookshops selling very nice coffee-table tomes, DVDs and maps of the country which can make great gifts. The Libraire Antoine bookshop in Hamra is a good starting point though there are many other good book stores in the capital (see page 117).

Outside the city, a less mainstream shopping aesthetic and souvenirs galore await in the souks of Byblos which is the place to buy rare books, fish fossils and stones. Further north, Tripoli's anachronistic markets are famed for their sweets, soap, herbs and spices and a range of metal products are still locally produced in medieval surroundings whilst the town of Jezzine is famous for its decorative hand-crafted cutlery and other utilitarian items. The southern city of Sidon is well known for its soap and is a great place to pick up all manner of 'smellies' to take home. For wine lovers, the Bekaa Valley has been home to a flourishing viticulture since Phoenician times and is the site of over 30 vineyards, including the renowned Kefraya, Ksara and Château Mussar labels, and these can also make excellent presents.

A local NGO, Consumers Lebanon (*9th Fl, Estral Centre, Hamra, Beirut;* ☏ *01 750 650;* e *info@consumerslebanon.org; www.consumerslebanon.org*) works to represent the interests of consumers and campaigns around a range of issues and rights and is a useful point of contact for any queries or problems regarding any purchases you may make whilst in Lebanon.

ARTS AND ENTERTAINMENT

Lebanon's diverse and eventful history has left the country with an equally eclectic and rich artistic and cultural legacy. Architecture adorns many parts of the country, left by a succession of conquering civilisations. Four of these sites – the Umayyad-era town of Aanjar, the Roman temples at Baalbek and the Phoenician ports of Byblos and Tyre – have been given prestigious World Heritage Site status by UNESCO. A variety of religious and other sites such as domed mosques, Druze hermitages, Christian Maronite churches and Crusader castles add extra interest. Supplementing these *in situ* cultural icons are some excellent museums such as the National and AUB museums in Beirut. Outside the capital Sidon's soap museum and the Khalil Gibran Museum in Bcharré (see page 184) are important reminders of Lebanon's artisanal and literary past. Museum opening hours differ across the country but many are closed on Monday, including Beirut's National Museum. There is no shortage of cultural pursuits and for those with an interest in the visual arts like cinema and theatre there are the mainstream Hollywood blockbusters together with more independent film showings. Theatres stage a wide range of Arabic, English and French productions from musicals to experimental plays. The long-established and world-renowned Caracalla Dance Theatre Company (*www.caracalladance.com*) is well worth seeing for their colourful and energetic dance routines. The Lebanese National Higher Conservatory of Music (*www.conservatoire.org.lb*) put on more than 100 concerts of oriental and world music annually, and have a flourishing educational programme designed to nurture young talent. Art galleries are also widespread, especially in Beirut, with many specialising in showing the work of young and upcoming Lebanese artists across a range of themes. Lebanon's mainly summer festivals stage performances of classical and contemporary music, poetry readings, puppetry and film and theatre. Many of these take place within the environs of the country's architectural buildings and palaces, which complement the regular arts scene very nicely. Full details of entertainments and festivals can be found in Lebanon's English-language newspaper *The Daily Star* and the monthly magazine *Time Out Beirut*.

Around the capital, Beirutis have a long-established and well-deserved reputation for being night owls. With an ever increasing number of bars, cafés, discos and nightclubs the *joie de vivre* rarely gets going until around midnight and continues often until dawn. The areas around Gouraud Street in Gemmayze, Achrafieh and the Downtown district are a pulsating mass of hedonism at weekends. Music ranges from house and techno to 80s pop, and jazz enthusiasts are catered for as well with a couple of great venues having regular live performances from established local and international artists in the Hamra area of Beirut.

Whilst Lebanon doesn't really have a national sport with the status of say, football (soccer) in the UK, Italy or Spain, it does have a great range of popular activities such as golf, horseracing and watersports from jet skiing to scuba diving. Basketball has a loyal following, and in 2010, the Lebanese national team won the FIBA Asia Stankovic Cup, beating Japan 97–59 in the final. Given Lebanon's undulating and rugged terrain locals and visitors alike are increasingly enjoying the many caving, hiking, kayaking, rafting, paragliding and trekking possibilities which exist around the country and there are now tour operators who specialise in just these activities. Lebanon is also one of the only places in the entire Middle East where you can ski (not counting the artificial 'snow' in places like Dubai), and the country's six resorts are hugely popular. Once again, there are tour companies who specialise in offering holidays catering to just these areas and activities.

PHOTOGRAPHY

During the country's long and bloody civil war years, pictures – both still and moving – had a great impact on shaping Lebanon's image to the world; bombed-out buildings and cars, pictures of corpses, the pain felt by both Lebanese and Palestinian refugees, etc defined Lebanon as a place to be avoided at all costs and such stereotypes persist to some extent to this day. Of course icons of war, such as the still-standing bullet and shell-shocked Holiday Inn hotel in Beirut remain a constant visual reminder of the country's battle-scarred past and it continues to be an oft-photographed subject. But like the transformed and pristinely manicured Downtown district of the capital – once a rubble of death and destruction – changed circumstances provide the visitor to the country with the chance to capture images which show another side of Lebanon, whether it's through the beauty of its natural and urban landscape or its architectural legacies in places such as Baalbek, Tripoli and Tyre.

Whilst the markets and shopping areas of Beirut won't yield authentic pictures of anachronistic Arab souks those in cities such as Sidon and Tripoli will, and they offer the photographer an opportunity to capture traditional day-to-day life in these areas which can say so much more than a pretty sunset postcard picture over the Mediterranean. Lebanon's architectural legacy is plentiful and extremely photogenic and any keen photographer would not want to miss the country's premier sites at Baalbek, Byblos, Deir al-Qamar or Tyre for example. Lebanon's plentiful year round festivals provide further opportunities to capture the Lebanese *joie de vivre* and cultured side of their country

EQUIPMENT AND TECHNICAL ISSUES Assuming that your photographic ambitions extend beyond capturing a few moments in time on your camera-ready mobile phone the following points should prove useful for those wishing to take home some treasured memories from their visit. Ideally, an SLR (Single Lens Reflex) camera with interchangeable lenses is the best equipment to take with you as it offers the most flexibility with regard to picture taking. To maximize your picture taking opportunities a couple of lenses which span the 20–200mm range should be sufficient to capture those mountain and valley vistas and some close up and intimate portraits. Although Lebanon has a good variety of wildlife this is not a Kenyan safari and you will not generally require an extreme (and extremely expensive!) 400–600mm telephoto lens. As digital image capture is now increasingly the norm in photography and here to stay, bring sufficient memory cards and batteries with you for the duration of your visit, though these are plentiful in Lebanon and easily obtained, especially at most of the photo stores which exist in Beirut. If you still use a film camera, black-and-white, colour negative and slide film are still available in Beirut and a few even offer E6 (slide processing).

Dust and humidity can be a problem in the summer months and it pays to look after your equipment by keeping it protected in a bag. Digital cameras are susceptible to dust which can easily implant itself onto the camera's sensor and show up later as spots and blotches on the image necessitating quite a bit of computer clean up time. To help prevent this try to keep your lens attached to the camera as it will help seal the camera from foreign intruders. Obviously this is easier if you have two camera bodies. A tripod, usually a useful accessory, can also be an essential item if you are particularly keen on photographing inside Lebanon's many museum's, the caves at the Ksara winery in the Bekaa Valley or have an interest in landscape and nighttime photography and don't want to use a flash gun which can potentially destroy the atmosphere of the shot.

As is the 'rule', the time of day at which you undertake the bulk of your outdoor picture taking has a marked affect on their quality. Generally speaking, early morning and late afternoon will provide more pleasing pictures as these times avoid the heat of the day and ensure the light is at its most attractive, and you will avoid the extremes of contrast in your images which can result from shooting during the day. Obviously indoor photography or picture-taking in the shade such as the covered area in a souk is another matter altogether and may necessitate the use of flash or even a tripod depending on the situation.

Although you should bring everything that you will need with you such as memory cards and/or film stocks, spare batteries, leads etc Beirut has a good supply of photographic shops where you can purchase additional items and many will burn your images to disc and provide prints with some offering the usual one-hour service. A couple of tried-and-tested shops in the capital worth noting are **Studio Gag** (*Rue Jean d'Arc, Hamra;* ℡ *01 354 255;* m *03 693 599;* e *studio-gag@hotmail.com;* ⊕ *09.30–20.00 Mon–Sat, closed Sun*) and **Photo Nubar** (*Makdissi St, Hamra;* ℡ *01 353 742;* ⊕ *09.00– 18.00 Mon–Fri, 09.00–15.00 Sat, closed Sun*) with the latter being an authorised Nikon reseller and offering a wide range of services including processing and sales of black-and-white and colour film. Passing your photographic equipment through airport X-ray machines is a mandatory aspect of the travel process. If you are still shooting film ask for a hand check (which may or may not be granted and much can depend on how busy or stressed the security personnel are), especially if you are travelling around the region by plane as part of a regional Middle Eastern tour. One pass of film through modern X-ray machines is usually OK but a number of bursts could fog your film, especially if shot at a high ISO (speed) rating. If, as most people now are, you are using digital equipment, X-ray machines will not present any problems.

PHOTOGRAPHIC ETIQUETTE Generally speaking, your picture taking experience in Lebanon will be a varied and pleasurable experience with boundless photographic opportunities and there are few areas of the country off limits to photographers. However, there are a few points to bear in mind when choosing where to aim your camera and lens and which could save you some hassle later. In a country where issues of security are paramount you would be advised to refrain from trying to take photographs at the airport, at military installations and of soldiers and at the many checkpoints that you will doubtless come across around the country. It is perfectly OK to ask to take a photograph of military personnel but the likely response will be a flat 'no' and if so you should heed the answer and not try to sneak a shot. Similarly, if you are seen taking photographs of the Grand Serail (prime minister's office) building and the area around Nejmeh Place in Downtown Beirut, which contains the parliament building, it is likely that you will to be told to stop by soldiers as this author was. The likely worst case scenario is that you will be questioned, asked for your ID and perhaps told to delete the image(s) on your memory card. If this happens it pays to be polite with the authorities and cooperate. With Lebanon's wide ranging groups and religious sects people photo opportunities abound. However, some common sense and sensitivity is required when photographing conservatively dressed women and religious groups in case of causing offence.

Lebanon has a long and established media history, which reached its zenith during the latter stages of the Ottoman era, and by 1914 Beirut had a prolific output of some 168 daily and weekly newspapers, journals and magazines. The country has always been well known for the freedom granted to print and other media outlets and was the first Arab nation to grant private-sector radio and television station broadcast rights. In 2010, Reporters Sans Frontières (Reporters without Borders; *www.rsf.org*) ranked Lebanon 78th out of 178 countries surveyed in its annual Press Freedom Index survey, which saw Finland top the list of countries enjoying the highest level of journalistic independence, and Eritrea the least. This gave Lebanon the highest press freedom in the Arab world. Despite these positive figures, however, dark clouds remain over issues of censorship and press freedom. The assassinations in 2005 in Beirut of prominent newspaper journalist and academic Samir Kassir and newspaper chief executive Gebran Tueni still remain unsolved crimes. Intermittent detention and interrogation, often without legal representation, by the authorities remains a sporadic but nonetheless salient fact of life for some Lebanese journalists.

NEWSPAPERS There are a wide range of daily newspapers published in Lebanon in the country's three main languages of Arabic, English and French together with a handful of Arabic and French weekly news digests. None are state-owned but nonetheless tend to reflect their owners' sectarian bias. Lebanon's sole English-language daily since 1952 is *The Daily Star* (LBP2,000; ☎ 01 587 277; www.dailystar. com.lb), with a circulation of 29,940 and offering national and international news coverage together with a good roundup of sport and cultural events in the country. This is the most useful newspaper for the English-speaking visitor and highly recommended for those seeking to keep up to date with current affairs and events whilst in Lebanon. The long-standing daily *L'Orient Le Jour* (LBP2,000; ☎ 05 956 444; www.lorientlejour.com) has a circulation of 18,000 and offers similar coverage, in French, to *The Daily Star*. The principal Arabic newspapers include *Al Akhbar, Al Anwar, Al Diyar, Al Liwaa, Al Mustaqbal, Albalad and An-Nahar*. The international press is also well represented in Lebanon with newspapers such as the UK's *The Independent, The Daily Telegraph, The Guardian* and *The Times* as well as the *International Herald Tribune* and the French dailies *Le Monde and Le Figaro* all easily available, though often a day or so after publication, in bookshops in Beirut such as *Libraire Antoine* or from one of the many street book and magazine vendors in the capital though expect to pay a little more than you would back home.

MAGAZINES Apart from the whole gamut of Lebanese magazines you will notice a huge range on street bookstalls, as well as bookshops, of glossy publications from all over the region but especially from the Gulf. These tend to be centered on celebrity, lifestyle and women's issues and featuring the ubiquitous attractive girl on the front cover. However, for the visitor the most useful magazines are likely to be those such as the English-language *Monday Morning* (LBP3,000; ☎ 01 200 961/2/3; e info@ mmorning.com; www.mmorning.com), a weekly glossy devoted to Lebanese and international current affairs, business, lifestyle and celebrity issues. For French speakers the weekly *Le Revue du Liban* (LBP3,000; ☎ 01 200 961; www.rdl.com.lb) offers similar coverage. The monthly *Time Out Beirut* (LBP5,000; ☎ 09 639 556; www.timeoutbeirut. com) is an invaluable source of what's on listings in the capital together with interesting features on a wide range of topics from around the country. The pocket-sized, bi-weekly, French-language *Agenda Culturel* (LBP5,000; ☎ 01 369 242/3;

www.agendaculturel.com) is another good source of what's on information. For the business visitor there are a handful of monthly English-language magazines which could prove useful reading including *Lebanon Opportunities* (*LBP9,000;* ⟍ *01 739 777; www.opportunities.com.lb*), which has a range of articles and features on the economic, business and real estate sectors in Lebanon. The *Lebanon Executive* (*LBP8,000;* ⟍ *01 611 696; www.executive-magazine.com*) has wide-ranging coverage of banking, corporations, finance, consumerism, real estate, etc, from both Lebanon and around the region. For all things property related *Real Magazine* (*LBP8,000;* ⟍ *05 455 755; www.realmiddleeast.com*) has comprehensive news, features, reports and forecasts on the real estate sector for prospective investors in Lebanon and the region.

As with newspapers, many of the major quality international magazines such as *Der Spiegel, The Economist, Newsweek, Paris Match* and *Time* are all obtainable from booksellers and stalls, especially in Beirut.

RADIO   The proliferation of radio stations which resulted from the civil conflict of 1975–90, producing anarchy across the airwaves as well as on the streets, is well and truly over and nowadays, following government regulation in the mid 1990s, the number of radio stations has been cut drastically to just over a dozen or so. The state-owned broadcaster is Radio Liban (96.2FM, 837MW), which broadcasts a wide range of music and programmes, including an hourly news service, in Arabic, Armenian, English and French. Of the privately owned stations, Sawt El Ghad (96.7FM, 97.1FM) broadcasts 24/7 broad-based entertainment and educational programmes in Arabic and English. Other stations of most interest to the visitor and broadcasting a mix of news, music and entertainment include Voice of Lebanon (93.3FM, 93.6FM, Arabic, English and French), Pax Radio (103.0FM, 103.3FM, 103.4FM, 24/7 Arabic, English and French pop music), Melody FM Lebanon (99.5FM, 99.7FM, 99.9FM, 24/7 chart and pop music in Arabic, English and French), and Radio One (105.5FM, Lebanon's version of the UK's mainstream station). The BBC World Service is available in Lebanon on MW1323kHz and the BBC Arabic station is available on 93.1FM. Radio Sawa (*www.radiosawa.com*), which replaced Voice of America in 2002, broadcasts regional and world news in Arabic, along with a mix of Western and Arabic pop music 24/7 to its mainly youthful Arabic audience. In Lebanon you can tune in on the following frequencies: 87.7FM (Beirut, Sidon, Tripoli and Zahlé), and 98.7FM (western Bekaa Valley).

TELEVISION   Like the radio stations, television was completely unregulated until the mid 1990s when the government stepped in and made it obligatory for television companies to possess a licence to broadcast. The result of these stricter controls is that there are now only seven TV stations in the country with all serving up a diet of the usual entertainment, films, news, sport, documentaries and news coverage. The state-run broadcaster is called Tele Liban which screens its programmes in Arabic, English and French. The remaining stations are privately owned but are usually pegged to a sectarian or political bias. Thus Al Manar TV (*www.almanar.com.lb*) or 'the beacon' has a strong ideological attachment to Hezbollah and has been frequently targeted by the Israelis during periods of conflict between the two foes. A favourite of Sunni Muslims is Future TV (*www.futuretvnetwork.com*), launched and formerly owned by Rafiq Hariri in 1993 during his political tenure, and which broadcasts in Arabic, Armenian, English and French. A popular choice among the Christian community and probably the country's most popular channel is the Pan-Arab LBC International (*www.lbcgroup.tv*), broadcasting mainly family programmes in Arabic. The remaining stations include Murr TV (*www.mtv.com.lb*), owned by politician Gabriel Murr, the news channel NBN (*www.nbn.com.lb*) sympathetic to the Amal movement (*www.amal-movement.com*), and Orange TV (*www.otv.com.lb*), with programmes in Arabic, English and French. Satellite television is widespread in homes and in the numerous hotels so it is usually no problem to tune in to the likes of CNN, BBC World, and EuroNews, together with a whole host of sports channels.

INTERNET The advent of the internet has been embraced in Lebanon with as much enthusiasm as many other countries in the world. According to latest 2010 figures from Internet World Stats (*www.internetworldstats.com*), Lebanon's 'connected' population numbered around one million in 2010, with around a quarter having broadband connections. There are innumerable internet cafés around the country with even the smallest town usually having at least one 'wired' establishment and many, particularly in the capital, stay open 24/7. Reliable Internet Service Providers are plentiful should you be thinking of opening an account whilst in Lebanon. Connection speeds are more often than not fast, though be prepared on occasions to experience depressingly slow response times. The costs for hourly internet access range from LBP1,000 to LBP3,000 in the majority of internet cafés but many of the more expensive hotels will charge you a whopping LBP10,000–15,000 per hour.

MOBILE PHONES Mobile-phone use in Lebanon is widespread and even many companies and organisations prefer cellular contact to that of landline communication. In 2008, there were 1.43 million mobile users in the country, compared with only 714,000 fixed telephone lines. National and international coverage and reception is excellent and you will have no problem using your own mobile in the country for making and receiving calls and sending and receiving text messages (assuming you don't mind the size of the bill that will land on your door mat when you arrive home). For those who do, it is easy to buy a Lebanese SIM card (and consequently a new number), and this will save you money if you plan to make a lot of calls. Lebanon's two mobile operators are Alfa (m *03 391 111; www.alfa.com.lb*) and MTC Touch (m *03 800 111; www.mtctouch.com.lb*), and both provide a range of pay-as-you-go and other services. The whole process involves a minimum of bureaucracy to get yourself set up on the Lebanese mobile network. For those using a BlackBerry, MTC Touch is seen as a slightly better option. Prices can vary widely and it is a good idea to shop around for the best deal which usually involves paying for the SIM card and receiving a certain amount of phone credit included in the price.

TELEPHONES Lebanon's state-owned telecommunications provider is OGERO (*Organisme de Gestion et d'Exploitation de l'ex Radio Orient;* ✆ *01 840 000, 1515 (call centre within Lebanon); www.ogero.gov.lb*), which was founded in 1972. Since the end of the civil war it has transformed the country's battered and antiquated telephone system into a modern and reliable service with a full range of digital and internet services available to subscribers. All landline and mobile telephone numbers in Lebanon consist of six digits preceded by the two-digit code for the area you are dialling (see *Local area/regional codes within Lebanon*, page 80). The current tariff for national landline-to-landline calls is LBP100 per minute, and the cost of a landline call to a local mobile network is LBP300. Calls to international landlines are, with a few exceptions such as those to Antarctica and Western Samoa, standardised at LBP600 per minute at peak times (07.00–22.00), and LBP400 per minute off-peak (22.00–07.00). For those needing to make internal or international calls from Lebanon without incurring the often extortionate costs of using their own mobile-phone provider, OGERO offer two types of pre-paid calling cards, widely available

2

from OGERO offices, stores displaying the OGERO sign, supermarkets, post offices and many internet cafés. The Kalam card, available as a pre-paid LBP15,000 (valid for two months), or LBP45,000 (valid for six months) card, can be used from any fixed-line phone, private or street payphone, and which is activated by inputting a Personal Identification Number (PIN) and then dialling the number you want to call; the Telecarte card, available in LBP10,000 and LBP30,000 denominations, can only be used from one of the many street payphones and is valid for 12 months from first use. Very few places seem to stock the larger-denomination Kalam and Telecarte phonecards.

Telephone codes and numbers To call Lebanon from the UK it is necessary to dial 00 (international access code) then 961 (Lebanon country access code) followed by the regional code omitting the initial 0 and then the actual number. Unless essential it is a good idea to avoid making calls from your hotel, especially the mid-range and luxury establishments, as they can work out very expensive.

Some common country codes (from within Lebanon)
UK	00 + 44 + the number itself minus the 0
Canada and the US	00 + 1 + the number itself
Australia	00 + 61 + the number itself

Local area/regional codes within Lebanon
Unlike in many cities, such as London for instance, where telephone codes can vary widely from one area of the city to another, codes in Lebanon cover a wide geographic area. Thus the code for the Bekaa Valley (08) covers the areas of Baalbek, Chtaura, Hermel and Zahlé. Similarly, the area code for Beirut (01) applies to east, west, north and south Beirut. If making phone calls within Lebanon you need to dial the initial zero for both area and mobile-phone codes. If calling internationally, the initial zero of both mobile and landline codes are omitted.

Beirut	01
Bekaa Valley	08
Byblos (including Jounieh and Kesrouan)	09
Northern Lebanon (Tripoli and environs)	06
Southern Lebanon (Sidon and Tyre)	07
Northern Mount Lebanon	04
Southern Mount Lebanon (Chouf region)	05
Mobile-phone codes	03, 70, 71, 76
International operator	100
Directory enquiries	120

Emergency and other useful telephone numbers
Beirut–Rafiq Hariri International Airport ✆ 150	**OGERO (Telephone company)** ✆ 1515
Car breakdown SOS Auto; ✆ 01 216 376; www.sosauto.net	**Police** ✆ 112
Civil defence ✆ 125	**International operator** ✆ 100
Fire brigade ✆ 175	**Australian embassy** ✆ 01 960 600
Lebanese Red Cross ✆ 140	**British embassy** ✆ 01 960 800
Ministry of Tourism Police ✆ 01 752 428/9	**Canadian embassy** ✆ 04 713 900
Ministry of Tourism hotline ✆ 1735	**US embassy** ✆ 04 543 600
	Weather forecast ✆ 1718

ARABIC-LANGUAGE TUITION AND TRANSLATION IN BEIRUT

American Language Centre (ALC) 4th Fl Alam El Deen Bldg, Makdissi St, near the American University of Beirut (AUB) Hamra, Beirut; ✆ 01 741 262; e alc@alc.edu.lb; www.alcbeirut.com. Runs a 25-hour Spoken Levantine Arabic course catering to beginners & more advanced speakers.

American Lebanese Language Centre (ALLC) 7th Fl, Confidence Centre, Dimitri Hayek St, Beirut; ✆ 01 500 978; e info@allcs.edu.lb; www.allcs.edu.lb. Part of the worldwide network of International House World Organisation (IHWO) of adult education schools, this centre offers a range of short courses in Arabic, from beginner to advanced speaking level.

Talk Beirut m 03 436 261; e talk@bebeirut. org; www.talkbeirut.org. Amongst its range of other activities & courses for the Beirut visitor this company offers a 5hr Crash Course (LBP100,000) in Lebanese Arabic & a Regular Course of one-to-one tuition (LBP22,000/hr).

Berlitz Language Centre Marbella Bldg, Sidani St, Hamra, Beirut; ✆ 01 751 689/90; e info@berlitz-lebanon.com, berlitz@berlitz-lebanon.com; www.berlitz-lebanon.com. This long-established & internationally renowned school founded in 1878 offers over 50 language courses, including Arabic & French.

Magda Gholam m 03 746 571; e el_tradivarius@live.com. A Lebanese freelance translator with a Masters degree & over 15 years of general & specialised translation experience for individuals & companies. A native Arab speaker, she can provide written & verbal translation services in Arabic, English & French & also offers one-to-one & group tuition for those wanting to master the everyday basics of Arabic during their stay.

Saifi Institute 1st Fl, Saifi Urban Gardens Bldg, Pasteur St, Gemmayze, Beirut; ✆ 01 560 738; e kifak@saifiarabic.com; www.siafiarabic.com; ⏰ 08.00–20.00 Mon–Fri & by appointment only on Sat, closed Sun. Located adjacent to the Saifi Urban Gardens Hotel (see *Chapter 3*, page 107) the institute offers a range of excellent courses from beginner to advanced level. Take a look at their website for the latest course schedules & pricing together with useful information on living & studying in the capital.

POST Lebanon's national postal service, Libanpost (✆ *01 629 629*; e *customercare@ libanpost.com; www.libanpost.com.lb*) operates over 70 post office branches nationwide and has undergone a considerable amount of modernisation since the 1975–90 civil war, and can now boast a modern and efficient system on a par with those in western Europe and North America. In 2010, Libanpost won two awards for Innovation and Transformation at the World Mail Awards held in Copenhagen, Denmark. They have many distinctive **yellow postboxes** dotted around the city streets and on buildings where you can post mail to towns and cities both within Lebanon as well as destinations overseas. The system offers a full range of services including parcel posting, mail tracking, poste restante, mail redirection services as well as a point of sale for mobile and pre-paid phonecards. Libanpost is also an agent for Western Union for international money transfer. Sending a 50g postcard to the UK and Europe costs LBP1,500 and to the US and Canada LBP2,000. The price of sending a 20g letter to Europe, Canada and the US is LBP2,250 (50g is LBP4,250). Delivery times for letters and postcards to most overseas destinations are generally between four and seven days. To send mail within Lebanon a 20g letter costs LBP750 and to other countries within the Middle East LBP1,500. If posting mail from the yellow postboxes there are daily collections except on Saturday, Sunday and public holidays. Generally, post offices are open from 08.00 to 17.00 Monday to Friday, and from 08.00 to 13.00 or 13.30 Saturday, and are closed on Sunday.

ELECTRICITY

Lebanon's power supply is run by the state-owned Electricité du Liban (✆ *01 442 720; customer service Hotline* ✆ *1707;* f *01 443 828;* e *info@edl.gov.lb; www.edl.gov.*

lb) and uses the same voltage as that within continental Europe (220v, 50Hz). The electrical system is the usual European style round two-pin plugs. Power cuts and electricity rationing, however, are still a part of everyday life in Lebanon. In Beirut they occur daily for three hours, usually alternating between the hours of 06.00 and 09.00, 09.00 and 12.00, or 12.00 and 15.00. Outside the capital, power cuts and rationing can last considerably longer, and outages of up to ten or even 20 hours per day is not unheard of. The larger hotels, restaurants, cafés and stores often have their own generators which usually kickstart supplies within a few minutes.

BUSINESS

Lebanon offers many advantages for the aspiring foreign businessman including its greatest asset, the country's highly literate, skilled and often trilingual workforce. Although many Lebanese have emigrated over the years, they have maintained close links with their country through the income they send 'home' and the business acumen and experiences that they have gained overseas have often percolated through to their homeland. They can be shrewd and perceptive businesspeople and much business activity can be expected to be conducted within a very hospitable and social atmosphere, including lunches and dinners, before any deal is done. Dress codes are often formal though in the heat of summer it is common to dress down into more informal attire and common greetings such as handshaking are accepted etiquette. The Lebanese, like many in the Arab world, also have a love of business cards, so bring plenty with you. The liberal economic system in Lebanon is an extension of the cosmopolitan nature of the country itself; a long established *laissez-faire* economy, strict banking secrecy laws, little or no restrictions on the movement of capital and a highly competitive corporation tax of just 15%.

It is true, however, that periodic internal political and regional instability remains the salient factor undermining investor confidence. As with many other Arab countries, however, Lebanon has been largely immune from the global economic downturn which has afflicted the world's major economies, and the country remains ripe for foreign business activity, especially in the fields of electricity, education, roads, ports, water and other major ongoing infrastructure projects. Authoritative and up-to-date economic analysis, data and risk forecasting can be obtained from the **Economist Intelligence Unit** (*26 Red Lion Sq, London WC1R 4HQ;* ✆ *020 7576 8181;* e *emea@eiu.com; www.eiu.com*) and the **Oxford Business Group** (*131 Great Titchfield St, London W1W 5BB;* ✆ *020 7403 7213;* e *consultancy@oxfordbusinessgroup. com; www.oxfordbusinessgroup.com*), whilst the **Arab British Chamber of Commerce** (*43 Upper Grosvenor St, London W1K 2NJ;* ✆ *020 7235 4363;* e *info@abcc.org.uk; www.abcc.org.uk*) is another excellent resource publishing a range of business magazines, hosting events and offering a variety of export and translation services to prospective investors and businessmen. The following list of Lebanese government departments and organisations should prove useful for those visitors arriving in Lebanon for business. Working hours of government departments are generally 08.00–14.00 Monday–Thursday, 08.00–11.00 Friday, 08.00–13.00 Saturday.

The monthly *Lebanon Executive* magazine (*LBP8,000; www.executive-magazine. com*) is widely available in Beirut and a good source of information across the gamut of business and economic issues throughout Lebanon and the wider region.

Central Bank (Banque du Liban) Masraf Lubnan St, Hamra, Beirut; ✆ 01 750 000; www.bdl.gov.lb

Chamber of Commerce, Industry & Agriculture of Beirut & Mount Lebanon CCIABML Bldg, 1 Rue Justinien,

Sanayeh, Beirut; ☏ 01 353 390/1/2/3/4;
e information@ccib.org.lb; www.ccib.org.lb
**Council for Development &
Reconstruction** Tallet al-Serail, Riad al-Solh,
Beirut; ☏ 01 980 096; e infocenter@cdr.gov.lb;
www.cdr.gov.lb
Euro Info Correspondence Centre (EICC)
1 Rue Justinien, Sanayeh, Beirut; ☏ 01 744 163;
www.euroinfocentre.net
**Investment Development Authority of
Lebanon** 4th Fl, Azarieh Tower, Bechir St, Riad
al-Solh, Beirut; ☏ 01 983 306/7/8; e invest@idal.
com.lb; www.idal.com.lb
Lebanese Customs ☏ 01 700 115; e info@

customs.gov.lb; www.customs.gov.lb
Ministry of Economy & Trade Artois St,
Hamra, Beirut; ☏ 01 982 360/1/2/3/4/5;
www.economy.gov.lb
Ministry of Finance Riad al-Solh Sq, Beirut;
☏ 01 981 001; e infocenter@finance.gov.lb;
www.finance.gov.lb
Ministry of Industry Sami Solh Av, Badaro,
Beirut; ☏ 01 423 338, 01 427 006, 01 427 046;
e ministry@industry.gov.lb; www.industry.gov.lb
Ministry of Telecommunications 1st Fl,
Ministry of Telecom Bldg, Riad al-Solh Sq, Beirut;
☏ 01 979 161; www.mpt.gov.lb

In Beirut especially, there are now a number of regular and annual trade conferences, shows and exhibitions across a wide range of industries and business concerns as Lebanon is well embarked on making the country once again a regional hub for business and investment in the Middle East. A couple of well-known organisations and venues are given below:

**Beirut International Exhibition & Leisure
Centre (BIEL)** Downtown, Beirut; ☏ 01 995
555; e info@bielcenter.com; www.bielcenter.
com

Promofair Media Centre Bldg, Accaoui,
Achrafieh, Beirut; ☏ 01 561 600/1/2/3/4;
e promofair@inco.com.lb, info@promofair.com.
lb; www.promofair.com.lb

BUYING PROPERTY

Lebanon's real estate sector, along with tourism, is one of the many economic success stories in recent years and a walk around the capital reveals endless construction sites and cranes building a range of apartment blocks and new residential developments. In the first quarter of 2010, Lebanon achieved a record number of over 22,000 transactions worth more than US$2 billion, and there are some 350 building projects under construction in Greater Beirut alone. This flourishing market is complemented by favourable interest rates and competition amongst the banks who offer loans of between 50% and 85% of a property's value. The good news for the prospective foreign purchaser is that there are no restrictions on foreign property ownership in line with Lebanon's liberalised economy and the desire to encourage foreign investment. Overseas purchasers are permitted to own land up to a maximum of 3,000m^2 with larger plots requiring prior permission from the Council of Ministers. If you don't have your own personal contacts you will probably need to avail yourself of the services of a reputable real estate broker whose usual 5% commission is payable only when a sale is agreed, with the cost split evenly between buyer and seller. The property-buying process in Lebanon is not dissimilar to that in Western countries with all the usual formalities being broadly similar. A good starting point for your forays into the Lebanese property market is the classified advertising section of *The Daily Star* newspaper, which has a range of apartments and houses for sale and will give a good idea of asking prices. For more in-depth details about the real estate sector there are a couple of good monthly publications worth seeking out in Beirut: *Lebanon Opportunities (LBP9,000;* ☏ *01 739 777;* e *opportunities@infopro.com.lb; www. opportunities.com.lb)*, and *REAL magazine (LBP8,000;* ☏ *05 455 755;* e *real@imccom.*

com; *www.realmiddleeast.com*). The property portal www.lebanon.com/realestate is a cornucopia of nationwide properties for sale and rent whilst the *Global Property Guide* (*www.globalpropertyguide.com/middle-east/lebanon*) has a range of data on the current state of the market together with a guide to the buying process. Another useful website is www.realestate.com.lb, which advertises properties for sale and for rent. The site also has a list of real estate agents and developers.

CULTURAL ETIQUETTE

The Lebanese are a very tactile people and greetings usually commence with a series of three kisses on the cheek and a handshake. This may come as a surprise to the more reserved cultures of the UK and North America. The main exception to this occurs in more traditional areas and amongst married or traditional Muslim women, who will refrain from kissing or shaking hands with another man; a lowering of the head and the placing of their arm and hand across their chest normally indicates this. Displays of more overtly romantic affection, however, are more variable. In Beirut couples can often be seen holding hands and kissing, especially in the Downtown and east Beirut districts of the city. Yet in areas such as Tripoli, Sidon and the Bekaa Valley such behaviour would be frowned upon and could offend Muslim sensibilities. In these areas, discretion or abstinence is therefore advised. Although Lebanon is often seen as one of the most liberal and open minded of Arab societies, traditional values and family are entrenched, and Lebanese adore their children who often live with them until getting married. If visiting as a family you can expect a lot of interest and fuss to be made of your offspring; this is simply an extension of the Lebanese love of children and a display of genuine hospitality. If you get invited to someone's home for a drink or meal, do not hesitate to accept.

Many Lebanese are trilingual, speaking English and French in addition to their native Arabic. '*Hi habibi, ça va?*' ('Hi baby, how are you?') may be a cliché of many a Lebanese marketing brochure but can often be heard around the youthful areas of Hamra and Bliss streets in the capital. Learning a few words and phrases of Arabic will not only enhance your visit and win you a few friends, but will also often assist you in negotiating daily situations with hotels, buses, taxis, etc. One form of non-verbal etiquette you will encounter, especially when using taxis, is the word for 'no', which becomes a 't'-type sound accompanied by a slight tipping of the head backwards and raised eyebrows. Whatever language you converse in, certain subjects such as politics and religion are obviously hot potatoes in this part of the world and need to be approached with caution. Whilst certainly not taboo, it is best to steer clear of controversial topics unless you know the person well.

Among both males and females there is a high number of smokers in the country and although a 2011 law prohibited lighting up in public places, the fact remains that at present cafés, bars, restaurants, taxis and internet cafés can all be quite smoke-filled places which is not welcome news for those trying to quit. If using an internet café in the evening be prepared for an often smoke-filled environment.

Driving standards leave much to be desired in a country where the car and bus are such ubiquitous modes of transport. Traffic lights, road markings and signs are becoming more widespread but are generally ignored by motorists and even bus drivers. Driver temperament is often one of tunnel vision with speeding commonplace, and a general lack of anticipation or courtesy towards other road users. In the frequent traffic jams of Beirut the atonal symphony of vehicle horns testifies to an absence of patience being a virtue.

Despite being a very tolerant country, Lebanon remains a Muslim destination, where certain modes of dress and behaviour are essential for a rewarding visit. The most obvious of these is to adapt your type of clothing to the situation. In terms of visiting religious shrines such as mosques this means 'dressing down'. Women should adorn a headscarf and both males and females must remove their shoes before entering. Revealing and skimpy attire appropriate to a night out in Downtown or east Beirut is completely unsuitable (and offensive) when visiting a holy site.

Lebanon is an extremely photogenic country and generally speaking you will have no problems photographing any of the main tourist sites. However, for those who deem the airport, government buildings, army checkpoints or soldiers themselves as equally photogenic 'sites', this view will not often be shared by the Lebanese authorities, so exercise caution if turning your lens to these subjects or be prepared to be questioned, and possibly to delete your pictures from your memory card.

TRAVELLING POSITIVELY

Walking around the immaculately restored buildings of Downtown Beirut or gazing up at the plethora of glittering high-rise five-star hotels which dot the city, you could be forgiven for thinking that Lebanon is far from being a needy nation. Similarly, with its high adult literacy rate, advanced health care facilities and billions of dollars which pour into the country each year from the Lebanese diaspora, Lebanon can evoke an aura of prosperity, and street beggars are a rarity compared with many other countries in the region. However, appearances can be deceiving and beneath the wealthy veneer Lebanon remains an emerging country, following the cessation of civil war hostilities, with issues of human poverty, the environment and sectarian divides. All these concerns ensure that there are plenty of opportunities for the visitor to ponder if they want to put back into the country at least as much as they take out. It may be a cliché, but buying Lebanese produce, such as at Beirut's weekly farmers' market, Souk el Tayeb, or purchasing your souvenir craft items from Lebanese artisans at the city's L'Artisan du Liban, is a fantastic way of ensuring that your money goes to some of those who need it most. Furthermore, buying organic produce is one way of offsetting Lebanon's excessive use of pesticides.

You will doubtless see at some point during your visit the red and white vehicles of the **Lebanese Red Cross** (*Spears St, Kantari, Beirut;* ☏ *01 371 391; www.redcross. org.lb*), who operate their free emergency service throughout the country. Although volunteering opportunities for non-Lebanese citizens are limited, they are always in need of funds and medical supplies.

An increased awareness in recent years of man's impact on the natural world has led to a consequent increase in organisations campaigning on behalf of the environment and you may want to help them with a donation or by volunteering. One organisation, founded in 2006 after the Jiyeh plant oil disaster (see page 7), is **Indyact** (*4th Fl, Jaara Bldg, Nahr St, Rmeil, Beirut;* ☏ *01 447 192;* e *info@indyact.org; www.indyact.org*), an umbrella group who address environmental, social and cultural issues and who are in need of both financial and volunteer assistance. Another organisation which was formed after disaster struck, this time following devastating forest fires in 1992, is the **Association for Forests, Development and Conservation** (*1st Fl, Bldg 26, Sagesse St, Jdiedeh, Beirut;* ☏ *01 898 475/6;* e *afdc@ afdc.org.lb; www.afdc.org.lb*), who run a wide range of rural development and educational programmes with volunteering opportunities available. In addition,

2

there are many other organisations working for various good causes in the country and the following should provide useful pointers to your own particular area or areas of interest:

Association for Volunteer services 6th Fl, Chawkatli Bldg, Saifi, Beirut; office ☉ 09.00–16.00 Mon–Fri; ☎ 01 449 470; m 03 757 098; e avs@avs.org.lb; www.avs.org.lb. An umbrella NGO working with a wide range of charities & organisations across a range of issues from children, the elderly & the disabled, to rights for women. An extensive listing of organisations is available on their website.

Caritas Lebanon Dr Youssef Hajjar St, Sin el Fil, Beirut; ☎ 01 499 767, 01 483 305; e executive@caritas.org.lb; www.caritas.org.lb. Caritas is Latin for 'charity', & this long-established & worldwide network of organisations with a Catholic ethos works nationwide providing health, social & humanitarian programmes for the less fortunate, including assistance to Lebanon's migrant workers.

Children's Cancer Centre of Lebanon Bldg 56, American University of Beirut Medical Centre, Clemenceau St, Beirut; ☎ 01 351 515, 01 366 052; m 70 351 515; e cccl@cccl.org.lb; www.cccl.org.lb

René Moawad Foundation 844 Alfred Naccache St, Achrafieh, Beirut; ☎ 01 613 367/8/9; e rmf@rmf.org.lb; www.rmf.org.lb. Set up in 1991 as an NGO by MP Nayla Moawad & named after her former Lebanese president husband, René, who was assassinated in 1989 only 17 days after being sworn in, the foundation carries out its work in the fields of economic, health, social & rural development remaining true to her husband's principles of unity & equality.

Probably the most visible area of concern is that of Lebanon's 400,000+ Palestinian presence in the country. Scattered across refugee camps around the country, their living conditions are not what any human being should have to endure. Consequently, there are quite a few organisations, including of course the UN, operating around the country that work to improve the lot of the Palestinians and the following are a useful starting point if you wish to partner up with a charitable group.

Canadian-Palestinian Educational Exchange 612 Markham St, Toronto, ON M6G 2L8, Canada; e info@cepal.ca; www.cepal.ca. A range of volunteering opportunities for Canadian nationals only, to live & work in the Palestinian camps at Bourj al-Barajneh & Shatila in Beirut, & the Wavel refugee camp near Baalbek in the Bekaa Valley.

Children & Youth Centre Shatila (CYC) Shatila Camp, Beirut; ☎ 03 974 672; e info@cycshatila.org; www.cycshatila.org. An NGO striving to better the lot of Palestinian children & youths with ample opportunities for volunteering as well as donations to the organisation. CYC also run a guesthouse where, for around US$10 pp per night in clean, but basic accommodation, travellers & volunteers can experience life at the camp first hand.

Palestinian Human Rights Organisation Mar Elias Camp, Beirut; ☎ 01 306 740; f 01 301 549; e info@palhumanrights.org, phro@palhumanrights.org; www.palhumanrights.org

Prior to departing for Lebanon, a worthwhile website to look at is www.stuffyourrucksack.com, a charitable initiative by TV broadcaster and journalist Kate Humble whose mantra is 'pack a bag, change a life', designed to show visitors how a small item or donation can make a big difference to a range of organisations such as charities and schools in the country in which they are travelling.

Part Two

THE GUIDE

3

Beirut

Telephone code 01

Framed by the blue waters of the Mediterranean Sea and the often snowy peaks of Mount Sannine, Lebanon's capital and most populous city, Beirut, the 'Bride of the East' to the ancient Phoenicians, commands a proud and enduring presence at the midway point on the Lebanese coastline. This much-vilified city of almost two million people boasts more than 5,000 years of recorded history. However, it is only the last few decades with which most foreigners are acquainted as sectarian divisions and foreign interference thrust Beirut and Lebanon onto the international stage with the onset of the country's 15-year civil war. Lebanon's descent into anarchy soon made the country a byword for man's inhumanity and the very notion of Beirut and tourism became one of the modern era's best-known oxymorons.

The *al hawadith* or 'events', as the Lebanese call the 1975–90 debacle, which left 85,000 people dead in Beirut alone and forced another 700,000 to flee the country, effectively cut Lebanon off from the outside world. The city's notorious Green Line, which demarcated Christian east and Muslim west, became an icon of smouldering resentment. Similarly, the Downtown district sunk into a maelstrom of death and destruction not seen in any Arab city in the modern history of the Middle East conflict. With the onset of peace, however, came the inexorable drive towards rebuilding the city – both physically and psychologically – and Beirut today is probably the most transformed city in the entire region.

Whilst present-day Beirut may lack the old-world charm of Cairo, Marrakesh or Tangier, a visit to the high-octane Achrafieh and Gemmayze districts suggests the city is once again flaunting the cosmopolitan and hedonistic lifestyle that gave the capital its pre-war reputation as 'the Paris of the Middle East'. The epicentre of reconstruction is Downtown which now boasts beautifully restored Ottoman- and French-era architecture, souks and a plethora of five-star hotels complemented by a chic café culture and modern restaurants. On bustling Rue Hamra, once known as Beirut's Champs Elysées, coffee and conversation take precedence while further east the neighbourhood of Bourj Hammoud is an example of an integrated diaspora, a displaced Armenian people who have made Beirut their home whilst preserving their own cultural identity. In upmarket Verdun, Beirut bling competes with international designer fashion labels. The southern suburbs of the city, however, provide a poignant reminder of a city still wearing its past on its sleeve. Here, thousands of Palestinian and Shi'ite Muslim refugees live in abject poverty; posters of martyrs killed fighting Israel in the south of the country line the streets together with effigies of Iran's Ayatollah Khomeini, providing the most visible reminders that for all its renaissance, Beirut remains embroiled in the wider Middle East peace process.

For decades Beirut was touristically a no-man's-land. With the capital now restored it merits at least a few days of any visitor's time. Put aside any preconceptions of drug-crazed gunmen and terrorists roaming the streets and experience a city and a people who are among the friendliest, tolerant and varied in the entire Middle East.

Beirut

3

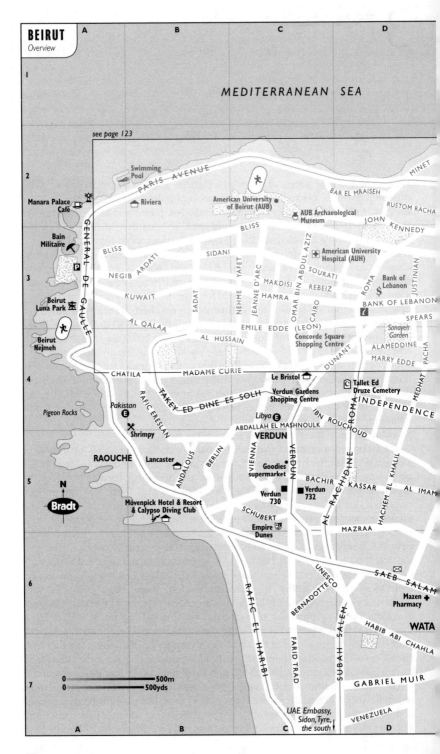

see page 123

MEDITERRANEAN SEA

BEIRUT
Overview

Swimming
Pool

PARIS AVENUE

Riviera

Manara Palace
Café

Bain
Militaire

Beirut
Luna Park

Beirut
Nejmeh

American University
of Beirut (AUB)

AUB Archaeological
Museum

BAR EL MRAISEH

MINET

RUSTOM RACHA

JOHN KENNEDY

BLISS

American University
Hospital (AUH)

GENERAL DE GAULLE

BLISS

NEGIB

ARDATI

SIDANI

NEHME

YAFET

JEANNE D'ARC

OMAR BIN ABDUL AZIZ

MAKDISI

SOURATI

REBEIZ

ROMA

JUSTINIAN

Bank of
Lebanon

KUWAIT

SADAT

HAMRA

CAIRO

BANK OF LEBANON

SPEARS

AL QALAA

EMILE EDDE (LEON)

Sanayeh
Garden

AL HUSSAIN

Concorde Square
Shopping Centre

DUNANT

ALAMEDDINE

MARRY EDDE

PACHA

CHATILA

MADAME CURIE

Le Bristol

Tallet Ed
Druze Cemetery

MEDIAT

Verdun Gardens
Shopping Centre

TAKEY ED DINE ES SOLH

RAFIC ERESLAN

Pakistan

Shrimpy

Libya

ABDALLAH EL MASHNOULK

ROMA

INDEPENDENCE

IBN ROUCHOUD

Pigeon Rocks

VERDUN

RAOUCHE

Lancaster

ANDALOUS

BERLIN

VIENNA

Goodies
supermarket

VERDUN

AL RACHIDINE

HACHEM EL KHALIL

AL IMAM

N

Bradt

Mövenpick Hotel & Resort
& Calypso Diving Club

Verdun
730

Verdun
732

BACHIR

KASSAR

SCHUBERT

Empire
Dunes

MAZRAA

SAEB SALAM

UNESCO

Mazen
Pharmacy

BERNADOTTE

SUBAH SALEM

WATA

RAFIC EL HARIRI

FARID TRAD

HABIB ABI CHAHLA

GABRIEL MUIR

0   500m
0   500yds

UAE Embassy,
Sidon, Tyre,
the south

VENEZUELA

I

see pages 104–105

BIEL

PORT OF BEIRUT

Beirut Waterfront Park

Saint-George Yacht Club & Marina

EL HOSN

MIR MAJIDD ARSALAN

2

Intercontinental Phoenicia

LONDON

AHMAD CHAOUQI

FRENCH

ALLENBY

TRIESTA STREET

Holiday Inn

DOWNTOWN (SOLIDERE)

Beirut Souks

Beirut Municipality building

OMAR DAOUK

BAB IDRISS

MELKI

AHMAD DAOUK

WEYGAND

US Embassy, Canadian Embassy, Antelias, Dora, Jounieh, Byblos, the north

Charles Helou Bus Station

CHARLES HELOU

3

FRANCE

RIAD EL SOLH

Place de Etoile (Nejmeh Square)

St George Cathedral (old)

ARMY

AL SHOUHADA

DAMASCUS

KADISHA

GEORGE HADDAD

LEBANON

PASTEUR

GOURAUD

St Nicholas Steps

SURSOCK

Sursock Museum

BUSTROS

GEN FOAAD CHEHAB

AMIR AMINE

AYSRA

Al Zahre Mosque

Al Imam Ali Mosque

TYANE

Lebanese National Higher Conservatory of Music

Lebanese Museum of Prehistory

MONOT

CHARLES MALEK

SALIM BUSTROS

Switzerland

St Nicholas Gardens

MICHEL

4

ALGERIA

SALIM SALAM

MOMOUN

PETRO TRAD

HUVELIN

ACHRAFIEH

MAR ELIAS

ABI HANIFA

Beirut Museum & Urban Cultural Centre

ABDUL WAHAB EL INGLIZI

ACHRAFIYE

Hotel Albergo & Al Dente Restaurant

INDEPENDENCE

Empire Sodeco

DAMASCUS

Sioufi Garden, Sunday market, Hazmieh Rotana, Acid nightclub, Beit Mery

5

BASTA

ABDUL GHANI ARAYSSI

OMAR BIN EL KHATTAB

MOHAMMAD EL HOUT

HABIB BACHA EL SAAD

Hotel Dieu de France

BURJ ABI HAIDAR

MAZRAA

BECHARA EL KHOURY

see page 129

France

British Council & Goethe Institute

HOTEL DIEU

6

BOULEVARD

French cultural centre

Bus 7 to Beit Mery & Broummana

ABDALLAH EL YAFI

AFIF EL-TIBEH

ABU CHAKER

MOHAMMAD ALI BEYHUM

OUZAI

Hippodrome (horseracing)

National Museum

MUSEUM

BADARO

SAHT-EL-SOLH

Finland consulate

7

Cola Intersection

SALIM SALAM

SOLEIMAN

OMAR BEYHUM

Pine Forest (Horsh Beirut)

Sunflower Theatre

Camille Chamoun Sports City Stadium, Sabra & Shatila Palestinian camps, Sahel General Hospital, Kuwait Embassy, airport, Golf Club of Lebanon, southern suburbs

Baabda, Damascus

E   F   G   H

Beirut

3

Although Beirut has shown signs of settlement dating back to the Stone Age, the first city-state was founded by the Phoenicians c3000BC. And although Beirut was upstaged by the southern cities of Sidon and Tyre, the city was nonetheless a significant trading port for this ancient mercantile civilisation. Beirut's rise to prominence had to wait until the advent of the Roman epoch in 64BC. Thanks to Pompey's successor, Augustus, the city was named after his daughter, Julia, and given the rather flamboyant title of Colonia Julia Augustus Felix Berytus. The Roman era witnessed the city's School of Law gain a reputation for being one of the finest in the empire, and with its Justinian code was a precursor to much of our current Western legal system. The city continued to flourish during the eastern or Byzantine Roman period until a massive earthquake and tsunami in AD551 killed some 30,000 Beirut citizens, shortly after which the School of Law was relocated to the city of Sidon for safety.

Beirut sunk into relative obscurity until the rise of Islam and the conquest by the Arabs in AD635. Although the Maronite Christian sect were forced to flee the city and take refuge in the Lebanese mountains, the transition to Arab rule was a largely peaceful one and ushered in a range of dynasties which have left an indelible mark on the city. Arab rule was briefly interrupted in 1110 by the Crusaders whilst on their way to Jerusalem to liberate the Holy Land from Muslim rule. The Crusaders assumed control of Beirut, along with Lebanon's other coastal towns, until Arab rule was reinstated by the Mamluks in 1291.

Following the sacking of the Mamluk caliphate by the Turks in 1516, Beirut came under the banner of the Ottoman Empire who remained the principal power broker for the next 400 years. During the formative years of Ottoman rule, Beirut and its environs were mainly controlled by indigenous Druze and Christian emirs who were granted considerable autonomy by the Sublime Porte (Ottoman Government) in Istanbul in return for prompt and full payment of taxes. From 1839, however, the Ottomans, wary of increasing European domination, implemented the Tanzimat, a series of constitutional, economic and legal reforms aimed at increasing the prosperity of the capital and to help stave off European colonialism. Beirut became an important centre for the export of Lebanese silk to Europe, especially France, which in turn attracted foreign investment for major infrastructure projects such as roads and telecommunications. The city also attracted the attention of Protestant Missionaries who, in 1866, founded the Syrian Protestant College, later renamed the American University of Beirut, which to this day remains one of the most prestigious educational institutions in the Middle East. Beirut also underwent a *nahda* or cultural renaissance and the capital became a major centre for a wide-ranging printing and publishing industry.

The advent of World War I once again changed the fortunes of the city. Ottoman control had by this time reached its nadir against Arab rebellion and the governor, Jamal 'the butcher' Pasha, publicly hanged several Lebanese in 1915 in the Downtown district for siding with the Allies. An Allied blockade of the port followed, in an attempt to bring the Ottomans to their knees, together with a devastating locust plague which engendered widespread famine. This, combined with outbreaks of bubonic plague, meant that by the end of the war tens of thousands of Beirutis had perished.

Following World War I, the European victors proceeded to divide up much of the Levant between them and the League of Nations gave France a mandate to rule over Lebanon; its linguistic and architectural influence can still be discerned in the city today. French rule continued until 1943, when Lebanon finally gained full independence from France. The city once again became a financial, cultural and intellectual centre of the Arab world, until simmering discontent finally boiled over and culminated in the tragic events of 1975, plunging the city into a lawless state for the next 15 years. Tit-for-tat killings, a mêlée of foreign involvement, bombings and hostage-taking created feelings of general insecurity that percolated through the city to become a way of life for the majority of the people. After the 1989 Taif Accord which ended the fighting, the capital embarked on the Herculean task of reconstruction, much of it inaugurated by the country's then prime minister Rafiq Hariri, whose initiatives have largely transformed the city into some semblance of its former prosperous self. Hariri's assassination on Valentine's Day 2005 ushered in the Cedar Revolution, a mass protest of Lebanese in the Downtown district which blamed Syria for the murder of their former prime minister and demanded the withdrawal of all Syrian military and security personnel from Lebanese territory. The following year, a month-long confrontation between Israel and Hezbollah once again threatened to destabilise the entire country. Yet since the cessation of hostilities Beirut and Lebanon have enjoyed considerable stability and hopes are high for continued peace. Democratic and peaceful elections in the summer of 2009 saw the advent of a Government of National Unity, led by Saad Hariri, the son of former prime minister Rafiq Hariri. It would be foolhardy to think that all of Lebanon's problems have been solved, however, and the country continues to face many challenges. This was nowhere more demonstrated than in January 2011, when several members of the cabinet resigned, leading to the collapse of the pro-Western coalition government over impending indictments by a UN-backed tribunal investigating the murder of former prime minister Rafiq Hariri in 2005. This action prompted fears of a return to sectarian violence, which so far has failed to materialise despite heightened tensions in the country. Following a five-month period of political stalemate the new incoming prime minister, Najib Mikati, finally managed to form a new cabinet in June 2011.

In 2010, Lebanon received its highest ever number of visitors with more than two million people arriving in the country. With *The New York Times* listing Beirut as the first of 44 destinations to visit in 2009, and UNESCO designating the city World Book Capital in the same year for 'emphasising cultural diversity and dialogue', Beirut is at last regaining its reputation for events other than death and destruction.

GETTING THERE

BY AIR Lebanon is served by over 40 international airlines from major cities in Europe, the Middle East, Africa and the Far East and this is the way the vast majority of visitors to the country will arrive. There were no budget airlines serving the capital at the time of writing, but in 2011, the Ministry of Tourism announced it was keen to attract low-cost carriers such as easyJet and Ryanair to Beirut and with the former recently commencing flights to the Jordanian capital Amman, bucket shop deals could become a reality in the not-too-distant future. At the present time, however, there is sufficient competition amongst the major carriers to ensure that cut-price deals are often available and with a little shopping around a return airfare from London to Beirut can be obtained for under £400. In the UK the weekly free *TNT Magazine* (www.tntmagazine.com) has listings for cheap flight deals. Online, it is worth browsing www.tripadvisor.co.uk, www.expedia.co.uk, www.lastminute.com, www.travelbuddy.com, www.travelrepublic.co.uk, www.travelsupermarket.com and www.travelocity.com for cut-price deals.

As has been the case for many years now, there continues to be no direct flights to Beirut from/to the US and Canada. However, the national carrier, Middle East

3

Airlines (MEA), has code-share agreements with partners such as Air France, American Airlines, Continental Airlines and Air Canada to ensure efficient connections with Montreal, Toronto, New York, Los Angeles, Washington and Beirut. If you are considering flying to Lebanon from neighbouring Syria there is at the time of writing only one flight per week on Saturday, from the Syrian capital Damascus to Beirut operated by Syrian Arab Airlines (*in Damascus;* ✆ *03 11 168; www.syriaair.com*), with a flight time of around 45 minutes. The flight departs Damascus at 07.20, arriving in Beirut at 08.05. At the time of writing, this flight operates only between 7 July and 22 October.

Beirut Rafiq Hariri International Airport (airport code: BEY) [90 F7]

(✆ *01 628 000, dial 150 from within Lebanon; www.beirutairport.gov.lb*) Lebanon's only commercial international airport is located in the southern suburbs of the city in the district of Khaldeh, some 7km from Beirut's Downtown area. It's bright and airy, and the modern interior is the result of a decade-long reconstruction plan which has totally transformed the former drab and outdated interior, and it is now used by many of the world's major international airlines. Upon arrival, formalities are usually quick and efficient. A white entry form for foreigners, supplied by your cabin crew prior to landing, must be filled out with your personal and passport details together with the address of where you are staying in Lebanon. Once at passport control, your passport will be stamped with a **one-month Lebanese visa** permitting you to stay in the country for up to two months before you need to apply for an extension.

Once through customs and passport control the arrivals area is very well organised. To your right is a plethora of car-hire companies and opposite is a duty-paid shop selling stationery, newspapers and magazines, postcards and local Alfa and MTC touch mobile-phone services. Opposite the shop is Café Akle, open 24/7, serving a range of hot and cold drinks and snacks and, in theory, is the only area where you are permitted to smoke inside the airport. To your left in the arrivals hall is the office of the **Ministry of Tourism** (✆ *01 629 769;* ⏰ *08.30–17.00 Mon–Thu, 08.00–14.00 Fri, 08.30–15.00 Sat, closed Sun & public holidays*), which has helpful staff and a range of printed material which you can take away in a variety of languages. Across the hall from the tourist office is the 24/7 Café Matik and next to this is another duty-free shop selling a range of confectionery, cold drinks, biscuits, tobacco and a range of fluffy toys. There are also numerous public payphones located in the arrivals hall with a bank of seven located adjacent to the Sûreté Générale opposite Café Matik. BankMed (✆ *01 623 624, 01 628 622; www.bankmed.com.lb*) is the current official airport bank and they have a couple of 24/7 ATMs in the arrivals hall.

There are **bus links** from the airport to the city centre, although the main bus stop is located an inconvenient 1km from the terminal, necessitating a probably unwelcome walk if arriving in the height of summer. Although more expensive, it is probably a better option to take a **taxi** to the city centre which can cost anywhere between US$15 and US$25 depending on your haggling abilities (see pages 97–8), but be prepared to be quoted around US$40. Another option is to arrange for a pre-booked hotel to organise your transfer from the airport. Most of the hotels, even the budget ones, now offer this service which can work out considerably cheaper than using the airport taxis. The journey time to Downtown Beirut is about 15–20 minutes, depending on traffic.

Upon your departure from Beirut a pink exit form must be completed with the same details as the white entry form. This is submitted to passport control, which will then place an exit stamp in your passport. The departures terminal is similarly very well organised and has a branch of Libanpost (✆ *01 629 369*), and also a large and extremely well-stocked duty-free shop where you can pre-order any items you wish to purchase (✆ *01 629 520; customer service* m *03 145 465;* e *preorder@pac. com.lb; www.beirutdutyfree.com*).

Major airline offices in Beirut

✈ **Air France (airline code: AF)** [104 F4] Foch St, Downtown; ✆ 01 977 977; www.airfrance. com

✈ **Alitalia (AZ)** [123 E4] 8th Fl, Liberty Tower Bldg, Rome St, Hamra; ✆ 01 754 883; www. alitalia.com

✈ **British Midland International (BD)** [123 E2] Block B, 10th Fl, Gefinor Centre, Clemenceau St, Hamra; ✆ 01 347 007; e beytobd@flybmi. com; www.flybmi.com

✈ **Cyprus Airways (CY)** [104 C4] Block B, Ground Fl, Starco Bldg, Downtown; ✆ 01 371 136; www.cyprusair.com

✈ **EgyptAir (MS)** [104 E5] Riad al-Solh Sq, Downtown; ✆ 01 981 809; www.egyptair.com

✈ **Emirates (EK)** [123 E2] Block D, Ground Fl, Gefinor Centre, Clemenceau St, Hamra; ✆ 01 734 500; www.emirates.com

✈ **KLM-Royal Dutch Airlines (KL)** [123 E4] Foch St, Downtown; ✆ 01 977 977; www.klm. com

✈ **Lufthansa German Airlines (LH)** [123 E2] Block B, 10th Fl, Gefinor Centre, Clemenceau St, Hamra; ✆ 01 347 007; e beyteam@dlh.de; www. lufthansa.com

✈ **Malaysia Airlines (MH)** [123 E2] Block D, 2nd Fl, Gefinor Centre, Clemenceau St, Hamra; ✆ 01 741 344/5/6; www.malaysiaairlines.com

✈ **MEA (ME)** [123 E2] Gefinor Centre, Clemenceau St, Hamra; ✆ 01 628 888; e gefinor@mea.aero; www.mea.com.lb

✈ **Oman Air (WY)** [123 E2] Block D, Ground Fl, Gefinor Centre, Clemenceau St, Hamra; ✆ 01 753 581/2/3/4; e resbey@omanair.com; www. omanair.com

✈ **Royal Jordanian Airlines (RJ)** [123 B2] Bliss St, Hamra; ✆ 01 379 990/1; e beytsrj@ rj.com; www.rj.com

✈ **Syrian Arab Airlines (RB)** Mar Elias St; ✆ 01 375 636; m 03 388 018; e rb.beirut@syriaair.com; www.syriaair.com

BY ROAD Lebanon shares land borders with both Israel and Syria. However, in the absence of a comprehensive Middle East peace settlement it is not possible to enter or exit Lebanon from Israel, despite Israel's military withdrawal from the majority of the south of the country in May 2000. Currently, then, Syria remains the only option for direct entry to Beirut by land. A **bus or service taxi** from the Syrian capital Damascus will cost about 700–800 Syrian pounds (SYP) from the Samaria bus station in Damascus, arriving at Beirut's Charles Helou bus station close to the Downtown district of the capital. The journey time is around four–six hours depending on traffic conditions and border control delays. It is also possible to catch a bus or taxi from other cities in Syria such as Aleppo (known locally as *Halab*), Lattakia, Hama and Homs to Beirut. At the time of writing an exit tax of SYP500 was payable on departure from Syria. There are also **taxis from Jordan** (Amman) and **buses and taxis from Turkey** (Antakya, Istanbul) arriving at Beirut's Charles Helou bus station (see page 96).

BY SEA For details on cruise companies visiting Beirut, see pages 51–2.

GETTING AROUND

The combination of being a small city with a plentiful and well-developed private transportation system means that Beirut is quite an easy place to get about. That said, there is a dearth of street signs and finding your exact location can be a real headache. For those planning on an extended stay or tour of the city and its environs, by whatever transport mode, who want to correctly navigate Beirut's often nameless streets, a very useful companion to have in hand is *Zawarib Beirut & Beyond* (e *info@zawaribbeirut.com; www.zawaribbeirut.com*), which is akin to a London A–Z street map. The latest 2010 edition of this invaluable road and street atlas (scale: 1:4,500/1:9,000) covers some 150km² of Beirut plus the outlying areas of Aley, Beit Mery, Broummana and Jounieh. The book also contains a directory of emergency and useful telephone numbers, a bus map and a list of banks, foreign embassies, government departments and hospitals along with their telephone details. Available in bookshops throughout the capital and by international mail order, it costs LBP18,000 (US$12). Stanford's travel bookshop in London is also a stockist with mail order available (£13.95).

BY BUS The main bus company serving Beirut is the privately owned **Lebanese Commuting Company (LCC)** (*Main Rd, Choueifat, opposite Sultan Steel;* ⅋/f *05 810 510;* ⅋ *05 810 610;* e *info@lccworld.com; www.lccworld.com*), with its red-and-white-coloured buses which commenced operations in 1995 to bring some semblance of order and efficiency to Beirut's hitherto archaic and inefficient public transport system. The generally excellent LCC fleet of around 225 buses operate throughout Beirut as well as to outlying areas in Mount Lebanon such as Aley, Broummana, Beit Mery, Byblos and Jounieh. Although there are no published timetables or official bus stops, buses generally run at intervals of between five and 20 minutes, depending on the route, between the hours of 05.30 and 21.00 but be aware that buses can stop running earlier on some routes in more remote areas of LCC operation. Depending on the distance travelled, fares range from LBP1,000 to LBP1,500, and you normally pay the driver upon boarding the bus. Ticket inspectors regularly operate on LCC buses so remember to keep hold of your ticket for possible inspection. If time is not of the essence the buses provide a cost-effective and great way to get around the city and its environs. Pocket-sized LCC bus route maps are often available from drivers, inspectors and at the Ministry of Tourism office in Hamra, but for convenience the latest available 2010 route details are provided below (see box, pages 100–1). Note that at the time of writing bus number 9 (Barbir–Nahr El Mott) was suspended but it could be operational again by the time you read this.

The state-owned blue-and-white buses of the **OCFTC** (*Office des Chemins de Fer et du Transport en Commun* (*Railway & Public Transportation Company*); *Ibrahim Pasha St* (*near Electricité du Liban*), *Mar Mikhael;* ⅋ *01 587 215*) formerly operated a similar comprehensive network of routes within the city but operations were suspended in 2009 owing to a lack of government funding; it remains uncertain at the time of writing whether services will resume. There is also a range of other privately run minibuses, vans and other vehicles which ply many routes within and outside the city; it is best to just ask the driver where he is going and be prepared to wait until the vehicle fills up before departing.

Bus stations Beirut's network of buses and stations has grown extensively over the last few years and now covers most areas of Lebanon and a number of countries beyond. The following stations all double up as taxi stations, which mean that entering and exiting the capital has never been easier. Just bear in mind that in many cases, whether travelling by bus or service taxi, you will often have to wait until the vehicle fills up with other passengers before departing, though this does not necessarily mean a long wait.

Charles Helou bus station [129 B1] (*Charles Helou Av, Rmeil*) Named after a former Lebanese president, this station is just a few minutes' walk east from

Downtown, but this busy, drab and grey-looking terminus is anything but stately and is long overdue for a facelift. Clearly signposted '*gare routière*', the station is, however, quite well organised compared with the others, and is for transport to areas north of the capital, along with buses and taxis to international destinations. There are a number of companies who operate services and they have ticket booths where you can purchase your ticket in advance of travel. Timetables were scarce at the time of writing and it is best to just ask at one of the ticket booths. Services to all destinations are plentiful and frequent.

Charles Helou station is divided into three clearly signposted zones based on the destinations served: **Zone A** is for buses and taxis to Jordan (Amman, but only by taxi at the time of writing), Syria (Aleppo, Damascus, Homs, Latakia) and Turkey (Antakya, Istanbul); **Zone B** for buses to Syria, Tripoli and Turkey; and **Zone C** for bus and taxi services to Jordan, Syria, Jounieh, Byblos and Tripoli. Prices vary between the different companies, but the following sample fares from Beirut were applicable: Aleppo (US$13, bus); Antakya (US$33, bus); Amman (US$40, taxi); Damascus (US$12 bus, US$18 taxi); Tripoli (LBP4,000, bus).

Cola intersection [90 E7] (*Pl de la Resistance et de la Liberation, Salim Salam St, Wata*) More open plan and chaotic than Charles Helou station Cola is generally for buses, minivans, service taxis and taxis to destinations in southern Lebanon including the Chouf, Sidon and Tyre. Minivans and taxis, however, also go to the Bekaa Valley and you can additionally catch the LCC bus number six from here which passes by the National Museum, Bourj Hammoud, Dora and Jounieh *en route* to its final destination at Byblos.

Dora [90 H3] (*Dora Highway, near Bourj Hammoud*) A little more remote than the other stations Dora, like Charles Helou station, is a hub for minivans and taxis travelling to destinations generally north of the capital, including to Byblos, Jounieh and Tripoli.

BY TAXI Taxis – usually pre-1975 Mercedes with **red number plates** – are ubiquitous and a good way to travel around the city as they cover all areas of the capital and operate on the usual hail-and-ride principle. You basically have three choices: a taxi, a *servees* (collective/shared) taxi or a *serviceain*. With the first option you flag down a taxi and ask for 'taxi' and agree a price to your destination before getting inside the car. The fare for journeys to most places within the city should be around LBP5,000–10,000. To outlying suburbs the cost can be upwards of LBP10,000. The cheaper option is to flag down a passing taxi and ask for *servees* to your destination and, once again, agree the price in advance before setting off. Unlike with a taxi, the driver is at liberty to pick up and put down passengers *en route* but the upside is that you often get the opportunity to chat to the locals. The current cost of a *servees* taxi within the central Beirut area is around LBP2,000, but can be more if travelling to the outskirts of the city in which case a *serviceain* fare will apply, which equates to twice the price of a servees (LBP4,000).

If you wish to pre-book a taxi, the following selection of companies all have good reputations but it is still a good idea to agree the price to your destination over the phone before confirming your booking. Many of these companies also offer car hire and tours around the country.

Allo Taxi Kurban Daouk Bldg, Army St, Kantari; ℡ 01 366 661; m 03 325 772; dial 1213 within Lebanon; e operation@allotaxi.com.lb, info@allotaxi.com.lb; www.allotaxi.com.lb. With over

3

200 cars, this large & well-established company is a good option.

Banet Taxi Adliyeh St, Downtown; ☏ 01 422 229, 04 419 006; m 70 286 896; e info@banettaxi.com, banettaxi@gmail.com; www.banettaxi.com. A 24/7 nationwide taxi service, for women & families only, driven by ladies in pink cars.

Jesuit Taxi Jesuit Gardens, Achrafieh; ☏ 01 586 400

Lebanon Taxi Rome St, Hamra; ☏ 01 340 717/8/9, 01 353 152/3; m 03 207 283 (emergencies); e taxi@lebanontaxi.com; www.lebanontaxi.com

National New Dawn ☏ 09 854 370, 09 857 300; e info@nndleb.com; www.nndleb.com. Londoners will be thrilled that they can now hail or book a black cab in Lebanon. Reliable & competitive prices, a taxi from Beirut's Downtown area to the airport will cost around LBP25,000.

Taxi Premiere 4th Fl, Kaiss Bldg, Sami El Solh St, Badaro; ☏ 01 389 222; e info@taxipremiere.com; www.taxipremiere.com

Trust Taxi Sassine St, near Hotel Dieu, Achrafieh; ☏ 01 613 573, 01 613 398; m 03 601 806; e info@trust-taxi.com; www.trust-taxi.com

CAR HIRE Renting a car in Beirut couldn't be easier as there are plenty of companies offering the service, both with and without a driver. Whichever firm you choose you will need to be over 21 years old (in some cases over 23) and have a valid – preferably international – driving licence. Car hire is a great alternative to a taxi if you are planning an extended tour of the country but not really worth your while for travelling around the capital's congested streets. In Beirut stick to taxis and buses. The following list of companies is not exhaustive, but represents those agencies which have good reputations and deliver reliable and friendly service. Rates can start for a small car from around US$30 per day rising to over US$300 for a luxury vehicle with all the bells and whistles. In all cases it is best to check whether insurance is included in the price of car hire.

🚗 **Advanced Car Rental** Azarieh Bldg, facing Jerious Cathedral, Downtown; ☏ 01 999 884/5; m 03 500 855, 70 151 510; e rent@advancedcarrent.com; www.advancedcarrent.com

🚗 **Avis** [104 A3] Achrafieh; ☏ 01 611 000; airport; ☏ 01 629 890; Downtown; ☏ 01 367 124; Ain al-Mreisse (inside the Phoenicia Intercontinental Hotel); ☏ 01 363 848; e reservations@avis-lebanon.com; www.avis.com.lb

🚗 **Beirut Car Rental** Minkara Centre, Rue Madame Curie, Hamra; ☏ 01 356 000, 01 740 741; e reservation@beirutrentacar.com; www.beirutrentacar.com

🚗 **City Car** Al Oraifi Bldg, Kalaa St, Ras Beirut; ☏ 01 780 000, 01 803 308; m 03 316 111; e citycar@citycar.com.lb; www.citycar.com.lb

🚗 **Europcar** Saarti Bldg, Fouad Chehab St, Sin El Fil; ☏ 01 480 480; e lenacar@lenacar.com; www.lenacar.com

🚗 **Hala Rent a Car** Sami El Solh Av, Badaro; ☏ 01 393 904; m 03 318 432; e rent@halacar.com; www.halacar.com

🚗 **Hertz** Sami El Solh St, Badaro; ☏ 01 427 283; e hertz@cyberia.net.lb; www.hertz.com

🚗 **Nasrallah Rent a Car** Slav St, Hayek Sq, Dekwaneh; m 03 811 051, 03 740 804; e info@nasrallahrentacar.com; www.nasrallahrentacar.com

🚗 **Thrifty Car Rental** Obeid Bldg, Dekwaneh (opposite Mirna Chalouhi Centre); ☏ 01 510 100; m 03 290 399, 03 339 009; e info@thriftylebanon.com; www.thriftylebanon.com

BY BIKE Cycling is growing in popularity as people want to get and keep fit together with an awareness of the growing problem of congestion and pollution in the city. You will see many cyclists around the Corniche and the 'classic' bike route is from Ain al-Mreisse and along the Corniche all the way to Raouche and beyond. The following companies hire bikes and/or organise city tours:

♪ **Beirut By Bike** [123 F1] Abdel Nasser St, behind the mosque not far from McDonald's, Ain al-Mreisse; ☎ 01 365 524; f 01 375 524; m 03 435 524, 70 435 524, 71 435 524; e info@beirutbybike.com; www.beirutbybike.com; ⏰ 07.00–midnight daily. Bikes & accessories are available for hire (LBP5,000/hr, LBP15,000/half day & LBP30,000/day), catering for all age groups & they also organise biking events around the city, often in aid of good causes. They also have 2 other branches in the Downtown area at the entrance to the Beirut International Exhibition & Leisure Centre (BIEL) & at the Beirut Souks. It's also worth keeping an eye on their website for details of up & coming cycle events.

♪ **Cyclosport** [129 B1] Gouraud St, Gemmayze; ☎ 01 446 792; e cyclosport@cyberia. net.lb, info@cyclosport-lb.com; www.cyclosportlb.com; ⏰ 10.00–22.00 daily. This long-established & respected shop offers a wide range of pedal power from road to mountain bikes which can be rented by the hour for LBP5,000 & by the day for LBP25,000. They also run a cycling club catering to both the beginner & seasoned bike rider.

♪ **LebCycling** 7th Fl, La Princesse Bldg, Haret Sakher, Jounieh; m 03 226 713; f 09 637 144; e info@lebcycling.com; www.lebcycling.com. Although they are based just outside the capital, this organisation of amateur bike enthusiasts aims to promote the joys & benefits of cycling as a healthy & enjoyable pastime countrywide. In addition, they also organise & run a wide range of other summer & winter pursuits including caving, hiking, kayaking, scuba diving, skiing & snowboarding.

BY FOOT Beirut's compact size makes it an ideal city to explore by foot, though the summer heat and humidity can be uncomfortable, therefore walking either early in the morning or late afternoon can make travel by foot more bearable. Seeing the city this way also has the advantage of bypassing the capital's often congested traffic, especially around the narrow roads of the Hamra area in west Beirut. Any concerns you may have about street crime are unwarranted as Beirut is an incredibly safe city to walk around, day or night, and you will feel safer here than in many Western cities such as London or New York. The *What to see and do* section (see page 122) provides pointers to the main areas of interest in the city which you can reach by foot but the company BeBeirut, which commenced walking tours of the city in April 2009, comes highly recommended, taking in areas not on the normal tourist trail – from Yasser Arafat's once café of choice to the little-explored Jewish quarter – and gives an edifying view of the city by local people who actually live there.

BeBeirut (m *70 156 673*; e *walk@bebeirut.org; www.bebeirut.org*) was founded by Ronnie Chatah in 2009, a former American University of Beirut (AUB) student. The company conducts an approximately 3½-hour WalkBeirut tour of the city, in English. In winter 2011, the tours ran twice weekly on Saturday and Sunday from 16.30–20.30, leaving from the Gefinor Centre in Hamra, opposite the offices of Middle East Airlines. The cost in 2011 was LBP30,000, which includes a map of the walking tour area.

TOURIST INFORMATION

Lebanon's official Ministry of Tourism office is at 550 Central Bank St, Hamra [123 E3] (☎ *01 340 940*; e *mot@destinationlebanon.gov.lb; www.destinationlebanon.gov.lb*; ⏰ *08.30–17.00 Mon–Thu, 08.30–14.00 Fri, 08.30–15.00 Sat*). The Ministry also has an office in the arrivals hall at Beirut airport (☎ *01 629 769*; ⏰ *08.30–17.00 Mon–Thu, 08.00–14.00 Fri, 08.30–15.00 Sat, closed Sun & public holidays*), where visitors can obtain information on all regions of the country and advice from the helpful staff. In addition to their range of brochures and pamphlets the Ministry also produce some weightier tomes with extended listings of hotels, cafés and

BUS 1: HAMRA–KHALDEH Caracas, Radio Lebanon, Syar Darak, Verdun, UNESCO, Mar Elias Betina, Cola Roundabout, Sports City, Bir Hassan, Airport Bridge, Ghobeire, Mucharafieh, Said Hadi Highway, Hay El Abiad, Al Rouais, Kafaat, Saqui El Hadath, Lebanese University, Kfarshima, Choueifat, Khaldeh

BUS 2: HAMRA–ANTELIAS Hamra (Emile Edde St), Radio Lebanon, Tallet Druze, Karakoul Druze, Mar Elias, Basta Tahta, Bechara El Khoury, Nasra, Sassine Square, Mar Mitr, Ekawi, Rmeil, Mar Mikhael, Quarantina, Bourj Hammoud, Dora Roundabout, Mar Youssef, Jdaide, Nahr El Mott, Zalka, Jal El Dib, Antelias

BUS 5: AIN AL-MREISSE–CHOUEIFAT Ain al-Mreisse, AUB Beach, Manara, Bain Militaire, Raouche, Ramlet al-Bayda, Verdun, UNESCO, Mar Elias Betina, Wata Moussaitbeh, Cola Roundabout, Malaab El Baladi, Sabra, Shatila Roundabout, Airport Bridge, Horch El Qatil, Al Rassoul Al Aazam, Ain El Delbeh, Cocodi, Airport Roundabout, Tahwit al-Gadeir, Meraija, Hay El Seloum, Choueifat

BUS 6: COLA–JBAIL (BYBLOS) Cola Roundabout, Mazraa, Abed al-Nasser, Makassed, Barbir, Museum, Adlieh, Fiat Bridge, Corniche El Nahr, Nahr Bridge, Quarantine, Bourj Hammoud, Dora Roundabout, Nahr El Mott, Zalka, Jal El Dib, Antelias, Dbayeh, Jounieh, Maameltain, Tabarja, Boire, Aquiba, Nahr Ibrahim, Fidar, Jbail (Byblos)

BUS 7: MUSEUM (MATHAF)–BHARSSAF Museum, Adlieh, Fiat Bridge, Jisr El Wati, Hayek Roundabout, Mkalles Roundabout, Mansourieh, Mountazah, Monteverde, Ain Saade, Beit Mery Roundabout, Broummana, Baabdat, Bhaines, Bharssaf

restaurants and other useful contact information. Ask them for a copy of their annual *Lebanon Tourist Guide* or the yearly *Lebanon Official General Tourism Guide*, which provides similar information but in a slimmer, pocket-sized format. Their generally excellent website also provides a wealth of information for all regions of the country which can help you to plan and tailor your visit to your own interests, though the website could be updated a little more frequently. There are also local tourist information offices in Baalbek, Batroun, Byblos, Jeita Grotto, Sidon, Tripoli and Zahlé (for further details, see the respective regional chapters).

LOCAL TOUR OPERATORS

Ariane Travel & Tourism 1st Fl, Ariane Bldg, New Jdeideh St, Jdeidet El Metn; ↘ 01 888 148, 01 890 005, 01 897 833; e ariane@ariannetravel.com; www.ariannetravel.com. Operates a range of nationwide tours ranging from 6 to 15 days.

Barakat Travel Block A3, Ground Fl, Azarieh

Bldg, Downtown; ↘ 01 972 111; m 70 972 111; e tours@barakat-travel.com; www.barakat-travel.com. Although not offering the widest selection of tours, this is a well-respected company in Lebanon.

Beirut Urban Adventures ↘ 09 237 011; m 70 102 333; e info@

BUS 8: BAIN MILITAIRE–AIN SAADE Sporting Club, Radio Lebanon, Tallet Druze, Karakoul Druze, Mar Elias, Basta Tahta, Bechara El Khoury, Nasra, Sassine Square, Karm Zeitoun, Nahr Bridge, Nabaa, Bourj Hammoud, Mar Youssef, Jdaide Square, Fanar Crossroad, Fanar, Ain Saade

BUS 9: BARBIR–NAHR EL MOTT Barbir, Museum, Adlieh, Furn El Chebbak, Chevrolet, Sin El Fil Roundabout, Mkalles Roundabout, Hayek Roundabout, Saloumeh Roundabout, Dekwaneh, Sabtieh, Mar Takla Square, Jdeideh (Fanar Crossroad), Rouaisset El Jdaide, Nahr El Mott

BUS 12: HAMRA–BOURJ EL BARAJNEH Wardieh (Hamra), Radio Lebanon, Tallet Druze, Karakoul Druze, Mar Elias, Selim Salam, Cola Roundabout, Malaab El Baladi, Sabra, Chatila Roundabout, Chiyah, Mucharafieh, Ghobeire, Haret Hreik, Bourj El Barajneh

BUS 14: COLA–ALEY Cola Roundabout, Mazraa, Barbir, Tayoune Roundabout, Furn El Chebbak, Chevrolet, Galerie Semaan, Assyad Roundabout, Hazmieh, Yarze, Fayadiyeh, Jamhour, Aaraiya, Kahhale, Dahr El Wahsh, Aley

BUS 14: MUSEUM (MATHAF)–ALEY Adlieh, Furn El Chebback, Chevrolet, Galerie Semaan, Assyad Roundabout, Hazmieh, Yarze, Fayadiyeh, Jamhour, Aaraiya, Kahhale, Dahr El Wahsh, Aley

BUS 15: COLA–ALEY Cola Roundabout, Sports City, Bir Hassan, Airport Bridge, Ghobeire, Mucharafieh, Mar Mikhael Church, Galerie Semaan, Assyad Roundabout, Hazmieh, Yarze, Fayadiyeh, Jamhour, Aaraiya, Kahhale, Dahr El Wahsh, Aley

beiruturbanadventures.com; www.beiruturbanadventures.com. Offers 2 walking tours of Beirut: a 2hr guided walk around the restored Downtown district (US$45) & a 4hr tour of the traditional Armenian quarter of Bourj Hammoud (US$79).

Campus Travel [123 D2] Maktabi Bldg, Rue Makhoul, Hamra; ☏ 01 744 588; m 03 900 902; e campus@campus-travel.net; www.campus-travel.net. Geared to the student/budget market, this company offers very affordable nationwide tours including eco & religious tourism.

Commodore International Services (CIS Tours) [123 F3] Commodore St, near Commodore Hotel, Hamra; ☏ 01 354 229, 01 349 597, 01 347 699; e cistours@cyberia.net.lb, cistours@cistours.com; www.cistours.com. Offers half-day tours of Beirut plus a range of full-day

tours to Baalbek, Aanjar, Byblos, Jeita Grotto, Sidon & Tripoli.

Concord Travel [123 F3] 8th Fl, Saroulla Bldg, Hamra St, Hamra; ☏ 01 730 074; m 03 334 337; e tours@concordtr.com; www.concordtr.com. Tour operator offering a range of individual & group tours from 3 to 8 days to most areas of Lebanon & also tours combined with Jordan & Syria. This company can also arrange airport transfer, hotel & apartment bookings.

Esprit Nomade ☏ 01 201 950, 09 933 552; m 03 223 552; e coord@esprit-nomade.com; nomade@esprit-nomade.com; www.esprit-nomade.com. Specialist ecotourism operator.

Kurban Tours Downtown; ☏ 01 368 958; m 03 510 333; e info@kurbantours.com; www.kurbantours.com. Nationwide tours taking in all the highlights of Lebanon. As a destination management company, they also specialise in events & group tours for business.

○ **Lebanese Adventure** m 03 360 027, 03 214 989, 03 454 996; e infos@lebanese-adventure. com; www.lebanese-adventure.com. As its name suggests, specialises in weekend activity-based tours including trekking, camping, hiking & rafting.

Lena Tours & Travel Ground Fl, St George's Centre, Sin El Fil; ✆ 01 496 696; m 03 070 728; e info@lenatours.com; www.lena-tours.com. A one-stop shop for countrywide tours, car hire & hotel bookings.

 Liban Trek ✆ 01 329 975; m 03 291 616; e info@libantrek.com; www.libantrek.com. Founded in 1997, this is Lebanon's first ecotourism operator, providing a varied countrywide programme of birdwatching, camping, biking, hiking, caving, skiing, snowshoeing, etc.

LIBA Tours & Travel ✆ 09 541 547; m 03 527 555; e info@libatours.com; www. libatours.com. Specialising in a range of nationwide daily tours including belly-dancing Lebanese nights.

Mont Liban Travel & Tourism 4th Fl, Noor El-Hayat Bldg, Verdun; ✆ 01 811 666; m 03 871 666; e nhz2000@dm.net.lb; www.montlibanonline.com. Geared more to the corporate & VIP market, this company provides a range of services to the travelling businessman including private tours, luxury car rental, hotel reservations, conference & translation services.

Nadia Travel & Tourism New Jeddah, Monte Lebanon Centre; ✆ 01 887 878; m 03 220 398; e nadiatravel@nadiatravel.com; www. nadiatravel.com. A good range of full- & half-day tours of the main sites.

Nakhal Ghorayeb Bldg, Sami El Solh Av; ✆ 01 389 389, dial 1270 within Lebanon; e tours@nakhal.com.lb; www.nakhal.com.lb. One of Lebanon's longest-established travel companies specialising in mainly daily tours

encompassing most of the main sites in Lebanon.

Rida Travel & Tourism 4th Fl, Al Arz Centre; ✆ 04 718 790; e ridaint@ridaint.com.lb; www. ridaint.com.lb. Variety of tours nationwide ranging from 3 to 6 days. Also arranges car hire. The company's international arm offers tours combining Lebanon, Syria & Jordan.

SAAD Tours Haddad Bldg, Amine Gemayel St, Achrafieh; ✆ 01 429 429; e inbound@saadtours. com; www.saadtours.com. Range of daily & extended tours throughout Lebanon. Also arranges car rental.

Skywaystours 4th Fl, Aramex Centre, Main Rd, Sin El Fil; ✆ 01 510 185/6; m 03 660 899; e info@skywaystours.com; www.skywaystours. com. Geared mainly to the corporate market, this company provides tailor-made individual & group travel tours throughout Lebanon together with car rental & hotel reservations.

Tania Travel [123 C2] Sidani St, opposite Jeanne d'Arc cinema, Hamra; ✆ 01 739 682; m 03 686 121; e taniahamra@taniatravel.com; www.taniatravel.com. Daily tours visiting Aanjar, Baalbek, Bcharré, Cedars, Jeita Grotto, Byblos, Beiteddine, Sidon & Tyre. US$60–70 including transport, lunch, guide & entrance fees to sites. Excellent value.

Target Travel 4th Fl, Sadat Home Bldg, Sadat St, Hamra; ✆ 01 743 440; e info@targettravel. com; www.targettravel.com. A one-stop shop from meeting & greeting at the airport, hotel bookings, car rental, theatre & restaurant bookings together with a range of excursions throughout Lebanon.

Vent Nouveau 30 Badaro St; ✆ 04 712 037; e info@ventnouveau.com.lb; www.ventnouveau. com.lb. Specialist tour packages including ecotourism, skiing & sport.

Wild Discovery [129 C1] Pasteur Bldg, Pasteur St, Gemmayze; ✆ 01 565 646; m 71 202 727; e dailytours@wilddiscovery.com.lb; www. wilddiscovery.com.lb. Daily half- & full-day tours from a respected adventure tour operator throughout Lebanon at very competitive prices.

WHERE TO STAY

LUXURY

⌂ **Four Seasons Hotel** [104 C2] (230 rooms & suites) 1418 Professor Wafic Sinno Av, Minet al-Hosn; ✆ 01 761 000; e res.beirut@fourseasons. com; www.fourseasons.com/beirut. Opened in Jan 2010, this seafront hotel offers everything you would expect from this chain – classy, ultra luxurious & sleek with rooftop pool & spa, great service & fantastic sea views. **$$$$$**

⌂ **Gefinor Rotana** [123 E2] (159 rooms & suites) Clemenceau St, Hamra; ✆ 01 371 888, 01 371 999; e gefinor.hotel@rotana.com; www.rotana.com. An excellent & luxurious hotel well suited to business travellers with extensive business & conference facilities, easy access to Downtown & the Hamra district & with good leisure facilities & a scenic rooftop pool. **$$$$$**

⌂ **Hotel Albergo** [129 A3] (33 suites) 137 Rue Abdel Wahab El Inglizi, Achrafieh; ✆ 01 339 797; e albergobeirut@albergobeirut.com, albergo@relaischateaux.com; www.albergobeirut.com. For those seeking luxury with individuality, this boutique hotel offers it in spades. Each room has been meticulously & individually furnished with its own character. More sedately & nicely located than most, the hotel also has a small but great rooftop pool with an adjacent bar & lounge area surrounded by greenery. A delightful place you won't easily forget. **$$$$$**

⌂ **Intercontinental Le Vendome** [123 G1] (73 rooms & suites) Minet El Hosn, Ain al-Mreisse; ✆ 01 369 280; e iclevendome@levendomebeirut.com; www.levendomebeirut.com. Scenically located overlooking the Corniche, this small, luxurious boutique hotel has a classic French flavour & feel. **$$$$$**

⌂ **Intercontinental Phoenicia Hotel** [123 G2] (506 rooms & suites) Minet El Hosn, Downtown; ✆ 01 369 100; f 01 369 101; e phoenicia@phoeniciabeirut.com; www.phoeniciabeirut.com, www.ichotelsgroup.com. A favourite of well-heeled Gulf Arabs & the venue for many a high-profile political meeting, this marble adorned hotel is in a great location & oozes luxury, with terrifically spacious rooms & great sea views. Royal Suite US$15,000 per night (b/fast inc). **$$$$$**

⌂ **Le Bristol** [90 C4] (151 rooms & suites) Rue Madame Curie, Verdun; ✆ 01 351 400; e lebristol@lebristol-hotel.com; www.lebristol-hotel.com. Elegant, luxurious & classically styled with business centre & rooftop pool. **$$$$$**

⌂ **Le Commodore** [123 C3] (204 rooms & suites) Commodore St, Hamra; ✆ 01 734 700, 01 734 734; e info@lecommodorehotel.com; www.lecommodorehotel.com. A home from home for foreign journalists during the civil war, this is a

much-renovated but still decent 5-star option in the centre of Hamra for business & leisure travellers alike. **$$$$$**

⌂ **Le Gray** [104 F5] (87 rooms & suites) Martyrs' Sq, Downtown; ✆ 01 971 111; e info@legray.com, reservations@legray.com; www.legray.com, www.campbellgrayhotels.com. In an excellent central Downtown location this latest boutique offering from hotelier Gordon Campbell Gray evokes minimalist chic with all the luxurious accoutrements you would expect for the price, such as rooftop pool & Bar 360 affording panoramic views. An ideal hotel for business travellers & tourists alike. **$$$$$**

⌂ **Le Royal Beirut** (231 rooms & suites) PO Box 70-1010, Dbayeh; ✆ 04 555 555; e info@leroyalbeirut.com; www.leroyalbeirut.com. An imposing & classically furnished luxurious hotel on the outskirts of the city, ideal for business travellers, with excellent facilities as well as a ballroom adjoining the Aqua Park for families. **$$$$$**

⌂ **Palm Beach Hotel** [123 G1] (87 rooms & suites) Ain al-Mreisse; ✆ 01 372 000; e info@palmbeachbeirut.com; www.palmbeachbeirut.com. There is no denying this hotel is in a great location overlooking the Corniche with fantastic Mediterranean vistas, but the rooms seemed a little tired & in need of a makeover. Nonetheless, this is a decent enough hotel with good facilities & a superb rooftop pool with bar & lounge area. **$$$$$**

⌂ **Raouché Arjaan by Rotana** [123 A4] (176 rooms & suites) Raouche Bd, Raouche; ✆ 01 781 111; e raouche.arjaan@rotana.com; www.rotana.com. Another excellent hotel from the Rotana chain with all their usual high-quality business & leisure facilities & in a great location overlooking the Mediterranean & Pigeon Rocks. **$$$$$**

⌂ **Riviera Hotel** [90 B2] (120 rooms & suites) Av de Paris, Corniche El Manara; ✆ 01 373 210; e info@rivierahotel.com.lb; www.rivierahotel.com.lb. First opened in 1956, the name & ambience continue to evoke the era when Beirut was a hedonist's playground, nowhere more apparent than its famed Beach Lounge, reached by underground walkway beneath the Corniche, which has swimming pools, Jacuzzi & sun beds, with jet skiing &

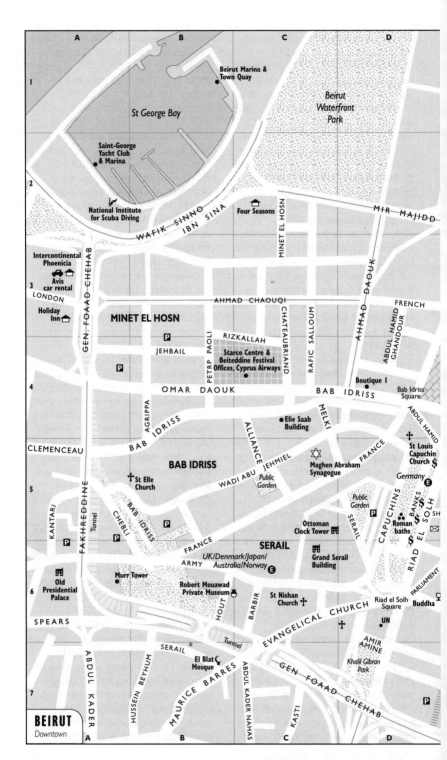

Beirut Marina & Town Quay

St George Bay

Beirut Waterfront Park

Saint-George Yacht Club & Marina

National Institute for Scuba Diving

Four Seasons

MIR MAJIDD

WAFIK SINNO

IBN SINA

MINET EL HOSN

Intercontinental Phoenicia

Avis car rental

LONDON

Holiday Inn

GEN-FOAAD-CHEHAB

AHMAD CHAOUQI

FRENCH

MINET EL HOSN

JEHBAIL

RIZKALLAH

PETRP PAOLI

CHATEAUBRIAND

RAFIC SALLOUM

AHMAD DAOUK

ABDUL HAMID GHANDOUR

Starco Centre & Beiteddine Festival Offices, Cyprus Airways

OMAR DAOUK

BAB IDRISS

Boutique 1

Bab Idriss Square

CLEMENCEAU

BAB AGRIPPA

BAB IDRISS

Elie Saab Building

MELKI

ALLIANCE

BAB IDRISS

WADI ABU JEHMIEL

† St Elle Church

Public Garden

Maghen Abraham Synagogue

FRANCE

† St Louis Capuchin Church $

Germany **E**

CAPUCHINS

Public Garden

Roman baths $

BANKS

RIAD EL SOLH

SH

KANTARI

FAKHREDDINE

Tunnel

CHEBLI

BAB IDRISS

FRANCE

Ottoman Clock Tower

SERAIL

SERAIL

P

ARMY

UK/Denmark/Japan/ Australia/Norway E

Grand Serail Building

PARLIAMENT

Old Presidential Palace

Murr Tower

Robert Mouawad Private Museum

HOUT

BARBIR

St Nishan Church †

Riad el Solh Square

Buddha

SPEARS

EVANGELICAL CHURCH

UN

†

AMIR AMINE

Khalil Gibran Park

ABDUL KADER

HUSSEIN BEYHUM

SERAIL

MAURICE BARRES

Tunnel

El Blat Mosque

ABDUL KADER NAHAS

KASTI

GEN FOAAD CHEHAB

P

BEIRUT
Downtown

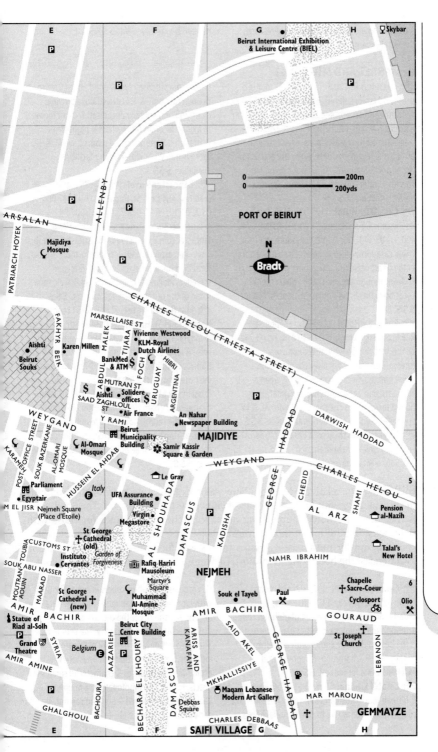

Skybar

Beirut International Exhibition
& Leisure Centre (BIEL)

E   F   G   H   I

P   P   P

ARSALAN

Majidiya
Mosque

200m
200yds

PORT OF BEIRUT

N

Bradt

PATRIARCH HOYEK

FAKHYR BEIK

CHARLES HELOU (TRIESTA STREET)

MARSELLAISE ST

ALLENBY

MALEK

ABDUL

TIJARA

FOCH

HIBRI

URUGUAY

ARGENTINA

Vivienne Westwood
KLM-Royal
Dutch Airlines

Aishti
Karen Millen

Beirut
Souks

BankMed
& ATM

MUTRAN ST

Aishti   Solidere
offices

Air France

SAAD ZAGHLOUL ST

Y RAMI

An Nahar
Newspaper Building

WEYGAND

KARAMEH

POST OFFICE STREET

SOUK BAZERKANE

AL-OMARI MOSQUE

HUSSEIN EL AHDAB

Al-Omari
Mosque

Beirut
Municipality
Building

MAJIDIYE

Samir Kassir
Square & Garden

WEYGAND

HADDAD

DARWISH HADDAD

CHARLES HELOU

Le Gray

Parliament

Egyptair

M EL JISR

Nejmeh Square
(Place d'Etoile)

Italy

UFA Assurance
Building

Virgin
Megastore

AL SHOUHADA

DAMASCUS

GEORGE

CHEDID

KADISHA

SHAMI

AL ARZ

Pension
al-Nazih

St George
Cathedral
(old)

Garden of
Forgiveness

Instituto
Cervantes

Rafiq Hariri
Mausoleum

NEJMEH

NAHR IBRAHIM

Talal's
New Hotel

CUSTOMS ST

TOUBIA

SOUK ABU NASSER

MOUTRAN

MAARAD

Martyr's
Square

Muhammad
Al-Amine
Mosque

St George
Cathedral
(new)

AMIR   BACHIR

AMIR BACHIR

Souk el Tayeb

Paul

SAID AKEL

GOURAUD

Chapelle
Sacre-Coeur

Cyclosport

Olio

Statue of
Riad al-Solh

Grand
Theatre

SYRIA

Belgium

AAZARIEH

Beirut City
Centre Building

ARISS AND KANATANI

St Joseph
Church

LEBANON

AMIR AMINE

BACHOURA

BECHARA EL KHOURY

DAMASCUS

MKHALLISSIYE

GEORGE HADDAD

GHALGHOUL

Maqam Lebanese
Modern Art Gallery

Debbas
Square

MAR MAROUN

GEMMAYZE

CHARLES DEBBAAS

SAIFI VILLAGE

E   F   G   H

scuba diving available. At the time of research the hotel's rooms were undergoing a much-

needed & extensive refit. **$$$$$**

UPMARKET AND MID RANGE

⌂ **Hazmieh Rotana** [90 H5] (151 rooms & suites) Bd Emile Lahoud, Hazmieh; ☎ 05 458 000; e hazmieh.hotel@rotana.com; www.rotana.com. A bright & warm hotel offering excellent business & leisure facilities & attentive service to both the business & leisure traveller with easy access to the airport, Downtown & local shopping mall. This hotel offers good value. Comprehensive buffet b/fast inc. **$$$$**

⌂ **Casa D'Or Hotel** [123 D3] (76 rooms) Rue Jeanne D'Arc, Hamra; ☎ 01 347 850, 01 746 400; m 03 348 300; e info@casadorhotel.com; www.casadorhotel.com. Long-established hotel in the heart of Hamra, the rooms are functional & clean, though unremarkable, given the price. Location is this hotel's greatest asset. B/fast inc. **$$$**

⌂ **Embassy Hotel** [123 D3] (48 rooms) Rue Makdissi, Hamra; ☎ 01 340 814; m 03 242 281; e info@embasyhotellebanon.com, reservations@embassyhotellebanon.com; www.embassyhotellebanon.com. A clean & adequate mid-range offering in a great central Hamra location but the rooms, all with AC & TV, are quite ordinary considering the price. **$$$**

⌂ **Hayete Guesthouse** [129 B2] (4 rooms) Furn al-Hayek St, Achrafieh; ☎ 01 331 530; m 70 271 530; e info@hayete-guesthouse.com; www.

hayete-guesthouse.com. A good alternative to mainstream hotels, this guesthouse provides charming, individually decorated & clean rooms in a good location for the bars & nightlife of Achrafieh & Gemmayze. All rooms have AC & there is free Wi-Fi with laundry facilities available. **$$$**

⌂ **Lancaster Hotel** [90 B5] (75 rooms & suites) Australia St, Raouche; ☎ 01 787 004, 01 790 810; m 70 878 787; f 01 790 820; e lancasterhotel@lancaster.com.lb, sales@lancaster.com.lb, reservation@lancaster.com.lb; www.lancaster.com.lb. Very comfortable & nicely furnished hotel ideal for business & leisure travellers looking for more comfort & style than some of the other mid-range options. **$$$**

⌂ **Mayflower Hotel** [123 D2] (81 rooms) Nehme Yafet St, Hamra; ☎ 01 340 680; e mayflo@dm.net.lb; www.mayflowerbeirut. com. A long-established hotel in the heart of Hamra which has had some well-known guests over the years including the former British/Russian spy Kim Philby, former Formula 1 world champion Graham Hill & the writer Graham Greene. The rooms, however, are quite ordinary & unexciting but there is a small rooftop pool & the atmospheric Duke of Wellington British-style pub. **$$$**

BUDGET Until relatively recently there was a dearth of accommodation options in this category with little in the way of choice for the backpacker. The good news is that there are now a burgeoning number of cheaper lodgings for those with tight belts. In addition to those reviewed below, the following websites are worth checking out for both existing places to stay and for future developments at the lower end of the hotel scale: www.hostelslebanon.com and www.hostelsclub.com.

⌂ **Cedarland Hotel** [123 D2] (77 rooms) Abdel Aziz St, Hamra; ☎ 01 340 233/4; e info@cedarlandhotel.com; www.cedarlandhotel.com. Although the rooms have rather bland décor, this is the best mid-range choice with all rooms having AC, TV & bathroom & representing excellent value for money. **$$**

⌂ **L'Hotel Libanais** m 03 513 766; e hotelibanais@hotmail.com; www.hotelibanais. com. A great alternative to conventional hotels,

this organisation offers rooms in private houses with local families, enabling a more intimate insight into the city & the country & you are welcomed as part of the family. The company also run a nationwide network of private lodgings, accommodation in monasteries ecolodges, guesthouses & characterful small hotels. For B&B accommodation, a minimum 2-night stay is required & booking can only be done online via their website. **$$**

🏠 Port View Hotel [129 D1] (28 rooms) Rue Gouraud, Gemmayze (opposite Electricité du Liban); ☎ 01 562 722, 01 567 500; e portviewhotel@hotmail.com; www. portviewhotel.com. Well located for Gemmayze's nightlife, the rooms are clean & comfortable with AC & TV. Internet access is charged at US$5/day, & a new bar area was under construction at the time of research. B/fast inc. **$$**

🏠 Regis Hotel [123 G1] (20 rooms) Rue Razi Ain al-Mreisse, near Palm Beach Hotel; ☎ 01 361 845; e regishotel@regishotel-lb.com; www.regishotel-lb.com. Good central location with excellent proximity to the Corniche &

SHOESTRING

🏠 Al Shahbaa Hotel [129 B1] (5 rooms) Pasteur St, Gemmayze (behind Charles Helou bus station); ☎ 01 562 812; m 03 056 048, 71 219 472; e alshahbaahotel@gmail.com; www. alshahbaahotel.com. A cheerful & jolly place with basic but clean rooms with fan & TV. Internet & Wi-Fi access available & there is a good communal area for guests. The rooftop terrace is available for US$10 per night. Airport collection (US$20) & drop off (US$15) is available. Dorms US$10pp. **$**

🏠 Hotel Mushrek [123 D3] (48 rooms) Rue Makdissi, Hamra; ☎ 01 345 773. Very basic but fine for 1 night. Often full with students, so best to call ahead to check availability. Good central Hamra location. **$**

🏠 Pension al-Nazih [129 A1] (10 rooms) Charles Helou Av, Gemmayze; ☎ 01 564 868; m 03 475 136; e halaassali@hotmail.com; www.pension-alnazih.8m.com. A rarity in Beirut: a non-smoking & spotlessly clean budget hotel, with AC & TV in all rooms, making this an excellent choice & conveniently located for the Charles Helou bus station & Downtown area. Wi-Fi (US$9/day) & laundry facilities (US$5 for small loads) are available. An airport pickup service is available for US$25 & a taxi to the airport is US$15. B/fast US$6 extra. Dorm room US$17pp. **$**

🏠 Pension Home Valery [123 G2] (15 rooms) 2nd Fl, Saab Bldg, Phoenicia St, Ain al-Mreisse; ☎ 01 362 169; m 03 725 348; e homevalery@hotmail.com. A slightly bleak-

Hamra district. Clean & basic. TV & AC in all rooms. The hotel also arranges airport pickup to the hotel for US$25 & hotel to the airport for US$15. B/fast US$3 extra & a laundry service is available. **$$**

🏠 University Hotel [123 D2] (28 rooms & suites) Bliss St (opposite the main gate of the AUB), Hamra; ☎ 01 365 390/2; e info@ university-hotel.net; www.university-hotel.net. A good budget option on this busy street. Clean & presentable rooms, all with AC & TV. Internet access available. Used by many AUB students but manages to retain a reasonably quiet ambience! **$$**

looking entrance & interior, though renovations were underway at the time of research. This is one of the cheapest budget options in town with shared bathrooms & toilets, & reasonably clean rooms with a TV in the communal area. Fan cooled in summer but an AC system is promised. **$**

🏠 Saifi Urban Gardens [129 C1] (15 rooms & dorms) Pasteur St, Gemmayze; ☎ 01 562 509; e hello@saifigardens.com; www.saifigardens. com. A gem of a place ideally located for Charles Helou bus station, Downtown & Gemmayze's nightlife. Excellent, clean rooms with a rooftop bar & on-site Arabic-language school for all levels, this friendly, family-run establishment only opened in Jul 2010, & comes highly recommended. Free Wi-Fi. Discounts are available for weekly & monthly stays. Possibly Beirut's best budget option. B/fast inc. Dorm room US$18pp. **$**

🏠 San Lorenzo Hotel [123 C3] (45 rooms) Hamra St, Hamra; ☎ 01 348 604/5. Extremely basic & could be cleaner, but in a good central Hamra location. **$**

🏠 Talal's New Hotel [129 A1] (22 rooms) Charles Helou Av, Gemmayze; ☎ 01 562 567; m 70 562 567; e info@talalhotel.com; www. talalhotel.com. A basic but popular option for backpackers with free internet access & Wi-Fi. Guests also have complimentary use of kitchen facilities. If the hotel is full the rooftop is available for US$8 per night. B/fast US$4 extra. Very close to Pension al-Nazih. **$**

Beirut has a burgeoning eating and drinking scene and new establishments are sprouting up all the time. There is a huge choice both in terms of price and also the type of cuisine, including the famous Lebanese *mezze*. Most of the international fast-food and drink chains such as KFC, McDonald's, Nandos, TGI Fridays, Costa Coffee and Starbucks, Hard Rock Café et al are all represented in the city as are more independent eateries serving French, Italian, Chinese and Japanese food, including sushi. As with shopping, different areas of the capital tend to have their own distinct flavour and the following selections of restaurants and watering holes are by no means exhaustive; in Beirut you are never far from somewhere to eat or drink and, unlike in many Arab or Middle Eastern countries, alcohol consumption is not taboo. Bear in mind though that some of the places listed get very busy at certain times, especially at weekends, and it is probably always best to book a table in advance.

EXPENSIVE

✗ **Al Dente** [129 A3] 137 Abdel Wahab el-Inglizi St, Achrafieh; ✆ 01 339 797; e restaurant@albergobeirut.com; www. albergobeirut.com; ⏱ 13.00–15.00 & 20.00–23.00 Sun–Fri, 20.00–23.00 Sat. Legendary restaurant, part of the Albergo Hotel, serving excellent Italian cuisine in surroundings every bit as luxurious as the hotel itself. $$$$$

ABOVE AVERAGE

✗ **Abdel Wahab** [129 A3] 51 Abdel Wahab el-Inglizi St, Achrafieh; ✆ 01 200 550/1; e ghia@ghiaholding.com; www.ghiaholding. com; ⏱ 12.00–midnight daily. Often touted as the best place to experience a wide variety of Lebanese cuisine amid authentic Ottoman-era décor with the grills & mezze amongst the best in the city. $$$$
✗ **Le Rouge** [129 B1] 15 Gouraud St, Gemmayze; ✆ 01 442 366; e info@lerougebeirut. com; www.lerougebeirut.com; ⏱ 10.00–00.30 Mon–Sat, 17.00–00.30 Sun. A good, homely French bistro serving excellent international cuisine including a delicious smoked salmon

MID RANGE

✗ **Barometre** [123 D2] Makhoul St, Hamra; ✆ 01 367 229; m 03 678 998; ⏱ 19.30–late daily. Great intimate Latino atmosphere in this small, friendly bar with nice, rustic appeal & decent menu of chicken & hummus. $$$
✗ **Gemmayze Café** [129 A1] Gouraud St, Gemmayze; ✆ 01 580 817, 01 447 319;

✗ **La Table d'Alfred** [129 C2] 360 Sursock St, Achrafieh; ✆ 01 203 036; e info@latabledalfred. com; www.latabledalfred.com; ⏱ 13.00–15.00 & 20.00–23.00 Mon–Fri, 20.00–23.00 Sat. Upmarket & luxuriously decorated with a huge cellar stocking hundreds of Lebanese & world wines to accompany the fine French menu. Very impressive – bring your credit card. The adjacent Lounge Bar has nightly live piano music. Ideal venue for business visitors. $$$$$

pizza. This place can get very busy, so advisable to book ahead. $$$$
✗ **Manara Palace Café** [90 A2] Manara, opposite Riviera Hotel, Corniche; ✆ 01 364 949; m 03 753 887; e palacecafe@hotmail.com; ⏱ 24/7. A large & excellent eatery by the lighthouse on the Corniche for inside & al fresco dining whilst watching fishermen cast their nets into the Mediterranean. Great food including a wide selection of fresh fish & there is live Arabic music & dancing from 22.00. This is also a good place to puff on a nargileh (LBP9,000–12,000). $$$$

⏱ 09.00–01.00 Mon–Sat, 16.00–01.00 Sun. Akin to a traditional English tea room, this long-established & atmospheric venue serves decent food & offers the chance to try a nargileh (sheesha pipe). Hosts live Arabic music after 22.00. $$$
✗ **Kababji** [123 E3] Saroulla Bldg, Hamra St,

Hamra; ☎ 01 741 555; m 03 265 100; e kabab-ji@kabab-ji.com; www.kabab-ji.com; ⊕ 09.00–01.00 daily. Tasty & filling Lebanese food from this chain eatery in unpretentious surroundings. $$$

✗ **De Prague** [123 D3] Makdissi St, opposite Vinci clothing store & HSBC Bank, Hamra; ☎ 01 744 864; m 03 575 282; ⊕ 09.00–late daily. With its colourful & low cushioned seating this is a cosy & homely venue for a good coffee, cakes & croissants. Patronised by a predominantly young, intellectual clientele, this is also a good place for Wi-Fi users in a quiet café without the distraction of daytime music. $$$

✗ **Laziz** [123 D3] Hamra Sq, Hamra St, Hamra; ☎ 01 353 433; www.laziz.me; ⊕ 07.00–02.00 daily. A great informal '100% Lebanese' eatery in the heart of Hamra serving a range of dishes & delicious desserts including a fantastic orange cake. $$$

✗ **Napoletana** [123 C3] Hamra St, Hamra; ☎ 01 345 444, 01 355 117; ⊕ 09.00–midnight daily. An excellent & family orientated pizzeria serving generous portions accompanied by excellent service in the heart of Hamra. $$$

✗ **Olio** [129 B1] Gouraud St, Gemmayze;

☎ 01 563 939; www.lotus-group.net; ⊕ 12.00–midnight daily. Great Italian restaurant serving pizzas from their wood ovens & equally delicious risotto in relaxed surroundings. Advisable to book ahead as it gets very busy. They also have another branch off Makdissi St, Hamra (☎ 01 741 133). Delivery to hotel/home is also available. $$$

✗ **Paul** [129 A1] Gouraud St, Gemmayze; ☎ 01 570 170, 01 582 222; ⊕ 08.00–midnight daily. Hugely popular, & justifiably so, large French bakery & café serving delicious cakes, pastries & coffee in a great atmosphere. A good place for breakfast. There is a pleasant outdoor seating area for people-watching on this busy street & the toilets are wheelchair-user friendly. $$$

✗ **Simply Red Café** [123 E3] Estral Bldg, Hamra St, Hamra; ☎ 01 353 986; e simplyredbeirut@gmail.com; www.simplyredbeirut.com; ⊕ 08.30–late Mon–Sat, 10.00–late Sun. Patronised by a predominantly young, artistic & intellectual crowd, its retro-style red seating offers a good range of alcoholic & non-alcoholic drinks, salad, snacks & tapas with live bands on 1 of its 3 floors in an overall cordial atmosphere. $$$

CHEAP AND CHEERFUL AND ROCK BOTTOM

✗ **Barbar** [123 D4] Spears St, Hamra; ☎ 01 379 778/9; ⊕ 24/7. Beirut's quintessential street snacking experience with a delicious array of meat, fish & rice dishes & sandwiches. $$

✗ **Bliss House** [123 D2] Bliss St, Hamra, opposite American University of Beirut; ☎ 01 366 290/1/2; ⊕ 06.30–02.00 daily. Very popular & good-value fast-food take-away, serving burgers, sandwiches, juice & ice cream. $$

✗ **Bread Republic** [123 C3] Hamra St, Hamra (opposite Bank Audi); ☎ 01 739 040; e info@breadrepublic.com; www.breadrepublic.com; ⊕ 07.30–23.00 daily. Excellent bakery/café with outdoor seating that use organic ingredients for their delicious range of pastries & snacks. The coffee is good here too & located in the same alleyway as the weekly Tue Earth Market (see page 115). $$

✗ **Captain's Cabin** [123 B3] Adonis St, near the TSC Supermarket on Sadat St, Hamra; ☎ 01 740 516; m 03 431 749; ⊕ 17.00–late daily. Opened in 1964, this atmospheric & terrific

nautical-themed bar resembles a British pub complete with pool table, dartboard & summer garden area. Owned & run by the friendly André, this is a great place for an easy-going few drinks or even a night out. $$

✗ **Godot** [129 B2] Gouraud St, Gemmayze; ☎ 01 575 770; e cocoelio@hotmail.com; ⊕ 15.00–03.00 daily. Unusually for Beirut & Lebanon, Wed is no-smoking night in this lovely, welcoming little hostelry which serves a range of draught beer & cocktails; bar snacks are also available. $$

✗ **Kadche** [123 D2] Bliss St, Hamra (opposite American University of Beirut); ☎ 01 377 872; ⊕ 08.00–midnight Mon–Sat. A decent Lebanese eatery with an excellent selection of breakfast, lunch & dinner menus. The plat du jour is good value. $$

✗ **Le Chef** [129 B1] Gouraud St, Gemmayze; ☎ 01 445 373, 01 446 769; ⊕ 07.00–midnight Mon–Sat. A delightful & unpretentious intimate little restaurant with rustic charm & fantastic home-cooked Lebanese cuisine with a new menu daily. Highly recommended. $$

✘ **Shrimpy** [90 B4] Raouche, Corniche; ☎ 01 790 878, 01 796 667, 01 804 488; ⏰ 09.00–02.00 daily. A no-frills seafood diner but makes up for this with serving an excellent range of seafood at good prices. A kind of slightly more upmarket McDonald's, but with fish. $$

✘ **Torino Express** [129 B2] Gouraud St, Gemmayze; m 03 248 606; ⏰ 09.30–late daily. A small, laid-back bar by day, it gets very busy in the evenings serving beers, champagne, spirits & cocktails accompanied by a good range of music. Also sells a small selection of bar snacks. $$

✘ **Whistles Snacks** [123 C2] Sidani St, Hamra; ☎ 01 747 110; m 70 484 567; ⏰ 09.30–21.00 Mon–Sat. A small, friendly little eatery serving tasty burgers, sandwiches, coffee & cake & snacks. $$

✘ **Rabbit Hole** [123 C3] Makdissi St, Hamra; m 03 534 787, 03 803 912; ⏰ 15.00–late daily, happy hour 17.00–20.00. With free Wi-Fi, this small, intimate but lively bar caters to a predominantly young Beiruti crowd with the low-key lighting adding a nice atmosphere. An Almaza beer costs LBP5,000 & bar snacks including chicken & steak sandwiches are around LBP9,000–12,000. $

ENTERTAINMENT AND NIGHTLIFE

Unlike many countries in the Arab world and the Middle East, Beirut is very much a place which embraces hedonistic pursuits in all their infinite variety. In fact, if your penchant was just for these aspects of the city alone, and given the sheer range of offerings, you could easily spend a week in the capital and not set foot inside a museum and still leave feeling you have had a good time. New places and nightspots are opening up at a frenetic rate and the monthly *Time Out Beirut* magazine keeps itself updated with the latest venues. The following places, therefore, are not exhaustive but represent a selection of venues for a contrasting evening's entertainment. A useful website, www.BeirutNightlife.com, has listings for all things nocturnal in Beirut (well, almost), plus a host of other attractions and events in the city.

MUSIC AND NIGHTCLUBS

☆ **Acid** [90 H5] Sin el Fil, adjacent to the Futurscope Exhibition Hall; m 03 115 777; e acidnightclub@hotmail.com; www.acidnightclub.blogspot.com; ⏰ 22.00–06.00 Fri/Sat; admission US$20 before midnight. A popular, tactile & gay-friendly club with a spectacular sound & laser show. Very loud & crowded with the DJ spinning a range of techno, house, funk & oriental discs.

♀ **Bar Louie** [129 B1] Gouraud St, Gemmayze; ☎ 01 575 877; m 03 791 998; ⏰ 20.00–late Mon–Sat. Live jazz, blues & Latin music nightly in this popular & friendly venue. Like The Blue Note Café, this bar has a slightly more relaxed atmosphere than some others in the city. Good Spanish, French & American food is also served.

☆ **Behind the Green Door** [129 D1] Nahr St, Mar Mikhael (opposite the Lebanese Electricity Authority bldg); ☎ 01 565 656; m 70 856 866; ⏰ 20.00–late daily. The name apparently derives from a cult 1980s 'artistic' porn movie & its green,

purple & red velvety & boudoir-like interior does have a certain seductive appeal. Attracting a predominantly student & 25+ clientele this venue has character & is certainly less mainstream than most & worth a visit especially if your musical tastes embrace loud dance, indie & rock music to the wee hours. Fri nights in Aug get very busy & it's advisable to book ahead.

☆ **B018** [129 F1] Charles Malek Av, Karantina, near Forum de Beyrouth; ☎ 01 580 018; m 03 810 618; ⏰ 20.00–03.00 Thu–Sat; www.b018.com. The brainchild of Lebanese architect Bernard Khoury, this club pounds out the tunes until the wee hours when the retractable roof opens to reveal the city skyline at dawn. A Gothic-like interior with seating resembling coffins, this place is something of an institution & like Acid above, is a gay-friendly establishment.

♀ **Buddha Bar** [104 D6] Asseily Bldg, Riad al-Solh Sq, Downtown; ☎ 01 993 199;

e buddhabar@buddhabarlebanon.com; www.
buddha-bar.com; ◷ 20.00–04.00 daily. Part of
the international French chain, this spacious &
lavishly decorated venue over 2 floors is overseen
by an imposing effigy of a Buddha & a good
restaurant serving international food to music
which switches from kama to dance as the evening
progresses. Not cheap, bring a credit card (or 2).
☆ **Cloud 9** [129 C1] Gouraud St, Gemmayze;
↘ 01 566 376; www.cloud9beirut.com;
◷ 19.00–late daily. Inspired by New York lounge
bars the décor is ultra-modern & cocktails & food
are aiso served in a less high-octane ambience
than many other bars in the city.
♀**Mojo Jazz Club** [123 D3] Rbeiz Bldg, Hamra
St, facing old Hamra Theatre near Costa Coffee,
Hamra; m 70 796 279, 03 443 033; e mojo@
mojobeirut.com, waleed@musikuest.com; www.
mojo-beirut.com; ◷ 15.00–02.00 Mon–Sat,
20.00–02.00 Sun; Happy Hour (buy 1 drink get 1
free) 18.00–21.00 daily; music charge LBP10,000
(local artists), LBP22,000 (international artists).
Live nightly jazz & blues music in more modern
& spacious surroundings than The Blue Note Café
below, & patronised by a more lively 30s crowd.
Their website has a weekly events calendar.
☆ **Pacifico** [123 A2] Monot St, Achrafieh;
↘ 01 204 446; ◷ 19.00–01.30 daily, happy hour
19.00–20.00. Jazz 19.30–21.30 Mon. A highly
popular venue with a Latino atmosphere serving

decent Mexican fare as well as cocktails & other
drinks. Prices are a little on the high side.
☆ **Palais by Crystal** [129 A3] Monot St,
Achrafieh; ↘ 01 338 964; m 03 854 455; www.
thecrystalgroup.net; ◷ 23.00–late Thu–Sat. Set
in a very modern, chic venue, this place caters to
an equally chic & sophisticated glamorous,
clubbing clientele belting out a wide range of
sounds.
♀**Sky Bar** [104 H1] BIEL (Beirut International
Exhibition & Leisure Centre) Downtown; ↘ 03
939 191; e info@sky-management.net; www.
sky-bar.com; ◷ summer 20.00–late Tue–Sun.
This very glitzy rooftop bar & club, with great
views over the city & mountains, is very much the
'in' place to go for thrill seekers. Voted best bar in
the world in 2008. Booking advisable as it gets
packed & admission is a steep US$100+pp for a
table for 8.
♀**The Blue Note Café** [123 D2] Rue Makhoul,
Hamra (near the American University of Beirut);
↘ 01 743 857; www.bluenotecafe.com;
◷ 12.00–01.00 Mon–Sat; 'music charge'
LBP10,000–18,000 depending on the artist.
Long-established, intimate & homely venue for
live jazz, oriental & Latin music most nights. They
also serve a good selection of Lebanese mezze &
steak dishes which make this a popular haunt for
dining amid the live music. Reservations
recommended at weekends.

CINEMAS These mainstream multi-complex cinemas mostly serve up the usual
mainstream diet of Hollywood blockbusters and such like. The English-language
The Daily Star newspaper and the monthly *Time Out Beirut* magazine contain
details of current showings.

🎬 **Empire Cinema City** (9 screens)
City Mall, Dora Highway; ↘ 01 899 993;
www.circuit-empire.com
🎬 **Empire Dunes** [90 C5] (5 screens) Dunes
Centre, Verdun St, Verdun; ↘ 01 792 123;
www.circuit-empire.com
🎬 **Empire Sodeco** [129 A3] (6 screens) 3rd Fl,
Block A, Sodeco Sq, Damascus Rd, Achrafieh;
↘ 01 616 707; www.circuit-empire.com
🎬 **Grand ABC** [129 C3] (7 screens) ABC Mall,
Achrafieh St, Achrafieh; ↘ 01 209 109, 01 209
208; m 03 164 625; www.grandcinemas.com

🎬 **Grand Concorde** [123 E4] (8 screens)
Concorde Centre, Dunant St, Verdun;
↘ 01 343 143; m 03 374 491;
www.grandcinemas.com
🎬 **Metropolis Empire Sofil** [129 C2]
(2 screens) Ground Fl, Sofil Centre, Av Charles
Malek, Achrafieh; ↘ 01 204 080; e info@
metropoliscinema.net; www.metropoliscinema.
net. An exception to the rule, this venue screens
films across a wide range of genres including
art-house movies & is a venue for film showings
during Beirut's annual film festivals.

Cinema clubs The venues below all offer a more independent and avant-garde
film experience.

Academie Libanaise des Beaux-Arts (ALBA Cineclub) ALBA Campus, Av Emile Edde, Sin El Fil; ☎ 01 480 056; admission free. Screens alternative & modern classic films every Fri at 19.00.

Cine Club 43 Club 43, Gouraud St, Gemmayze; m 03 708 811; admission LBP2,000. Screenings every Sun at 19.15. All profits go towards providing a weekly free lunch for Beirut's less fortunate.

De Prague Cineclub [123 D3] 166 Makdissi St, Hamra; m 03 575 282; admission free. Nightly screenings at 21.00 but note that the films are shown without sound but subtitled in Arabic, English or French.

L'Ecole Superieure des Affaires (ESA) [123 F2] ESA Auditorium, Clemenceau St, Hamra; ☎ 01 373 373; admission free. Screenings every Tue at 20.30, usually in French or with French subtitles.

Simply Red Café [123 E3] Estral Bldg, Hamra St, Hamra; m 03 181 585, 03 563 804; admission free. Screenings on Thu at 19.30 with each month featuring a different director's work.

THEATRES All of the venues listed below put on shows in Arabic, English and French and tickets can be bought at the venues themselves and occasionally, depending on the type of performance, from the Virgin Megastore in Downtown (see page 115). Apart from visiting the theatre in person be sure to take a look at the monthly *Time Out Beirut* magazine and the back page of the English-language *The Daily Star* newspaper for details of current and up and coming performances and cultural events.

Al Madina Theatre [123 F3] Saroula Bldg, Hamra St, Hamra; ☎ 01 753 010/1; e masmad@cyberia.net.lb; www. almadinatheatre.com. Having recently undergone an extensive refit at the time of research, including new seating, it is now once again staging concerts, dance, plays & educational workshops, in Arabic, English & French.

AUB (American University of Beirut) Theatre [123 C2] Bliss St, Hamra; ☎ 01 374 374 ext 4350 (Dept of Fine Arts & Art History); www. aub.edu.lb. Students & faculty members put on a handful of shows annually, usually during May, in the 250-seat West Hall auditorium on the AUB campus. The works performed range from concerts to dance, & plays are mostly in English though Arabic & French plays are also performed.

Babel Theatre [123 E3] Marignan Centre, Cairo St, Hamra; ☎ 01 744 033/4; m 71 144 767; e info@babeltheatre.com; www.babeltheatre. com. An excellent 300-seat theatre, founded in 2007 & converted from an old cinema, stages performances across a range of genres including plays, stand-up comedy & experimental works. Holds drama workshops & acts (no pun intended) as a vehicle for self-expression for writers & artists from Arab countries where this is often problematic.

Monnot Theatre [129 A2] University St Joseph St, Achrafieh; ☎ 01 202 422; e monnot@usj.edu.lb; www.usj.edu.lb; Aug closed. Extremely active theatre staging about 60 eclectic productions annually, mainly in French & Arabic, together with concerts & dance.

The Sunflower Theatre [90 H7] Sami Solh Av, Tayouneh; ☎ 01 381 290; m 03 035 298. Another theatre with a prolific output of performing arts, around 3 performances per month, & it is also the venue for the Lebanese Puppet Theatre.

CONCERTS

Lebanese National Higher Conservatory of Music (LNHCM) [91 G4] Achrafieh; ☎ 01 489 530/1/2/3; f 01 500 996; e info@ conservatory-lb.com; www.conservatoire.org.lb. In addition to being a centre of excellence for the education & training of future musicians, the orchestra has a very prolific output & between Oct & Jun performs in excess of 100 concerts across both Arabic & World Music genres. Times, venues & performance details are usually available on the LNHCM website.

SPORT AND ACTIVITIES The beautiful game – **football** – though not as religiously followed as in countries like Italy, Spain or the UK, nevertheless enjoys a popular following in Beirut though there are no players who are household names outside the country, whilst Lebanon's July 2011 FIFA World Ranking of 177 (out of 203 countries) does not exactly make the country one of the giants of the sport. The city's two most famous football (soccer) teams are Beirut Al-Ansar and Beirut Al-Nejmeh; the former holding the Guinness World Record for winning the most consecutive domestic league titles (11 between 1988 and 1999). The best place to find out when and where they are playing is to have a look at *The Daily Star* newspaper or *Time Out Beirut* magazine for venues and kick-off times.

Although primarily a male preserve, **horse racing** is a passionately followed sport with seven to eight races per meeting at Lebanon's only racecourse, the Hippodrome du Parc de Beyrouth [90 G7] (*Abdallah Al-Yafi Av, just behind the National Museum;* ✆ *01 632 515;* e *sparca@cyberia.net.lb, sparca.leb@gmail.com; www.beiruthorseracing.com; during Jul/Aug races commence at 13.30 Sat, the rest of the year at 12.30 Sun; admission LBP5,000–15,000*). This is a great way to spend an afternoon amongst the raucous Beirutis betting with a frenzy, but don't expect facilities characteristic of Newmarket or Ascot in the UK.

For aficionados of **golf** the Golf Club of Lebanon [90 F7] (*Ouzai, Bir Hassan, a short distance north of the airport;* ✆ *01 826 335/6/7;* f *01 822 474;* m *03 609 412;* e *info@golfclub.org.lb; www.golfclub.org.lb;* ⏰ *07.00–19.00 daily*) is located in a very scenic and tranquil setting and has the country's sole 18-hole championship course. Non-members are permitted to use the course, which costs US$40 during the week and US$60 on weekends and public holidays. Equipment hire is available as an optional extra. The club also has tennis and squash courts, snooker and billiard tables, a swimming pool, restaurants and a children's playground which can also be used by visitors.

For those with a penchant for **sub-aqua** there are plenty of opportunities for both novice and experienced divers to don wetsuit and aqualung. The National Institute for Scuba Diving (NISD) [104 A2] (*Beirut Marina, Solidere area;* ✆ *01 739 203;* m *03 204 422;* e *info@nisd-online.com; www.nisd-online.com*) has been running courses and dive expeditions since the 1980s and has three boats which conduct open dive visits around the waters of the capital as well as in the north and south of the country. The **Calypso Diving Club** [90 B5] (*Mövenpick Hotel & Resort, General de Gaulle Av, Raouche;* m *03 533 338, 03 876 057*) also has a good reputation for quality tuition and offers beginner courses and dives from shore and boat together with underwater videography and exploration of wrecks.

BEACH CLUBS With Beirut being a coastal city, the capital is a hedonist's and sun-worshipper's paradise, and in true Lebanese fashion beaches are places to be seen in as much as they are for rest and recreation. All of the following have ample facilities (except an abundance of sand) and although there is a free public beach at Ramlet al-Bayda it is distinctly lacking, and most people gravitate towards the private clubs simply for the caché of being private and stylish!

La Plage [123 F1] Ain al-Mreisse; ✆ 01 366 222; m 03 374 437; ⏰ 09.00–20.00 daily; admission LBP25,000. Not quite as good as the nearby St Georges but it has a nice open-air restaurant, jacuzzi & swimming pool.

Mövenpick Hotel & Resort [90 B5] General de Gaulle Av, Raouche; ✆ 01 869 666; e hotel. beirut@moevenpick.com; www.moevenpick-hotels.com; ⏰ 07.00–20.00 daily. Although it is only open to hotel guests, this has Beirut's sole beach club located directly onto the sea. Part of the Swiss hotel chain, it offers a varied experience with a marina, private beach, 4 swimming pools & a host of activities ranging from banana-boat rides to water skiing.

Riviera Hotel [90 B2] Av de Paris, Ras Beirut, Corniche; ✆ 01 373 210; m 03 322 600; e info@ riviera-yachtclub.com, prive@rivierahotel.com.lb; www.rivierahotel.com.lb; ⊕ 08.00– late daily; admission: adults LBP30,000 Mon–Fri, children LBP25,000 Mon–Fri, adults LBP40,000 Sat/Sun, children LBP25,000 Sat/Sun; hotel guests free. Once epitomising Beirut's 'Paris of the Middle East' image, their recently renovated Beach

Lounge has 3 swimming pools, jacuzzi, pool bar, a VIP lounge, jet skiing & scuba-diving activities. **Saint-George Yacht Club & Marina** [104 A2] Ain al-Mreisse; m 03 958 379; e hotel@ stgeorges-hotel.com; www.stgeorges-yachtclub. com; ⊕ 09.00–18.00 daily; admission: adults LBP25,000 Mon–Fri, children LBP20,000 Mon– Fri, adults LBP30,000 Sat/Sun, children LBP25,000 Sat/Sun. This former playground of the rich & famous & overlooked by the equally famous ruined shell of the St George Hotel remains one of the best options with adult & children's swimming pools, bar, restaurant & an overall cordial atmosphere.

SHOPPING

If the concept of retail therapy had a capital city then Beirut would certainly be among the shortlist of contenders. The Syrian poet and writer Nizar Qabbani once commented that it was *de rigueur* for any businessman to take his wife's shopping list with him when visiting Beirut. In fact, most Beirutis are inveterate shoppers and there is no shortage of opportunities to check out the latest Beirut bling, international fashion labels, textiles and crafts. The main thing to bear in mind when shopping in the capital is that, for the most part, it is not the traditional or exotic experience characteristic of many other Arab and Middle Eastern cities. If you think of Dubai, London's Oxford Street or New York's Fifth Avenue you will get some idea of the retail experience which awaits you in the city. The following areas are among the most popular shopping neighbourhoods in the city but new chains and stores are constantly opening so the shops mentioned represent just a selection of what's on offer. For what's hot on the current shopping scene have a look at *Shop Beirut* (2009) by Marwan Naaman, available via Amazon and at many Beirut bookstores.

ACHRAFIEH Situated just east of Downtown, this Christian area is an attractive district home to designer clothing, jewellery, antique and home furnishing stores, especially around the Sassine Square area. The one-stop **ABC Shopping Mall** [129 C3] (*Alfred Naccache St;* ✆ *01 212 888;* e *info@abc.com.lb; www.abc.com.lb;* ⊕ *10.00–22.00 daily*) sells a comprehensive range of international fashion labels for men, women and children. The complex also boasts cinemas, restaurants and free parking. Described as the 'social working class in Lebanon' is the weekly **Souk al-Ahad** [129 E4] or Sunday market (Jisr al-Wateh, Beirut River, near Achrafieh) which, unlike the majority of Lebanese shopping, sacrifices aesthetics for utility; the market is more akin to a car boot sale in the UK, selling almost everything imaginable from plugs to clothing at much cheaper prices than elsewhere. Take a service taxi from the museum or Dora station. If you want to buy local arts and crafts whilst at the same time supporting the endeavours of local craftsmen then visit **L'Artisan du Liban** [129 C1] (*Rue Montée Accawi, Achrafieh;* ✆ *01 364 880;* ⊕ *10.00–18.00 Mon–Sat*).

BOURJ HAMMOUD This area provides a contrasting shopping aesthetic to most other shopping districts in the city and is a world away from the malls and trendy streets of Verdun and Downtown. With its distinctive Armenian cultural identity, the area offers more competitively priced jewellery, clothing and craft stores centred on the busy Arax and Armenia streets where you can pick up more bargain-priced items (see page 131).

DOWNTOWN Beirut Central District (BCD) or Solidere, as it is also known, provides the core of the city's upmarket retail experience. Interspersed with luxury hotels and pavement cafés are a range of internationally known fashion labels and brands. Shopping highlights include:

Aishti [104 E4] Moutran St & Beirut Souks; ℡ 01 991 111; e info@aishti.com, customerservice@aishti.com; www.aishti.com; ⏱ 10.00–20.00 Mon–Sat

Beirut Souks [104 E4] Modern & glitzy market areas which, in addition to its shopping options, houses numerous cafés, restaurants & cinemas (see page 126).

Boutique 1 [104 D4] 2 Park Av; ℡ 01 981 666; e beirut@boutique1.com; www.boutique1.com; ⏱ 1 Jul–30 Sep 10.00–21.00 Mon–Sat, 15.00–20.00 Sun; 1 Oct–30 Jun 10.00–20.00 Mon–Sat, closed Sun

Elie Saab [104 C4] Elie Saab Bldg; ℡ 01 981 982; e boutiquelb@eliesaab.com; www.eliesaab.com; ⏱ 10.00–19.00 Mon–Sat. (See box, page 116, for details of Lebanese designer Elie Saab.)

Karen Millen [104 E4] Allenby St; ℡ 01 999 929; www.karenmillen.com, ⏱ 10.00–20.00 Mon–Sat

Saifi Village [104 F7] A short walk southeast of Martyrs' Sq; ℡ 01 980 650/660; e info@solidere.com.lb; ⏱ 10.00–19.00 Mon–Sat. Another Solidere initiative, this delightful little district is described as the 'artistic destination at the heart

of Beirut City Centre' containing an eclectic range of shops not found in many of the city's shopping malls. There are over 30 stores & the Quartier des Arts is full of art galleries, antique & craft shops.

Souk el Tayeb [104 G6] 266 Gouraud St, Gemmayze, in the car park just north of Saifi Village; ℡ 01 448 129; m 03 340 198; e info@soukeltayeb.com; www.soukeltayeb.com; ⏱ 09.00–14.00 Sat. Launched in 2004, this is Lebanon's first weekly farmers' market, selling a wide range of organic & non-organic local produce from farmers all over the country.

Virgin Megastore [104 F5] Opera Bldg, Martyrs' Sq; ℡ 01 999 666; ⏱ 10.00–midnight daily. Part of the international chain of shops, this one is reputedly the largest outside the UK, stocking the usual range of music & movie DVDs, books, magazines & newspapers. This is also the place to book tickets for a wide range of festivals & theatrical events.

Vivienne Westwood [104 F4] Bldg 127, Foch St; ℡ 01 971 315; www.viviennewestwood.co.uk; ⏱ 10.00–20.00 Mon–Sat

HAMRA Although usurped in recent years by the rapidly developing areas of Downtown, Achrafieh and Verdun, this is still a hive of retail activity with some 200 stores, and its hustle and bustle is more akin to a Western high-street shopping experience. The main streets for all kinds of goods, including clothes, are Rue Hamra and Bliss Street. There is also the **ABC Shopping Mall** [123 C3] (*Hamra St;* ℡ *01 344 740;* e *info@abc.com.lb; www.abc.com.lb;* ⏱ *10.00–20.00 Mon–Sat*), which specialises in women's wear. For those seeking less mainstream items, the **Oriental Art Centre** [123 D2] (*Rue Makhoul, Hamra;* ℡ *01 349 942;* ⏱ *09.00–13.00 & 15.30–18.00 Mon–Sat*) sells retrospective items such as old postcards and photographs of a bygone age in the Middle East. Just north of Hamra **Artisans du Liban et d'Orient** [123 G1] (*Ain al-Mreisse, Corniche;* ℡ *01 362 610;* ⏱ *10.00–18.00 Mon–Sat*) specialises in souvenir items from the region. The **Earth Market** ([123 C3] *alleyway joining Hamra St & Makdissi St, facing Bread Republic; www.earthmarkets.net*) takes place every Tuesday between 09.00 and 14.00. Farmers and other vendors sell their wares including homemade honey and jam, fresh fruit and vegetables, new and secondhand books, DVDs and other electronic devices, etc.

VERDUN A very modern development since the 1990s boasting predominantly luxury boutiques and related outlets from many of the world's top-end designer brands, Rue Verdun is the place to start your forays into high-class chic. The beast of a shopping mall, **Dunes Centre** [90 C5] (*Verdun St;* ☎ *01 785 310/1; www.dunes. com.lb;* ⊕ *10.00–20.00 daily*) offers designer brands plus a range of international eateries, cinemas and ATMs. **Verdun 730** [90 C5] and **Verdun 732** [90 C5], either side of Rachid Karame Street, are other ultra-modern shopping malls.

SUPERMARKETS Although there are many corner shops and minimarkets dotted around the city, for more extensive food and grocery shopping Beirut is also well supplied with supermarkets offering both local and international products. Those listed below are just a snapshot of what's available and the Hamra neighbourhood has a particularly plentiful supply.

Consumers Co-op [123 C3] Rue Name Yawed, Hamra; ☎ 01 348 465; e hamracoop@sodetel. net.lb; ⊕ 07.00–23.00 Mon–Sat, 09.00–21.00 Sun. Good range of groceries, household & clothing items. Free delivery.

Dekkaneh Jeanne D'Arc St, Hamra; ☎ 01 739 699, 01 739 701; ⊕ 06.30–00.30 daily. Good range of groceries & produce with free delivery.

Goodies [90 C5] Rue Verdun, Verdun; ☎ 01 796 797; www.goodies.com.lb; ⊕ 08.00–20.00 Mon–Sat. Part of the nationwide chain of supermarkets selling a comprehensive range of groceries & general household & cosmetic items.

Idriss Supermarket [123 D3] Sourati St, Hamra (opposite Bank of Beirut); ☎ 01 743 770; m 70 918 441; e info@idriss.net; ⊕ 07.30–22.00 Mon–Sat, 08.00–17.00 Sun. A long-established & well-stocked supermarket with a range of fruit, vegetables & meats. They also offer free delivery to home or hotel.

Spinneys [129 C2] Mar Mitr St, Achrafieh; ☎ 01 210 110; e info@spinneys-lebanon.com, customer_service@spinneys-lebanon.com; www.spinneys-lebanon.com; ⊕ 08.00–23.00

ELIE SAAB

Born in Beirut on 4 July 1964, Elie Saab is Lebanon's best-known couturier famous for his modern, elegant and feminine designs. With boutiques in Beirut, Paris and Harrods in London, his career direction appeared to be sewn up at the tender age of nine. Utilising his mother's curtains and tablecloths, he would sketch designs and make items of clothing for his sisters. Following a brief sojourn to Paris in 1981 to study fashion, he returned to Lebanon after a year to open his first atelier in Beirut. Later that year he enjoyed instant success with his first collection shown at the Casino du Liban. In 1997, he became the first foreign designer to become a member of the Camera Nationale Della Moda (The National Chamber for Italian Fashion), and showcased his first collection outside Lebanon in Rome. Renowned for his evening gowns, Saab also became the first Lebanese designer to have one of his creations worn by an Oscar winner, Halle Berry in 2002, when she won the Best Actress award. Other 'A' list celebrities who have adorned themselves with Saab's finery include Angelina Jolie, Catherine Zeta-Jones, Elizabeth Hurley, Gwyneth Paltrow, Helen Mirren and Queen Rania of Jordan. Recently, Saab has made the journey from the runway to the shipping lanes, designing luxurious yachts evoking the same chic and elegant designs for the high-end boat market and extending 'the experience of luxury beyond the conventional limits of fashion'.

daily. A branch of the nationwide Lebanese chain, this supermarket stocks the full range of everyday groceries.
TSC Plus [123 C3] Sadat St, Hamra; ☎ 01 746 989, 01 746 874; ⏲ 07.00–00.00 daily. Recently opened, this is a good, mid-sized supermarket selling a wide range of items including fruit, vegetables, toiletries, beers & spirits, newspapers & magazines at competitive prices.

BOOKSHOPS Beirut has a great selection of bookshops stocking a wide range of English-language reading matter, and they are also a great place to catch up with newspapers and magazines. The following stores are among the best in the city and all stock books in English, Arabic and/or French.

Bachoura Public Library 3rd Fl, Iswas Al Baladi Bldg, Bachoura; ☎ 01 667 701; ⏲ 09.00–13.00 & 15.00–18.00 Mon–Fri, 09.00–17.00 Sat. This is Beirut's first & biggest public library holding books in many different languages in addition to Arabic, English & French.
Books & Pens [123 C2] Jeanne D'Arc St, Hamra; ☎ 01 741 975; ⏲ 08.00–22.00 Mon–Fri, 08.00–20.00 Sat. Although predominantly specialising in art supplies & stationery, they also sell a decent range of books, newspapers & magazines.
L'Arche de Noé Sadat St, Hamra; ☎ 01 742 663; ⏲ 09.30–18.00 Mon–Fri, 09.30–14.00 Sat. Extensive range of books in Arabic, French & English together with a café & readers' lounge area.
Librairie Antoine [123 D3] Hamra St, Hamra; ☎ 01 341 470/1; ⏲ 08.30–19.00 Mon–Sat; Sassine Sq, Achrafieh; ☎ 01 331 811; e contact@antoineonline.com; www.antoineonline.com. This store has been established for well over 70 years & sells an eclectic range of travel & non-fiction books in Arabic, French & English. Antoine also has 8 other branches around the country. Quite possibly Lebanon's finest & best-stocked bookshop.
Libraire Orientale [129 C3] Achrafieh St, Achrafieh; ☎ 01 200 875, 01 333 379; ⏲ 08.30–19.00 Mon–Fri, 08.30–14.00 Sat; www.librairieorientale.com.lb. Maps, travel books, newspapers & magazines in Arabic, English & French. They also have another good branch on Hamra St (opposite Bread Republic), Hamra; ☎ 01 736 524; ⏲ 08.30–19.00 Mon–Fri, 08.30–14.00 Sat.
Maliks [123 D2] Bliss St, Hamra (opposite main gate of the AUB); ☎ 01 741 975; e maliks@maliks.com; www.maliks.com; ⏲ 08.00–22.00 Mon–Fri, 08.00–17.00 Sat. Stocks mainly academic books but will order any title. Also sells office supplies & provides a while-you-wait passport photo service as well as copying, courier & internet facilities. Has other branches in Verdun & Achrafieh.
Virgin Megastore (see *Downtown*, page 115)

OTHER PRACTICALITIES

FOREIGN CONSULATES AND EMBASSIES IN BEIRUT AND ENVIRONS
🄴 **Australia** [104 C6] Embassy Complex, Serail Bldg, Downtown; ☎ 01 960 600, 01 960 670 visa section; f 01 960 601; e austemle@dfat.gov.au; www.lebanon.embassy.gov.au; ⏲ 08.30–16.00 Mon–Thu, 08.30–13.30 Fri
🄴 **Austria** [129 B2] 8th Fl, Tabaris Bldg, Charles Malek Av, east of Saifi Village, Achrafieh; ☎ 01 213 017, 01 213 052; f 01 217 772; e beirut-ob@bmeia.gv.at; www.bmeia.gv.at/en/embassy/beirut; ⏲ 07.30–15.30 Mon–Fri, 08.30–13.00 for visas & other services
🄴 **Belgium** [104 E7] Amir Bachir St, Downtown; ☎ 01 976 001; f 01 976 007; e beirut@diplobel.fed.be; www.diplomatie.be/beirut; ⏲ 07.30–15.00 Mon–Fri; ⏲ 08.00–10.00 Mon–Fri for the visa section
🄴 **Canada** [90 H3] 1st Fl, Coolrite Bldg, Jal al-Dib; ☎ 04 713 900; f 04 710 593; e berut-cs@international.gc.ca; www.lebanon.gc.ca; ⏲ 08.30–11.30 Mon–Fri
🄴 **China** 72 Nicolas Sursock St, Mar Elias; ☎ 01 856 133; f 01 822 492; e chinaemb_lb@mfa.gov.cn; www.lb.china-embassy.org; ⏲ 09.00–15.00 Mon–Fri
🄴 **Denmark** [104 C6] Embassy Complex, Serail Bldg, Downtown; ☎ 01 991 001/2/3; f 01 991

006; e beyamb@um.dk; www.ambbeirut.um.dk;
⏰ 08.00–16.00 Mon–Thu, 08.00–14.00 Fri

❸ Finland (Consulate) [90 H7] 3rd Fl,
Chaoui Bldg, Badaro St, Badaro; ☎ 01 396 704;
f 01 387 307; www.finlandconsulate.gov.lb;
⏰ 09.00–15.00 Mon–Fri

❸ France [90 H6] Rue de Damas, Achrafieh,
near University of St Joseph & French Cultural
Centre; ☎ 01 420 000; f 01 420 013; www.
ambafrance-lb.org; ⏰ 08.00–13.00 & 14.00–
16.30 Mon–Fri

❸ Germany Maghzal Bldg, near Jesus & Mary
School, Mtayleb, Rabieh; ☎ 04 935 000;
m 03 600 053 (24/7 emergency number);
f 04 935 001; e info@beirut.diplo.de; www.
beirut.diplo.de; ⏰ 07.30–16.30 Mon–Tue,
07.30–15.15 Wed–Thu, 07.30–13.30 Fri during
summer, 07.30–16.45 Mon–Thu, 07.30–13.30 Fri
during winter

❸ Ireland (Consulate) Badaro St, opposite
Chevrolet, Badaro; ☎ 01 395 005;
☎/f 01 392 005; e irishcon.leb@hotmail.com;
⏰ 09.00–13.00 Mon–Fri

❸ Italy Rue du Palais Presidentiel, Baabda;
☎ 05 954 955; f 05 959 615/6; e amba.beirut@
esteri.it; www.ambbeirut.esteri.it;
⏰ 09.00–13.00 Mon–Fri

❸ Japan [104 C6] Embassy Complex, Serail
Bldg, Downtown; ☎ 01 989 751/2/3; f 01 989
754; www.lb.emb-japan.go.jp; ⏰ 08.00–16.00
Mon–Fri, visa section ⏰ 08.00–12.00 Mon–Fri

❸ Jordan southeast of the Presidential Palace,
Baabda; ☎ 05 922 500;
☎/f 05 922 502; ⏰ 08.30–14.30 Mon–Fri

❸ Kuwait [90 C7] Bir Hassan; ☎ 01 822 515;
f 01 840 613; e info@kuwaitinfo.net; www.
kuwaitinfo.net; ⏰ 08.30–14.00 Mon–Fri

❸ Netherlands [129 C2] Netherlands Tower,
Charles Malek Av, Achrafieh; ☎ 01 211 150; m 70
189 389 (24/7 emergency number) f 01 211 173;

e bei@minbuza.nl; www.netherlandsembassy.
org.lb; ⏰ 07.30–15.30 Mon–Fri; consular & visa
section ⏰ 09.00–12.30 Mon–Fri by prior
appointment only

❸ Norway [104 C6] Embassy Complex, Serail
Bldg, Downtown; ☎ 01 960 000; f 01 960 099;
e emb.bey@mfa.no; www.norway-lebanon.org;
⏰ 09.00–16.30 Mon–Fri, consular section
⏰ 10.00–13.00 Mon–Fri

❸ Republic of South Korea Rue du Palais
Presidentiel, Baabda; ☎ 05 953 167;
f 05 953 170; e lbkor@mofat.go.kr; www.lbn.
mofat.go.kr; ⏰ 08.00–16.00 Mon–Fri

❸ Spain Palace Chehab, Hadath; ☎ 05 464 120;
f 05 464 030; e emb.beirut@maec.es; www.
embajadaenlibano.maec.es; ⏰ 08.00–15.00
Mon–Fri

❸ Switzerland Bourj al-Ghazal Bldg, General
Fouad Chehab Av, Achrafieh; ☎ 01 324 123, 01
324 129; f 01 324 167; e bey.vertretung@eda.
admin.ch; www.eda.admin.ch/beirut; ⏰ 08.30–
11.00 Mon–Fri

❸ Turkey 3rd St, Rabieh; ☎ 04 520 929, 04 520
939; f 04 407 557; www.beirut.emb.mfa.gov.tr;
⏰ 09.00–15.00 Mon–Fri

❸ UK [104 C6] Embassy Complex, Serail Bldg,
Downtown; ☎ 01 960 800 (24/7); f 01 990 420,
01 960 855; e visa.beirut@fco.gov.uk (visa
queries); www.ukinlebanon.fco.gov.uk;
⏰ 08.00–16.00 Mon–Thu, 08.00–14.00 Fri

❸ United Arab Emirates (UAE) [90 C7]
Ramlet el-Baida, Jnah; ☎ 01 857 000; f 01 857
009; e eembassy@uae.org.lb; ⏰ 08.30–12.00
Mon–Fri

❸ USA [90 H3] Rue Amin Gemayel, opposite
Awkar Municipality Bldg, Awkar; ☎ 04 542 600,
04 543 600; f 04 544 136, 04 544 861;
e beirutacs@state.gov, beirutpd@state.gov;
www.lebanon.usembassy.gov; ⏰ 08.00–11.00
Mon, Tue, Thu

BANKS Given the importance of financial institutions as the mainstay of the
Lebanese economy it will come as little surprise to learn that banks proliferate
throughout the city and country and transactions are usually carried out very
efficiently with services easily up to the standards of most European and US banks.
There are also innumerable 24/7 ATM machines for cash withdrawals throughout
Beirut dispensing money in either LBP or US$. Opening hours can vary between
different banks and even between different branches of the same bank but generally
speaking, they are open between 08.00 and 15.00 Monday to Friday and 08.00–
12.00 or 13.00 on Saturday. The following are a small selection of some of Lebanon's
main banks and their conveniently located branches in the capital.

$ **Bank Audi** [123 C2] Bliss St, Hamra; 01 361 714/5; www.banqueaudi.com. Lebanon's largest bank with 80 branches nationwide & over 20 in the capital.

$ **Bank of Beirut** [123 E2] Ground Fl, Block A, Gefinor Centre, Hamra; 01 738 767/8/9; www.bankofbeirut.com.lb

$ **Bank of Beirut & Arab Countries (BBAC)** 250 Clemenceau St, Hamra; 01 364 883; www.bbacbank.com

$ **Banque Bemo** Banque Bemo Bldg, Elias Sarkis Av, Achrafieh; 01 200 505; www.bemobank.com. One of Lebanon's smallest banks with just 9 branches located nationwide but most

have an ATM machine.

$ **Blom Bank** Rachid Karami St, Verdun; 01 738 938; www.blom.com.lb. Voted Best Bank in the Middle East in 2009.

$ **Byblos Bank** Rachid Karameh St, Verdun; 01 805 100; www.byblosbank.com.lb

$ **BankMed** [104 F4] Weygand St, Downtown; tel/f 01 992 061/2/3/4; www.bankmed.com.lb. At the time of writing BankMed has 51 branches countrywide, including 25 in Beirut, & whose market share is around 10% of Lebanon's banking system.

$ **HSBC** [123 D3] Rbeiz Bldg, Abdul Aziz St, Ras Beirut; 01 760 000; www.hsbc.com.lb

COURIER SERVICES When time is of the essence, or bulky or valuable items need to be sent, there are a number of courier companies which can arrange this. The 'big three' all have offices in Beirut.

DHL 01 629 700; www.dhl.com.lb. DHL has a plentiful supply of offices throughout the city & these are listed on their website.

Federal Express (FedEx) 01 987 000; www.fedex.com/lb

UPS Azouri Bldg, 711 Alfred Naccache St, Achrafieh; 01 218 575; e info@unitedcouriers.net; www.ups.com/lb

CULTURAL AND INFORMATION CENTRES

British Council [90 H6] 8th Fl, Berytech Bldg, Damascus Rd; 01 428 900; e general.enquiries@lb.britishcouncil.org; www.britishcouncil.org/lebanon; ⏰ 09.00–18.00 Mon–Fri

Centre Culturel Français de Beyrouth [90 H6] Espace des Lettres, Rue de Damas, near the National Museum; 01 420 200, 01 420 230; f 01 420 207; www.ccf-liban.org. A very active cultural centre which hosts a regular range of conferences, events & lectures together with dance, film & theatre showings & a range of language courses.

Instituto Cervantes [104 E6] 2nd Fl, Bldg 287, Rue Maraad, Downtown; 01 970 253; e cenbei@cervantes.es; www.beirut.cervantes.es. Runs a range of Spanish language courses & hosts many cultural events from concerts to films.

Goethe-Institut Beirut [90 H6] 7th Fl, Berytech Bldg, Damascus Rd; 01 422 291/2;

f 01 422 294; e info@beirut.goethe.org; www.goethe.de/beirut; ⏰ 09.00–17.00 Mon–Thu, 09.00–13.00 Fri. Offers a number of German language courses as well as a varied range of events across the cultural spectrum. Also has a well-stocked library.

Italian Institute of Culture Beirut Najjar Bldg, Rue de Rome, Hamra; 01 749 801/2; e iicbeirut@esteri.it; www.iicbeirut.esteri.it; office ⏰ 09.00–16.30 Mon–Thu, 09.00–15.00 Fri. In addition to running Italian language courses the institute works in partnership with many of Lebanon's most prestigious universities & organisations including UNESCO, Sursock Museum & the National Conservatoire & has its own stand at the annual Beirut International Book Fair.

Ministry of Culture [90 E4] Hatab Bldg, Rue Madame Curie, Verdun; 01 744 250/1/2/3; www.culture.gov.lb

DOCTORS AND HOSPITALS

✚ **American University of Beirut Medical Centre (AUBMC)** [123 D2] Cairo St, Hamra; 01 374 374, 01 350 000; e aubmc@aub.edu.lb;

www.aubmc.org. This private 420-bed hospital provides a full range of medical services, including accident & emergency, & has a prestigious reputation throughout Lebanon & the Middle East.

✚ **Clemenceau Medical Centre** [123 F3] Rue Clemenceau, Hamra; ☎ 01 372 888; hotline ☎ 1240; e info@cmc.com.lb; www.cmc.com.lb. With its glass façade, mature leafy trees & salubrious interior, you could be forgiven for thinking that this is the latest 5-star offering from an international hotel chain. In fact this is a well-respected hospital, affiliated with John Hopkins International, utilising state-of-the-art medical facilities.

✚ **Doctors at Home** [129 B1] Pasteur St, Gemmayze (near Charles Helou bus station); ☎ 01 444 400; m 03 609 998. A 24/7 emergency call-out service with doctors charging US$60 for a day/evening visit. Nursing care charged at US$40/day.

✚ **Dr Rizk Clinic** [129 B4] Rue Zahar, Ashrafieh; ☎ 01 200 800; e info@cliniquerizk.com.lb; www.cliniquerizk.com

✚ **Home Visiting Doctor** Achrafieh; hotline m 70 112 116; e drghabre@hotmail.com; www.homevisitingdoctor.com. Offers a 24/7 call-out service to homes & hotels with full nursing support.

✚ **Hôtel-Dieu de France** [129 C4] Rue Alfred Naccache, Achrafieh; ☎ 01 615 300; e hdf@usj.edu.lb; www.hdf.usj.edu.lb

✚ **Najjar Hospital** [123 E3] Abdul Baki St, close to Gefinor Centre, Hamra; ☎ 01 340 626; e najjarhp@inco.com.lb. A 61-bed private modern hospital offering a comprehensive & state of the art range of medical facilities including emergency admissions.

✚ **Sahel General Hospital** [90 F7] Airport Av, Ghobeiry; ☎ 01 858 333; e info@sahelhospital.com.lb; www.sahelhospital.com.lb

✚ **St George Hospital University Medical Centre** [129 D2] Rue Rmeil, Achrafieh; ☎ 1287 (within Lebanon); 01 441 000, 01 575 700 (outside Lebanon); www.stgeorgehospital.org

EXCHANGING TRAVELLERS' CHEQUES
At the time of research there was a dearth of places willing to exchange travellers' cheques, with only the following bureaux happy to do so, upon production of a receipt and your passport.

Friends Exchange [123 C3] Hamra St, Hamra; ☎ 01 348 469; m 03 217 515/6; ⏰ 09.00–19.00 Mon–Sat. Situated directly opposite Caribou café, they charge a flat-rate 5% commission.

Lebanon Exchange [123 C3] Hamra St, Hamra; ☎ 01 749 309; m 03 219 953, 03 363 080; ⏰ 09.00–21.00 Mon–Sat, 11.00–20.00 Sun. This exchange bureau is located opposite Vero Moda & Caribou café. They charge US$10 per transaction.

INTERNET
Ubiquitous throughout Beirut and other cities in the country, you should have no problem gaining access to the internet, including Wi-Fi, at most hotels, cafés and restaurants. The area around the vicinity of the American University of Beirut (AUB) is an especially good source of internet cafés and there is an increasing number of Internet Service Providers (ISPs) for those with wireless-enabled laptops. A selection of ISPs and internet access locations is listed below.

e **Cyberia** ☎ 01 744 101; www.cyberia.net.lb
Destination ☎ 01 577 222, 01 234 716; www.destination.com.lb
e **Iconet Data Management (IDM)** ☎ 01 512 513; www.idm.net.lb

e **Lynx Internet** ☎ 01 296 096, 01 296 090; e info@lynx.net.lb; www.lynx.net.lb
e **Terranet** ☎ 01 577 511; e info@terra.net.lb; www.terra.net.lb

Internet cafés
The following cafes are just a small selection of the many available in the capital, with all offering decent internet facilities and charges generally hovering around LBP3,000/hr. In the evening especially some cafes are often patronised by the younger generation playing computer and video games with a consequent increase in noise (and smoke) levels so choose your time carefully if you require more sedate email checking and surfing time. As well as these dedicated

internet venues see also the *Where to eat and drink* section, as an increasing number of cafes offer free Wi-Fi for those with laptops.

e Bits 'n Bytes [123 C2] Rue Jeanne D'Arc, Hamra; ✆ 01 742 211; ⊕ 24/7. Good, high-speed access with plenty of computers & refreshments available.
e Firewall Sidani St, Hamra; ✆ 01 739 497; ⊕ 11.00–02.00 Mon–Sat, 18.00–02.00 Sun
e PC Club [123 C2] Sidani St, Hamra; ✆ 01 745 338

e Sky Net St 53 (off Mahatma Gandhi St), Hamra, Beirut Smith's Info Village, 49 Rue Sadat, Hamra
e The Net Mahatma Gandhi St, Hamra
e Web Café [123 C2] Rue Makhoul, Hamra; ✆ 01 348 881

LAUNDRETTES Although there is no shortage of places offering a dry-cleaning service, including many hotels, the city is not exactly awash with laundrettes. The following friendly and efficient establishment is a tried-and-tested option, and is highly recommended if you want to avoid the steep costs charged by the high-end hotels for washing your clothes.

Laundromatic [123 C3] Jabre Doumit St, off Jean D'Arc St, near Mayflower Hotel & La Cigale Patisserie, Hamra; ✆ 03 376 187; ⊕ Jul–Sep 09.00–17.00 Mon–Sat, Oct–Jun 08.00–18.00 Mon–Sat, closed Sun & public holidays. This excellent laundry, Lebanon's 'first coin-operated laundromat' according to their carrier bag, will collect (LBP1,500) & deliver (LBP1,500) your laundry within the Hamra area & they also offer an ironing & free delivery of dry-cleaning service within the Hamra district. For self-service wash loads less than 4.5kg the cost is LBP5,500 & for loads of 4.5–8kg LBP7,000, excluding detergent, with the dryer costing LBP3,000/10mins.

PHARMACIES

✚ Berty Pharmacy [129 C3] Achrafieh St, near Librairie Orientale & Sassine Sq; ✆ 01 200 767; f 01 327 744; e info@phberty.com; ⊕ 08.00–23.00 Mon–Sat, 09.00–22.00 Sun. An excellent pharmacy with a comprehensive supply of drugs & medicines.
✚ Mazen Pharmacy [90 D6] Bd Saeb Salam, Mazraa; ✆ 01 313 362; ⊕ 24/7
✚ Pharmacie Vitale [129 B1] Gouraud St, Gemmayze; ✆ 01 446 043, 01 564 037; ⊕ 08.00–22.00 Mon–Sat
✚ Phoenicia Pharmacy [123 G1] Near Regis & Phoenicia hotels, Ain al-Mreisse; ⊕ 08.00–midnight daily. Excellent selection of cosmetics & general medicines.
✚ Ras Beirut Pharmacy [123 B3] Sadat St (facing Lebanese American University), Hamra; ✆ 01 788 383, 01 869 830; ⊕ 08.00–midnight daily. Good range of prescription & non-prescription drugs.
✚ Sami Pharmacy [123 A3] Manara, opposite Beirut Luna Park; ✆ 01 343 888; m 71 343 888; e sami@samipharmacy.com; www.samipharmacy.com; ⊕ 24/7. A well-stocked, newly opened & ultra-modern pharmacy with staff who can also check blood pressure & glucose levels; there is also a small consulting room for treatment of minor ailments.
✚ Wardieh Pharmacy [123 E3] Wardieh Sq, Rue Sourati, Hamra; ✆ 01 343 679, 01 751 343, 01 751 345; ⊕ 24/7. Good pharmacy. Close to the American University Hospital (AUH) & Clemenceau Medical Centre (CMC).

POST Lebanon's national postal service is **Libanpost** (✆ *01 629 629; www.libanpost. com.lb*) and their branches and post boxes are easily recognised by their distinctive yellow signs. The company have numerous branches and post boxes throughout the city and nationwide providing an efficient and comprehensive range of postal services including *post restante* and redirection of mail. Some will even change US$ to LBP. Post office opening hours are generally 08.00–17.00 Monday to Friday and from 08.00 to 13.00 or 13.30 on Saturdays with all branches closed on Sunday. The following outlets are in convenient and central locations in the city's main areas and districts.

✉ **Achrafieh** [129 C3] Ogero Bldg, Sassine Sq; ☎ 01 321 657, 01 202 019

✉ **Bourj Hammoud** [129 G2] Armenia St; ☎ 01 260 543

✉ **Downtown** [104 D5] Ogero Bldg, Riad al-Solh St; ☎ 01 992 777. At the time of research this branch was in the process of installing an internet café which will go a long way to making

up for the current dearth of such facilities in the Downtown area.

✉ **Gemmayze** [129 B1] Gouraud St; ☎ 01 442 902

✉ **Hamra** [123 D3] 1st Fl, Matta Bldg, Makdissi St; ☎ 01 354 706

✉ **Rafiq Hariri International Airport** [90 F7] upstairs in Departure Terminal; ☎ 01 629 369

WHAT TO SEE AND DO

The Lebanese capital is not exactly endowed with a *mezze* of historical sights and attractions in the traditional sense. Whilst icons of the rejuvenation of the city are a key feature of Downtown and icons of war like the still-standing but bullethole-ridden Holiday Inn Hotel in Ain al-Mreisse possess a certain war kitsch, the city's pull lies in its people and its quartet of neighbourhoods. These highlights offer the visitor a fascinating and insightful glimpse into a people and a city which continues to fall victim to stereotypes based on events which occurred over 20 years ago. A visit to the National Museum should help to emphasise the diversity and richness of the country's history whilst a night out in the districts of Achrafieh or Gemmayze will dispel notions that the main preoccupation of the Lebanese is guns and conflict. Here life is lived with a capital 'L', from clubbing to shopping. Strolling the treelined Corniche in west Beirut is to experience a cosmopolitan and laid-back feel to the city as both Christians and Muslims freely mingle.

WEST BEIRUT This predominantly Muslim area broadly covers that part of the city west of Downtown between Ain al-Mreisse and Ras Beirut – the 'headland' of the city – and along the Corniche south to the public beach at Ramlet al-Bayda and incorporating the busy district of Hamra.

Hamra The beating heart of west Beirut takes its name from the word 'Ahmar', a reference to the reddish hue of the area's soil. This commercial and financial district has always been the hangout for a cosmopolitan, artsy, intellectual and student population. Thronged with shops, cafés, restaurants and moneychangers along the main Hamra Street the district is also the location for most of Beirut's mid-range hotels, cinemas, theatres, late-night bars and art galleries. Once eclipsed by Gemmayze in east Beirut for its nightlife, Hamra is once again beginning to reassert itself as the haunt for night owls. If proof were needed that Beirut was once a thriving publishing centre, a stroll along Hamra Street with its innumerable magazine and book stands together with a whole range of quality bookshops selling both mainstream and specialist titles will surely dispel any doubts. Hamra's main downside for the visitor is the sheer density of vehicular traffic which packs into its many narrow streets and where the atonal symphony of horn honking is constant. Such is the upbeat feel to this area that in 2010, the annual Hamra Street Festival (see box, page 133) was held for the first time since 1998. The whole area reverberates with life and is one of the best places in the city for a tour by foot for its atmosphere alone, though there are a few engaging sites, such as the American University of

KEY

1 Mayflower Hotel
2 Whistles Snacks
3 Laundromatic
4 Rabbit Hole
5 San Lorenzo Hotel
6 Consumers Co-Op
7 Bread Republic
8 Napoletana
9 Friends Exchange and Lebanon Exchange
10 ABC Shopping Mall
11 Hotel Mushrek
12 De Prague Café
13 Oriental Art Centre
14 Barometre
15 Bliss House
16 Idriss Supermarket

BEIRUT West

MEDITERRANEAN SEA

RAS BEIRUT

MANARA

KOREITEM

SANAYEH

KANTARI

JOUMBLAT

AIN EL MREISSE

JAMAA

HAMRA

American University of Beirut (AUB)

AUB Archaeological Museum

Lebanese American University

Intercontinental Le Vendome
La Plage
Hard Rock Café

Artisans du Liban et d'Orient
Palm Beach
Phoenicia Pharmacy
Regis
Intercontinental Phoenicia
Holiday Inn

Pension Home Valery

Al Madina Theatre
Concord Travel

Beirut Theatre

L'Ecole Supérieure des Affaires
Gefinor Rotana

Clemenceau Medical Centre

Bank of Lebanon
Ministry of Tourism

Liberty Tower, Alitalia & KLM
Concorde Square Shopping Centre
Ministry of Culture

Sierra Leone
Lebanese Red Cross HQ

Sanayeh Garden (René Moawad Public Garden)

Lebanese Red Cross HQ

Gefinor Centre & airline companies
American University Hospital
HSBC Hospital

Najjar Pharmacy
Babel Theatre
Kababji & Simply Red Café
Mojo Jazz Club
Hamra
Barbar
Montreal

Wardieh Pharmacy

Books & University Pens
Web Café
Bits 'n Tania Bytes Travel

Malitis
Hotel
Campus Travel

Librairie du Liban
Kadche
Blue Note Café
Agial Art Gallery
Cedarland

Casa D'Or

Librairie Antoine
Hamra Mosque

Art Circle Caribou Café
Le Commodore

PC Club
Police
Royal Jordanian Airlines
Captain's Cabin

Sami Pharmacy
Raouché Arjan by Rotana

Beirut by Bike

0   200m
0   200yds

Denmark
UK
Finland
Saudi Arabia
Bahrain
India
Michel Chiha
Paraguay

Poland
Embassy
Mexico
America

PARIS AVENUE
BAR EL MRAISEH
JOHN KENNEDY
CLEMENCEAU
MOHAMAD ABDUL BAKI
MAAMARI
CAIRO
SOURATI
AZIZ
SITT NASSAB
MAKDISI
OMAR BIN ABDUL AZIZ
IBRAHIM ABDUL AAL
JEANNE D'ARC
HAMRA
NEHME YAFET
BLISS
SIDANI
YAMOUT
CHIEKH ELIAS GASPARD
ANTOUN GEMAYEL
MAHATMA GHANDI
BAALBAK
SADAT
MADAME CURIE
EMILE EDDE (LEON)
AL HUSSAIN
WADI SABRA
MOUSTAFA KAMAL
ALFRED NOBEL
TABARI
ROMA
DUNANT
ROOSEVELT
REBEIZ
AMINE MNEIMNEH
GEORGE ASSI
ALAMEDDINE
MARRY EDDE
MEDHAT PACHA
HALAMANI
JUSTINIAN
AMIR OMAR
SPEARS
BOUTHOUR
WATWAT
SANAYEH
Al QALAA
El Jazari Square
BLISS
NEGIB ARD TANNOUKHIYEN
MANARA
VENUS
BAHRAIN
CALIFORNIA
KUWAIT
LABBAN
ADONIS
MANSOUR JURDAK
Versailles
BOLIVAR
KHALED CHEHAB
BADR DEMACHKIEH
SALAH ED DINE EL AYOURI
AL QALA
CHATILA
LAMMENS
AMIR OMAR
MICHEL CHIHA
KAMAL ZOBEL
KANTARI
RUSTOM RACHA
IBN SINA
RAZI
WHINET-EL-HOSN
STREET
LONDON
PHOENICA
MAY ZIADEH
Jamal Abd El Nasser Square
Rustom Racha

Beirut (see following section), which shouldn't be missed. For a bit of peace and quiet from Hamra Street, head for the **Sanayeh Garden** [123 F4] (*Emile Edde St, opposite the law faculty of the Lebanese University, Sanayeh;* ⊕ *winter 06.00–18.00 daily, summer 06.00–19.30 daily*), which first opened in 1907, and is the city's oldest public garden with children's play areas and an all-round jovial family atmosphere – a perfect setting for a family picnic.

Less than 2km south of Hamra is the relatively new area of **Verdun**; an exclusive residential and shopping district which dates from the latter part of the 1990s and which is often described as Beirut's version of New York's Fifth Avenue. Packed with expensive apartment buildings, cafés and restaurants, Lebanese and international designer clothing stores, it has a rather soulless feel despite its affluence but if upmarket retail therapy is your thing then you will be in shopaholic heaven here. The epicentre of the area is around Rue Verdun and Rachid Karami, where there are a number of large department stores in addition to the smaller and no less expensive boutiques.

American University of Beirut (AUB) [123 D1] (*Bliss St, Hamra;* ⤥ *01 340 460, 01 350 000;* e *information@aub.edu.lb; www.aub.edu.lb;* ⊕ *09.00–17.00 Mon–Fri, 09.00–13.00 Sat; admission free; upon entering proceed to the security office & leave your passport & you will be given a visitors' card which you present on leaving & your passport will be returned. The Visitors' Bureau on your right down the steps after the entrance offers free half- & full-hour tours of the campus conducted by students 09.00–16.00 Mon–Fri, 09.00–13.00 Sat, though a donation is appreciated*) Since its founding in 1866, this private, non-sectarian university which teaches all classes in English has become one of the most prestigious seats of higher education in the Middle East. It is a well-respected institution worldwide, with many well-known people having been educated there including the new Lebanese prime minister-designate Najib Mikati.

Founded by the Reverend Daniel Bliss, it was originally called the Syrian Protestant College prior to adopting its present name, and its 74 buildings extend over 61 acres of beautifully manicured landscaped grounds with its verdant scenery extending to the coast where it has its own student and public beach. In what must be a delightful place to study, the campus grounds are well worth a couple of hours of wandering to get a glimpse of student life and take in the attractive neo-Ottoman architecture. It is also worth checking out the university's website as they hold regular lectures on a range of topics which visitors are often welcome to attend. The campus is also home to a varied collection of fauna and flora and an excellent archaeological museum.

AUB Archaeological Museum [123 D2] (*Bliss St, Hamra;* ⤥ *01 340 549;* e *frndmuse@aub.edu.lb; www.aub.edu.lb/museum_archeo;* ⊕ *summer 10.00–16.00 Mon–Fri, winter 09.00–17.00 Mon–Fri, closed during university & public holidays; admission free; audio guide LBP3,000. For wheelchair users there is disabled access to the museum's 2nd floor*) This museum, one of the oldest in the Middle East, was founded in 1868, and is organised over two galleries. The first gallery exhibits large archaeological finds from the Stone-Age and Bronze-Age periods in Lebanon and the wider region. The second, and more archaeologically extensive, displays a range of smaller artefacts from the Iron Age, Hellenistic, Roman, Byzantine and Islamic eras.

In addition to housing a fine collection of antiquities, the AUB Museum is also engaged in ongoing archaeological digs in Downtown Beirut, the Bekaa Valley and in neighbouring Syria. The museum also runs regular exhibitions, organises a programme of events for children and holds regular lectures by professors and visiting archaeologists between October and June each year and in 2010, held a children's 'make your own mummy day'. Although not as extensive as the National Museum, the exhibits are all well presented and labelled in Arabic and English, and it is well worth visiting for its hive of information such as the stages of manufacture employed by the ancient Phoenicians to manufacture purple dye for garments sold to the rich and the royal.

CORNICHE A good place to start what is almost a Beirut ritual, and obligatory stroll for any visitor, is from opposite the Palm Beach Hotel in Ain al-Mreisse and then walk west along this 8km strip of promenade dotted with palm trees to the public beach at Ramlet al-Bayda. It's an attractive walking tour at any time of day but early morning is usually dominated by joggers and strollers with women sporting designer tracksuits and men fishing from the Corniche. Itinerant tea and coffee vendors clunk their cups whilst others cycle or push their carts along to tempt you with *ka'ik*, a circular type of bread with sesame seeds. But the people mosaic really comes to the fore in the evenings and at weekends when cyclists, rollerbladers, couples and families all take to the Corniche for what becomes one big social occasion with people bringing their own chairs to sit and smoke the *nargileh*.

Shortly after passing the famous Riviera Hotel, which basically epitomises the area you are now walking along, you come to the Manara Lighthouse which, I was told by a hotelier, the Israelis spared during the 2006 July War with their helicopter gunship only interested in taking out the light. The **Beirut Luna Park** [90 A3] is unmissable, dominated by its large colourful Ferris wheel (LBP2,000 per person), which illuminates the night sky. This compact funfair is a haven for families and couples with a smattering of rides including dodgem cars and a café. A little further along this western stretch of the Corniche is the appropriately named Raouche, which is the Arabic version of the French word *rocher* meaning 'rock'. These two 60m-high **Pigeon Rocks** [90 A4], the city's sole geological attraction, are relics from one of the numerous earthquakes which have afflicted the city and are an enchanting and romantic sight come sunset where courting couples can often be seen leaning over the Corniche's railings admiring these natural wonders. There are a couple of small cafés which overlook the rocks, offering a great vantage point and setting at sunset. It is also possible to walk down the steep 100m path from the cliff edge for a closer look at these natural rock formations from sea level, and boat owners will take you around and through the rocks' inlets for a fee of around US$15–20 day or night.

DOWNTOWN Once the anarchic arena for rival militias during the 1975–90 civil war, the Downtown area of the city, also known as Beirut Central District (BCD) or Solidere, became the focal point of the war, devastating the former prosperous commercial district. This area was also the location for the most notorious symbol of the conflict, the Green Line, which divided the city into Muslim west and Christian east Beirut, making the area effectively a no-go zone for civilians and visitors alike. Since the mid 1990s, however, the sound of machine gun and sniper fire has been replaced by the clattering machinery of reconstruction filling the void of a once-desolate wartime landscape. The totally transformed area which you see today has been undertaken by **Solidere** (*The Lebanese Company for the Development & Reconstruction of Beirut Central District; Bldg 149, Saad Zaghoul St;* ✆ *01 980 660;* e *solidere@solidere.com.lb; www.solidere.com*) since 1994, which was initiated by former prime minister Rafiq Hariri. Hariri poured millions of his own personal fortune into this ambitious and futuristic project, which envisaged a completely new city of commercial and residential developments to drive Lebanon's economic rejuvenation and percolate through to other spheres of the economy following 15 years of negative economic fortunes.

Ironically, it also took 15 years of conflict to help unearth the city's more illustrious past with archaeologists who have worked with Solidere in tandem with the bulldozers to uncover important ramparts from antiquity to the Crusader eras, some of which are still visible in Downtown, such as the Roman baths, whilst others are on display in Beirut's National Museum. The heavily restored and pristine expanse of real estate which you see today has undoubtedly transformed this once-barren landscape and contributed to the oft-quoted cliché of Beirut's Phoenix-like revival from the ashes of war. However, the reconstructed French and Ottoman façades, plush designer stores, cafés and restaurants have not met with universal approval. Locals often bemoan the lack of character to the place and the almost clinical feel of reconstruction. Nowhere is this more the case than the recently opened **Beirut Souks** [104 E4] on the northern section of Downtown. Here, spread over 128,000m², are a plethora of expensive boutiques, clothing and jewellery stores, an entertainment complex with 14 cinemas and more designer labels than Avery! Don't let the word 'souk' fool you into visions of traditional Arab markets full of intrigue and the aroma of spices – this area is a pure glitzy and modernist shopping mall through a concrete jungle of walkways with not a hint or whisper of *1,001 Arabian Nights.*

To the south of the Beirut Souks is **Nejmeh Place** [104 E5], often also referred to as Place de Etoile or Stars Square, where a series of roads radiate out from the central Art-Deco clock tower containing cafés, restaurants and shops. The clock tower, with its Rolex face, dates back to the French Mandate era and is a stone's throw away from the Lebanese **Parliament Building** [104 E5] where soldiers may not always appreciate you taking photographs. The **Grand Serail Building** [104 C6], just west of Nejmeh Place, is the office of the prime minister. It has been nicely restored since its Ottoman roots but again, at the time of writing, photographing this building could result in a telling off from soldiers. The nearby **Ottoman Clock Tower** [104 C5] was built in 1897 in honour of the tenth anniversary of the coronation of Sultan Abdel Hamid. Just below and in front of the Serail are the quite extensive remains of some **Roman baths** [104 D5] which were discovered in the late 1960s but only restored since the late 1990s, with archaeologists carefully removing the rubble from the civil war to reveal these ancient finds. They are in remarkably good condition, with the heating system devised by the Romans (hypocaust) clearly visible. Set in delightfully manicured gardens with seating, they are well worth a look for the fabulous restoration work done by the archaeological team. Though sectarian groups battled it out for supremacy here, Christian and Muslim architecture continues to stand in contented juxtaposition.

Lebanon's largest mosque, the distinctive blue-domed **Muhammad Al-Amine Mosque** [104 F6], resembling the Blue Mosque in Istanbul, is unmissable southeast of Nejmeh Square, with its four 65m-high minarets, and is particularly impressive when lit up at night; a ray of light arrows its beam towards Mecca. Financed by former premier Rafiq Hariri the mosque is also atmospheric during Friday prayers with the overflow congregation filling the area outside the mosque giving a moving display of the importance of faith. The ornate interior of the mosque is also worth a visit. Adjacent to the mosque is the **mausoleum** of the former Lebanese premier who was slain by a car bomb on Valentine's Day 2005. The shrine is free to visit and enveloped by the national flag and numerous large-scale photographs of

Hariri which make for a moving tribute to the man once the driving force behind Lebanon's post-war regeneration and the Downtown district you see today. More than six years on from his death the site continues to be one of pilgrimage for many Lebanese from across the sectarian divide to a man still regarded by many as a national hero. Its Christian neighbour is the neoclassical **St Georges Maronite Cathedral** [104 E6], dating from the 19th century, which has undergone extensive renovation since the war and is now the city's principal base for Maronite reverence.

Once the epicentre of the Downtown district, the former **Beirut City Centre** [104 F7] building variously known as 'the blob', 'dome', 'egg' or 'bubble' by locals on account of its distinctive shape, is one of the only remaining examples of pre-war architecture in Downtown and sits just a short stroll behind the Muhammad Al-Amine mosque. This grey looking structure dates back to the mid-1960s and was the brainchild of the Lebanese architect Joseph Philippe Karam (1923–76), a leading exponent of modernism. The building was designed as a multi-purpose complex complete with cinema and could once boast the Middle East's largest shopping mall, but the intervention of the civil war halted construction and final completion of the project. Nowadays, the austere structure remains an icon of modernist architectural endeavour and a reminder of war amidst the restored facades of Downtown, much like the similarly iconic and shell-shocked former Holiday Inn hotel in Ain al-Mreisse. The future of the building remains uncertain with continual talk of demolition and, latterly, preservation, by such organisations and pressure groups as Save Beirut Heritage.

To the north of the Al-Amine Mosque opposite the large **Beirut Municipality Building** on Weygand Street stands the **Al-Omari** or **Grand Mosque** [104 E5] (*Weygand St;* m *03 433 513, 03 730 064;* e *info@omarimosque.com; www.omarimosque.com*), which has had the builders in several times over the years. Originally the site of a Byzantine church, then a Roman bathhouse, it was converted by the Crusaders into a cathedral to St John in 1150, before finally being transformed into a mosque in 1291 by the Mamluks. In the author's view, this is the best of the mosques to visit in the area with a fine interior and very friendly staff, but be sure to dress appropriately if visiting. Women visitors must cover their hair.

A few minutes' walk east from the mosque and opposite the Le Gray Hotel is the attractive **Samir Kassir Square and Garden** [104 F5], a compact and quiet little space containing a pool shaded by trees and containing a statue of the former *An-Nahar* newspaper journalist who was assassinated by a car bomb in 2005, and whose employers' towering building is also opposite.

Although it recently acted as an atmospheric backdrop to a fashion-show extravaganza by Lebanese fashion designer Tony Yaccoub, **Martyrs' Square** [104 F6], across the road from the Al-Amine Mosque, has also been the setting for far less salubrious occasions over the years. This three-person statue, the creation of Italian Realist artist Marino Mazacurati (1907–69), stands in honour of the Lebanese nationalists murdered by the Ottomans in 1915–16; the woman holding aloft a torch symbolising an array of light for the future. The square was the setting for the 2005 Cedar Revolution, when a quarter of the country's population descended on the square demanding the truth about the slaying of Rafiq Hariri and calling for an end to Syrian interference and military presence in Lebanon.

A short walk southeast of Martyrs' Square is the newly built **Saifi Village** [104 G7], a leafy, commercial and residential enclave with just a hint of chocolate box-type appeal with its pretty pastel hues giving a nice respite from the hustle and bustle of the main Downtown area. Also referred to as the *quartier des arts*, this pristine area of French colonial-style architecture is home to a variety of eateries, high-end boutiques and Lebanese designer fashion outlets together with a number of art galleries. This small, serene space, another Solidere initiative intended to evoke an urban village, comes alive each Saturday when the car park just north of the village is transformed into a farmers' market (see page 115).

An unlikely presence, perhaps, but Beirut formerly had quite a thriving Jewish community with some 17 synagogues in Downtown alone and over 20,000 Jews living in Lebanon at one time. Today, estimates vary, but the Jewish population in Lebanon is now only somewhere between 20 and 200. Tucked away between the less than kosher streets of France Street and Wadi Abu Jehmiel just north of the Grand Serial, is the remains of the **Maghen Abraham Synagogue** [104 C5] (e contact@ thejewsoflebanonproject.org; www.thejewsoflebanonproject.org), which dates back to 1926. Plans are afoot to renovate the ruins of this important symbol of Jewish identity which still has a discernible Star of David on its walls. The website has a mine of information on the former Jewish community in the country together with details of the restoration project which is just the start of what is hoped to be an ongoing project to restore other synagogues and Beirut's run-down Jewish cemetery.

Robert Mouawad Private Museum [104 B6] (*Army St;* ⅂/f *01 980 970;* e *info@ rmpm.info; www.rmpm.info;* ⏱ *09.00–17.00 Tue–Sun; admission: adults LBP9,000, students LBP1,500*) Not far from the Grand Serail, this cornucopia of opulence contains an eclectic mix of jewellery, metalwork, antiques, carpets, Chinese porcelain, Islamic pottery and books dating from the 12th to the 20th centuries. A former home of Lebanese art collector and connoisseur Henri Pharaon (1901–93), it was transformed by the prominent artist and jeweller Robert Mouawad who has continued to expand the collection. The building itself is also of grand proportions and the extensive gardens, often the location for concerts and weddings, are adorned with Greek and Roman figurines.

EAST BEIRUT Situated to the east of Downtown, this is the traditional heartland of Beirut's Christian community, and evinces a less frenetic daytime pace than many other areas of the capital. This district is home to innumerable cafés, restaurants and shops and is the main hub for the city's nightlife when at weekends, especially in Achrafieh's Rue Monot and Gemmayze's Rue Gouraud, it buzzes with affluent young and style-conscious Beirutis. It also makes a pleasant place for a stroll to admire traditional neighbourhood houses, which have a very French ambience, and the well-respected Francophone St Joseph University (USJ), founded in 1875 by the Jesuits and housing a very engaging prehistory museum.

Gemmayze A few minutes walk east from Downtown's Martyrs' Square, Gemmayze is basically defined by its main Gouraud Street. This long, narrow road is festooned with bars, cafés and restaurants and its traditional old houses with balconies give the area a very rustic and faded sense of grandeur, a nice contrast if you have just emerged from Downtown. Although it is slowly losing its night-time dominance, due in part to pressure from local residents who have managed to get a curfew introduced to curb late-night noise in the area, the street makes for an interesting stroll and is a great place to eat or drink at any time. Just past the excellent Le Chef Restaurant and on the same side of the road are the **St Nicholas Steps** [129 B1–2], which will take you up to Achrafieh. Held twice a year since the early 1990s, these 125 steps and walls are festooned with Lebanese and international artists displaying their creations at the **Gemmayze Stairs Art Festival (Festival Escalier des Arts)** every June and October.

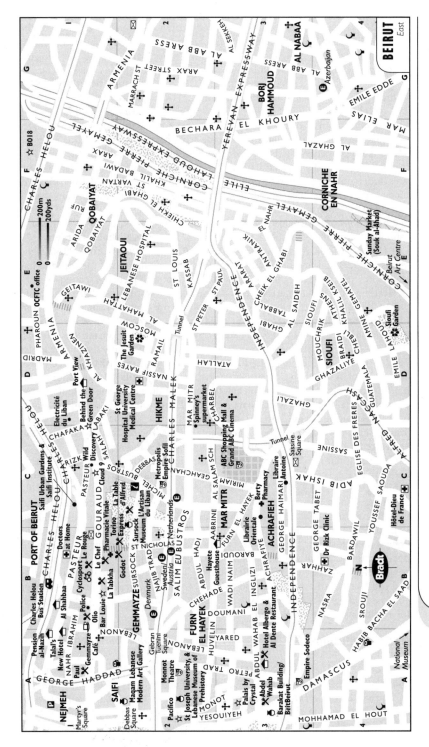

BEIRUT East

Key locations on map:

NEJMEH
SAIFI
PORT OF BEIRUT
GEMMAYZE
FURN EL HAYEK
MAR MITR
ACHRAFIEH
HIKME
JEITAOUI
QOBAIYAT
SIOUFI
BORJ HAMMOUD
AL NABAA
CORNICHE EN NAHR

0 ___ 200m
0 ___ 200yds

Martyr's Square
Debbas Square
Charles Helou Bus Station
Pension al-Mazih
New Hotel
Talal's
Al Shahbaa
Gemmayze Café
Bar Louie
Olio
Le Chef
La Tabkha
Cyclosport Le Rouge
Police
Doctors at Home
Electricité du Liban
Pharmacie Vitale
Torino
Express
L'Artisan du Liban
Sursock Museum
La Table d'Alfred
Wild Discovery
Behind the Green Door
Port View
St George Hospital University Medical Centre
The Jesuit Garden
Lebanese Hospital
Metropolis Empire Sofil
Cloud 9
Godot
Magam Lebanese & Modern Art Gallery
Gebran Tueini Square
Monnot Theatre
Pacifico
St Joseph University, & Lebanese Museum of Prehistory
Palais by Crystal
Abdel Wahab
Barakat Building/ BeitBeirut
Empire Sodeco
Hotel Albergo & Al Dente Restaurant
Hayete Guesthouse
Librairie Orientale
Berty
Pharmacy
Librairie Antoine
Dr Rizk Clinic
Hôtel-Dieu de France
Sassine Square
ABC Shopping Mall & Grand ABC Cinema
Spinney's supermarket
Azerbaijan
Stoufi Garden
Sunday Market (Souk al-Ahad)
Beirut Art Centre
National Museum
Pharoun OCFTC office

129

Achrafieh Broadly, Achrafieh extends from Damascus Road in the west to the banks of the Beirut River in the east and reaches as far south as the National Museum with its northern limit roughly coinciding with Charles Malek Avenue. If visiting the area from the top of the St Nicholas Steps after walking along Rue Gouraud, you will arrive on Sursock Street which, on your left, has arguably the most beautiful building in the whole city, the **Sursock Museum** [129 C1] (*Rue Sursock, Achrafieh;* ⟍ *01 201 892, 01 334 133;* e *museesursock@idm.net.lb;* ⊕ *call in advance of visit for opening times; admission free)*.This ornate and impressive house dating from 1912, with its white façade built in an Italianate-Lebanese style, has a graceful winding staircase which is supplemented by its stained-glass windows which enhance the beauty of this building when illuminated at night. At the time of writing, however, the museum was undergoing a major refurbishment and is currently dwarfed by a massive, incongruous crane and surrounding residential development, which means that its equally elegant interior of dark wood furnishings, marble floors and range of Islamic and other *objets d'art* are closed to the public until the early part of 2012. Behind the museum and facing St Nicholas Church, the 22,000m² **St Nicholas Gardens** [129 C2] (*Charles Malek Av;* ⊕ *winter 06.00–17.00 daily, summer 06.00–20.00 daily; admission free*) makes for a pleasant pause if on a walking tour of the area and has statues of Greek goddesses and a colourful tiled pool with plenty of seating.

Heading west along Charles Malek Avenue back towards west Beirut will bring you to the francophone St Joseph University which operates the **Lebanese Museum of Prehistory** [129 A2] (*University of St Joseph, St Joseph University St, near intersection with Monnot St;* ⟍ *01 421 860/1/2;* e *mpl@usj.edu.lb; www.usj.edu.lb/mpl;* ⊕ *09.00–15.00 Tue, Wed, Fri & Sat; admission: adults LBP3,000, students & under 18s LBP1,000*). Opened in 2000, this museum holds an extensive archaeological collection of more than 500 artefacts, gathered by Jesuits, of agricultural and hunting implements from Lebanon and the wider Middle East. The intriguing array of mainly small artefacts which date from the Paleolithic to Chalcolithic periods offer a fascinating insight into a rich history dating back some one million years. The museum also screens a short documentary film. The nearby Rue Monot is the epicentre for the area's nightlife and boasts several cafés and restaurants.

If you continue heading south from the university or from Monot Street towards Sodeco Square, you will eventually come across the large war-damaged **Barakat Building** [129 A3] (*Sodeco Sq; www.beitbeirut.org*), which less than eloquently illustrates what it meant to be located right on the Green Line between east and west Beirut during the civil war. Known as the Yellow House, the bullet-ridden structure is currently appropriately draped with yellow tarpaulin and is planned to open sometime during the early part of 2013 as a museum and major cultural centre documenting the civil war and history of the city. A major project, undertaken in conjunction with the city of Paris, BeitBeirut will also stage exhibitions and lectures and will house a café, restaurant and a state of the art multimedia library. A further 10–15- minute walk down the Damascus Road will bring you to Beirut's must-see, the world class National Museum.

National Museum [90 H6] (*Corner of Damascus Rd & Av Abdallah al Yafi;* ⟍ *01 612 295;* e *info@beirutnationalmuseum.com; www.beirutnationalmuseum.com;* ⊕ *09.00–17.00 Tue–Sun, closed Mon, Christmas & New Year's Day, & Muslim holidays; admission: adults LBP5,000, students & under 18s LBP1,000. The Ministry of Tourism office in Hamra has free brochures about the museum but for more extensive information the shop inside the museum has more detailed publications for sale. All exhibits within the museum are labelled in Arabic, English & French;*

disabled access for wheelchairs at the entrance & lifts to the 1st floor) Without a doubt Lebanon's premier-league museum and arguably the first site to visit in the country in order to gain an overview of the history and peoples which have helped shaped the development of this multi-faceted country.

Construction of the museum commenced in 1930 and was completed in 1937, and the museum, known as *matHaf* in Arabic, finally opened to the public in 1943. Located right on the former Green Line, which divided the warring factions during the civil war, it was forced to close in 1975 with the onset of hostilities. In order to protect the larger items such as statues, sarcophagi and friezes, they were encased in concrete but still some were destroyed from a combination of neglect and saltwater corrosion. The imposing façade also suffered a heavy pounding from gun and shellfire and the pillars were riddled with bullet holes. Restoration work on the building itself and the artefacts began in 1995, and the museum finally reopened to the public in 1999 after lengthy and costly reconstruction work. A fascinating 15-minute documentary film, *Revival*, is screened every hour between 09.00 and 16.00, offering a poignant insight into how the museum was painstakingly restored by its staff and volunteers. Today, the museum's extensive archaeological collection spans the salient eras from prehistory and the Bronze Age to the Mamluk period.

The ground floor contains over 70 of the largest items in the museum's collection, including a beautifully preserved mosaic just inside the entrance depicting the Seven Wise Men from AD300 that hails from Baalbek and once adorned a Roman villa. The other important exhibits include a marble statue of Hygeia, the goddess of health from the Roman period, 2nd-century AD Roman sarcophagi decorated with inebriated cupids and scenes of battles with the Greeks, and a bas-relief of Pharaoh Ramses II. From the Phoenician era statues of children associated with Echmoun, the god of healing are particularly impressive, but the most prestigious relic from this period is the sarcophagus of King Hiram, the 10th-century King of Byblos, which contains the earliest inscriptions of the Phoenician alphabet. Continuing up to the first floor, around 1,000 smaller, delicate and more ornate items are no less impressive for their exquisite craftsmanship. Artefacts here date from prehistory, the Neolithic and Chalcolithic eras. There, Bronze-Age figurines depict hippopotami, hedgehogs, cats, dogs, sphinxes and various grotesque faces found in Byblos and Beirut. From the Iron-Age and Greek Hellenistic periods, pottery, copper and flint tools together with terracotta figurines testify to the rich archaeological heritage left by Lebanon's early civilisations. One of the highlights of this floor is the display of lithe Phoenician figures with their gold-leaf pointed hats arranged in platoon-like fashion.

BOURJ HAMMOUD The location for Beirut's Armenian community who fled here in great numbers following the 1915 genocide in eastern Turkey, this district is often overlooked by visitors, yet provides another perspective on the city. Though the area has few specific sites of note except for a few traditionally built Armenian churches, the attraction of this part of town, easily reached by LCC bus numbers 2 and 8 or by walking from Downtown and continuing along Gouraud Street, is its distinctive Armenian identity evidenced in its food, the Armenian script on shop and street signs, and the shopping. A wander through the area's streets, especially around the main busy Armenia and Arax streets, you will encounter traditional Armenian embroidery such as scarves and tablecloths, spices, fruit and vegetable vendors, wandering tea sellers and a range of other bric-a-brac items.

The narrow streets off the main drag are also worth a wander for the aroma of spices and cheap goods. What is striking about this enclave is the understated prosperity of the area and the friendly and welcoming people. The small **Square Café** (🕒 *11.00–*

01.00 daily) is a pleasant place to sit for a drink amidst some nice greenery and to watch the world go by although there are numerous other decent cafés and cheap eateries all within easy walking distance. The area also has a good supply of banks and pharmacies. If you are visiting the area on a Sunday the nearby market **Souk al-Ahad** [129 E4] (*Corniche al-Nahr, parallel to Emile Lahoud Av;* ☕ *07.00–17.00 Sun*) could be worth a visit either *en route* to or on the way back from Bourj Hammoud as this large busy market sells everything from books to wedding dresses. Guided half-day tours of this district are conducted by Beirut Urban Adventures (see page 101).

Cilicia Museum (*Armenian Catholicosate of Cilicia, Antelias;* ✆ *04 410 001;* e *museum@armenianorthodoxchurch.org; www.armenianorthodoxchurch.org;* ☕ *10.00–17.00 Tue–Sat, 10.00–13.00 Sun; admission free*) Although located outside Bourj Hammoud, this museum is interesting for the light it sheds on a fascinating and traumatic aspect of Armenian history. The museum takes its name from the See in Sis church in Cilicia, former Armenian Turkey, following the genocide of

EVENTS AND FESTIVALS IN BEIRUT

What the capital lacks in historical sights it more than makes up for in its sheer range of annual cultural offerings with something to cater for most interests all year round. The following details and listings comprise the current principal events of most interest to the visitor and tickets can usually be purchased from the festival organisers themselves or at the Virgin Megastore in Downtown Beirut.

Beirut Fashion Week Beirut International Exhibition & Leisure Centre (BIEL), Downtown; e info@beirutfashionweek.com; www.beirutfashionweek.com. Proclaiming itself to be the 'first international fashion show in the entire Middle East', the event is held in Mar with regional & international designers showing off their latest collections & haute couture.

Beirut International Film Festival Ground Fl, Bechara Aoun Bldg, St Nicholas, Sursock St, Achrafieh; ✆ 01 202 411; m 70 141 843; e info@beirutfilmfoundation.org; www. beirutfilmfoundation.org. Held annually in Oct, this well-established & largest film festival in the Middle East screens both short & feature films from Lebanon & the wider MENA (Middle East & North Africa) region.

Beirut International Marathon 4th Fl, Makateb Bldg, Mar Takla, Hazmieh; ✆ 05 959 262; www.beirutmarathon.org. Since its inaugural run in 2003 which attracted 6,000 runners from 49 countries, this event has grown year on year with some 30,000 runners from 85 countries taking part in 2010. As well as the full marathon (42.195km) for over 17s only, there is a 10km Fun Run for those over 9, a 3km run for politicians & those aged 9–17 years, & a 1km family run. Wheelchair users can also participate in the 10km race & full marathon. The marathon is usually held in Nov or Dec each year.

Beirut International Platform of Dance 2nd Fl, Estral Centre, Hamra St, Hamra; ✆ 01 343 834; e info@maqamat.org; www.maqamat.org. Tickets can be purchased at all branches of Virgin Megastores & at www.ticketingboxoffice.com. This festival takes place annually between the months of Apr & May at various Beirut theatres, showcasing a range of performers from Lebanon & the Middle East & beyond. The organisers, Maqamat Dance Studio, also run dance classes across a range of styles including contemporary, oriental, dabke & hip-hop.

Beirut International Tango Festival ✆ 01 511 894; m 03 872 013; e info@ tangolebanon.com; www.tangolebanon.com. Held annually towards the end of Apr (check

Armenians by the Turks in 1915. Hastily removing their artefacts from their monastery, the monks transported what they could of their treasures and travelled to Syria before finally arriving in Antelias and making it their home in 1930. The beautiful artefacts on display in the museum, which is continually receiving new exhibits, includes the first ever Armenian printed Bible, tapestries and sculptures, along with exquisitely decorated gold and silver metal items.

Getting there The museum is located about 30 minutes north of Beirut but is easily reached by LCC bus number 2 from Hamra which terminates at Antelias. Alternatively, you can take LCC bus number 6 from Cola station to Byblos, alighting at Antelias for the short walk to the museum.

SOUTHERN SUBURBS Often referred to locally as the 'Belt of Misery', this sprawling mass of poverty and urban degradation couldn't be more different from the glitz and glamour of the Downtown area of the city. Reached by following the road

website for the schedule), this event runs dance classes as well as concerts & shows & is one of Lebanon's more recently established festivals which was first held in 2009.

Docudays PO Box 113-7222, Hamra; m 03 167 824, 03 075 870; e info@docudays.com; www.docudays.com. Founded in 1999, the Beirut International Documentary Festival usually takes place in Nov/Dec & is a celebration totally devoted to the non-fiction film genre which attracts filmmakers from the Arab & international film world.

Hamra Street Festival m 03 617 112, 70 502 370; e hamrafestival@hotmail.com; www.discoverhamra.com. Held during the 2nd week of Sep in 2010 for the first time since 1998, this 3-day festival is one big street party (with roads closed to vehicular traffic) with music, artists & other performers, a range of stalls selling all range of wares together with plenty of NGOs keen to show off their charitable good work.

International Festival for Experimental Music in Lebanon (Irtijal) m 03 323 339; e sound@irtijal.org; www.irtijal.org. Usually held over 4 days in Apr, this is currently Lebanon's only showcase of innovative music across a variety of music genres. Check the website for dates & prices of upcoming events.

Souk el-Bargout This huge & eclectic twice-yearly flea market adorns the streets of Downtown every evening for around 2 weeks between May/Jun & Nov/Dec.

Sunflower Theatre Spring Festival Sami Solh Av, Tayouneh; ☎ 01 381 290; m 03 035 298, 70 126 764; 2010 ticket prices LBP10,000, available from the venue. Held in May each year, this month-long festival showcases music, song, contemporary dance, theatre, puppetry & drama workshops from throughout the Arab world as well as from Europe.

The Garden Show & Spring Festival Beirut Hippodrome; ☎ 01 480 081; e garden@the-gardenshow.com; www.the-gardenshow.com. Lebanon's answer to London's Chelsea Flower Show, this floral delight is held annually over 5 days in May with around 200 exhibitors from Lebanon, the Arab world & beyond showing off their finest floral wares.

Vinifest Beirut Hippodrome ☎/f 01 280 085; m 03 260 985; e eventions.one@googlemail.com; www.vinifestlebanon.com, www.eventions-one.com. This annual 4-day celebration of Lebanese wine is usually held from the 1st week in Oct & in addition to the obligatory tasting sessions & Lebanese food the festival hosts a wide range of cultural & musical events, games, quizzes, exhibitions & film screenings. The organisers also arrange various wine tasting tours to the vineyards in Batroun & the Bekaa Valley through their summer Vinitour scheme. Take a look at the festival website for full itineraries & prices.

Unveiled in August 1995, and coinciding with the 50th anniversary of the founding of the Lebanese army, outside the Lebanese Ministry of Defence at Yarze is one of the world's largest modern sculptures, the *Hope for Peace*. A monument to the debacle of the 1975–90 civil war, it was the brainchild of the French New Realist artist Armand Fernandez (1928–2005) who believed that art is a vital requirement for peace and prosperity in any society. In his trademark style of using found objects for his assembled creations – which have previously included household waste, car and bicycle parts, buttons, musical instruments and typewriters to aid social commentary and challenge received ideas about art and society – Fernandez's creation is a 100ft-high structure weighing in at over 5,000 tonnes and designed to transform objects of death and destruction and turn them into symbols signifying peace and a hope for the future. The ten-storey memorial contains real Soviet T-55 tanks, guns and armoured vehicles encased in masses of concrete: relics of endless militia battles. Each piece of military hardware was sandwiched between the concrete sandbags. Then, once the concrete had set, the tanks, guns and artillery pieces were given a fresh coat of camouflage paint. The artist believes that: 'embedding objects in something else changes the time of the object. Instead of a present object, you have a fossil of the object, as you might find an organic fossil in a rock formation… objects are by their nature rather impermanent, and I like that. I also like fossils.'

To visit the monument either take a taxi from Beirut for around LBP10,000 or LCC bus number 14 or 15 (from Cola station or the National Museum) to Yarze and ask to be dropped off outside the Ministry of Defence. There is no charge to visit the monument.

further south from the public beach at Ramlet al-Bayda and then turning inland, this area is 'home' to thousands of Palestinian refugees at the Bourj al-Barajneh and the infamous Sabra and Shatila refugee camps which witnessed appalling massacres during Israel's 1982 occupation of the city. These shanty-type dwellings accommodate the unfortunate thousands forced to flee their homeland in Palestine following the creation of the State of Israel in 1948. Supplementing these camps are those areas housing Shi'ite refugees from south Lebanon who have migrated north to escape the conflict between Israel and Hezbollah.

This area was also formerly where many foreigners were kidnapped during the civil war and lost their liberty for years, including the UK's John McCarthy. As a Hezbollah stronghold the area was heavily bombed during the 2006 July War with Israel, and continues to show the effects to this day. The suburbs are by no means on the traditional tourist trail and the 'sites' in this area are predominantly ones of poverty with posters and placards of martyrs killed fighting Israel. It is more of an edifying, albeit sombre, experience of the effects of war and conflict on displacing people and destroying their livelihoods. It is perfectly safe to wander around the streets and area, but bear in mind that with a large Shi'ite population, this is a more conservative part of Beirut and you should dress appropriately. Although it is perfectly possible to visit the Palestinian camps as a lone traveller or on a group visit, it can sometimes be a good idea to be accompanied by a bona fide local guide or to make contact with UNRWA (*Public Information Office;*

\ *01 840 461; www.unrwa-lebanon.org*), the United Nations humanitarian agency responsible for the provision of education, health and social services to registered Palestinian refugees.

GREEN SPACES AND PUBLIC PARKS

Gibran Khalil Gibran Garden [104 D7] (*Near General Av, adjacent to the Roman Baths, Downtown;* ⊕ *24/7*) Named after the revered Lebanese poet and philosopher, this 6,000m² garden contains a bust of the famed writer plus a fountain, lawns, trees and plants.

Horch Tabet Garden (*Off Fouad Cheab St, Horch Tabet;* ⊕ *07.00–21.00 daily*) A good area for a picnic with immaculately cut lawns and, a rare sight in the city, bins for recycling.

Horsh Beirut (The Pine Forest) [90 G7] (*Opposite the Hippodrome, entrance on Hamid Franjiye Av, Tayouneh;* ⊕ *07.00–17.00 daily*) A lovely green diversion from the hustle and bustle of the city, this 40,000m² space is adorned with pine trees and also has a children's playground, tennis and basketball courts and football pitches.

Sin El Fil Municipality Garden (*Es Sadye St, next to Sadye Church, Sin El Fil;* ⊕ *08.00–19.30 daily*) A compact park with hedges, paths, pine trees and a small fountain.

Sioufi Garden [129 D4] (*Jean Jalkh St, Sioufi;* ⊕ *07.00–17.00 daily*) Perfect for kids with its swings and climbing activities, together with a range of sculptures, plants and great views. In June 2011 the garden became Lebanon's first Wi-Fi internet park offering free, high speed internet access with further zones planned for the capital and beyond in the future.

The Jesuit Garden [129 D2] (*Moscou St, off Charles Malek Av, Achrafieh;* ⊕ *07.00–17.00 daily*) One of the city's smaller parks and mainly patronised by the mature generation of Beirutis, but worth a look/stroll for the slice of life which takes place here, such as men playing backgammon.

ART GALLERIES Beirut has a flourishing arts scene showcasing a range of Lebanese and non-Lebanese art across a variety of genres and themes. The venues below represent a small selection of those available which range from small-scale spaces to the large expanse of the cutting-edge Beirut Art Centre below. All the galleries below are free to visit. Both *The Daily Star* newspaper and the monthly *Time Out Beirut* magazine often publicise details of present and forthcoming exhibitions together with profiles and interviews with artists.

Agial Art Gallery [123 D2] (*63 Abdel Aziz St, Hamra, near the American University of Beirut;* \ *01 345 213;* m *03 634 244;* e *agial@cyberia.net.lb; www. agialart.com;* ⊕ *10.00–18.00 Mon–Fri, 10.00–13.00 Sat*) Puts on seven–eight exhibitions per year which showcase the work of young and emerging 'Lebanese and Arab Contemporary Art' and artists across a range of genres. The gallery also houses a permanent collection of works from across the Arab world.

Art Circle [123 C3] (*Assaf Bldg, Antoine Gemayel St, Hamra;* m *03 027 776, 03 774 510;* e *info@art-circle.net; www.art-circle.net;* ⊕ *11.00–19.00 Tue–Fri, 11.00–15.00*

Sat) Hosts a whole range of artworks and multi-media installations by Lebanese artists with around 12 different exhibitions annually.

Beirut Art Centre [129 E4] (*Bldg 13, St 97, Zone 66, near Jisr el Wati (off Corniche Al Nahr & Emile Lahoud Av);* \ *01 397 018;* m *70 262 112;* e *info@beirutartcenter. org; www.beirutartcenter.org;* ⊕ *12.00–20.00 Mon–Sat*) Opened in January 2009, this not-for-profit gallery is one of the newest major galleries on the city's art scene. The bright and airy 1,500m² space puts on around five solo and themed exhibitions per year specialising in contemporary Lebanese art across a variety of media. Past exhibitions have included work by famed Lebanese architect Bernard Khoury. In addition to its gallery space, the centre houses a bookshop, a multi-media digital database of contemporary art, and holds regular workshops ranging from art history and theory to photography and video. The website contains full details of both past and present exhibitions and forthcoming shows.

Maqam Lebanese Modern Art Gallery [104 G7] (*Saifi Village, al-Mkhallasiya St, Downtown;* \ *01 991 212;* e *info@maqamart.com; www.maqamart.com;* ⊕ *14.00– 19.00 Tue–Fri, 12.00–17.00 Sat*) A nice intimate little gallery in the delightful setting of this quaint restored district showing up to six exhibitions a year on social, political, artistic & musical themes, including multi-media installations.

Zamaan Art Gallery [123 B3] (*Ground Fl, Abou El Hasan Bldg, Sadat St, Hamra;* \ *01 745 571/2;* e *info@zamaangallery.com; www.zamaangallery.com;* ⊕ *10.00–19.00 Mon–Sat*) This gallery specialises in young and emerging Lebanese and Arab artists with around two–three exhibitions per month. It is also home to a private collection of some 1,700 paintings.

4

Mount Lebanon

Telephone code 09 (except where otherwise indicated)

Probably Lebanon's most varied region, the country's western range of mountains, which often climb steeply from the coastal districts, extends geographically practically the entire length of the country, but administratively stretches from Beirut to just south of the coastal town of Batroun in the north. The area encompasses a diverse range of terrain including forests, rivers, valleys and waterfalls and also contains Lebanon's highest point at Qornet es Saouda (3,083m) in the northeast portion of the territory. This is also the region from which the country derives its name, Lubnan, which is Arabic for 'white', a reference to the snowy peaks of Mount Lebanon. Given its undulating landscape and relative remoteness, the area has long been a safe haven for both the Christian and Druze populations seeking refuge from persecution and during the Ottoman period managed to retain a semi-autonomous status.

Today, the region is predominantly Christian, with the effects of altitude lending the area a more cordial and temperate feel in many parts. In summer there are a range of offerings for the visitor including the summer resort towns of Beit Mery and Broummana, the ancient sites and charming fishing port at Byblos which has resisted modernisation over the years, and the geological wonders at Jeita Grotto. The ski season runs from December through to April and sometimes even later, with the Mount Lebanon region home to five of the country's main resorts catering for the beginner and intermediate skier, together with superb après-ski facilities for individuals and families alike. Although the Chouf Mountains fall geographically within the southeast section of Mount Lebanon, owing to the area's distinctive history, landscape and culture, they merit separate treatment with their own chapter (see page 217).

BEIT MERY AND BROUMMANA *Telephone code 04*

These two towns, lying to the east of Beirut in the group of mountains known as the Metn, are Mount Lebanon's quintessential summer playgrounds and resort towns, just as they were for the Romans who also appreciated the cool mountain air and breezes for their pleasant respite from sultry summer conditions on the coast. Beit Mery, Arabic for 'House of the Master', is just 16km from the capital and sits 800m above sea level in the Metn offering commanding views over Beirut and the Mediterranean coastline, which are even more spectacular at night.

The town boasts a good range of eateries, an internationally renowned hotel which hosts a similarly famous annual winter festival, and a couple of historical sites which make Beit Mery an extremely easy and pleasant day trip at least. Nearby Broummana, about 6km to the northeast, has a far less tranquil feel and in summer sees its population balloon fourfold to some 60,000 as pleasure-seeking Lebanese and well-heeled Gulf Arabs flock here for the food, drink and often pulsating music

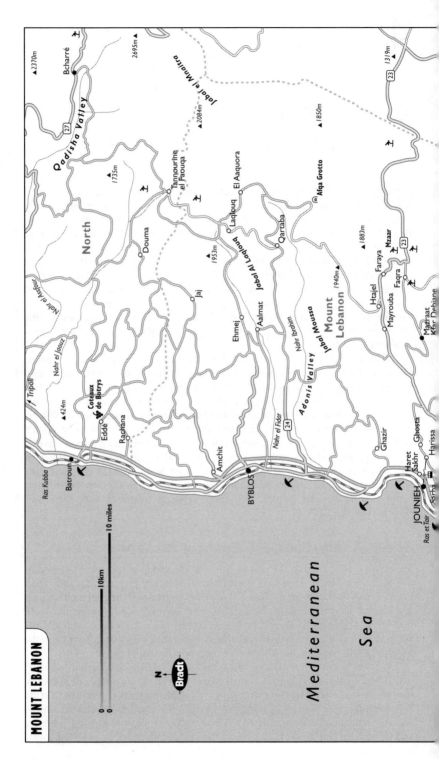

0 10km

0 10 miles

N

Bradt

Mediterranean

Sea

Ras Kubba

Batroun

Ras et Tair

Tripoli

Nahr el Jaouz

▲424m

Coteaux de Botrys

Eddé

Rachana

Nahr el Assfour

North

Qadisha Valley

Bcharré

▲2370m

27

2695m ▲

Jabal el Mnaitra

▲2084m

▲1735m

Douma

Jaj

▲1953m

Tannourine el Faouqa

Laqlouq

El Aaquora

Jabal Al Laqlouq

Qartaba

Afqa Grotto

▲1850m

23

1319m

▲1883m

Mzaar

Htajel

Faraya

Mayrouba

Faqra

23

Mazraat Kfar Debiane

Ehmej

Aalmat

Jabal Moussa

Mount Lebanon

1940m▲

Nahr Ibrahim

Adonis Valley

Amchit

BYBLOS

Nahr el Fidar

24

Ghazir

Ghosta

Haret Sakhr

JOUNIEH

Harissa

Sarba

138

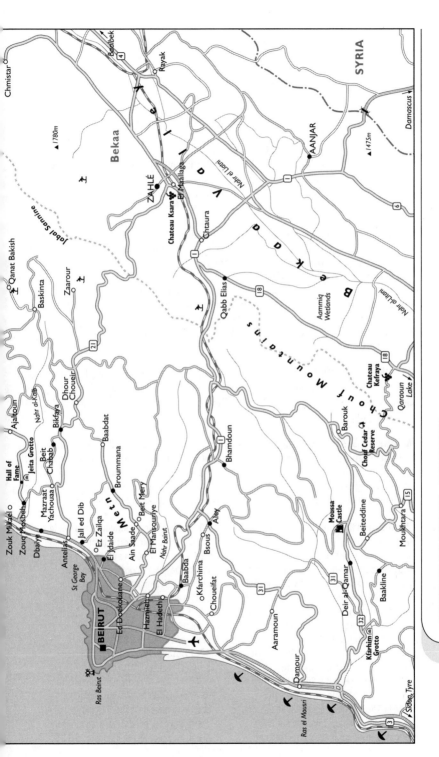

4

scene. Although Broummana has equally good, if not better, panoramic views over the capital and coast, it has a dearth of historical sites to engage the visitor. However it does hold a couple of annual summer festivals which are worth attending if you happen to be in town at the time.

GETTING THERE From Barbir, a short walk behind the National Museum (MatHaf), you can take LCC bus number 7 which travels through both Beit Mery and Broummana (LBP1,000). The journey takes about an hour and is an extremely pleasant one with terrific views down to Beirut as you ascend Mount Lebanon. At Beit Mery the bus will drop you off at the roundabout where the sites and amenities are all within easy walking distance. It should also be possible to catch a minivan or service taxi leaving from Beirut's Dora intersection. Expect to pay upwards of LBP20,000 for a taxi. It is worth noting, however, that as buses stop running around 20.00 at the time of writing, you will need to get a service taxi or taxi back to Beirut, which can cost anywhere between LBP5,000 and LBP20,000 depending once again on your negotiating skills. If planning to visit the Splash Land activity park (see page 143) in Mansourieh, LCC bus number 7 can drop you off right outside the entrance which passes through here *en route* to Beit Mery and Broummana or, in the author's experience, breaks down right outside. To reach Beit Mery and Broummana by the self-drive method from Beirut drive eastward from the capital towards the large roundabout at Mkalles and continue travelling east towards Mansourieh, Ain Saade and finally Beit Mery with Broummana a further 6km northeast from Beit Mery.

GETTING AROUND Both Beit Mery and Broummana are easily and best explored by foot as both towns are quite compact, and it's also a pleasant though slightly elevated 6km walk from Beit Mery to Broummana; taxis and of course LCC bus number 7 are available.

WHERE TO STAY Given their resort status both Beit Mery and Broummana are, not surprisingly, well catered for in terms of accommodation but they are geared mainly towards well-heeled visitors. However, there is a reasonable range of prices to suit different budgets. Outside the high summer season, it is worth enquiring about possible discounts though it is, of course, worth asking at any time.

Al Bustan Hotel (117 rooms & suites) Beit Mery; ☎ 04 972 980/1/2; m 03 752 000; e hotel@albustan-lb.com; reservations@ albustan-lb.com; www.albustanhotel.com. This hotel's unique selling point is its unrivalled views over Beirut & the surrounding mountains & it plays host to the prestigious annual Al Bustan Festival (see pages 142–3) each Feb/Mar. A pricey alternative to the area's other hotels, but can boast the intimate & scenic Scottish Bar & its popular French & Italian restaurants. **$$$$$**

Grand Hills Hotel & Spa (118 rooms & 54 apartments) Main Rd, Broummana; ☎ 04 868 888; e info@grandhillsvillage.com; www.grandhillsvillage.com. A beautifully decorated, luxurious hotel & resort offering

every conceivable accoutrement you would expect for the price. Oozes charm & immaculate elegance with the bonus of fantastic views. Part of the Robert Mouawad Group, owner of the Robert Mouawad Private Museum in Beirut (see page 128), the hotel holds the Guinness World Record for having the largest hotel suite; yours for only US$50,000 per night (b/fast inc). **$$$$$**

Printania Palace Hotel (86 rooms & suites) Chahine El Achkar St, Broummana; ☎ 04 862 000; e printania@printania.com; www.printania.com. A large, traditional hotel with pleasant & spacious rooms, hotel swimming pool, good views from the rooms & a pleasant outdoor seating area. **$$$$**

🏠 Bellevue Palace Hotel (50 rooms) Main Rd, Broummana; ☎ 04 865 000; www.bellevuepalacehotel.com. More lively than most of the other hotels with 3 restaurants, nightclub & live loud music. Nice, large rooms with great mountain views. **$$$**

🏠 Garden Hotel (42 rooms) Chahine El Achkar St, Broummana; ☎ 04 860 444, 04 860 777, 04 960 579; e info@gardenhotellb.com; www.gardenhotellb.com. A decent enough hotel with clean & spacious, if unexciting, rooms, a swimming pool & pleasant outdoor bar area. Not all rooms have AC. **$$$**

🏠 Hotel Belvedere (27 rooms) Main Rd, Broummana; ☎ 04 861 192; m 03 050 610. Although the rooms are a bit pricey for basic & bland, but clean accommodation, it is in a good central location & all rooms have AC & TV. **$$$**

🏠 Le Crillon Hotel (58 rooms) Main Rd, Broummana; ☎ 04 865 555; e c@lecrillon.com; www.lecrillon.com. Situated in a nice secluded setting just off the main road, this place caters mainly for older, expat Lebanese. Pleasant & clean rooms with swimming pool & lovely views over Mount Sannine. For those wanting a cosy, peaceful & quiet stay this is a good choice. **$$$**

🏠 Hotel Kanaan (17 rooms) Main Rd, Broummana, facing Broummana High School; ☎ 04 960 084, 04 960 025; m 03 826 725. This hotel, family run since 1955, represents the best value in town. Though the en-suite rooms are a little simple with rather bland décor, this place has lovely old-world charm with a guest lounge area akin to a Victorian drawing room. Between Jul & Sep guests are permitted to use the Broummana High School swimming pool opposite for LBP10,000/day. **$$**

✗ WHERE TO EAT AND DRINK Broummana has by far the widest choice of drinking and eating options and all are very close together, on or just off the town's main road; the following establishments represent a good selection.

✗ Deir al-Kalaa Country Club Beit Mery; ☎ 04 972 989; m 03 655 958; e club@dakcc.com; www.dakcc.com; ⏰ winter 08.00–23.00 daily, summer 08.00–midnight. An extremely pleasant club with terrific views & open to non-members which every Sun provides a buffet meal for US$24pp. Very family friendly, the swimming pool & other facilities are open to non-members for a charge. **$$$$$**

✗ Mounir Just off Main Rd, Broummana; ☎ 04 873 900; e Hffadel@mounirs.com; www.mounirs.com. Delightful Lebanese food in equally delightful & picturesque surroundings. **$$$$$**

✗ Calvados Fabraka St, behind Le Gargotier, Broummana; m 03 487 150, 03 979 597; ⏰ 19.30–late daily. Lively & atmospheric with a Spanish feel, located in a converted 300-year-old house. Good pub atmosphere serving decent steaks & other pub food. **$$$$**

✗ Le Gargotier Main Rd, Broummana; ☎ 04 960 562; ⏰ 12.00–15.00 & 19.00–midnight Tue–Sun. A favourite with locals

serving nice French food with an equally nice French ambience. Can get very busy at weekends so best to book ahead. **$$$$**

✗ Manhattan Centre Main Rd, Broummana; ☎ 04 961 967, 04 963 370; ⏰ 09.00–00.30 daily. Serves Lebanese & international dishes & a good place to sit outside & watch the world go by. **$$$$**

✗ Crepaway Main Rd, Broummana; ☎ 04 964 965; e info@crepaway.com; www.crepaway.com; ⏰ 10.30–00.30 daily. Part of the nationwide chain serving decent standard fare of burgers, salads, pizza & pasta in the heart of the town. **$$$**

✗ Restaurant Tiger close to Deir al-Kalaa, Beit Mery; ☎ 04 870 564, 04 870 264; ⏰ 12.00–midnight daily. Serves decent Lebanese cuisine in a great rooftop setting with superlative views of Beirut below. **$$$**

✗ Chez Nassim Main Rd, Broummana; ☎ 04 964 137; ⏰ summer 06.30–23.00 daily, winter 06.30–20.00 daily. Great pâtisserie serving Arabic sweets. **$**

ENTERTAINMENT AND NIGHTLIFE You are spoilt for choice in Broummana but the following are two of the best places in the author's view; there are plenty of others on or just off the main street.

☆ **Cheers** Main Rd, Broummana; m 03 211 420; ⊕ 18.00–late daily. Next door to Moods, this hostelry caters to a young crowd bopping away to pop & dance music.

☆ **Moods** Main Rd, Broummana; m 03 796 814, 70 233 322; ⊕ 21.00–late daily. Opened in May 2010, this small, intimate & lively watering hole has karaoke on Mon & a DJ spinning techno, house & Arabic discs on Fri/Sat nights. Doesn't serve food.

SHOPPING Whilst both towns have a range of general shops and stores there is nothing here that you would travel especially to buy, but the following supermarket should meet most travellers' daily needs.

Bechara Supermarket Main Rd, Broummana; ⟍ 04 960 617; 04 862 330; m 70 175 050; ⊕ 07.00–21.00 Mon–Sat, 07.00–13.00 Sun.

A well-stocked supermarket selling a wide range of groceries, fresh meat, frozen foods, dairy products & pastries.

OTHER PRACTICALITIES On Broummana's Main Road, the **Bank of Beirut** and **Bank Audi** both have 24/7 ATMs for cash withdrawals. There are also pharmacies.

Broummana Post Office (*Ogero Bldg, Rue Central, Broummana;* ⟍ *04 960 005;* ⊕ *08.00–17.00 Mon–Fri, 08.00–13.30 Sat*) provides a full range of postal services, including money transfer.

WHAT TO SEE AND DO

Beit Mery The town's small but engaging historical sites, which you can visit any time free of charge, revolve around the 18th-century Maronite monastery to St John of **Deir al-Kalaa (Monastery of the Fortress)**. Built c1748, it is thought to occupy the site of a much earlier Phoenician sanctuary and temple where they honoured their god of music and dance, Marqod, which the Romans later adapted to their own temple in the 1st century AD after their god Baal Marqod or Lord of the Dance, a reference to his power to control earthquakes and thunder and the ritual-like dances which worshippers engaged in his honour. Until 2005, the site was used as an army barracks by the Syrian army who looted and vandalised many of the artefacts before their departure, and graffiti by the former occupiers can still be seen.

Restoration of the monastery and interior, which is well worth seeing, is ongoing and there are a series of photographs inside the monastery which show the extent of the destruction by the Syrian soldiers. In the reception area there is also a stone statue of Baal Marqod. A short walk downhill from here reveals a small, unattended site where there are some fine and well-preserved **mosaics** which form the floor of a former 5th-century Byzantine church. In the vicinity are also the remains of some **Roman baths** with the tiles that formed the heating system clearly visible, together with the remnants of a small temple dating from the reign of the emperor Trajan and dedicated to Juno, the Roman goddess who is reputed to have had a variety of roles, including guardian of women and fertility.

Al Bustan International Festival of Music and the Arts (⟍ *04 972 980/1/2;* m *03 752 000;* e *festival@albustan-lb.com; www.albustanfestival.com; tickets can be purchased from the Al Bustan Hotel & from various venues in Beirut. See the festival website for full details*) This annual themed winter festival, which is held over a five-week period during February and March, celebrates its 19th year in 2012 and takes place mainly at the 483-seat Emile Bustani Auditorium next to the Hotel Al Bustan as well as in the hotel itself. This showcase of highbrow culture is a platform for a wide range of performing arts, from chamber and choral music to dance, jazz and theatrical productions with many international artists having performed here including Spanish flamenco guitarist Paco Peña, the English Shakespeare Company, and cellist Julian Lloyd Webber. In 2012, the festival dates are from 21 February until 25 March with *The Music of Latin America* as the year's theme.

Broummana Although Broummana is a pleasant town to walk around with lovely scenic views, it lacks any real sites of note, but it partially makes up for this by hosting a couple of well-established events which take place annually in the town and are well worth attending if you are visiting Broummana around the same time.

Broummana Summer Festival (*www.brummana.org.lb*) This summer festival held throughout July each year sees Broummana's streets free of vehicular traffic and replaced with outdoor exhibitions of artists exhibiting and selling their work, sales of Lebanese food, and a variety of entertainers perambulating the streets including clowns, jugglers and stilt walkers.

Broummana Tennis Festival (*Broummana Sports Club, Broummana High School Campus;* \ *04 960 430;* m *71 641 743;* e *info@brummanasc.com; www. brummanasc.com*) Dating back to 1927, this annual tennis tournament takes place towards the end of July and the beginning of August using the tennis courts at Broummana High School. Over the years the competition has attracted players of international standing from Asia, Europe and the Americas. If you are staying at the Kanaan Hotel, which is opposite the tennis courts, you'll get a decent bird's-eye view of the action from its top-floor terrace; if not, entry to the tennis club for spectators is free of charge.

Activities
Splash Land (*Ain Saadeh, Main Rd, Mansourieh;* \ *04 531 166/7/8;* e *info@ splashlandlb.com; www.splashlandlb.com;* ⊕ *10.00–20.00 Mon–Sat; admission LBP10,000–50,000, depending on number of people & type of activities*) If you are travelling by LCC bus number 7 from Beirut, it passes by here and this family activity and theme park is a one-stop shop for indoor and outdoor family pursuits with nine water slides, pools and wall climbing. It also organises summer camps.

Sharewood Camp (*PO Box 1474, Beit Mery, Metn;* \ *04 870 592;* m *03 294 298;* e *info@sharewoodcamp.com; www.sharewoodcamp.com*) This is a well-respected, fully equipped camping and activity-based organisation based in the Metn geared towards families providing tents with a full range of facilities including electrical power, 24/7 hot shower and toilet facilities. Outdoor activities on offer include abseiling, archery, donkey rides, hiking and trampoline.

BSOUS *Telephone code 05*

This quaint Maronite mountain village is just 15km southeast from Beirut in the *caza* (district) of Aley in the Mount Lebanon Governorate. Although lower in height than Beit Mery and Broummana at between 200m and 700m, it is also a popular summer resort for Lebanese and Gulf Arabs alike with a cooler summer climate than the capital. The village's main appeal for the visitor is its silk museum which is less than an hour away by bus or taxi from Beirut.

GETTING THERE If coming from Beirut you can board LCC bus number 14 or 15 from Cola intersection or the National Museum which terminates at Aley. Depending on traffic, the journey time can take up to an hour with the bus costing LBP1,500. Alight at Jamhour and catch a taxi for the remaining 4km journey to the Silk Museum. Expect to pay around LBP40,000–45,000 for a taxi from Beirut; it would be a good idea to ask the driver to wait whilst you visit the museum which takes up to two hours to view at a leisurely pace. If you are on a self-drive visit, the museum's website has a clear map and directions to the entrance from Beirut.

WHAT TO SEE

The Silk Museum (Musée de la Soie) (*Bsous, Aley;* ↘ *05 940 767;* e *info@ thesilkmuseum.com; www.thesilkmuseum.com;* ⏲ *1 May–31 Oct 10.00–18.00 Tue–Sun; admission: adults LBP8,000, students LBP5,000, children under 4 years free*) This fascinating 'eco-museum' takes you through the history and processes of sericulture, which was once a flourishing, domestic and export industry during the Ottoman era. One of the most enduring legacies of the rule of the emir Fakhreddine Maan II was to cultivate a silk industry and under his reign *khans* were built from Sidon and Deir al-Qamar to Tripoli. Run by husband-and-wife team George and Alexandra Asseily, the museum is housed in a restored silk factory amidst delightful scented terraced gardens, mulberry trees and olive groves, and makes for a fascinating and edifying tour of what is a dying artisanal activity. There is a small gift shop selling silk garments, olive oil and soap, and the museum puts on periodic silk-related exhibitions from around the globe.

Animal Encounter (*Al-Zouhour St, Ras al-Jabal, Aley;* ↘ *05 558 724;* m *03 667 354/5;* e *mabisaid@cyberia.net.lb; www.animalencounter.org;* ⏲ *11.00–18.30 Sat/ Sun; voluntary contribution of around US$10 for family of 3–4 appreciated*) This non-profit organisation is dedicated to the welfare of abused and abandoned animals, and runs educational and lecture programmes together with hiking and camping during the summer months. This is a great venue for families, which houses a wide range of animals such as bears, deer, foxes, jackals, ostrich, pelicans, imperial eagle and wild boar amongst others.

SKIING AND SKI RESORTS

Lebanon has at the time of writing six ski resorts (a seventh is in the planning stage at Sannine Zenith with state of the art facilities, including a helipad), with the season running from around mid-December to early or mid-April. Bear in mind that climate change has, and will continue to have, an impact on the ski season, with recent years having seen a marked decrease in its duration. Transport to the slopes other than in winter is, like the snow, sparse and many of these resorts have little to offer the visitor outside the ski season. Even during the ski season, at the time of writing, there are no direct bus routes serving the resorts, and your transport options are confined to self-drive or taxis which will mostly have to be negotiated. **Ski Lebanon** (m *70 103 222;* e *res@skileb.com; www.skileb.com*) offers excursions and a range of ski-related packages and tours, and is highly recommended if you want someone else to take care of the travel and ski arrangements.

QANAT BAKISH AND ZAAROUR These two resorts, on the foothills of Mount Sannine, are not only the closest to the capital, at 45km and 54km respectively, but also two of Lebanon's smallest and most laid-back resorts; ideal for beginners, families and cross-country skiers. For climbing enthusiasts, the town of Baskinta also makes a good starting point for a 6km journey east to Nebaa Sannine where in the summer months you can climb the 2,628m-high Jebel Sannine. This requires an ascent of around three hours if you are in reasonable health, and no special equipment is required except a plentiful supply of water. Be aware that the mountain has two peaks, with the higher summit, about 1km away, less interesting than its lower neighbour. From the top of the lower peak the views are stunning, affording panoramas all over Lebanon including the Bekaa Valley, Anti-Lebanon Mountains, and the country's highest mountain at Qornet es Saouda (3,083m).

Qanat Bakish (*North of Baskinta Village;* \ *04 340 300;* ⏰ *08.00–15.30 Mon–Fri, 08.00–16.00 Sat/Sun; adult ski lift pass prices: US$10 Mon–Fri, US$18 Sat/Sun*) First opened in 1967, this resort ranges from 1,910m to 2,050m above sea level with three ski lifts and five slopes.

Zaarour (*South of Baskinta Village;* \ *04 310 010;* ⏰ *08.00–15.30 Mon–Fri, 08.00– 16.00 Sat/Sun & public holidays; adult ski lift pass prices: US$17 Mon–Fri, US$27 Sat/ Sun*) Destroyed on two occasions during the 1975–90 civil war, this tiny, privately run resort has been completely rebuilt, but owing to its lower altitude of between 1,700m and 2,000m, has a shorter season than the others. Its main advantage is the excellent quality of its snow and a good 4km trail for lovers of cross-country skiing along Mount Sannine. There are seven ski lifts catering for the beginner and advanced skier.

Getting there Both Qanat Bakish and Zaarour are best reached by car or taxi. Expect to pay somewhere around LBP60,000–75,000 for a taxi from Beirut. If on a self-drive visit from the capital take the road to Sin al-Fil passing through Mansourieh, Beit Mery, Broummana, Baabda and Bikfaya, before turning east towards Dhour Choueir and Mrouj, and keep an eye out for the signs to the Snow Land Hotel. Alternatively, take the coast road north from Beirut and turn inland at Antelias towards Bikfaya and then follow the route above.

Where to stay The options are fairly limited at present to the sole venue below for the best access to the slopes at Qanat Bakish and Zaarour.

Snow Land Hotel (35 rooms & suites) Qanat Bakish; \ 04 252 222; m 03 345 300; e info@snowland.com.lb; www.snowland.com. lb. A clean, no-frills hotel with dated décor but with good access to the ski slopes. The hotel can provide ski tuition for beginners, equipment hire & purchase. Use of the nice outdoor pool is free to guests. B/fast inc. *Dorm US$27pp.* **$$**

LAQLOUQ (*Ihmij Village, between Mzaar & Cedars ski resorts;* m *03 441 112;* ⏰ *08.00–15.30 Mon–Fri, 08.00–16.00 Sat/Sun & public holidays; adult ski lift pass prices: US$16 Mon–Fri, US$23 Sat/Sun*) Located at between 1,650m and 1,920m above sea level, Laqlouq first opened as a ski resort in 1958 and offers nine slopes catering mainly for the beginner and intermediate skier. This is probably the best resort for cross-country skiing and an ideal choice for families and those content with more laid-back and sparser après-ski facilities amid stunning alpine scenery. Ski equipment and lessons for the novice to intermediate skier are also available.

Getting there Laqlouq is 62km from Beirut and 28km east from Byblos. For a taxi from Byblos, expect to pay somewhere around US$30–35 for a one-way trip.

The journey time by car is around 1½ hours from the capital. A taxi from Beirut should cost somewhere in the region of LBP65,000–75,000. If on a self-drive visit take the coast road from Beirut to Byblos (Jbail) and then turn inland eastwards towards Annaya past St Charbel Monastery. Laqlouq ski resort is around 2km north of the main town of Laqlouq.

Where to stay

🏠 **Hotel Shangri-La** (20 rooms) Ihmij Village; m 03 441 112; e info@lakloukresort. com; www.lakloukresort.com. Conveniently located less than 5mins' walk from the slopes, this is a decent & popular choice with a nice homely feel. It is also open outside the ski season & offers a range of summer outdoor activities including archery, horseriding, mountain biking & tennis, as well as swimming in the hotel's own pool. **$$$**

What to see Apart from the skiing Laqlouq is reasonably close to some interesting natural rock formations at Balaa, about 3km northwest of Laqlouq, which comprise a series of ancient dwellings cut into the rock face. A further 3km along from here is the **Balaa Sinkhole**, only discovered in 1952, a series of Jurassic limestone caverns separated by a natural rock bridge carved by water and over 250m deep. Although an extraordinary sight, the utmost care is needed if exploring close up as there are no barriers or fences and the drops are sheer.

MZAAR (*Kfardebian;* ✆ *09 341 501;* 🕐 *08.00–15.30 Mon–Fri, 08.00–16.00 Sat/Sun & public holidays; ski lift pass prices: adults US$27–33 Mon–Fri, children under 16 years US$20–27 Mon–Fri, adults US$40–57 Sat/Sun, children under 16 years US$30–43 Sat/Sun*) Previously known as Faraya Mzaar, this is Lebanon's premier, most modern, glitzy and best-equipped ski resort situated just above the village of Faraya. A relative ghost town in summer, it gets very busy in winter and has by far the country's best facilities, including a well-developed après-ski scene to international standards. With its 80km of ski trails and 42 slopes Mzaar is also Lebanon's largest ski resort, varying in height from 1,850m to 2,465m above sea level and affording outstanding views over the Bekaa Valley, the Cedars and Beirut from its zenith. The resort's slopes are split into three categories based upon their access and are known as *Refuge, Jonction* and *Wardeh.*

Getting there Mzaar is 46km from Beirut and the journey time by taxi from the capital is around 1½ hours. Expect to pay around LBP68,000–75,000 for a taxi from the capital. If driving yourself from Beirut, take the coast road north until you get to Dog River (Nahr al-Kalb) and turn right to follow the road to Jeita Grotto. Keep following the roads ahead through the villages of Ajaltoun, Raifoun, Faitroun, Mayrouba and Faraya village and on to Aoyoun al-Simane.

Where to stay

🏠 **Intercontinental Mzaar Mountain Resort & Spa** (131 rooms & suites) Ouyoun El Simone, Mzaar; ✆ 09 340 100; e mzaar.resort@ icmzaar.com; www.ichotelsgroup.com. The classiest & most expensive place in town has everything you would expect from this luxurious chain. The hotel has direct access to the slopes from the Refuge category slope. **$$$$$**

🏠 **Tamer Land Hotel** (54 rooms) Faraya Village, Faraya; ✆ 09 321 268; m 03 818 981; e tamerland@hotmail.com. A good, friendly & simple no-frills option, with all rooms having en-suite facilities & TV. Ski passes can be purchased from reception. Free Wi-Fi & there is a bar & restaurant. **$$$**

🏠 **Coin Vert** (20 rooms) Main Rd, Faraya; 📞 09 950 903; **m** 03 724 611. Simple, clean rooms with dated décor & dark wood panels, this friendly hotel is a good budget option with bar & restaurant. **$**

What to see and do

Mzaar Winter Festival (*Mzaar Kfardebian Resort, Faraya;* 📞 *09 231 611;* **e** *info@ skimzaar.com; www.skimzaar.com*) Each February, Lebanese and international skiers and snowboarders take part in a competitive display of their skills at the resort which also plays host to a fashion and lingerie show at the foot of the ski slopes.

Mzaar Summer Festival (*Mzaar Gardens, Faraya;* 📞 *09 340 100*) Held annually each August, this festival plays host to a range of Lebanese-based art, fashion show, music, fireworks display and previous events have included trips in a hot-air balloon.

FAQRA CLUB (*Kfardebian;* 📞 *09 300 601;* 🕐 *08.00–15.30 Mon–Fri, 08.00–16.00 Sat/ Sun & public holidays; ski lift pass prices: US$12 Mon–Fri, US$20 Sat/Sun, night ski pass US$12 Sat/Sun only*) Some 45km from Beirut and with only four slopes, Faqra, at between 1,735m and 1,980m above sea level, is one of the smaller resorts. As the club is for private members only, you will only be permitted to ski here if you take out membership of the club or are a guest of a member. Staying at the club's hotel does not permit you to use the slopes, though on quiet days the club may make an exception. It would be sensible to call the club before visiting and certainly before booking a room. The club can provide ski tuition for beginners and also organises non-ski events such as hiking and horseriding.

Getting there A taxi from Beirut to Faqra should set you back between LBP60,000 and LBP80,000. If on a self-drive trip take the coast road from Beirut north until just after the Nahr al-Kalb (Dog River), and turn right towards Jeita Grotto to follow the road ahead, passing through Ajaltoun, Raifoun, Faitroun, Mayrouba, through Faraya, and follow the signs to Faqra.

🏠 **Where to stay**

🏠 **L'Auberge de Faqra** (28 rooms) Faqra; 📞 09 300 600; **e** info@faqraclub.com; www. faqraclub.com. This hotel underwent extensive renovation in 2010, & offers rooms of a decent size & comfort with all the modern accoutrements you would expect for the price; guests can use the hotel's outdoor swimming pool. **$$$$$**

🏠 **Terre Brune Hotel** (40 rooms & suites) Kfardebian Main Rd; 📞 09 300 060, 09 300 065; **m** 03 030 301; **e** info@terrebrunehotel.com; www.terrebrunehotel.com. Tasteful décor with lovely warm & cosy rooms is supplemented by the hotel's stunning mountain vistas, gym, pool & spa. Wi-Fi charged at US$5/hr. **$$$$$**

What to see One of the most interesting of Faqra's sites is its 35m-long limestone Natural Bridge or Jisr al-Hajar, on the road between Faqra and Faraya, which looks so beautifully sculpted as if to be the work of skilled craftsmen but is in fact the work of nature. Apart from its Natural Bridge and of course its skiing, Faqra possesses the most extensive archaeological remains in all of the Mount Lebanon region; during the Roman epoch it functioned as an important centre of ecclesiastical worship. On his forays around Lebanon in the 19th century the French archaeologist Ernest Renaan observed that Faqra's remains were 'the most spectacular ruins on the mountain' with the site comprising a broad array of lithe-like columns, altars, tombs and temples. The most intriguing, although its origins remain the subject of some scholarly debate, is the cube-like 15m-long Claudius Tower. The structure contains a weathered Greek inscription over its portal stating that it was renovated by the Roman emperor Claudius in AD43–44 in homage to the 'very great god,' whom is widely believed to be Adonis. At one time this cube-shaped building contained a pyramid-shaped top, resembling the one at Hermel in the Bekaa Valley (see page 215) but today it is the views from the top of the tower accessed by a staircase which will most interest the visitor.

ADONIS VALLEY AND AFQA GROTTO

Legendary associations and scenic beauty aside for one moment, if you want to live the cliché and ski in the morning and swim in the afternoon, this is as good a spot as any to do it. The pure waters of the Nahr Ibrahim or Adonis River rush over a 200m-high cliff and are ideal for bathing, as well as being in close proximity to the ski resort at Laqlouq (see page 145). In addition to appreciating the area's stunning natural beauty, it is also possible to supplement the swimming and skiing with some hiking along the banks of the river. In the spring and summer months when the water level and flow is at its lowest you can explore inside the cave.

The area is ideal for exploring on foot and has numerous caves, inlets and a Roman temple near the cave. Feeding the river is the 3,600m-long cave at Afqa Grotto, which has an even longer mythological history, and like many a Hollywood movie has spawned a number of sequels. According to the Phoenician version, this is where Adonis met Astarte – Afqa means 'source' in Arabic – and stole his first passionate kiss with her (Aphrodite to the Greeks, Venus to the Romans). Unfortunately for Adonis, by the next date things turned rather Oedipal and Astarte's jealous husband despatched a wild boar to kill Adonis, who died in her arms, but not before they had managed to exchange one last kiss. Astarte succeeded in her quest for Adonis's reincarnation, well for part of each year anyway, and each spring the river takes on a reddish tint believed to be the blood of Adonis, which allegedly is responsible for the carpet of crimson anemones which adorns the landscape during this season. A more likely explanation, however, for the hue of the river and seasonal blooms is the speed of the flowing water picking up mineral deposits from the soil as it flows downstream, which also just happens to be the best time to visit this spot.

GETTING THERE As the valley and grotto are somewhat isolated and remote from any bus or service taxi route, the best option for getting there is to negotiate a taxi from Byblos. Expect to pay somewhere in the region of LBP40,000–50,000 for the return fare.

 WHERE TO STAY Although the area is often visited as part of a day trip the nearby option below, Lebanon's premier eco-resort, is highly recommended for adventurous travellers seeking an authentic ecotourism experience.

La Reserve (campsite) Afqa; ☏ 01 498 775/6; m 03 727 484; e info@lareserve.com.lb; www.lareserve.com.lb; ⊕ May–Oct only. Accommodation in 4-person tents with all bedding & linen supplied (except sleeping bag) with separate WC & shower facilities. In 2011, prices were LBP15,000 for adults & LBP10,000 for children under 10 years. There is also a range of activities on offer here including archery, caving, climbing, hiking & mountain biking. **$**

NAHR AL-KALB (DOG RIVER) This 7km-long river, the Lycus or Wolf River to the ancient Greeks, originates at the nearby Jeita Grotto and forms the natural boundary between the Metn and Kesrouan administrative districts. It has witnessed, literally, the march of history for more than 3,000 years since the Egyptian pharaoh Ramses II felt the need to record and perhaps give thanks for his successful crossings. The route through the narrow, steep gorge for invading armies was potentially a precarious one owing to the barriers created by mountain and water, which necessitated a single-file march by the invaders leaving them vulnerable to attack. One journeyman in 1232 remarked that 'a few men could prevent the entire world from passing through this place'.

Continuing the tradition set by Ramses II, subsequent foreign conquerors left their own calling cards. The result is that Dog River is a kind of a cross between an art gallery and open-air museum, with some 22 stelae (stone slabs with a commemorative inscription) in their native scripts serving as commemorative documents to the presence of icons from history. With the exception of one stela on the north or left bank of the river by the 6th-century neo-Babylonian king Nebuchadnezzar II, all of the stelae are on the right or south bank of the river. Some stelae are located higher up on the mountainside, and it is a short walk up a specially constructed footpath with railings. Many of the stelae are labelled in Arabic, English and French, which is especially useful for those which have been weathered over time. Among the fascinating inscriptions to see are those depicting Assyrian kings, the pharaoh Ramses II with a prisoner about to be sacrificed to the god Harmarkhs, and Emperor Napoleon III, which overlays a former stela by Ramses II, commemorating his 1860 presence during the Christian–Druze conflict. There is also a selection of stelae from the more modern era, including the 25 July 1920 entry of French troops under General Gouraud into Damascus, whilst another documents French troops going the other way with their final withdrawal from Lebanon in 1946. Not all of the stelae deal directly with conflict. For instance, one commemorates construction work on the road during the Roman period under Emperor Caracalla.

Getting there The Nahr al-Kalb is 12km north of Beirut and if travelling from the capital you can catch the LCC bus number 6 from Cola intersection (LBP1,500), which can drop you off just past the clearly signposted bridge to the stelae (look out for the sign on the bridge saying *Vallé Historique de Nahr El Kalb*), which are impossible to miss and on your right when you alight from the bus.

Activities

Rio Lento (*1,500m from Nahr al-Kalb;* ℡ *04 915 656;* e *info@riolento.com; www. riolento.com;* ⏰ *summer 09.00–19.00 daily*) Lebanon's first water park offers a diverse family experience, with a host of water rides ranging from the Lazy River to the vertical Kamikaze and a 700m² children's pool amongst its many attractions.

JEITA GROTTO (*Main Rd, Jeita;* ℡ *09 220 841/3;* e *info@jeitagrotto.com; www. jeitagrotto.com;* ⏰ *Oct–May 09.00–17.00, Jun 09.00–18.00, Jul–Sep 09.00–19.00, closed Mon except during Jul/Aug; admission fee: adults LBP18,150, children 4–11 years LBP10,175, children under 4 free. Allow 2hrs for your visit. Photography & video recording is strictly forbidden inside the grotto & cameras & mobile phones have to be deposited in secure lockers*) Outside the capital itself, Jeita Grotto is the country's

4

biggest tourist attraction, receiving well in excess of 250,000 visitors annually. Situated 22km north of Beirut and the source of the Nahr al-Kalb or Dog River, this karstic limestone landscape, fashioned by geology, time and water has resulted in a stunning array of stalactite and stalagmite rock formations. Human habitation of the caves dates back to the Palaeolithic period, but it wasn't until a chance encounter led to the discovery of its lower cavern by the American missionary Reverend William Thomson in 1836, whilst out on a hunting expedition. Upon hearing the rush of water he fired his gun and the resultant echo from inside the cave seemed proof enough that this was a substantial and important structure, which he reported back to the Ottoman authorities in Beirut. However it wasn't until 1873 that a team of engineers from the Beirut Water Company began to explore the caverns over a two-year period, who concluded that there was sufficient water present to supply much of the capital's needs, which it continues to do to this day.

Additional explorations of the caverns took place in 1902 by a team from the American University of Beirut (AUB), a French team in 1927 and, most intensely, by the Speleo-Club of Lebanon in the 1940s and 1950s, who were responsible for discovering the upper cavern in 1958 with the lower cavern opening as a tourist attraction in the same year. When the upper cavern opened in January 1969, it did so to great fanfare. Exploiting the acoustic potential of the caves, a concert was held featuring the music of French composer François Bayle, and later the same year the cavern hosted a concert at which the German composer Carl-Heinrich Stockhausen performed. With the onset of civil war in 1975, the caverns changed from tourist site to munitions dump for the Lebanese Forces militia and the grotto was forced to close, not reopening until July 1995, following completion of extensive renovation and modernisation work.

A visual feast for both adults and kids alike, a visit to the 9km-long grotto is divided into two parts: an upper and a lower cavern, which are separated by some 108m. The upper cavern, reached by a short cable car ride and then a 120m-long walkway, can be toured on foot for some 750m of its 2,200m length, where the temperature is kept constant at 22°C, and reveals a series of eerily peaceful and beautifully lit chambers containing bizarre rock formations, including the world's longest stalactite of 8.2m. The 7,000m lower grotto, as the origin of the Nahr al-Kalb, can only be visited by way of a short boat ride through 500m of its accessible length and is equally beautiful, though cooler at 16°C, but is sometimes closed in winter when the level of the water level is too high. Currently on the shortlist of 28 finalists to become one of the 'New 7 Wonders of Nature' (www.new7wonders.com), Jeita was in 14th place at the time of writing with the final results due to be announced in November 2011. What definitely won't win any awards, however, is the manmade and superfluous Disney-esque toy train ride outside the grotto. Apart from the obligatory gift shop there are also cafés and restaurants serving decent enough food.

Getting there The best way to get to Jeita if using public transport is to take LCC bus number 6 from Beirut's Cola station (LBP1,500) and ask to be dropped off just past the Nahr al-Kalb Bridge, which is about a 50-minute journey, traffic permitting, from the capital. Over the road to your right will be a legion of taxis all waiting to convey you on the last leg of your journey to the grotto. The taxi fare should cost around LBP12,000–15,000 one-way, though be prepared to be quoted more! If you are visiting the grotto by hire car from the capital take the coast road heading north and turn right shortly after passing Nahr al-Kalb and stay on this (scenic) road which will also take you past the Hall of Fame (see page 151) en route to Jeita which is c5km from the turn off.

Tourist information

HALL OF FAME (*Main Rd, Jeita;* ☏ *09 225 202, 09 225 303; www.halloffamelb.com;* ⏱ *Aug–May 09.00–19.00 daily, Jun/Jul 09.00–20.00 daily; admission: adults LBP12,000, children under 9 years LBP8,000*) Proclaiming itself to be the world's 'first animated silicone museum', this manmade attraction makes for an amusing and entertaining side trip when visiting Jeita Grotto as it is located on a side turning, clearly signposted, just off the same road to the grotto. Home to some 50 very lifelike moving and talking silicone figures from the worlds of celebrity, politics and culture, together with other more bizarre and famous people, the collection includes former Lebanese premier Rafiq Hariri, Fidel Castro, Tony Blair, Yasser Arafat, Lebanese singer Sabah, Bill Clinton, the towering frame of the world's tallest man, Robert Wadlow, and a shifty-eyed, former US president George W Bush among its immortalised incumbents. There is also a small gift shop inside the museum selling souvenirs.

JOUNIEH

Just 20km north up the coastal highway from Beirut in the Kesrouan *caza* or district to the north of the Metn region, this Maronite Christian town, with its picturesque 5km bay with mountains tumbling down into the sea, is a hedonist's paradise with its twin towns of Las Vegas, Monaco and Rio de Janeiro more than hinting at the town's main preoccupation. Unfortunately, Jounieh has also become a developers' paradise with an urban sprawl of tower blocks of concrete jungle proportions, and these monstrosities cascade down the mountainside as you approach from Beirut, with the town itself now dominated by hotels, restaurants, nightclubs and resorts. How times change. Prior to the civil war Jounieh was a green and quiet, almost anonymous little town with banana plantations and citrus groves.

With the onset of hostilities in 1975 and the divisive Green Line, Christians flocked here *en masse* and the area became a haven for uninhibited development as well as a party capital both during the war and after. Although usurped somewhat by the ongoing reconstruction and ever-expanding nightlife options in the capital, Jounieh remains a popular summer resort retreat for Lebanese and wealthy Gulf Arabs alike, keen to indulge in luxurious retail therapy at nearby Kaslik, and visit expensive restaurants, nightclubs and that icon of glamour and wealth, the Casino du Liban. Given its primarily decadent culture, Jounieh is a little light on sites to visit but a cable car ride on the Téléférique and a visit to the Christian shrine at Harissa make a visit worthwhile, made easier by the fact that the town is on the route to other important attractions such as the stelae at Nahr al-Kalb (Dog River) and the essential Jeita Grotto.

GETTING THERE From Beirut's Cola intersection, LCC bus number 6 (LBP1,500) departs regularly from the eastern side of the station and takes around an hour, depending on traffic, to the centre of Jounieh *en route* to Byblos. It is also possible to catch a minivan or service taxi from Cola or Dora for around LBP2,000. If on a self-drive trip, just take the coast road north from Beirut and Jounieh is clearly signposted. The journey up the coastal highway will not be the most scenic travail you can undertake in Lebanon, consisting mostly of huge advertising billboards marketing every conceivable product and service, together with large shopping malls.

Mount Lebanon JOUNIEH

4

GETTING AROUND Jounieh is easily managed on foot from the main town with everything from eateries to nightclubs all close together. You shouldn't have any need to take a bus or taxi unless you are planning to visit the Casino du Liban, which is a longish walk along the main Rue Maameltain, where the majority of hotels, clubs and restaurants are located as well as the Téléférique. If you do decide to continue walking this long road, you will eventually reach the Casino du Liban, with its superlative view over the Bay of Jounieh. Further north, this coast road continues all the way to Byblos and beyond.

TOUR OPERATOR

Lebanon Roots Opposite Holy Spirit University of Kaslik, Kaslik; ☎ 09 638 128; m 03 199 338; e info@lebanonroots.com; www.lebanonroots. com. This Christian Maronite-based tour operator specialises in religious tours & pilgrimages throughout the area & country. Their website also has a useful downloadable brochure of 'alternative lodgings' in Lebanon, such as those in convents & schools providing a different option from the hotels.

WHERE TO STAY
Jounieh is by no means short of accommodation options, though there is little to bring a smile to the face of the budget traveller. The hotels here do not really offer anything out of the ordinary, with the following being pretty representative. In any case, unless you find the sea and mountain views so irresistible that you feel compelled to stay overnight, Jounieh is best visited as a day trip.

Bel Azur (53 rooms) Port entrance; ☎ 09 937 752, 09 932 162, 09 930 621; e info@belazur.com, reservation@belazur.com, belazurhotel@hotmail.com; www.belazur.com. The quite average rooms, all with TV & AC, are a little overpriced, but this hotel has a full complement of resort-type facilities, including swimming pool, jet & water skiing, & paragliding. **$$$$**

Aquarium Hotel (43 rooms & suites) Rue Maameltain; ☎ 09 936 858, 09 936 860, 09 936 863; e info@hotelaquarium.info; www. hotelaquarium.info. Although there is no denying the fine sea views, the rooms look a little tired & dated, but all have TV & AC & there is a swimming pool in this resort complex. Otherwise it is a clean & adequate hotel for 1 or 2 nights. **$$$**

Hotel Arcada Marina (70 rooms & suites) Rue Maameltein; ☎ 09 640 597; m 03 117 667, 03 118 778; e reservations@arcadamarina.com; www.arcadamarina.com. Wonderfully spacious rooms, all with sea or mountain views, popular with business travellers though they don't quite match the grandness of the lobby. The US$500 suite, however, with its vast expanse of window, does invite you to plunge into the pool below! **$$$**

Hotel La Medina (45 rooms) Rue Maameltain; ☎ 09 918 484; m 03 274 011; e lamedina@lamedinahotel.com; www. lamedinahotel.com; ⏰ May–Oct only. A slightly cheaper option than the others, this hotel is pleasant & clean enough with large rooms but not all have sea views. There is a nice communal lounge for relaxing. **$$$**

WHERE TO EAT AND DRINK
What Jounieh lacks in sights and historical interest, it more than makes up for in its eating and drinking options. Cheap and convenience food including KFC and Dunkin' Donuts is supplemented by a whole host of cafés, restaurants and watering holes within easy walking distance of each other; the selection below is just a slice of the gastronomic choices on offer.

Chez Sami Rue Maameltain; ☎ 09 910 520; m 03 242 428; e info@chezsamirestaurant.com; www.chezsamirestaurant.com; ⏰ 12.00– midnight daily. Specialising in fresh seafood & established for over 40 years, this is one of those rare places where fine dining is complemented by the equally fine surroundings, whether it is the sea views from its terrace tables or the traditional *right* Aanjar is, uniquely in Lebanon, the product of only one historical period: the 8th-century Umayyad caliphate (PD) page 204

below The Crusader Sea Castle at Sidon was built by the Crusaders in 1228, using the foundations of a much earlier Phoenician temple (SS) page 240

bottom The Qadisha Valley was fashioned into a plethora of caves and rock-cut monasteries in the 7th century (SS) page 182

left   As an in-situ open-air and subterranean museum of war, the 60,000m² complex at Mleeta must rank as one of the most unique and extraordinary shrines to military endeavour in the world (PD) page 248

below   Once dubbed the 'Queen of the Seas' for its mercantile and seafaring activities, Tyre was previously a flourishing commercial centre for international trade and appears in the classical writings of Herodotus and Homer (PD) page 249

bottom   The pretty town of Deir al-Qamar preserves its rich legacy of Ottoman-era architecture in one of Lebanon's most serene settings (PD) page 219

right The reward for visitors who have survived the 600m ascent on the Téléférique from Jounieh to Harissa is the 19th-century 15-tonne statue of the Virgin Mary (SS) page 154

below After Cairo, Tripoli contains the largest and most significant set of Mamluk-period architecture in the world (SS) page 172

<table>
</table>

above   Sidon's atmospheric souks offer a range of foodstuffs and traditionally crafted products (PD) page 242

left   Druze man; the Druze sect was founded in Cairo in the 11th century as a splinter group from the Shi'ite Ismaili faith (SS) page 32

below   Carpet makers, Tripoli; Tripoli's souks are well worth a look, even if it's just to watch the craftsmen at work (SS) page 177

above Traditional Arabic or Turkish coffee is drunk very strong with copious amounts of sugar in small cups or glasses (KE/A) page 71

above right The Lebanese favourite, and main meal of the day, is the eclectic *mezze*, a wide array of small savoury dishes, served hot or cold (PD) page 69

right A popular Lebanese dessert is *baklava*, a very sweet and syrupy pastry with pistachio nuts (SS) page 69

below *Ka'ik* bread is sprinkled with sesame seeds and sold by the many street vendors who perambulate the Corniche in Beirut (PD) page 125

above   Château Ksara celebrated its 150th anniversary in 2007, and is Lebanon and the Middle East's oldest winery and largest producer (PD) page 201

left   The 35m-long limestone Natural Bridge, or Jisr al-Hajar, on the road between Faqra and Faraya, looks as if it's the work of skilled craftsmen but is in fact the work of nature (SS) page 147

below   Mzaar is Lebanon's premier, most modern, glitzy and best-equipped ski resort (EK/D) page 146

right Lebanon's most famous flora, and the country's national symbol, is the cedar tree (*Cedrus libani*) (PD) page 230

below Separated by the Mount Lebanon and Anti-Lebanon mountain ranges, the Bekaa Valley is an elongated plateau that reaches up to 1,000m above sea level in places (SS) page 195

bottom The 12km² Tannourine Cedars Forest Nature Reserve is rich in biodiversity and well worth a visit (EK/D) page 187

stone interior of this converted house. Highly recommended with great service. $$$$$

Makhlouf Rue Maameltain; 09 645 192; 24/7. One of the cheaper eateries, the Lebanese food served here is tasty & filling with burgers & pizzas also available. The plat du jour is LBP12,000. Has pleasant sea views; just a pity that the KFC opposite partially obscures the mountains, but there's always the sea on the other side. $$

Ociento Rue Maameltain; 09 830 252; m 70 686 339; 12.00–late daily. Decent snack bar selling sandwiches, soup & a tasty 'special offer' of half a chicken, hummus, Arabic salad, sweet & Pepsi for US$10pp. There is a pleasant outdoor seating area & free Wi-Fi access. $$

Rafaat Hallab Patisserie Rue Maameltain, opposite Chez Sami Restaurant; 09 635 351; e hallab@hallab.com; www.hallab.com; 07.00–midnight daily. One to avoid for weight-watchers, but this branch of renowned sweet makers from Tripoli who have been established since 1881 have a delicious range of speciality sweets such as baklava, cakes, pistachios, jams, coffee & ice cream. Ironically, they also stock diet products! $$

ENTERTAINMENT AND NIGHTLIFE You didn't decide to spend an evening in Jounieh for the peace and quiet which is just as well, as there isn't much. It may have been usurped by Beirut's ever-evolving and pulsating club and pub scene, but Jounieh certainly knows how to have a good time and the options are numerous. Of course, for those with large wallets there is always the Casino du Liban a little further up the road (see box, page 154) for a decadent night out, as well as a plethora of super nightclubs.

SHOPPING Jounieh has a bog-standard range of retail outlets including men's and women's clothing boutiques, pharmacies and supermarkets that between them stock enough items to cater for most daily needs, but there are few, if any, things you would come here to buy.

OTHER PRACTICALITIES ATMs, banks, and pharmacies abound, but the following useful and centrally located services are all clustered near to the Municipality Building.

$ BLC Bank Stephan Bldg, opposite the Municipality; 09 910 800; www.blcbank.com; 08.00–17.00 Mon–Fri, 08.00–13.00 Sat. Has a 24/7 ATM.

Middle East Airlines Khoury Bldg, Main Rd, facing Municipality Bldg; 09 932 120; e spu-jouso@mea.aero

Post office Fouad Chehab St, behind Municipality Bldg; 09 832 563, 09 914 984; 08.00–17.00 Mon–Fri, 08.00–13.30 Sat

WHAT TO SEE AND DO

Téléférique (*Téléférique Station, Rue Maameltain; 09 936 075, 09 914 324; e comments@teleferiqelb.com; www.teleferiquelb.com; summer 10.00–23.00 Tue–Sun, winter 10.00–19.00 Tue–Sun; admission: adults: return trip LBP9,000, one-way LBP5,000, children: return trip LBP5,000, one-way LBP3,000, children under 4 free if accompanied by adult*) Without doubt the highlight – with the emphasis on high – of a visit to Jounieh is this nine-minute ride by cable car from the town centre to Harissa (see below). A white-knuckle experience for those who suffer from vertigo but voyeuristic heaven for others who will enjoy the 'peeping Tom' experience of glimpses into people's kitchens, bedrooms and living rooms as the cable car climbs between the mountainside apartments. The final part of the journey is completed by funicular railway to Harissa and culminates in a fantastic symmetrical vista of the Bay of Jounieh, where you can sit down at the newly opened café and enjoy the view over a drink.

Harissa and Our Lady of Lebanon Shrine (*Harissa;* ☎ *263 660, 09 263 893, 09 263 895;* m *70 203 040;* e *info@ololb.com; www.ololb.com, www.ololb.org;* ⏲ *24/7; admission free*) The reward for vertigo sufferers who have survived the 600m ascent on the Téléférique is this important 19th-century 15-tonne bronze statue (painted in white) of the Virgin Mary with her arms outstretched, an icon of Christianity and of Jounieh's Maronite religious persuasion. The base of the structure houses a tiny chapel and when you reach the top of the 8.5m shrine via its spiral staircase, there are fine panoramic views over the Bay of Jounieh. There is a small souvenir shop close by Harissa and the Maronite Notre Dame du Liban basilica, which can seat a congregation of 3,500 worshippers, is worth visiting.

Jounieh Summer Music Festival This annual music festival, held during July and August in the streets of the town, sees a range of dancers, DJs, musicians and entertainers help party the night away. The website www.liveinbeirut.com often carries full details for the upcoming season's programme of events.

Adventure activities For adrenalin seekers and sporty types, paragliding (US$125) and waterskiing (US$110) can be undertaken daily around the Bay of Jounieh offered by **Skileb** (m *70 103 222; www.skileb.com*).

ZOUK MIKAEL If whilst in Jounieh you can tear yourself away from the nearby designer shopping outlets at Kaslik, a detour a little further inland to the attractive town of Zouk Mikael is well worth considering. This little 17th-century town has a

CASINO DU LIBAN

(*Maameltain Highway, Jounieh;* ☎ *09 859 999, 09 855 888, 09 853 222;* e *customerservice@cdl.com.lb; www.cdl.com.lb;* ⏲ *10.00–06.00 daily, except Good Friday*) This iconic showcase of 1960s and 1970s glamour and prosperity is nestled high up on the mountains commanding stunning views over the Bay of Jounieh. Lebanon's sole gambling venue, the 34,000m² casino complex, first opened in 1959, continues to evoke the era of extravagance and hedonism which saw the likes of Johny Halliday, Julio Iglesias, Sasha Distel and, of course, Lebanon's very own diva, Fairuz, entertain the famous and the wealthy. Forced to close for much of the civil war, the casino reopened in December 1996 following a US$50 million restoration project. Amid the chandeliers, grand entrance and plush décor, the casino boasts over 400 slot machines, four restaurants, three gaming rooms offering American Roulette, Black Jack, Punto Banco and stud poker and including the ultra-exclusive and private six-table Cercle D'Or Room for the gambling elite where the minumum bet is LBP250,000. If you think Las Vegas which, coincidentally, just happens to be Jounieh's twin town, you will have a good idea of the general ambience.

Assuming you haven't just lost all your money on the gaming tables or slot machines, the casino offers equally lavish entertainment in the form of a 1,000+ seat theatre and the 600+ seats of the Salle des Ambassadeurs, the venue for many a lavish and elegant cabaret and piece of performance art. Whilst Lebanese nationals have to prove they have an annual income in excess of US$20,000 in order to gain entry, all foreigners over the age of 21 years are welcome to the tables in smart dress.

nicely restored souk area and was once of some importance in the silk trade. Today, it retains many of its traditional old houses and village ambience, and you can still see artisans at work and selling the fruits of their hand crafted labours. Although the town has a reasonable smattering of restaurants and decent accommodation an overnight stay is not really warranted unless you are attending the annual summer festival (see below) and prefer to stay overnight rather than make the journey back to Beirut or elsewhere.

Getting there Zouk Mikael is situated around 20km north from Beirut. If you are on a self-drive visit take the coast road north from the capital and when you reach Kaslik head inland and follow the signs for Zouk. The total journey time, as always depending on traffic conditions, should be around half an hour. Expect to pay around LBP20,000 for a taxi from Beirut and obviously considerably less for a taxi from nearby Jounieh or Kaslik which should cost no more than LBP5,000.

Other practicalities In addition to the branch of Libanpost below there is a good supply of banks, pharmacies, petrol stations and shops around the town catering for most visitors needs.

✉ **Post Office** Ogero Bldg, Main Rd; ☎ 09 214 516

What to do
Zouk Mikael International Festival (*www.zoukmikaelfestival.org; Tickets can be purchased from branches of Virgin Megastore or online at www.ticketingboxoffice. com*) Held annually for a week in July this summer festival brings together musicians and singers from Lebanon and overseas and takes place within the confines of the town's Roman ampitheatre. In 2011 the festival featured Plácido Domingo, the Argentinian soprano Virginia Tola, the Lebanese Philharmonic Orchestra and the aptly named US blues band Roomful of Blues.

BYBLOS (JBAIL)

As the saying often goes, the more things change, the more they stay the same. This certainly applies to the town of Byblos (Jbail in Arabic) where, despite its 7,000 years of existence making it one of the contenders for the oldest continuously inhabited town in the world, this town and port continues to evoke the past as much as the present. Whilst the legends and myths of Adonis and Astarte were revered here for some 3,000 years from the Phoenician to the Roman eras, physical reminders of the town's past can be found in the wealth of archaeological layers of civilisations which span the Phoenician, Greek, Roman and Crusader periods. This historical importance was recognised by UNESCO in 1984 when it bestowed World Heritage Site status on the town. Byblos was also the town, under the Phoenicians, which gave birth to the alphabet upon which our modern version is based and was suitably named by the ancient Greeks as 'Byblos' after their word for papyrus, which was traded here and shipped to Egypt.

As a nation founded by its port cities and settlements, Byblos must rank as Lebanon's finest. Charming and picturesque by day and night, the port is the quintessential chocolate-box and picture-postcard scene. It would be a great shame to visit the country without stopping by here to see the still-functioning workaday harbour and the tastefully restored souk (easily better than Beirut's), offering some of the most unusual and best souvenir items in the country. Byblos is dotted with

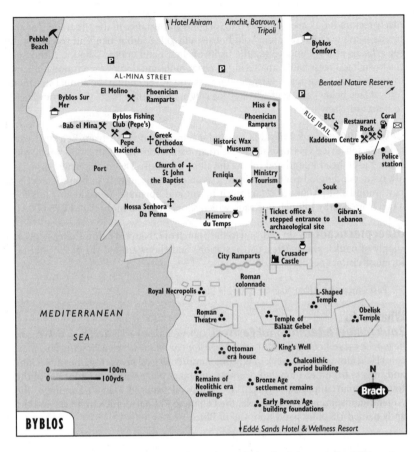

BYBLOS

Map labels: Hotel Ahiram · Amchit, Batroun, Tripoli · Pebble Beach · Byblos Comfort · AL-MINA STREET · El Molino · Phoenician Ramparts · Byblos Sur Mer · Bentael Nature Reserve · Miss é · Phoenician Ramparts · Byblos Fishing Club (Pepe's) · RUE JBAIL · BLC · Restaurant Rock · Coral · Bab el Mina · Pepe Hacienda · Greek Orthodox Church · Historic Wax Museum · Kaddoum Centre · Byblos · Police station · Port · Church of St John the Baptist · Feniqia · Ministry of Tourism · Souk · Nossa Senhora Da Penna · Souk · Mémoire du Temps · Ticket office & stepped entrance to archaeological site · Gibran's Lebanon · City Ramparts · Crusader Castle · Roman colonnade · Royal Necropolis · L-Shaped Temple · Obelisk Temple · MEDITERRANEAN SEA · Roman Theatre · Temple of Balaat Gebel · Ottoman era house · King's Well · Chalcolithic period building · 0 100m · 0 100yds · Remains of Neolithic era dwellings · Bronze Age settlement remains · Early Bronze Age building foundations · N · Bradt · Eddé Sands Hotel & Wellness Resort

fine seafood restaurants, including the Fishing Club which has a splendid location by the port and offers a museum of photographs dedicated to the rich and famous who indulged their heady passions by day and night during the 1960s and 1970s. At some 37km north from Beirut, Byblos is an easy day trip from the capital, though equally it is a delightful place to spend a couple of nights.

HISTORY From its humble beginnings as a modest Neolithic fishing port with small agricultural holdings some 7,000 years ago, Byblos's stature, like its coastal tides, have ebbed and flowed during its hosting of successive civilisations. During the Phoenician period the town was called Gubla and the Greeks renamed the town 'Byblos' in recognition of the town's importance in the paper trade, papyrus being the Greek word for paper. It wasn't until around 3000BC, however, with the arrival of the Canaanites, that Byblos expanded its sea trade and began to specialise in the export of Lebanese cedarwood to Egypt, receiving papyrus, gold and linen from the Egyptian pharaohs as part of the barter deal, which ushered in a period of economic prosperity for the town. Around 2300BC, the Amorite tribe descended on the town, disrupting trade relations for the next two centuries which was further exacerbated by the arrival of another Asiatic clan from the desert lands of Syria and west Asia, the Hyksos, who introduced new equipment and tools of warfare hitherto unseen in the area such as horse-drawn chariots and the composite bow. Following 500 years of Hyksos domination, the Egyptians finally managed to overcome them and restored economic and maritime prosperity that was accompanied by a new period of cultural and religious osmosis between Byblos and Egypt.

From around 1200BC, the Sea Peoples, probably from north Africa, arrived on the coast and after a period of struggle became assimilated into the fabric of the Phoenician city-states. Although this was the start of a golden era of overall Phoenician prosperity, Byblos very much played second fiddle to other ports such as Sidon and Tyre in the south. But this was also the period which witnessed perhaps the Phoenicians' greatest and enduring cultural legacy, the birthplace and development of the first 22 letter phonetic alphabet that was adopted by the Greeks in 800BC and is the foundation of our modern alphabet. Inscriptions discovered on the sarcophagus of King Ahiram, including a curse on grave robbers, ranks as one of the most important archaeological discoveries in Byblos (now in the National Museum). By 1000BC, Byblos was once again a victim of outside powers, this time by the Assyrians under King Ashurnasirpal II who, along with the other Phoenician states, forced Byblos into paying annual tributes of precious metals and cedarwood in return for a semblance of economic and political independence.

Despite ongoing invasions by more powerful states, Phoenician prosperity continued apace and under Persian rule in 539BC, following Cyrus the Great's defeat of the Babylonians, the two entered into a pragmatic alliance with Phoenician maritime skills and vessels utilised by the Persians in the Persian Wars against the Greeks. This mutually acceptable arrangement ended following Alexander the Great's defeat of Darius III in 333BC at the Battle of Issus, paving the way for the Hellenisation of Byblos in which Greek became the lingua franca along with other Greek customs and mores. This endured during the Roman occupation from 64BC under Pompey, when the town witnessed extensive Roman town planning and construction including colonnaded streets, temples and a theatre. With the partitioning of the Roman Empire in AD395 into an eastern and a western branch, following the emperor Constantine's conversion to Christianity, the paganism of antiquity which had hitherto held sway now came under the banner of Christianity during eastern or Byzantine rule and Byblos became, under the emperor Diocletian, a significant Christian bishopric, though there are few architectural remnants in the town from this period. The transition from Byzantium to Islamic rule which occurred cAD635, sustained this relatively uneventful and less illustrious period in Byblos's history. This was to change once more, with the arrival on Lebanon's shores of the Crusader knights from Europe in 1104, who exchanged the Arabic name Jbail to the more culinary Giblet. As in the other coastal towns, the Franks proved great early recyclers and utilised found Roman columns and stones to help construct the landmark Crusader fortress which you see today.

Byblos remained under the Crusader yoke for the next two centuries until the Mamluks finally ousted them in 1289. Byblos again reverted to its rather anodyne existence, and after the onset of Ottoman rule in 1516, Fakhreddine Maan II incorporated Byblos into his emirate which eventually became part of the Ottomans' northern administrative district. With the demise of the Turks following World War I, Byblos has become better known since for the efforts made by a number of archaeologists to unearth and document the town's rich historical legacy, which, though halted by the civil war, is still ongoing.

GETTING THERE From Beirut's Cola station LCC bus number 6 (LBP1,500) goes all the way to Byblos to the centre of town in around an hour, though traffic conditions can sometimes double the journey time. It is also possible to take a minivan from

Dora Roundabout (LBP1,500); LCC bus number 6 also passes through Dora. If you are staying in the Downtown area of Beirut it may be more convenient to take a bus from the nearby Charles Helou station going to Tripoli and ask to be dropped off at Byblos. Expect to pay around LBP45,000–60,000 for a taxi from the capital. If using a hire car, Byblos, at less than 40km north from Beirut, is an easy drive north along the coastal highway past Jounieh with the clearly signposted route (Jbail) taking 30–60 minutes, traffic permitting.

GETTING AROUND Byblos is small and easy to navigate around, centred on its small port, its archaeological ruins and souk area which are all close together; you should have no need to use buses or taxis. The main street, Rue Jbail, contains most of the banks, shops, cafés and restaurants and the post office, which is just off this main street. Slightly more outlying areas may require a service taxi or taxi and this is indicated in the appropriate sections.

TOURIST INFORMATION
🛈 Ministry of Tourism Old souk, facing Feniqia Restaurant; ☎ 09 540 325; ⏲ 08.30–17.00 Mon–Thu, 08.30–14.00 Fri, 08.30–15.00 Sat. This friendly office has an excellent range of brochures & pamphlets on Byblos & other areas of the country in Arabic, English, French, German, Italian & Spanish.

🏠 WHERE TO STAY
🏠 Byblos Sur Mer Hotel (30 rooms & suites) Port of Byblos; ☎ 09 548 000; e info@byblossurmer.com; www.byblossurmer.com. Byblos's most luxurious option has recently undergone a major renovation, with beautifully decorated & tasteful rooms. Its location overlooking the port is superb & there is free guest access to the beach opposite. **$$$$$**

🏠 Eddé Sands Hotel & Wellness Resort (28 rooms) Port of Byblos; ☎ 09 546 085; e info@eddesands.com; www.eddesandshotel.com. Nice smart rooms & part of the nearby resort which guests can use free of charge. Facilities include spa, massage, bars, restaurants, adult & children's swimming pools. A hedonist's paradise. **$$$$**

🏠 Byblos Comfort Hotel (45 rooms & suites) Main St; ☎ 09 942 200; e info@bybloscomforthotel.com; www.

bybloscomforthotel.com. Recently renovated & spacious hotel with clean, comfortable rooms all with AC, TV & fridge, but with a slightly clinical resort-type feel to the place. Not in the most central of locations. Wi-Fi is available for US$5/2hrs. **$$$**

🏠 Hotel Ahiram (23 rooms) ☎ 09 540 440, 09 944 726; e info@ahiramhotel.com; www.ahiramhotel.com. Most rooms have sea views at this decent enough hotel & there are discounts for extended stays. Free Wi-Fi & internet. **$$$**

🏠 Pepe Hacienda (8 bungalows) Harbour, behind Fishing Club; ☎ 09 540 213; e rogerppabed@hotmail.com; closed Jan. Run by Roger Abed of The Fishing Club these comfortable bungalows are all en suite with AC & TV. There is also a nice little garden for summer dining & drinking. **$**

✖ WHERE TO EAT AND DRINK
✖ Pepe's Fishing Club Pepe Abed St, Harbour; ☎ 09 540 213; m 03 635 850; e rogerppabed@hotmail.com; ⏲ summer 10.00–02.00 daily, winter 10.00–midnight daily. Although it doesn't quite match the glitzy décor of the Casino du Liban, this was the other main hangout in the 1960s & 1970s for a variety of international celebrities & the jet set who came here as much for the joie de vivre as the food. The owner, Pepe,

died in 2007, & the club is now run by his son Roger, who studied English in Hendon & lived in Golders Green. Although more sedate nowadays, the club is worth a visit to look at the gallery of black-&-white & colour photographs of past patrons which included Marlon Brando, Anita Ekberg, former French premier Jacques Chirac & Charles Aznavour to name but a few. The seafood served here remains excellent, though a tad overpriced, but the set meal for 2 of seafood mezze is good value for LBP66,000. $$$$$

✗ **Bab el Mina** Harbour; ☎ 09 540 475; m 03 540 475; e info@babelmina.com; www.babelmina.com; ⏰ 12.00–late daily. Located next door to Pepe's with a similarly nice port-side dining experience & the fresh sea food mezze every bit as good, but without the latter's ambience & history. $$$$

✗ **El Molino** Harbour; ☎ 09 541 555; ⏰ 12.00–midnight daily. Great Mexican restaurant with authentic atmosphere, excellent

service & superb margaritas. $$$$

✗ **Feniqia Restaurant** Old souk, facing Crusader castle & Ministry of Tourism office; ☎ 09 540 444; ⏰ 09.00–midnight daily. A good choice for a drink, snack or full-blown Lebanese mezze in the heart of the town with good & friendly service. $$$$

✗ **Restaurant Rock** Main St; ☎ 09 944 314, 09 546 667; ⏰ 08.00–02.00 Mon–Sat, 09.00–midnight Sun. This mainstream eatery serves decent burgers, seafood, shwarma, hot & cold beverages. $$$

ENTERTAINMENT AND NIGHTLIFE Back in the 1960s and 1970s, Byblos had a pulsating and vibrant nightlife centred on the famed Fishing Club (Pepe's) Restaurant patronised by the rich and famous. Nowadays, Byblos has a much more restrained entertainment and nightlife scene, far less frenetic than the capital and revolving essentially around dining at one of the harbourside restaurants whilst admiring the picturesque views of the port followed by an evening stroll around the harbour and nearby lanes. The town's annual festival (see page 163) ups the *joie de vivre* ante during the summer months with its diverse music offerings. As a coastal town Byblos has some clean and excellent beaches, notably the well-known Tam-Tam Beach south of the ruins, and the following resort venue is recommended for its range of relaxation and activity options.

Eddé Sands ☎ 09 546 666; m 03 997 688; e info@eddesands.com; www.eddesandsresort.com; ⏰ 09.00–19.00 daily; admission: adults LBP25,000 Mon–Fri, children LBP10,000 Mon–Fri, adults LBP33,000 Sat/Sun, children LBP10,000 Sat/Sun. Well suited to families, a range of activities are on offer here from jet skiing to water skiing. For those seeking more laid-back entertainment there are bars, spas & a range of pampering & therapy treatments available.

SHOPPING Although the main Rue Jbail in Byblos contains the vast majority of banks, pharmacies and shops, including those selling the usual tourist tack, by far the best place to browse and buy is in the recently restored souk area which offers a much more original and rewarding retail experience, with the following three outlets among the best options.

Gibran's Lebanon Old souk; ☎ 09 542 226; e gibranslebanon@idm.net.lb; www.eddeyard.com; ⏰ summer 09.00–21.00 daily, winter 09.00–19.00 daily. A superb bookshop in a lovely sandstone building & definitely worth a browse even if you are not buying. It sells a wide range of tomes on virtually every aspect of Lebanon including its history, culture, cuisine & politics in Arabic, English & French, including many rare titles. Also stocks a good selection of postcards.

Mémoire du Temps (Memory of Time) Old souk; ☎ 09 540 555; m 03 742 099, 03 378 901, 03 755 117; e abisaad@memoryoftime.com; www.memoryoftime.com; ⏰ summer 09.00–

20.00 daily, winter 09.00–18.00 daily. This fascinating, part museum part shop, sells ancient fossilised fish remains dating back about 100 million years. Though some of the smaller items sell for US$5, many of the fossilised slabs are large enough to start paving a patio. Owned & run by Palaeontologist Pierre Abi Saad, who carries on a tradition begun by his grandfather, excavating a number of mountain sites up to 800m above sea level east of Byblos chipping away at the geological timescale and sediment which encased these creatures, including sharks, turtles, stingrays & many other varieties which are then embedded in limestone rock & sold in

his shop. Each purchase comes with a numbered certificate of authenticity with detailed background information on the fossil. A gem of a shop.
Miss é Old souk; ☎ 09 943 023; m 03 370 007; e customerservice@miss-eboutique.com;

⏱ 10.00–20.00 daily. Sells some delightful & innovative clothing & accessories such as jewellery & handbags by Lebanese designers for the elegant & fashion-conscious woman.

OTHER PRACTICALITIES
$ BLC Bank Rue Jbail; ☎ 09 540 150; www.blcbank.com; ⏱ 08.00–17.00 Mon–Fri, 08.00–13.00 Sat. Has a 24/7 ATM.
$ Byblos Bank Rue Jbail; ☎ 09 945 252; www.byblosbank.com.lb; ⏱ 08.00–17.30 Mon–Fri, 08.00–13.00 Sat. Has a 24/7 ATM.
Green Line Taxi 1st Fl, Al-Haref Centre, Elysée St; ☎ 09 949 477; m 70 217 200; e info@greenlineleb.com; www.greenlineleb.

com. A 24/7 company charging around US$30 from Byblos to Beirut's Hamra district.
✉ **Post office** 2nd Fl, Rouhban Bldg, Rouhban St, off Rue Jbail near the Coral petrol station; ☎ 09 540 003; ⏱ 08.00–17.00 Mon–Fri, 08.00–13.30 Sat. As well as offering the usual range of postal services, they will also change US dollars to LBP.

WHAT TO SEE
Byblos Archaeological Site (☎ *09 540 001, 09 546 333;* ⏱ *08.00–sunset daily; admission: adults LBP6,000, students LBP1,500, children under 10 years free. In order to get the most from your visit set aside a minimum of 2 hours to view the site at a leisurely pace*) It wasn't until the latter period of the 19th century that Byblos's multiple layers of history began to be unearthed, when the French archaeologist Ernest Renan started his excavations of the ancient *tell*, or mound, of the town, which paved the way for the discovery of seven different layers of civilisations across 7,000 years of history. Renan's work was followed by his compatriot, the Egyptologist Pierre Montet (1885–1966), who was responsible for bringing to light the sarcophagus of King Ahiram as well as providing evidence of trading links between Egypt and Byblos during antiquity. The archaeologist Maurice Dunand (1898–1987) was the driving force behind more than 40 excavations between 1926 and the mid 1970s, before work was halted due to the onset of civil war. Today, ongoing archaeological work has resumed under the auspices of Lebanon's General Directorate of Antiquities.

From the ticket office, reached by walking through the old souk, the site's first and most conspicuous landmark is the omnipotent 12th-century **Crusader castle**, Château de la Mer to the Franks, which measures some 50m by 45m and was the final building in the Byblos historical jigsaw. At the top of the stairs after the ticket office, which leads to the castle's west entrance, it is definitely worth pausing to look in at the small museum on your left before proceeding further as it gives a great overview of the history of the town. The painstaking archaeological renovations, which have gone on since the 19th century, can also be seen, together with small items of pottery from the earliest-known Neolithic and Chalcolithic (6000–3200BC) periods, along with items of jewellery and other artefacts found in the area. The castle itself consists of five towers, one on each corner of the castle and a fifth centrally positioned in the north wall tower to protect the entrance, surrounding the courtyard and dungeon below. Constructed using pre-existing Roman columns and stones, the castle has been modified over the years with the Arabs, for instance, overlaying the moat with a bridge and adding vaulted ceilings and arches. Although the castle's monolithic appearance testifies to its once-strategic importance in guarding both port and town, for the visitor it is the commanding views over the entire archaeological site where its appeal lies.

Phoenician ramparts Once you exit the castle you are amidst the hub of the ancient Phoenician town dating from the 3rd and 2nd centuries BC. The defensive 25m-thick walls, which curve from the castle to the coast, would have been a difficult obstacle for an invader to overcome. The ramparts have been modified and strengthened by succeeding civilisations.

Roman theatre Originally located between the city gate and the Obelisk Temple, this amphitheatre, a third of its original size and with only five of its original seating tiers remaining, is now arguably in a much better position, situated right on the coast. It affords glorious views over the Mediterranean and looks very enchanting at sunset. The theatre dates back to AD218, and was once adorned with a fine mosaic depicting Bacchus, which is now on display in Beirut's National Museum.

Roman colonnade and the Temple of Baalat Gebel These six standing columns, dating from AD300, are all that remain of what was once a much more extensive collection of columns which were built to form the route to the Baalat Gebel Temple or 'Lady of Byblos'. Built in 2700BC, and located to the left of the colonnade, this is Byblos's most ancient temple and paid homage to Adonis's lover, the goddess Astarte, on a site considered so sacred it was built over many times and dedicated to Aphrodite under the Romans.

Obelisk Temple and the L-Shaped Temple These two temples, once revered as the dwelling of gods and used as sites where they were worshipped, date from the late Bronze Age. The Obelisk Temple, dating from 2150BC at the height of the Egyptian presence in Byblos, occupies its current position just a short distance away from where it was originally built on the site of the L-Shaped Temple in order to facilitate ongoing archaeological work. The temple comprises a sacred courtyard with a number of standing obelisks including one built in the 19th century BC at the behest of Abichemou, king of Byblos. The base of another obelisk is thought to honour Resheph, the Phoenician god of war. Aside from the obelisks, hundreds of other discoveries have been unearthed here, including iconic Phoenician figurines attired with gold leaf and wearing conical hats, providing further evidence of votive offerings to the gods; many of these are now on display in the National Museum in Beirut. The L-Shaped Temple, so named for obvious reasons, although not as ancient or as well preserved as that of Baalat Gebel, ranks as one of the oldest in Byblos. The temple was partially destroyed by fire during offensives by the nomadic Amorite tribe around 2150–2000BC and subsequently rebuilt with some design modifications. It is thought that this temple too may have been in honour of the Phoenician god Resheph.

King's Spring or 'Ain al-Malik' This is a large crater sited on a promontory near the sea which was the town's principal water supply until the Romans began utilising water from the surrounding mountains using specially constructed aqueducts. The water here was reserved only for use in sacred rituals such as those at the Temple of Baalat Gebel. According to ancient mythology, Isis was discovered weeping for Osiris here by maidservants by the pool.

Royal necropolis Dating from the 2nd century BC and located adjacent to the Colonnaded Street, these series of vertical burial shafts up to 10m deep represent probably the most significant archaeological find in Byblos. Of the nine tombs which have been unearthed, the most famous is that of the sarcophagus of the

1200bc King Ahiram, which contains the earliest-known Phoenician script, now one of the most cherished exhibits in Beirut's National Museum. Another tomb contains the resting place of the 19th-century bc King Yp-Shemou-Abi. If you can ignore the Phoenician curse, which reads 'Warning, here! Thy death is below', you can walk down some of the shafts and between them.

Prehistoric Byblos settlement Further south towards the coast, dotted around the attractive 19th-century red-tiled Ottoman-era house, is evidence of Byblos's claim to be the oldest town in the world in the form of dwellings, barely visible limestone floors and low walls from the Neolithic and Chalcolithic periods (5000–4000bc). Funerary or burial jars discovered here number around 1,500, with the skeletal remains arranged in the foetal position as if awaiting rebirth, and are now on display in the National Museum.

Medieval Byblos The arrival of the Crusader knights from Europe did much to revitalise Christianity in the town, and in 1115, construction commenced on the attractive Church of St John the Baptist built in a Romanesque style with an unconventional open-air baptistery. The church has seen later additions to its structure such as the 18th-century north door, which is of Arab origin, whilst the remnants of a mosaic in the garden west of the church date to the much earlier Byzantine period. The church suffered serious damage from an earthquake in 1170 and again in 1840 from British bombardments, but extensive restoration since 1947 has transformed the structure and the bell tower you see today was added during this period.

Nossa Senhora Da Penna If you turn left out of the Crusader castle ticket entrance *en route* down to the port, this pocket-sized Christian stone chapel with vaulted ceiling is a quaint and atmospheric shrine, with pictures of Mary and burning candles with nicely manicured gardens dotted with religious icons; well worth a quick look in.

ERNEST RENAN

Born at Tréguier in Brittany in 1823 into a family of fishermen, the archaeologist, historian, philosopher and theologian Ernest Renan was responsible for undertaking some of the most important archaeological discoveries in Lebanon. Probably best known in his native France for his 1863 work Vie de Jésus, this book was both critically acclaimed and controversial for its less than sacred arguments and views. In 1860, the learned Renan travelled to Lebanon at the request of Emperor Napoleon III to undertake archaeological research into the country's Phoenician past, and lived in the coastal town of Amchit. The meticulous work and discoveries he made in nearby Byblos and elsewhere in the country paved the way for future work, and added significantly to our understanding of ancient cultures and their visible remains which we can enjoy today. His year-long stay in Lebanon formed the basis for his 1864 work Mission de Phénicie, where he outlines the 'powerful impression' the country made on him. His treasured sister, Henriette, who accompanied him to Lebanon, died whilst they were staying in Amchit and she is buried in the town where her resting place can be seen. Renan himself died after a short illness in France in 1892 and is buried in the Montmartre Quarter of Paris.

(Bentael; Vf 09 738 330; m 03 227 174; e info@bentaelreserve.org; www. bentaelreserve.org; ⊕ summer 08.00–18.00 daily, winter 08.00–17.00 daily; admission: no obligatory entrance fee but donations of LBP5,000 to aid ongoing environmental work in the reserve appreciated) This is the first and smallest of Lebanon's protected natural environments, which was officially re   nised as such in 1999. Established by Bentael's local residents in orde   help safeguard the area from 'the misdeeds of development', this heavily   ooded area covers just 2km² and sits between 300m and 850m above sea level and some 8km northeast of Byblos. An area rich in biodiversity, its range of flora includes oak and pine trees, heather, orchids and cyclamen whilst squirrels, voles, porcupines, shrews, wild boar, jackals, porcupines and foxes roam the verdant landscape. Recognised by the Ministry of Environment in 1999 as a nature reserve, it was also given the status of Important Bird Area (IBA) in 2008 and the white stork is a common visitor to the area during its annual migratory pattern. Also within the reserve is the small St John's Hermitage which, during the 18th or 19th centuries, was home to a solitary monk of the Maronite order for some 40 years. The reserve is open all year and is ideal for hikers. For more information on the reserve and to arrange a visit, take a look at the official website www.bentael.org, which also has directions on how to get there.

Historic Wax Museum *(Opposite the castle;* ↘ *09 540 463; m 03 395 537; ⊕ summer 09.00–18.00, winter 09.00–17.00, both daily; admission: adults LBP8,000, children LBP5,000)* This small museum, opposite the Church of St John the Baptist, displays a range of waxwork tableaux showcasing a variety of scenes from Lebanese history. Phoenician glass blowing, Alexander the Great at the burning of Tyre, a traditional village wedding, the imprisoned cabinet during the French Mandate era, and quite a scary-looking mermaid are some of the 23 different slices of Lebanese life on display here. Worth a look in, but this is really one only for kitsch lovers.

Byblos International Festival *(UNESCO Sq;* ↘ *09 542 020; m 03 538 536; e info@byblosfestival.org; www.byblosfestival.org. Tickets can be booked via the festival website, at any branch of Virgin Megastore or online at www.ticketingboxoffice. com)* An annual event during the months of July and August since 2003, the Byblos International Festival is held in a beautiful setting with the stage overlooking the ancient Phoenician harbour and Crusader ruins. The performances include a range of musical sounds and styles from flamenco, jazz and rock to opera, by both Lebanese and internationally acclaimed artists. Well-known names who have performed here over the years have included Bryan Ferry, Placebo and Kool and the Gang. In 2010, best-selling UK band Gorillaz were the headline act here together with Lebanese folk-music icon Wadih el-Safi, who was celebrating 70 years in the music industry. Taking place in tandem with the main festival is the 'OFF-Byblos Festival', the first of its kind in Lebanon to nurture both young Lebanese and non-Lebanese artistic talent with bands, comedy and dance shows held at various venues in the old souk.

AMCHIT

The hometown of current Lebanese president Michel Suleiman, Amchit is around 3.5km north from Byblos and home, literally, to dozens of attractive Ottoman-period houses which are now all listed buildings and worth a wander around. The town's other main claim to fame is that the 19th-century French archaeologist and writer Ernest Renan (see box, page 162) once resided here, and described the town as 'paradise'. His sister, Henriette, is also buried here and both the house and her burial site can be visited.

GETTING THERE As Amchit was not served by buses at the time of writing, you can catch a taxi to the town from Byblos for around LBP5,000 or it's a good 30-minute walk to the town and Camping Les Colombes.

JEBAL MOUSSA

Located in the Kesrouan district northeast of Jounieh, Lebanon's newest biosphere reserve was referred to by UNESCO in 2009 as 'a true mosaic of ecological systems', and achieved Important Bird Area (IBA) recognition in the same year. Jebal Moussa encompasses an area of some 6,500ha, extending 500m north beyond the Nahr Ibrahim River and a similar distance beyond the Nahr al-Dahab River in the south. The undulating and wild terrain in this reserve on the western slopes of the Mount Lebanon range varies in height from between 350m in the west to 1,700m in the east. This region has paid homage to the legend of Adonis and Astarte and stairways were constructed to aid passing legions during the Roman occupation. During the 18th century, Jebal Moussa's cultural importance was supplemented by its economic significance in the silk industry, where the area's mulberry trees provided sustenance for the silkworms which were transported to the market villages at the bottom of the mountain. In the 2nd century AD, the emperor Hadrian practised an early type of environmental management when he prohibited the felling of specific trees. Today, the Association for the Protection of Jebal Moussa (APJM) has taken a few extra steps than the Romans in order to preserve the long-term sustainability of this region through its awareness and educational campaigns, research and field study programmes. The area's landscape of valleys, rivers and mountains are home to a variety of fauna including the hyena, the hyrax (the elephant's nearest living relative), porcupines, squirrels, wild boar, wolves and over 80 species of native and migratory bird. Of the genus of flora, cyclamen, Calabrian pine, kermes oak, manna ash, storax, maple, orchid, peony and the Lebanon marjoram dot the countryside.

As part of their environmental awareness programme, APJM operate a number of hiking trails of varying length and duration throughout the reserve with experienced and bilingual guides. They have a dedicated Ecotourism Officer (m 71 944 405), who can advise and arrange tours and visits. Alternatively, visit the APJM website below for further details on how to reach the reserve and hiking trail maps.

Association for the Protection of Jebal Moussa (APJM), Suite 205, 2nd Fl, Le Portail Bldg, Jounieh; \f *09 643 464; m 71 944 405; e info@jabalmoussa.org; www. jabalmoussa.org;* ⏱ *09.00–17.00 daily for walking tours but the reserve is open for visits 24/7; admission: adults & children over 16 yrs LBP8,000, children under 16 yrs LBP4,000; a guide to accompany groups of hikers costs LBP50,000.*

WHERE TO STAY

⌂ Camping Les Colombes (14 chalets
& 25 'tengalows') Amchit; ↘ 09 622 401/2;
e contact@campinglescolombes.com; www.
campinglescolombes.com. For something a little
different in an ultra-rural setting overlooking
the sea try this campsite, the first in Lebanon,
which offers a variety of sleeping options,
including camping (LBP10,000pp/night, supply
your own tent), chalets (from LBP50,000/night),
or a 'tengalow', a tent-shaped bungalow
(LBP30,000 per 2 people per night), with AC,
TV & fridge. At weekends, chalets must be
booked a week in advance & 2 days ahead
for tengalows. **$**

OTHER PRACTICALITIES

$ Bank of Beirut Main St, opposite IPT
station; ↘ 09 622 734; ⏱ 08.30–15.30
Mon–Fri, 08.30–12.00 Sat

$ Byblos Bank Main St; ↘ 09 620 815.
Has an ATM.

RACHANA

A further 17km north of Amchit, this compact and hilly village just off the main coastal highway is the location for some extraordinary street art. This was created by the trio of the now-deceased Basbous Brothers, who since the 1950s had created an eclectic outdoor museum of conceptual, religious and sensual art forms, working with stone and wood materials. Since 1994, they held the annual 'International Sculptor Atelier' during August and September, where sculptors from around the world could exhibit their work in a public setting and in 1997, prompted UNESCO to label Rachana the 'International Capital of Sculpture in Open Air'. The sculptures are still ubiquitous around the town.

GETTING THERE It is best to take a taxi from Byblos or Amchit as there were no buses operating to Rachana at the time of research; expect to pay around LBP30,000–40,000 for a return trip from Byblos.

The only British airline flying to Paris.

The Paris of the Middle East, that is.

London Heathrow nonstop to
beautiful Beirut. Bienvenue au Liban.

British Midland International
book at flybmi.com

5

North Lebanon

Telephone code 06

North Lebanon comprises the area roughly north from the coastal town of Batroun to the tip of the Syrian border and inland to the western slopes of the Mount Lebanon range. The region is centred on the bustling and traditional coastal Sunni Arab city of Tripoli where, unlike the capital, time has virtually stood still as witnessed by its beautiful old buildings, anachronistic souks and a much more conservative lifestyle. The food is good too, with Tripoli renowned for its pastries and sweets. A visit to this city should be on every traveller's itinerary, but equally it would be a shame to overlook the region's other main attractions, with some of the best opportunities in the country to 'get back to nature'. The Christian town of Bcharré, some 50km southeast of Tripoli, is the birthplace of and location for a museum dedicated to the country's greatest literary figure, Khalil Gibran (see box, page 192), ideally situated at the head of the natural and manmade beauty of the UNESCO World Heritage Site-listed Qadisha Valley. This rugged and wild region is home to numerous rock-carved chapels, grottos, monasteries and waterfalls, and is where the Maronites established their roots and shelter in the 7th century, fleeing their Arab persecutors; there are also innumerable opportunities for hiking and trekking in the area.

Above Bcharré is one of the last and oldest-remaining stands of Lebanon's iconic cedar tree. Once carpeting the Lebanese countryside, they provided the raw material for many a Phoenician trading vessel as well as helped to build King Solomon's Temple in Jerusalem. Today a fiercely protected species, some are estimated to be 2,000 years old, but age has not withered them, especially when snow-covered in winter. Adventurous travellers will find that the raw and rustic appeal of Lebanon's northernmost region offers a quite different experience from the chic and gloss of the capital. Modernisation *en masse* has been largely resisted, providing an opportunity to obtain an alternative view of Lebanon which goes beyond media and touristic clichés.

BATROUN

This attractive Christian Maronite coastal town, some 50km north of Beirut and 20km north of Byblos, is the first principal town you reach in the north. Batroun traces its ancient roots back to Phoenician times and its founder was King Ithobaal of Tyre, father of the infamous Jezabel. It is also referred to in the ancient 14th-century BC Egyptian *Armana Letters*. Under the Greeks, the town was called Botrys and in AD551, it succumbed to a massive earthquake which destroyed its prosperity and which is believed by some historians to have created its natural harbour. Today, Batroun has the look and feel of a charming traditional fishing port and provincial town with attractive streets and sandstone buildings, plus houses and a workaday souk.

Renowned for its lemonade from the citrus groves which surround the town, Batroun is now also a hub of nightlife for the north with a good range of bars and

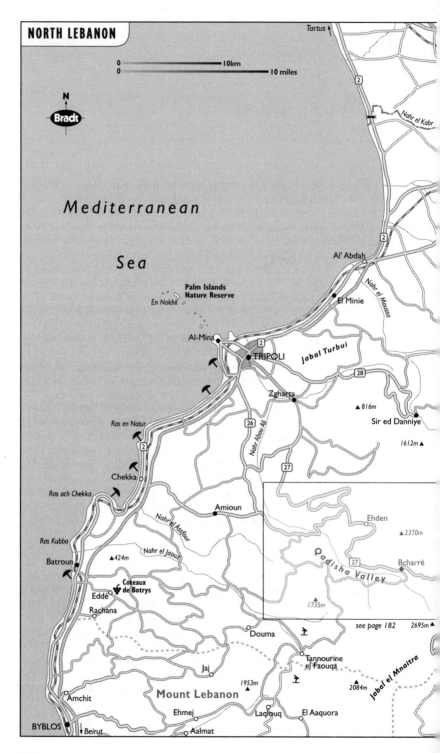

Mediterranean

Sea

Tartus

Nahr el Kabr

2

2

Al' Abdah

Nahr el Moussa

El Minie

Palm Islands
Nature Reserve

En Nakhil

Al-Mina

TRIPOLI

Jabal Turbul

28

Zgharta

▲816m

Sir ed Danniye

1612m▲

Ras en Natur

2

Nahr Abou Ali

26

Chekka

27

Ras ach Chekka

Amioun

Ehden

Nahr el Assfour

▲2370m

Ras Kubba

Qadisha Valley

27

Bcharré

Batroun

▲424m

Nahr el Jaouz

Coteaux
de Botrys

Eddé

Rachana

1735m

see page 182

2695m▲

Douma

Tannourine
el Faouqa

Jaj

1953m▲

2084m▲

Jabal el Mnaitra

Mount Lebanon

Amchit

Ehmej

Laqlouq

El Aaquora

BYBLOS

Beirut

Aalmat

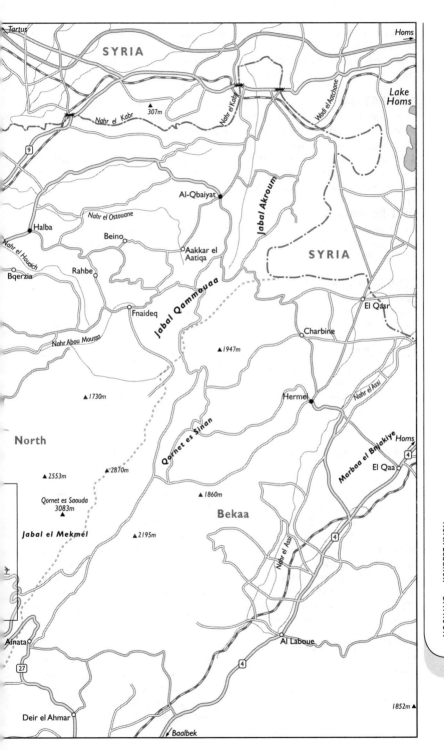

clubs and a number of beach club bars and cafés just a few kilometres south of town, which keep the Batroun party rolling until late. Despite its small-town feel, Batroun is certainly the most cosmopolitan and lively place in the region, and especially at night, is a lively contrast to Tripoli.

GETTING THERE Batroun is easily reached from the capital, being on the coast road to Tripoli. From Zone B or C of the Charles Helou bus station in Beirut you can board a bus to Tripoli and ask to be dropped off at Batroun. Depending on which bus company you use the one-way fare will be LBP2,000–4,000. Alternatively catch a bus or minivan from Dora station or a taxi from Byblos. If you are on a self-drive visit, just follow the coast road north from Beirut or Byblos. Expect to pay around LBP40,000–50,000 for a taxi from Beirut.

GETTING AROUND Like many of Lebanon's towns, Batroun is easily and best explored on foot covering a fairly compact area and walking will give you a much better feel for the town. Slightly more outlying areas and sites such as Batroun's beach clubs, Moussaslayha Castle and winery will require a short taxi ride.

TOURIST INFORMATION

◪ Ministry of Tourism Old souk, Batroun; ☏ 06 741 522; ⏱ summer 08.00–16.00 Mon–Sat, winter 08.00–14.00 Mon–Thu, 08.00–11.00 Fri, 08.00–14.00 Sat. This recently opened office has a good range of brochures & information on Batroun as well as other regions of Lebanon.

⌂ WHERE TO STAY As a principally summer resort town popular with local couples and families, Batroun's resort-type complexes are geared more towards this more affluent local market. For the budget conscious traveller, however, Batroun is an easy and affordable day trip from either Beirut or Tripoli and these two cities could make an ideal base, with their cheaper lodging options, from which to explore the town and its regions.

⌂ Batroun Village Club (23 rooms & suites) Off the highway about 2km from the centre of Batroun; ☏ 06 744 333; e info@batrounvclub.com; www.batrounvclub.com. Perched on a hill with lovely sea views, this is a fine & charming resort complex with some character, managing to avoid the often glitzy & plastic look of many resort complexes. Very family friendly with a nice tropical pool, horseriding, basketball & tennis courts among the summer activities, & there is a children's crèche. **$$$$**

⌂ San Stephano Resort (64 rooms & suites) Sea Rd, around 1km north of the town; ☏ 06 740 366, 06 642 366, 06 643 202; e info@sanstephano.com; www.sanstephano.com. Comfortable, though with less charm than the Batroun Village Club, with all the usual resort accoutrements such as swimming pool, beach bar & scuba-diving school. **$$$$**

⌂ Sawary Resort & Hotel (18 rooms & 150 chalets) Sea Rd; ☏ 06 642 100; e info@sawaryresort.com; www.sawaryresort.com. Nicely situated for Batroun's amenities; decent rooms with sea views, live music at the beach bar & swimming pool. All rooms have TV, AC & Wi-Fi. **$$$$**

✕ WHERE TO EAT AND DRINK

✕ Chez Maggie Makaad al-Mir; m 03 439 147; ⏱ 10.00–22.00 daily. Small & homely restaurant serving excellent fish mezze & a menu which changes daily. This place can get busy so book ahead. **$$$$$**

✕ Le Marin Bahsa St; ☏ 06 744 016; m 03 328 678; ⏱ 12.00–midnight daily. Popular, no frills & casual local haunt, serving excellent seafood & mezze with a nice outdoor terrace dining area with panoramic sea views. **$$$$**

✕ Le Garage Facing St Stephen's Church; m 03 323 897; ⏰ 06.30–midnight daily. A good place to try Batroun's speciality, lemonade, & a range of delicious Lebanese snacks such as man'oushe, Shish Tawouk & other quick eats. $$

✕ Chez Hilmi Main Rd, near the souk; ☎ 06 640 068; ⏰ 07.00–22.00 daily. Good patisserie selling Batroun's ubiquitous lemonade, pastries & sweets. $

ENTERTAINMENT AND NIGHTLIFE Batroun's nightlife offerings, whilst not quite as varied or grand as the capital's, are vibrant enough but still manage to evoke its small-town status. The following selections are all quite close together and represent a small selection of what's available.

☆ **Bank Music Club** Main St; ☎ 06 741 111; m 03 141 516; ⏰ 20.00–late Fri/Sat; admission US$20 minimum. Trendy & popular nightclub with top DJs spinning the discs from electronic & hip-hop to R&B.

☆ **Colorbar Pub** Main St; m 70 138 776; e contact@colorbarpub.com; www.colorbarpub.com; ⏰ 20.00–late Wed–Sun. Dark & cavernous with a lively crowd of regulars, this is a very atmospheric place for a drink or an evening of varying musical styles.

☆ **Mint Lounge** Main St; m 70 170 700; ⏰ 21.00–late Tue, Fri, Sat & Sun. A popular & fun hangout with DJ, karaoke & live music with a slightly more laid-back atmosphere than other venues.

The following beach clubs and facilities, around 5km south of Batroun and easily reached by taxi, offer a more chilled-out atmosphere than the bars and clubs in the main town and they all serve good seafood and *mezze* dishes. A range of water-based activities are also available such as kayaking, sailing, scuba diving and windsurfing.

Bonita Bay Tahoun; ☎ 06 744 844; e info@bonitabay.me; www.bonitabay.me; ⏰ 10.00–late daily; admission: adults LBP15,000, children under 15 free

Jammal Kfarabida, 1km south from Batroun; ☎ 06 740 095; ⏰ 11.00–19.00 Mon–Fri, 11.00–midnight Sat/Sun; admission free

Pearl Beach Tahoun; ☎ 06 743 941; m 03 300 941; e info@pearlbeachlebanon.com; www.pearlbeachlebanon.com; ⏰ 11.00–midnight daily; admission free

Pierre & Friends Tahoun; m 03 352 930; ⏰ 10.00–late daily; admission free

White Beach Tahoun; ☎ 06 742 404, 06 742 505; m 03 732 404; e info@whitebeachlebanon.com; www.whitebeachlebanon.com; ⏰ 08.00–23.00 daily; admission: LBP5,000 Mon–Fri, LBP7,000 Sat/Sun

SHOPPING Despite having an old and still-working souk, Batroun's retail offerings are pretty much geared to local needs, with few things that you would come here specifically to buy. If you are planning to venture further north to Tripoli, your money would be better spent in the souks of that city.

OTHER PRACTICALITIES Batroun's Main Street is home to all the banks, cafés, eateries, shops, banks and ATMs for cash withdrawals.

$ **BLC Bank** Main Rd; ☎ 06 642 166; ⏰ 08.30–13.30 Mon–Fri, 08.30–12.00 Sat. Has an ATM.

$ **Byblos Bank** Main Rd; ☎ 06 642 360/370; ⏰ 08.00–15.30 Mon–Fri, 08.00–12.00 Sat. Has an ATM.

✉ **Post office** Ogero Bldg; ☎ 06 740 302; ⏰ 08.00–17.00 Mon–Fri, 08.30–13.00 Sat

✚ **Red Cross** ☎ 06 741 588

WHAT TO SEE AND DO As a charming and scenic town, Batroun is best explored by walking the streets to admire its residential buildings and houses which, despite the renovations of recent years, remains an essentially traditional town. Start off by the pleasant old harbour where you can watch a slice of life with fishermen in their boats mending their nets. Behind the harbour which it overlooks is the triple-arched and imposing **St Stephen's Church** which dates from 1860. Nearby the **St George's Greek Orthodox Church**, built in a Byzantine style, dates from the latter period of the 18th century. There are many other religious buildings and icons dotted around this predominantly Christian Maronite town. Batroun's principal attraction is its sandstone **souks** where local shopkeepers ply their trade as fishmongers, grocers and woodworkers behind large wooden doors. Just under 4km north from Batroun is **Moussaslayha Castle**. This solitary and strategically located structure was once thought to be of Crusader origin but many authorities now attribute it to the work of Fakhreddine Maan II during the 17th century, intended to function as a lookout post to protect the coast road from Beirut to Tripoli. There are some rock-cut steps leading up to the top and the relatively steep climb is worth it for the views alone. The Nahr al-Jawz or Walnut River runs beneath an ancient bridge below the castle which is easily reached by service taxi or taxi from Batroun and easily accessible from the main road.

Coteaux de Botrys (*Main Rd, Eddé*; ☏ *06 721 300*; m *03 238 937, 03 517 508*; e *info@coteauxdebotrys.com; www.coteauxdebotrys.com*) A little further inland in the hills above Batroun, this château has been producing wine since 1998 and is now amongst the best known of the area's eight wineries. The brainchild of retired army general Joseph Bitar, the château produces three varieties of reds together with a white, and a rosé, and its Arak Kfifane has been hailed as the best in Lebanon. Spread over more than 16ha, production continues today by the late general's two daughters who, in 2009, corked some 40,000 bottles with output anticipated to increase to 65,000 within five years. Each year, from June until September on the first and last Sunday of each month, the château plays host to a lunch and wine-tasting event held in the picturesque and pleasant surroundings of the vines and overlooking the Mediterranean below. It is best to phone in advance for any tour of the winery or tasting session outside these days.

Getting there The winery is located inland around 10km southeast of Batroun in the village of Eddé; a taxi from Batroun should cost around LBP5,000.

Batroun International Festival (☏ *06 642 262*; m *03 105 700*; e *info@ batrounfestival.org; www.batrounfestival.org; tickets can be purchased from the Virgin Megastore in Downtown Beirut, online at www.ticketingboxoffice.com & from the Batroun Festival Office, Old souk, Batroun;* m *71 440 071*) Held annually during July and August, this festival has a much more local feel than many of Lebanon's other festivals and showcases dance, song, comedy acts, open-air party nights in the town's main street and Phoenician wall area, as well as a variety of exhibitions by visual artists, free coffee, lemonade and tours of the town and its sites. In 2011, the festival was headlined by Ali Campbell, former lead singer with UK band UB40.

TRIPOLI

With a population of around 250,000 and a heartland of the Sunni Muslim community, Tripoli is Lebanon's second-largest city and port and capital of the North Lebanon Governorate. Despite its size, it has recently been estimated that only some 2% of visitors to the country actually visit Tripoli and those who do

TRIPOLI

N

0 _____ 100m
0 _____ 100yds

Bradt

Al-Tawbat Mosque

Souk al-Haraj & Café Haraj

Madrasa al-Burtasiyat

RACHID KARAMI STREET

Abu Ali' River

Al-Attar Mosque

Khan al-Misriyin

Khan al-Khayyatin

EMIR FAKHREDDINE STREET

Khan al-Askar

AMIR BACHIR AL-CHEHAB STREET

Al-Tuwashiyat Madrasa

Khan al-Sabboun & Bader Hassoun & Sons

Souk al-Sayyagin

Citadel of Raymond de Saint-Gilles

Hammam al-Abed

Madrasa al-Nouriyat

Hammam al-Nouri

Al-Qartawiyat Madrasa

Great Mosque

RACHID RIDA STREET

Madrassa al-Saqraqiyat

Madrassa al-Khatoumiyat

AHMAD EL RIFFAL STREET

Al-Muallaq Mosque

Tall

Rafaat Hallab & Sons

Abdul Rahman Hallab & Sons

Palace

Koura

Municipality building

Bus services to Aleppo, Damascus & Turkey

RUE TALL

Café Fahim

Pension Haddad

Tall Square

El Koura Square

Al Nejmeh Square

CHEIKH NASIF AL-YAZIGI ST

Arghoun Mosque

Hammam al-Jadid

Al-Tinat Fountain

Clock Tower

Tripoli Express

Ahdab Company

Kotob

Abdel Hamid Karami Square

Ministry of Tourism office

Minivans to Bcharré

Sara.Net

Bab al-Ramel cemetery

Taynal Mosque

Al-Mina & Quality Inn Hotel

Al-Mina & boats for Palm Islands Nature Reserve, '46, Silver Shore, Beit al-Fann, Byblos Bank, post office, Quality Inn Hotel, British Council & Circuit Planète

Pharmacie Nadine

MARAAD STREET

Connexions Bus Company and Office

Beirut &Byblos

North Lebanon TRIPOLI

5

173

mostly arrive on organised coach tours as day trippers rather than on an extended tour of the city and its environs. Yet Tripoli, 85km north of Beirut, contains after Cairo the largest and most significant set of Mamluk-period architecture in the world, with other vestiges of its past highlighted by the anachronistic souks, as redolent of *1,001 Arabian Nights* as you will experience anywhere north of Sidon.

Here you can still see artisans from jewellers to tailors toiling over their labours in factories and workshops used by their forebears over the past five centuries. Keeping watch over this authentic Arab city is the Crusader castle of Raymond de Saint-Gilles which has seen many alterations over the years and is Tripoli's most recognisable monument. One 'monument' which hasn't seen much in the way of modification since construction started in the early 1960s is the large domed expanse of the Rachid Karami International Fair, which was intended to become a major international commercial and exhibition space. Located near the Quality Inn Hotel south of the Old City, it was commissioned in the early 1960s to enhance the profile of Tripoli as a business hub. The structure is the work of the renowned Brazilian architect Oscar Niemeyer (b1907) of *Brasilia* fame, but the onset of civil war in 1975 halted further construction and though there has been talk of restarting the project, it remains at the present time just a rather sorry blot on the landscape overlooked by the Quality Inn Hotel.

HISTORY Settlement in Tripoli dates back to the 14th century BC, and perhaps even earlier, but the foundations of a prosperous city-state were not established until the 9th century BC with the arrival of the Phoenicians. The city became part of a loose coalition of trading centres which included Sidon, Tyre and Arvad (along the coast of modern-day Syria), and grew into three separate districts which the Greeks later named Tripolis (Three Cities) and later amended to its current name Trablous with the inception of Arab rule. Tripoli has always been a centre for business and commerce activities though it never surpassed the importance of the southern cities of Byblos, Sidon or Tyre, and its Phoenician roots survive in name only. The roll call of conquerors and occupiers is a familiar one – Assyrians, Persians, Greeks, Romans, Byzantines, Arabs, Crusaders and Ottomans – all contributed to the city's general affluence over the centuries interrupted only by the devastating earthquake which afflicted the city and other coastal cities in AD551, and later rebuilt by the Byzantine emperor Justinian I. But it wasn't until the Middle Ages that Tripoli was to experience its greatest period of building and the fine architectural legacies which we see today. The arrival of the Crusaders from Europe in 1109 wreaked havoc on the city, including the burning of Tripoli's famous Dar il-ilm library which was once held in as high esteem as the famed Bibliotheca Alexandrina in the Egyptian city of Alexandria. But nearly two centuries of Frankish rule has left a magnificent castle which still oversees the city. Tripoli was the capital of the 'County of Tripoli' until 1289, when under Sultan al-Mansur Qalawun, the Mamluks sacked the knights and destroyed the city, building *hammams*, *madrasas* and the innumerable mosques which we see today.

The city's more recent history, however, has been marked more by destruction than construction. Tripoli suffered heavy Syrian bombardment in 1983 during the civil war and endured equally heavy fighting between Palestinian factions during the conflict. Tripoli is also the location for two of Lebanon's 12 Palestinian refugee camps, at Beddawi, 5km north of Tripoli, and at Nahr al-Bared some 16km north of the city centre. On 20 May 2007, fighting erupted for control of the latter camp between the militant group Fatah al-Islam and the Lebanese army, which in just over three months of struggle destroyed 95% of the camp's infrastructure and displaced around 27,000 Palestinians to nearby Beddawi camp. With the cessation of hostilities in September of that year, UNRWA has embarked on a wholesale renovation of the Nahr al-Bared camp which is due to be completed by the middle of 2012.

GETTING THERE As the capital of the north Tripoli is well connected with Beirut, and a number of bus companies offer services with an equally good selection of taxis regularly plying the route north and back south again. Tripoli is also the hub for transport to Bcharré and the Cedars and so is a good place to base yourself if planning a day trip(s) to these areas.

By car If you have a rental car, Tripoli is easily reached in less than two hours along the coastal highway north from Beirut, which is an extremely scenic and pleasant journey and clearly signposted.

By bus If you opt for the public transport method, there are numerous buses departing regularly from Zone C of Charles Helou bus station just east of Downtown Beirut. The following four companies are recommended:

Ahdab Company m 70 171 898. They have minivans departing daily for Tripoli every 15mins, from 05.00 to 21.30. The journey time is around 1hr 45 mins. One-way fare LBP3,000.
Connexion Transportation & Tourism
☎ 01 585 500; m 03 206 384 (Beirut); ☎ 06 626 969, 06 424 933; m 03 206 718 (Tripoli); e info@ connexion-transport.com; www.connexion-transport.com. This company operates a fleet of modern deluxe, AC coaches, taking around 1½hrs to Tripoli's Abdel Hamid Karami Sq. Buses run from 05.30 to 18.00 daily, with departures every 30min. One-way fare LBP4,000.

Kotob ☎ 06 444 986. This company also run minivans every 15mins from 05.00 to 19.00 daily, for the 1½hr journey to Tripoli. One-way fare LBP2,000.
Tripoli Express m 03 327 625 (Beirut); m 03 575 844 (Tripoli) Buses run from Beirut from 07.15 to 19.30 daily every 20mins, taking about 1½ hrs to Tripoli. One-way fare LBP3,000 Mon–Sat, LBP3,500 Sun & public holidays. Buses from Tripoli to Beirut run from 05.30 to 17.00 daily, & run every 20 mins. One-way fare LBP3,500 Mon–Sat, LBP4,000 Sun & public holidays.

By taxi There are numerous taxi companies in Beirut and expect to part with around LBP75,000–80,000 for a taxi to Tripoli from the capital.

Trust Taxi Achrafieh, east Beirut; ☎ 01 613 573, 01 613 398; m 03 601 806; e info@trust-taxi. com; www.trust-taxi.com. They operate 24/7
& their website has a useful tariff calculator for fares all over the country. They also offer car rental.

GETTING AROUND Although Tripoli is quite a large city, it is perfectly manageable by foot which is actually the best option to appreciate this busy Arabian metropolis and its sites. The city is divided into the contrasting medieval Old City around 3km inland from the coast, and the port or Al-Mina district which extends from the peninsula towards the Old City. As in Beirut, though, service taxis are readily available and prices are on a par with what you would pay in the capital.

TOURIST INFORMATION
🄸 **Ministry of Tourism** Abdel Hamid Rashid Sq; ☎ 06 433 590; ⏱ 08.00–16.00 Mon–Sat. A small, friendly branch of the Ministry offering
a range of brochures & pamphlets in Arabic, English, French & Spanish.

5

175

⌂ WHERE TO STAY

Tripoli is a budget traveller's paradise compared with Beirut, with only one hotel in the city at present catering to those seeking more salubrious or international-type accommodation.

⌂ **Quality Inn Hotel** (112 rooms & suites) Rashid Karami International Fair; ☎ 06 211 255/6/7/8; e info@qualityinntripoli.com, reservation@qualityinntripoli.com; www.qualityinntripoli.com. Although clean & boasting the usual range of tourist & business facilities you would expect of a 4-star hotel including 2 swimming pools & conference facilities, the rooms are quite bland & the stark, monochromatic bathrooms feel more on a par with budget offerings. The hotel's location is also about 2km from Tripoli's main city & attractions. **$$$**

⌂ **Koura Hotel** (8 rooms) Tall St; ☎ 06 425 451; m 03 371 041; e contact@alkourahotel.com; www.pensionalkoura.com. Tripoli's best-value hotel. Excellent, clean rooms, with character stone walls, flat-screen TV, AC, use of communal kitchen facilities & there is a fridge in every room. Laundry is an extra US$7–10 for a 5–6kg load. B/fast inc. **$$**

⌂ **Palace Hotel** (14 rooms) ☎ 06 429 993. The grandeur of its exterior belies a darker & bleaker interior & the rooms could be cleaner. The slightly bizarre family who run this hotel conjured up visions of the Addams Family. **$$**

⌂ **Tall Hotel** (17 rooms) Rue Tall; ☎ 06 628 407. Although this hotel can't spell its name correctly (look for the red-lettered 'Tell Hotel' on a yellow sign), this is still a reasonable, though very basic place, for a night or two. Most rooms have their own bathroom, are clean enough & the location is nice & central. **$$**

⌂ **Pension Haddad** (8 rooms) Tall St; m 03 507 709, 03 361 349; e haddadpension@hotmail.com; www.pensionhaddad.8m.com. A good & decent family run budget hotel hosted by a friendly grandma, mother, sister, aunt & daughter. A house of some character with simple, clean rooms. A good backpacker choice. Internet access charged at a very reasonable LBP1,000/hr. **$**

✗ WHERE TO EAT AND DRINK

Eating and drinking options are many in the city, but they tend to be more of the informal street snacking variety with few formal restaurants, which actually adds to the traditional charm of the city anyway. Just don't expect the options which you find in Beirut. Tripoli is famed for its sweets and in addition to the outlets below there are many others dotted around the city. The Al-Mina (port) area has an excellent seafood restaurant.

✗ **'46** Ibn Sina Rd, Al-Mina, Corniche; ☎ 06 212 223; e contact@restaurantfourtysix.com; www.restaurantsilvershore.com; ⊕ 11.00–23.00 Tue–Sun. If you don't like fish then this place, next door to Silver Shore, serves decent international & Italian cuisine with equally nice views. **$$$$**

✗ **Silver Shore** Ibn Sina Rd, Al-Mina, Corniche; ☎ 06 601 384/5; m 03 691 385; e contact@restaurantsilvershore.com; www.restaurantsilvershore.com; ⊕ 11.15–18.30 daily. Something of an institution, which means advance booking is recommended. This specialist seafood eatery is easily the best in town for ultra fresh-fish mezze accompanied by lovely sea views. This is a good place to try the local & popular spicy fish known as *samkeh harrah*. **$$$$**

✗ **Mustapha** Rear of Omar bin-Khattab Mosque, Al-Mina; ☎ 06 205 821; ⊕ 10.00–22.00 daily. An unpretentious café & restaurant serving freshly caught fish & mezze. A good value choice for filling & tasty food. **$$**

✗ **Café Fahim** Rue Tall, close to the Ottoman clock tower; ⊕ 06.30–22.00 daily. Anachronistic with old-world charm, this large indoor & outdoor café is the place to head to for a *nargileh* (LBP1,500–6,000), coffee, tea, soft drinks & to play (or watch) backgammon & cards amidst some traditional Arab atmosphere. This place doesn't serve food. **$**

✗ **Café Haraj** Souk al-Haraj; ☎ 06 440 154; m 03 956 458; ⊕ 09.00–sunset daily. Good homely feel about this place to watch the world go by in the souk, puff on a nargileh pipe or snack on a decent *falafel* or *Shish Tawouk* sandwich. **$**

ENTERTAINMENT AND NIGHTLIFE As a predominantly conservative city, Tripoli certainly doesn't exude nightlife options like the capital, with most places shutting up shop (and restaurant) by around midnight. The port area of Al-Mina has a handful of bars which stay open until midnight or thereabouts or for a night at the movies there is **Circuit Planète** (*City Complex, Rue Riad al-Solh;* \ *06 442 471;* e *cineklik@cineklik.com; www.cineklik.com*) , which is a typical multiplex cinema complex showing films in English, including the latest Western blockbusters.

SHOPPING The contrast with the glitz and glamour of Beirut couldn't be more pronounced in Lebanon's second city as the ubiquitous boutiques and shopping malls of the capital are largely absent in Tripoli giving way to a much more antiquated and authentic Arab shopping aesthetic. It probably goes without saying that the best and most satisfying shopping, unless modern designer labels are your thing, is in the city's anachronistic souks and *khans*, each of which has its own special character and products which are well worth a look even if you are not intending to buy but just to watch the craftsmen at work. The items for which Tripoli has long been most famous for the manufacture of are soap and sweets and the two shops below are well worth searching out, both for the products themselves and the still-traditional processes involved in their manufacture.

Abdul Rahman Hallab & Sons Kasr El Helou (Castle of Sweets), Riad al-Solh St; \ 06 444 445; e contact@hallab.com.lb; www.hallab.com.lb; ◔ 05.00–23.00 daily. Established since 1881, this is Tripoli's best-known & favourite sweet shop selling a huge variety of everything your dentist advised you against, including baklava, jams, nougats, the Lebanese favourite *knafeh* & the delicious Nammoura slice, containing a concoction of semolina, sugar, coconut, butter, syrup, milk & almonds. They also serve coffee.

Bader Hassoun & Sons Khan al-Saboun; \ 06 438 369; m 03 438 369; e info@khanalsaboun. net; www.khanalsaboun.net; ◔ 09.00–19.00 daily. The Hassoun family has been making soap for generations & a cornucopia of varieties are on sale at this 16th-century khan, ranging from a variety of aromatic soaps (amber, cinnamon, jasmine, etc) to those purporting to be for medicinal purposes. They also come in all shapes & sizes, including a double-page spread of the Koran, former prime minister Rafiq Hariri, & soap in the shape of a cedar tree. Highly recommended.

OTHER PRACTICALITIES There are numerous banks dotted around the roundabout at Place Abdel Hamid Karamé Square near the tourist office. They include Blom Bank and Gulf Bank, both of which have ATMs, and there are also branches of Banque Libano-Française and the Lebanese Canadian Bank.

British Council 2nd Fl, Safadi Cultural Centre, Maarad St (opposite Rachid Karami International Fair); \ 06 410 014; e general.enquiries@lb. britishcouncil.org; www.britishcouncil.org/ lebanon; ◔ 09.00–17.00 Mon–Fri, 09.00–14.00 Sat
$ **Byblos Bank** Jabadou Bldg, Chiraa Sq, Al Bawabe St, Al Mina; \ 06 205 943/4; ◔ 08.30–15.30 Mon–Fri, 08.30–12.00 Sat. Has an ATM.
✚ **Pharmacie Nadine** Maarad St; \ 06 440 470; m 03 809 480; e pharm_abboudeh@ hotmail.com; ◔ 08.00–22.00 Mon–Sat, 10.00–22.00 Sun. Next door to the post office this is a

friendly & well-stocked pharmacy selling a wide range of cosmetics, prescription & non-prescription drugs.
✉ **Post office** Maarad St; \ 06 425 690; ◔ 08.00–17.00 Mon–Fri, 08.00–13.30 Sat. Libanpost also has an additional branch in Al-Mina (*Batsh Bldg, Jamarek St;* \ *06 601 181*) & at the time of writing a couple of new branches were due to open in El Kobeh Sq (*Safsouf Bldg;* \ *06 388 107*) & at Abou Samra (*Al Siyadi Bldg, Saadoun Sq, behind the old mosque, Al-Bareed St;* \ *06 430 096*).

Sara.Net ☎ 06 626 089; m 70 367 376;
e best_bipo@hotmail.com; ⏱ 10.00–midnight
daily. Good, reliable, internet access charged at

LBP1,000/hr. Located up a side street on your
right just before Abdel Hamid Rashid Sq as you
are coming from Beirut.

WHAT TO SEE AND DO

Old Tripoli Although Tripoli has a history dating back to antiquity, the surviving architecture and principal historical sites are mainly those spanning the 14th and 15th centuries from the period of Mamluk rule, such as *hammams, khans, madrasas,* mosques and souks (see *Shopping*, page 177). Revered as fine warriors, this caste of former Ayyubid servants were equally fine designers and builders and the city possesses some of the finest examples of their handiwork outside their former capital in Cairo, with their trademark style utilising alternating layers of black and white stone, geometric shapes and highly decorated niches apparent in many of the city's buildings. There are some 45 buildings in the city which have been designated as listed monuments and although many are numbered, it may take some detective work to locate the often well-hidden plaques. The following sites are just a selection of the main places of interest in the city and just wandering around the alleyways and roads of the town will reveal many more. It is worth bearing in mind that as a traditional Arab city, a more modest mode of attire is very much the order of the day for both males and females so as not to offend local sensibilities and females may want to bring a headscarf if intending to enter any of Tripoli's mosques.

Citadel of Raymond de Saint-Gilles (*Old City;* ⏱ *08.00–sunset daily; admission: adults LBP8,000, children LBP4,000*) Tripoli's largest and most recognisable landmark covers some 10,000m² with its rectangular structure measuring some 140m by 70m. Known as Qalaa Sinjil in Arabic, this 12th-century Crusader fortress dates back to the time of the First Crusade and the Count of Toulouse, Raymond de St Gilles, who built the castle after entering the city in 1102. For the next 180 years of Crusader presence in Tripoli the castle's strategic location, on a hill which the Crusaders named Mount Pilgrim, kept watch over the city until the arrival of the Mamluk dynasty who laid siege to it and demolished the castle in 1289, only for it to be rebuilt two decades later by the Mamluk sultan Essendir al-Kurji. It was then destroyed once again by the Mamluks with the onset of Ottoman rule, and reconstructed under Suleiman the Magnificent whose stone-carved inscription which testifies to his hope for the eternal existence of this 'fortified stronghold' can still be read today over the large Ottoman gate through which you enter the castle. Once through the entrance gate, proceed across the bridge which is built over a moat constructed by the Crusaders. Once inside the vast castle complex you are confronted by an array of arches, courtyards and staircases that represent something of a mish-mash of architectural influences and styles, and are testimony to the castle's history. It is interesting to just wander around and look at the various ramparts. It is the views from the fortress's battlements, however, which make a visit most worthwhile with stunning panoramas over the Old City and the Abu Ali River.

Hammams

Hammam al-Abed (⏱ *08.00–22.00 daily; bath with 'full works' of steam bath, body scrub & massage around US$20*) Tripoli's sole working *hammam*, for men only, dates from the end of the 17th century and bears all the hallmarks of traditional bathing, with vaulted ceilings and sunlight shafting through the pierced Mamluk and Ottoman domes accompanied by the sound of running water, contributing to an almost hypnotic Arabian ambience and mood.

Hammam al-Nouri This now-obsolete public baths traces its origins back to 1333, when it was constructed by a former governor of the city, Nu red Din, and is notable for its cluster of perforated domes which allow light to percolate through to the baths below.

Hammam al-Jadid Although 300 years old, this public bath, also known as the 'New Bath' as, comparatively speaking, it is the newest of the city's baths, was a fully functioning *hammam* up until the 1970s. Located northeast of the Taynal Mosque, it was built during the Ottoman era in 1740 by the Damascus governor Asad Pasha al-Azem. It is also Tripoli's largest baths and still manages to evoke its former splendour. The huge stone interior with numerous recessed arches and central fountain is nicely complemented by the beautiful multi-coloured and geometrically decorated marble floor. The lofty-domed ceiling allows shafts of light to pierce through to the fountain below. Another fine feature of this *hammam* can be seen over the entrance which is adorned with a 14-link chain, from a single slab of hewn stone.

Madrasas

Al-Qartawiyat Madrasa Adjoining the Great Mosque, this Islamic school is an excellent and typical example of Mamluk architecture and a contender for Tripoli's most opulently decorated monument, with its prayer hall the city's sole building with an oval dome. The *madrasa* has an attractively adorned honeycombed pattern ceiling and the hallmark black and white, layered stonework on the building's façade is nicely complemented by its distinctive geometric patterning. Built by the Governor of Tripoli in the early period of the 14th century, after whom the building is named, it is thought that it may occupy the site of a former Frankish church with some of the stonework at the entrance typical of that period and style.

Al-Tuwashiyat Madrasa Built in 1471, this sandstone-constructed school is part *madrasa*, part mausoleum, with a nice example of layered black and white-striped stonework (*ablaq*), and the nicely decorated portal with zig-zag motifs is unique in that it is located above the main entrance.

Mosques

Al-Muallaq Mosque This simple and compact mosque, with an attractive garden in the courtyard, dates from the middle part of the16th century but is more famed for its location, on the second floor of a building. Hence its name, the 'Hanging Mosque'.

Burtasiya Madrassa-Mosque Situated on the bank of the Abu Ali River opposite the Khan al-Khayyatin, this impressive domed mosque dating from the beginning of the 14th century is well worth a visit to appreciate its large square minaret and the exquisite interior with its fine stonework and colourful mosaic-adorned *mihrab*.

Great Mosque Also referred to as Jami al-Kabir, the Great Mosque shows a fusion of Western and Mamluk styles of architecture, and was completed in 1315 after some 20 years under construction. It is built over the burnt remains of the St Mary of the Tower Cathedral and numerous porticos surround its sizeable courtyard. The interior of the mosque is typically Islamic with its large domed and vaulted prayer hall but vestiges of the former Frankish shrine can still be discerned at the mosque's northern entrance, together with the mosque's minaret, which was the former cathedral's Lombard bell tower.

Taynal Mosque If you visit only one mosque during your stay in Tripoli, make it this one; a superb and representative example of Mamluk architectural magnificence. Approximately a five–ten-minute walk southwest of the Great Mosque, this multiple green-domed shrine dates back to 1336, and was built by Saif ed-Din Taynal. It occupies the site of a former Carmelite church seen by the nave in the first prayer hall, and whose two granite columns support the large vaulted ceiling, which may themselves have been borrowed from an earlier Roman structure. It is the grand portico leading to the second prayer hall which is this mosque's greatest feature, with its use of layered black and white-striped stonework (*ablaq*), a decorative honeycomb-like niche, stone-carved geometric patterns and intricate Arab calligraphy.

Khans and souks
Khan al-Askar This early 14th-century *khan* was originally built as a garrison to house Mamluk soldiers, and thus is known as the 'Soldiers' Khan'. At its northern entrance it consists of two buildings which are connected to the southern building by a very narrow, vaulted alleyway. Although heavily restored during the 18th century, the original Mamluk architecture can still be discerned such as arches and columns, together with decorative palm leaf motifs.

Khan al-Khayyatin This elongated 'Tailors' Khan' is one of the oldest in the city dating back to the 14th century, and probably occupies a much earlier Byzantine and Crusader site. It is a great place to watch tailors fashioning all manner of clothing for locals and tourists alike.

Souk al-Haraj With a totally traditional and rustic atmosphere, this is Tripoli's only covered souk, dating to the 14th century. A series of 14 granite columns support its high vaulted roof and these are believed to be the remnants of much earlier Roman or Crusader structures. This workaday market specialises in a range of household utilities such as mats, mattresses and pillowcases.

Port (Al-Mina) Whilst the Old City has an abundance of medieval sites, the port area has just one site of any historical note, the **Burj es-Sabaa** or **Lion's Tower**, so-called owing to the carvings of lions which formerly adorned the building's façade. This large, rectangular mid 15th-century Mamluk defensive tower is the last remaining of a whole series of seven coastal fortifications which were once built to protect Tripoli. With its high vaulted ceilings and decoratively striped alternating monochromatic striped pattern, known as *ablaq*, it is typical of Mamluk architectural design. The monument is located about a 1km walk northeast of the coast just past the disused railway tracks.

Beit al-Fann (*Mar Elias St, Al-Mina, Corniche;* m *03 387 714;* e *beitelfann@ hotmail.com; www.azmculturalcenter.com, www.beitelfann.com;* ⏲ *08.00–18.00 daily; admission free*) Beit al-Fann means 'House of Art', and this centre for the promotion of culture is housed within a lovely old building full of character where they hold workshops, theatrical shows, concerts and exhibitions as well as working closely with local and overseas arts groups and organisations. Their patron is Lebanon's new prime minister Najib Mikati.

Palm Islands Nature Reserve Lebanon's only protected area which is not located on the mainland, this group of three flat islands located 5.5km off the northwest coast of Tripoli was designated protected area status by UNESCO in 1992 and is recognised as an Important Bird Area by BirdLife International. In 1993, the Lebanese Ministry of the Environment established the area as a National Nature Reserve. The largest of the three islands, covering some 180,796m² is Palm Island, formerly known as Rabbits Island, owing to its large population of the floppy-eared creatures, which have since been removed for the threat they posed to the local flora. Southeast of Palm Island is Sanani Island, covering an area of 45,503m² whilst the smallest of the three is Ramkine Island, at just 34,903m². Together, they comprise a unique and delicate ecosystem of flora and fauna and are a stop-off point for some 156 species of migratory bird including the Audouin's gull (*Larus audouini*), grey heron (*Ardea cinerea*), white wagtail (*Motacilla alba*) and the ruff (*Philomachus pugnax*). The area is also a preferred site for the green sea turtle (*Chelonia mydas*) and the loggerhead turtle (*Caretta caretta*) – both of which are globally endangered species – and the Mediterranean monk seal (*Monachus monachus*).

Of the prevalent species of flora on the islands are the rock samphire (*Crithmum maritimum*), sea poppy (*Glaucium flavum*), and sea daffodil (*Pancratium maritimum*). The islands have designated hiking trails and swimming and snorkelling can be undertaken. Normally, the islands are open for visitors from July until September

LEBANON MOUNTAIN TRAIL (LMT)

This is one of Lebanon's most exciting and recent major developments, intended to foster ecotourism in the country and bring economic development and improved prosperity to its rural towns and villages. The idea was conceived back in 2001 by Joseph Karam and Karim El-Jisr, who were inspired by the success of the 3,508km-long Appalachian Trail in the US. Although slightly less extensive in Lebanon at 440km, the LMT was finally given the green light to be put into practice in 2005, with the awarding of a two-year grant of US$3.3 million by USAID (US Agency for International Development) to ECODIT, the US company responsible for consultancy and developmental work on the project. The LMT finally opened in 2008, following delays caused by the 2006 July War between Israel and Hezbollah, and this hiking and walking trail now stretches down the spine of the country from Al-Qbaiyat in the north to the southern town of Marjayoun at the foothills of Mount Hermon. The signposted 26-section trail, which can be walked in its entirety or as day hikes individually, takes in the great variety of Lebanon's terrain and passes through over 75 towns and villages varying in altitude from 600m to 2,000m above sea level, two biosphere reserves and a UNESCO World Heritage Site. For aficionados of Lebanese literature, the LMT also incorporates the 24km-long Baskinta Literary Trail (BLT), whose route takes you through landmarks and sites associated with the country's most celebrated writers including Amin Maalouf, Abdallah Ghanem, Georges Ghanem and Khalil Gibran amongst others. The LMT website (*Lebanon Mountain Trail Association, 1st Fl, Ghaleb Centre, Baabda;* \ *05 955 302/3;* e *lmta@lebanontrail.org; www.lebanontrail.org*) contains a wealth of practical information for walkers, including advice and contact details on accommodation, child-and family-friendly routes, bike riding the trail, maps, etc.

North Lebanon TRIPOLI

5

when no special permit is required. Outside these times, a permit has to be obtained for which 48 hours' notice is required; contact the Palm Islands Nature Reserve Committee Office (*Al-Mina;* ✆ *06 615 938;* e *r-jaradi@cyberia.net.lb*) with the date of your proposed visit. There is no obligatory entrance fee to visit the islands but voluntary donations are welcome to aid with ongoing environmental work.

Getting there There are a number of boat owners at the Al-Mina port who can convey you to the islands in around half an hour. Fares can be negotiated with the port's fishermen but expect to part with up to US$20 for a return trip and be prepared to be quoted around US$100–130 as an individual to charter a boat. If you prefer to visit as part of an organised day cruise **Sharewood Camp** (✆ *04 870 592;* m *03 294 298;* e *info@sharewoodcamp.com; www.sharewoodcamp.com*) offer day trips to the islands, with opportunities for fishing, swimming, snorkelling and hiking. Lunch and a tour of Tripoli's Old City are usually included.

QADISHA VALLEY

This elongated steep-sided gorge extending for approximately 50km from Koura east of Batroun in the west to the town of Bcharré and the Cedars in the east possesses arguably the most spectacular scenery in the country. Unlike at many of Lebanon's natural and manmade attractions, the Qadisha Valley offers little in the way of concessions to tourists. Raw, rugged and wild with often treacherous and steep mountain passes dotted with waterfalls, the valley is a scenic place to visit at any time. In spring, Lebanon's varied and colourful flora like buttercups and poppies carpet the landscape with the melting snow drizzling down the mountain forming an extremely picturesque backdrop. Spring, along with summer, is ideal for hiking and trekking in this largely unspoilt and undulating terrain of outstanding natural beauty.

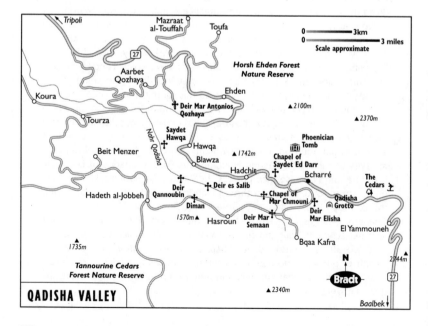

Translated from the Syriac language, Qadisha means 'Holy', and until a little over a century ago, this was the lingua franca of the valley and remains the language of the Maronite liturgy to this day. When UNESCO incorporated the valley into its World Heritage Site listing in 1998, it did so with the comment that Qadisha is 'one of the most important early Christian monastic settlements in the world'. Although not the first inhabitants in the valley, the Maronites sought refuge and spiritual solitude here from the dawning of Christianity as ecclesiastical debates and conflicts raged concerning the very essence of Christ and whether he had a divine or human will, or both. The arrival of the Arabs in the 7th century accentuated the exodus to the safety of the valley where the natural and inaccessible landscape was fashioned into a plethora of caves and rock-cut monasteries, which provided shelter from persecutors. The head of the valley is dominated by the town of Bcharré and with the Cedars close by, this picturesque town makes a logical and ideal choice for a base from which to explore the valley below.

BCHARRÉ

This small Maronite Christian town of red-roofed buildings with some 13,000 souls commands one of the most spectacular natural locations in the country. Situated 1,500m above sea level, the town sits above the Qadisha Valley and is framed by the snow-capped mountains and Cedars. Apart from its picturesque location, Bcharré is also well known as being the birthplace of Lebanon's most revered literary figure, Khalil Gibran (see box, page 192), who is also buried here, and there is a museum dedicated to his life and work. This is also the hometown of the Lebanese Forces (LF) leader Samir Geagea (b1952), who in 1995 stood trial for a series of political assassinations, including that of the rival Christian leader Dany Chamoun and former prime minister Rachid Karami. Sentenced to life imprisonment in 1995, he was released in 2005 following the Cedar Revolution. Located 110km from Beirut and 50km southeast of Tripoli, Bcharré is the obvious place to base yourself for a few days if planning an extended tour of the Qadisha Valley and the Cedars, and is a good transit stop if on a day trip to see the Khalil Gibran Museum (see page 184).

GETTING THERE If you are using a rental car from Beirut, take the coast road and drive north past Jounieh, Byblos and Batroun and then head inland at Chekka and pass through the town of Amioun on the road towards Bcharré.

From the capital's Dora station, the Estefan bus company (m *03 534 701*) have regular departures to Bcharré (LBP6,000), arriving in the centre of town in around two hours.

Minivans from Tripoli to Bcharré and the Cedars depart from just outside the Marco Polo travel agency near the Ministry of Tourism office and are operated by the Bcharré Transport Company (✆ *06 672 166*; m *70 353 135; LBP4,000 each way, 1hr 15mins, departures every 30min summer 07.30–19.30, winter 07.30–17.30*).

GETTING AROUND Bcharré is tiny and you certainly won't require a taxi to get around as it is easily navigated on foot. The nucleus of the town is the main square or Place Mar Sera, overlooked by the red-roofed Church of St Saba, which is also the main transport hub for taxis and vans. The main east–west road is where most of the amenities such as the bank, pharmacies, cafés and restaurants are situated, with the post office just to the north of this road.

5

WHERE TO STAY

Hotel Chbat (50 rooms) Khalil Gibran St;
06 671 270; m 03 292 494; e hotelchbat@
cyberia.net.lb, schbat@cyberia.net.lb; www.
hotelchbat.net. The most salubrious & sizeable of
the town's hotels, this is a nice, cosy option with
a restaurant serving Western & Lebanese food.
There is an outdoor swimming pool for the
summer season & also a gym & sauna. A good-
value stay with stunning views over the Qadisha
Valley. B/fast inc. **$$**

Palace Hotel (24 rooms) Main St;
06 671 460; m 03 468 606. A good central
& scenic location is this hotel's greatest asset,
with simple but clean rooms. Recently renovated.
$$

Bauhaus (12 rooms, suites & chalets)
Gibran Khalil Gibran St; 06 672 220; m 03 329
294; e info@bauhauslb.com; www.bauhauslb.
com. Run by the friendly owner Tony, this place is
nicely located for the Cedars, Qadisha & the Khalil
Gibran Museum. The rooms are spacious &
exceptionally clean with shared bathrooms.
2-person chalet US$70, inc Wi-Fi. Dorm room
US$10pp per night. **$**

Tiger House Hotel (8 rooms) Rue Cedre;
06 672 480; m 03 378 138, 03 429 463;
e tigerhousepension@hotmail.com. A small,
comfortable & friendly pension which certainly
lives up to its mantra 'home away from home',
this is a good option for a few days if exploring
the region. Dorm room US$10pp per night. **$**

WHERE TO EAT AND DRINK

Makhlouf Elie Main Rd; 06 672 585;
⊕ 11.00–23.00 daily. A cosy & simple eatery
serving standard fare such as *Shish Tawouk* &
mezze & there is a roof terrace open in the
summer months. **$$$$**

Mississippi Southern end of Bcharré;
06 671 225, 06 671 457; ⊕ 11.00–23.00 daily.
Affording terrific views from its location at the
head of the Qadisha River, this restaurant serves
decent *mezze* dishes, but the menu can't top the
location. **$$$$**

Abou Joseph Beneath the Qannoubin
Monastery; m 03 277 898; ⊕ mainly by
appointment only, call in advance to check.
A delightful place with superlative views
accompanied by excellent *mezze* in an
extremely soothing setting amongst
nature. Abou Joseph can also assist with
arranging transport around the valley
& nearby towns. **$$$**

OTHER PRACTICALITIES

$ BLC Bank Main Rd; 06 671 101;
⊕ 08.30–13.30 Mon–Fri, 08.30–12.00 Sat.
Has an ATM.

✉ **Post office** Just north of the Main Rd;
06 671 025; ⊕ 08.00–17.00 Mon–Fri,
08.00–13.30 Sat
✚ **Simona Pharmacy** 06 672 727;
⊕ 08.00–20.00 daily

WHAT TO SEE AND DO

Khalil Gibran Museum (*Main Rd;* 06 671 137; *e info@friendsofgibran.org;*
www.friendsofgibran.org; ⊕ *summer 10.00–18.00 daily, winter 09.00–17.00 Tue–Sun;*
admission: LBP5,000) A must-see museum for fans of Gibran's life and works, this
small but well-maintained museum houses hundreds of his original paintings and
drawings together with some of his original manuscripts and personal effects, and
in some ways resembles more a house than museum. Gibran's burial site and coffin
is located in the adjacent monastery and the museum is also home to the inevitable
gift and bookshop where his works are available translated into different languages.

Qadisha Grotto (*Off the top of the Old Rd between Bcharré & Cedars;* 06
671 088; ⊕ 08.00–17.00 daily; admission: LBP5,000) Like Jeita Grotto, this much
smaller, though still stunning and absorbing collection of stalactite and stalagmite

rock formations at the head of the Qadisha River, has been fashioned over millions of years but had a relatively recent discovery in 1903. It was to be another two decades before serious excavation of the cave started, and work is still ongoing. Although some 778m of the grotto have been explored, only a portion is currently accessible to visitors at present. A positive for visitors, however, is that unlike at Jeita photography is permitted inside the cave. A further plus point is that the views from outside the grotto over the valley are superb.

QADISHA VALLEY FLOOR: CHAPELS, CAVES AND MONASTERIES

GETTING AROUND To explore the most interesting and scenic 20km section of the Qadisha Valley from Tourza in the west to the source of the Qadisha River in the east at the Qadisha Grotto, you can walk down into the valley from roads which lead out of Bcharré. You should allocate a whole day to exploring the sites mentioned below independently, but if you would like a more guided and organised tour of the valley and its history, the following ecotourism organisations should be able to help.

Esprit Nomade ☎ 09 933 552; m 03 223 552; e coord@esprit-nomade.com; www.esprit-nomade.com
Lebanon Mountain Trail ☎ 05 955 302; e lmta@lebanontrail.org; www.lebanontrail.org. Part of the LMT goes through the valley & they can help organise a visit or put you in contact

with relevant tour operators. For more details on the LMT (see box, page 181).
Liban Trek ☎ 01 329 975; m 03 291 616; e info@libantrek.com; www.libantrek.com
Sharewood Camp ☎ 04 870 592; m 03 294 298; e info@sharewoodcamp.com; www.sharewoodcamp.com

WHAT TO SEE

Deir Mar Elisha This important monastery is where the Maronite Order of Lebanese Monks was founded in 1695, but is first mentioned back in the 14th century as the home of a Maronite bishop. As is apparent from its façade, the monastery underwent renovation in recent years and since 1991 is now part museum, with a number of exhibits explaining the history of the building. In one of its four chapels is the tomb of a French hermit, Father François de Chasteuil who died in 1644. One of the most picturesque and spectacularly located of the valley's many religious shrines, the monastery is cut into the rock face and almost appears part of the surrounding geology. Located south of Bcharré, a steep road takes you down into the monastery.

Deir Mar Semaan Located in the southern section of the valley this rock-cut hermitage, supposedly the former residence of Saint Simon (Mar Semaan), is reached by a 15-minute walk down a steep path just past the turning for the village of Bqaa Kafra. This hermitage dates from 1112 and was reputedly founded by Takla, the daughter of Basil, a priest from Bcharré. Although the hermitage contains a number of rooms built into the cliffs, the main points of interest are the remnants of some frescoes, cisterns for collecting and storing water, and terrific views over the valley.

Chapel of Mar Chmouni Occupying a position beneath a rocky ledge, this three-nave chapel – two manmade and one part of the local geology – dates from the Middle Ages. Until the late 1990s, the entire chapel walls were finely decorated with 13th-century Byzantine-style paintings. Regrettably, 20th-century artisanal endeavours have not been as creative, and the paintings are now obscured behind a layer of plaster.

Deir es Salib Though now abandoned and in a very poor state of repair, Deir es Salib, or Monastery of the Cross, still has traces of frescoes dating to the Byzantine era and a number of ecclesiastical scenes. In addition there is a chapel and a few caves formerly used as hermits' cells. The monastery can be reached by taking a 30-minute walk down a steep path down to the valley from the village of Hadchit.

Deir Qannoubin Partially cut into the rock face with lovely views over the valley in a serene and spectacular setting, Deir Qannoubin takes its name from the Greek word *kenobion* meaning 'monastery', and is reputedly the oldest Maronite monastery in the valley, dating back to the Byzantine period. Although a working convent nowadays, this was formerly the seat of the Maronite patriarchs between the 15th and 19th centuries, and there are frescoes dating from this time together with the remains of 17 Maronites buried in a nearby chapel to the west of the monastery. Also close by is the chapel-cum-cave dedicated to St Marina. According to local legend, St Marina entered the monastery disguised as a monk and following unfounded allegations of being the father of a child, decided to rear the baby herself using her own milk. Close to the monastery's entrance are the mummified remains reputed to belong to the 18th-century patriarch Yousef Tynan. Deir Qannoubin is about another hour's walk further along the valley floor from Deir es Salib.

Saydet Hawqa This compact cliff-side monastery, known as Our Lady of Hawqa, has a delightful little chapel and a number of monks' cells which date from around the end of the 13th century. It is mainly known for an attack by Mamluk forces and the betrayal by one of the local populace who suggested pouring water from a cistern, a cave and natural fortress called Aassi Hawqa above the monastery, to drown out the inhabitants. The fortress above the monastery is not easy to get to, and this is one place where you really need to be an experienced rock climber. Mainly secluded and unoccupied, the monastery comes to life each year on 14 August when it hosts the Feast of the Assumption of the Virgin, which culminates in a high mass during the evening. To reach here, continue along the valley past Deir Qannoubin. If you have a car you can drive from Blawza to Hawqa, which is then a 30-minute walk down a steep path.

Deir Mar Antonios Qozhaya A fully functioning monastery since the middle of the 12th century, this is one of the largest in the valley and its setting, partially cut into the rock face with lovely views, has one of the most attractive façades of all the area's monasteries. Since 1995, it has also housed a museum exhibiting ecclesiastical and ethnographic artefacts. Perhaps the most important object on display is the Arab world's first printing press which dates from the 16th century, and which was used to print the Book of Psalms in the Syriac language which remains in use by the Maronites today during their religious rituals. Close to the monastery's entrance is the 'Cave of the Mad' as locals refer to St Anthony's Grotto, where you can still see the chains that were used to restrain those deemed to be mentally ill or possessed by demons. If the chains eventually opened by themselves, it was believed that those they had been restraining had been visited and cured by St Anthony. If you are travelling on foot, continue along the valley floor. If driving, the monastery can be reached from Aarbet Qozhaiya, though you may need to ask locals for directions, as it is not clearly marked.

Chapel of Saydet Ed Darr A path down into this compact rock-cut sanctuary reaches the Our Lady of Abundant Milk, between Bcharré and Hadchit. Breastfeeding women, who would come here to give thanks, revered it. The walls of the chapel contain some 14th-century paintings, including a portrayal of the Baptism of Christ.

Diman Since the 19th century, this modern church at Diman has been the Maronite patriarch's summer residence. Located in the southern part of the gorge with lovely views over the valley from the rear of the church, it houses a nice collection of religious paintings from the 1930s and 1940s by the Lebanese artist Saliba Doueihy (1915–94).

Tannourine Cedars Forest Nature Reserve (*Main entrance: Tannourine al-Fawka;* \ *06 500 550;* m *03 815 029, 03 277 618;* e *info@arztannourine.org; www. arztannourine.org;* ⊕ *Apr–Nov 08.00–18.00 daily; admission: LBP5,000, LBP3,000pp for groups, optional guide LBP10,000)* A few kilometres south of Qadisha, Tannourine is one of Lebanon's less-visited nature reserves owing to its more rocky and undulating terrain making it more demanding for hikers and walkers than many of the other protected areas. Yet Tannourine is well worth a visit, with over three-quarters of the trees in the forest being cedars and, after those in the Chouf, it contains the largest number of the remaining cedar trees in Lebanon: around 25%. This 12km² reserve is also rich in biodiversity containing over 20 varieties of mushroom (of the edible and non-edible variety), the prickly juniper tree (*Juniperus oxycedrus*), the Lebanon prickly thrift (*Acantholiman libanoticum*), and the mountain tulip (*Tulipa montana*). In addition, the reserve is home to more than 16 species of mammal including hedgehogs, hyenas, cape hare, badgers, foxes, porcupine, wildcat, wild boar and the wolf. Both spring and summer are good times to visit, with the forest's flora in full bloom whilst autumn sees a variety of bird species stopping off here on their annual migratory routes. The reserve has a number of designated hiking trails of 1–4.5km in length, ranging from easy to difficult, and trail maps and further information can be obtained from the reserve's information office at the entrance.

Tour operators There are a number of ecotourism-based organisations who operate daily and periodic guided tours to the reserve (and other areas of Lebanon) if you prefer a more organised visit, with the following just a few of the possibilities worth contacting for further details.

Cyclamen \ 04 419 848; m 03 486 551; e contact@tlb-destinations.com; www.tlb-destinations.com
Lebanon Mountain Trail \ 05 955 302; e lmta@lebanontrail.org; www.lebanontrail.org.

They can organise trips for LMT members (see box, page 181).
Vamos Todos m 03 561 174; e info@vamos-todos.com, mark.aoun@gmail.com; www.vamos-todos.com

EHDEN

Like many of Lebanon's mountainous regions, Ehden is principally a resort town, often referred to as Lebanon's 'Summer Bride'. This attractive, friendly and pleasant little town is popular with residents from nearby Zgharta, many of whom have holiday homes in Ehden to take advantage of the town's more temperate summer climate, and between June and October the town is buzzing with couples and families enjoying the pleasant atmosphere of Ehden's main square and its gastronomy. Famed especially for its meat and in particular its variety of *kibbeh*, the popular and traditional Lebanese dish of raw or minced meat with cracked wheat, Ehden made it into the Guinness World Record book in 2009 for making the biggest-ever *kibbeh* which weighed in at a very filling 233kg (514lb). Outside the summer season, however, the town is extremely quiet with many cafés and restaurants closed for the winter, and there is little reason to visit unless you are exploring the nearby Horsh Ehden Nature Reserve.

GETTING THERE At an altitude of 2,000m above sea level, Ehden sits on the northern edge of the Qadisha Valley and is around 110km from Beirut and 40km southeast of Tripoli. The Horsh Ehden Nature Reserve is about a ten-minute drive (4km) north of the town.

If on a self-drive arrangement from Beirut, take the coast road north and turn inland at Chekka. Then follow the road that goes through Amioun, Kousba and Tourza towards Ehden.

If driving from Tripoli, take the road southeast towards Zgharta and continue on this road for around 26km, which will bring you to the town of Ehden. The reserve is then a further 4km or so from the town itself. This is a particularly scenic route.

Service taxis from Tripoli pass through Ehden *en route* to Bcharré and should cost around LBP8,000–10,000 for a service taxi. A service taxi from Bcharré to Ehden is around LBP15,000. Expect to pay around LBP45,000 for a taxi from Bcharré to Ehden.

GETTING AROUND Ehden's main area of interest is its central square or Al-Midan and is easily walkable, with all the main eateries, the town's handful of sites and watering holes all close by.

WHERE TO STAY

Ehden Country Club (85 rooms & suites) ✆ 06 560 651/2; m 03 252 700/1; e info@ehdencountryclubhotel.com; www.ehdencountryclubhotel.com. In many ways a typical resort complex with modern, spacious but minimalist rooms. The restaurant serves international & Lebanese food. A well-equipped gym, large outdoor pool & lively piano bar make this ideal for couples & families but there is little in the way of character. $$$$$

Hotel Ehden (36 rooms & suites) ✆ 06 560 100; m 03 560 100; e info@hotelehden.com; www.hotelehden.com. A new hotel with modern décor & spacious rooms with mountain views, TV, AC & Wi-Fi. The restaurant serves a good range of international dishes & there is a small pool & gym. $$$$$

Hotel Abchi (43 rooms & suites) ✆ 06 561 101/2; e info@abchi-hotel.com; www.abchi-hotel.com; ⊕ Jun–Oct. Within walking distance of Ehden's main square, this hotel has nicely decorated & comfortable rooms with all the usual modern accoutrements. There is a large outdoor pool & the hotel has a decent restaurant serving Lebanese & international cuisine. $$$$

WHERE TO EAT AND DRINK

The beating heart of the town is the pleasant Al-Midan or central square, shaded by trees and thronged with cafés and restaurants. The town in summer gets very busy, with couples and families enjoying the indoor and outdoor ambience of the town's setting.

Platanus Al-Midan; ✆ 06 360 442; m 70 117 058; ⊕ 10.00–late daily. Although the food served up here is standard pub fare of pasta, pizza & sandwiches, this attractive Ottoman-period café has a great local atmosphere & good service. $$$

OTHER PRACTICALITIES As primarily a summer bolthole for nearby residents from Zgharta, gastronomy and nightlife easily takes precedence over such practical matters as banking, post offices and pharmaceuticals in Ehden and the following are the best options located just over 20km away in Zgharta.

✚ Care Centre Pharmacy Zgharta; ✆ 06 550 655; ⏲ 08.30–22.00 Mon–Fri, 08.30–21.00 Sat, closed Sun
$ Credit Libanais Zgharta; ✆ 06 668 600; ⏲ 08.00–14.00 Mon–Fri, 08.00–13.00 Sat. Has an ATM.

✚ Ehden Governmental Hospital ✆ 06 561 701
✉ Post Office Zgharta; ✆ 06 660 001; ⏲ 08.00–17.00 Mon–Fri, 08.00–13.30 Sat

WHAT TO SEE AND DO Although Ehden functions predominantly as a resort town, it has a few engaging centrally located sites, in addition to the slightly further afield Horsh Ehden Nature Reserve, which are worth a look. To the west of the main square stands the AD749 Mar Mama or Saint Mamas Chapel, which is reputedly the oldest Christian Maronite church in Lebanon. The town's main St George's Church is also nearby, which houses the glass-topped sarcophagus of the local nationalist hero Youssef Bey Karam (1823–89), who led several military campaigns against the Ottomans but was finally killed by the Turks. His mummified body is dressed resplendently in his ceremonial finery of gold-embroidered costume and there is also a statue of 'Lebanon's hero', as the locals refer to Karam, on horseback next to the church. For a marvellous view of the surrounding valley and countryside, you can take a trip up to the 9th-century Our Lady of the Fort, or Saydet al-Hosn as she is known locally, which is perched atop a hill sitting atop a geometric structure in the shape of a star. Throughout the month of August, Ehden also holds its annual summer festival of **Ehdeniyat** (✆ *06 550 700;* 📱 *70 183 184; www.ehdeniyat.com*), with a wide range of activities for children, arts and crafts, concerts, film and theatre.

Horsh Ehden Forest Nature Reserve (*Zgharta;* ✆ *06 660 120, 06 663 120; www. horshehden.org; information centre* ⏲ *08.00–18.00 daily; admission: LBP3,000, LBP5,000 including guide*) This comparatively tiny nature reserve, varying in altitude between 1,200m and 2,000m, covers just 17km^2, but contains one of the most concentrated varieties of flora and fauna of any of Lebanon's natural reserves. Representing less than 1% of the country's total landmass, the reserve is home to 1,058 types of flora which account for 40% of the country's total species and contains some 20% of Lebanon's stands of cedar trees, the largest in the country. Of the varieties of fauna, 156 varieties of bird have been recorded in the reserve, including the globally endangered corncrake (*Crex crex*), greater spotted eagle (*Aquila clanga*), imperial eagle (*Aquila heliaca*), and lesser kestrel (*Falco naumanni*). In addition, there are 27 mammal species including badgers, deer, hyena, squirrels, wildcats and wolves, and 23 species of reptile such as the Lebanon viper (*Montivipera bornmuellen*), Palestinian viper (*Vipera palaestinae*), and the delightfully tongue-twistingly named Schreiber's fringe-fingered lizard (*Acanthodactylus schreiberi*). The reserve is best visited in spring and autumn when the variety of flowers are in full bloom and the trees are at their most vibrant. A stunning location for walking, the reserve has a number of short designated hiking trails that vary in length from just under 1km to just over 2km, with varying degrees of difficulty.

THE CEDARS

(✆ *06 672 562;* ⏲ *1 May–30 Nov daily; admission: voluntary contributions between LBP5,000 & LBP10,000 appreciated to aid ongoing preservation work*) Located around 4km above Bcharré on the slopes of Jebel Makmel between 1,900m and 2,050m above sea level, the Cedars is home to Lebanon's oldest stands of cedar tree, with only some 375 trees remaining of a copse which once carpeted the Lebanese mountains. But they are held in the most esteem for their grandiose proportions, attaining heights up to 40m and with a few dating back 1,500–2,000 years. With their huge girth of up to 14m, they are a scenic sight at any time of the year but particularly beautiful in winter when draped with snow against a mountain backdrop and it is arguably the best time to see them. Known locally as Arz al-Rab or 'Cedars of the Lord', numerous civilisations over the millennia have left their mark on the Cedars, from the ancient Phoenicians who felled the trees to build their trading vessels, to more latterly the British army in World War II who cut down the trees to build a railway line from Tripoli to Haifa.

Others decided to leave their mark in other ways including the English 19th-century poet Lord Byron, who saw fit to carve his initials onto one specimen, an example followed by the French aristocrat and poet Lamartine, whose tree has since been resculptured by the Bcharré artist Rudy Rahme. Perhaps following the conservationist example of the emperor Hadrian in the 2nd century, Britain's Queen Victoria was certainly not amused when she learnt that the cedar grove was under threat from goats with a taste for the young saplings, and personally financed the construction of a wall around the copse to protect the trees. Today it is the Maronite patriarchs who are the guardians and protectors of the cedar forest, and in 1843, they built a small chapel in the centre of the grove which is the location for a blessing and service to honour the trees in the first week of August each year.

GETTING THERE The Cedars are located around 5km from Bcharré. A taxi from outside the town's main St Saba church and square to the Cedars should not cost more than around LBP20,000 with a service taxi costing somewhere around LBP5,000–8,000. If driving from Beirut in a hire car take the coastal road north towards Tripoli and at Chekka, a few kilometres south of Tripoli, turn inland and follow the road towards Amioun, continuing towards Kousba, Tourza, Hadath el Joubbe and Bcharré with the Cedars just a few kilometres beyond Bcharré.

GETTING AROUND The Cedars are easily manageable by foot but if you prefer to visit by taxi it would be best to arrange this and negotiate a price in Bcharré as there is a distinct lack of public transport options in the Cedars.

WHERE TO STAY The accommodation options in the Cedars are very much geared towards the visiting skier and all offer a decent level of comfort. If coming here in the much quieter months outside the ski season, however, it could be worth enquiring about discounted room rates, where significant savings could be available. The hotels below all have food available.

Le Cedrus Suites Hotel (40 rooms & suites) Cedars; 📞 06 678 777, 06 678 077; e info@cedrushotel.com; www.cedrushotel.com. A salubrious & cosy option with warm décor & an excellent French 'Le Pichet' Restaurant & piano bar. $$$$$

L'Auberge des Cèdres (18 chalets, suites & luxury tents) Cedars; 📞 06 678 888; m 03 566 953; e res@smresorts.net; www.smresorts.net.

The Cedars' most luxurious option, with a great range of accommodation options & with all the bells & whistles you would expect for the price, including roaring fire & good restaurant menu. The hotel can also organise a range of winter & summer outdoor activities, including paragliding. $$$$

La Cabane Hotel (12 rooms) Cedars, above Bcharré; 📞 06 678 067; m 03 321 575; www.

lacabanecedars.com. In a superb location a minute's walk from the ski resort, with some of the best views over the Qadisha Valley. Rooms in this lodge are simple but spotlessly clean. Very friendly & helpful owner. B/fast LBP8,000 extra. **$$$**

🏠 **Hotel St Bernard** (25 rooms & suites) Above the Cedars; 📞 06 678 100; m 03 289 600, 70 979 769; www.hstbernard.com. Very homely

rooms & atmosphere combined with outstanding views over the Cedars. The hotel's Cedria Restaurant serves a Lebanese & international menu. **$$**

🏠 **Mon Refuge Hotel** (16 rooms) Main Rd, Cedars; 📞 06 671 397, 06 678 050. A comfortable hotel with more simple, but clean, rooms than the other options but has a nice friendly atmosphere. **$$**

✕ **WHERE TO EAT AND DRINK** In addition to the venues below, the hotel's reviewed above all have good restaurants for food and non-guests are welcome to eat in the hotel restaurant.

✕ **La Casa Night Club** Main Rd; m 03 555 829, 70 555 829; ⏲ Oct–Jun 21.00–late Sat, July–Sept 21.00–late Fri & Sat. A great fun & friendly venue serving a wide range of alcoholic & non-alcoholic drinks in a party atmosphere which includes karaoke & a DJ spinning discs from electro to R&B. **$$**

✕ **Tombe La Neige** Main Rd; 📞 06 678 800; m 70 953 577; ⏲ 07.00–00.00 daily. Very much a home from home eatery & pub with fireplace & welcoming atmosphere & a varied menu including fondue, steak & salad. **$$**

OTHER PRACTICALITIES For day to day practicalities such as banking, post office and pharmacies etc nearby Bcharré is your best option given the dearth of these facilities in the area (see page 184).

ACTIVITIES

Skiing (*Cedars; above Bcharré;* m *03 399 133;* ⏲ *08.00–15.30 Mon–Fri, 08.00–16.00 Sat/Sun; adult ski lift pass prices: US$23/day Mon–Fri, US$30 Sat/Sun, half-day pass after 12.00 US$17 Mon–Fri, US$23 Sat/Sun*) A couple of kilometres further up the road from the trees, the Cedars is also the location for Lebanon's oldest ski resort where skiers have been negotiating its slopes since the 1920s, well before its first ski lift was installed back in 1953. At nearly 2,000m altitude, the Cedars is also Lebanon's highest ski resort with the resulting higher altitude giving a longer ski season than the others in the country – it can run from as early as November or early December right through to April. The resort is probably the most picturesque of Lebanon's ski locations with superlative views over the cedar forest and Qadisha Valley. Of the resort's eight ski lifts, five are for beginners, making this an ideal choice for the novice. Although its après-ski facilities can't compete with those at Mzaar, there has recently been ongoing investment in the resort to the tune of US$15 million including new chair lifts, a six-person gondola to take skiers from base level to the highest accessible point of 2,870m, and a new road to reduce journey times from Bcharré to the slopes.

Qornet es Saouda Around 6km northeast of the Cedars, the northern portion of the Mount Lebanon range is Qornet es Saouda (the Black Horn), Lebanon's highest mountain at 3,083m, towering over the surrounding landscape. From its peak it affords unrivalled views over the coast, the Bekaa Valley and neighbouring Syria. A good time to climb this mountain is generally between late May and September and the climb should take around four–five hours to reach the summit, depending upon your level of fitness. It would be a good idea to allocate a whole day to making the

5

KHALIL GIBRAN

Born on 6 January 1883 in the mountainous region of Bcharré in northern Lebanon, Khalil Gibran is Lebanon's best-known and loved artist, philosopher and writer. After Shakespeare and Lao-tzu he is the best-selling poet of all time. Gibran was born into a poor Maronite family and was the second eldest of four children. His father was never a good family provider, opting instead to drink and gamble away what little income the family possessed. Whilst working as a tax collector he was imprisoned by the Ottoman authorities for embezzling funds in 1891, leaving the family destitute and homeless. In order to carve out a better life, his stronger-willed wife and mother, Kamila, took the children to the US in 1895, settling in the immigrant quarter of South End in Boston, Massachusetts. Although the family's financial hardships continued, despite Kamila working as a seamstress and peddler, Gibran began to attend school for the first time where his interest and talent for art, nurtured back in his native Bcharré, was recognised by his teacher. They introduced him to Fred Holland Day, a painter and photographer who was one of the first people to argue for photography as a fine-art form. Holland took Gibran under his wing as assistant and student, and the young man's cultural world blossomed. Gibran held his first exhibition in Boston in 1904, where he met and formed a life-long professional and personal association with the much older headmistress Mary Elizabeth Haskell. Following two years in Paris from 1908 studying art under August Rodin, who likened Gibran's works to that of William Blake, he moved to New York to concentrate on painting and writing. Until 1918, most of Gibran's written works were in Arabic, but after this time he began to write in English and of his 17 published books, nine are in Arabic and eight in English, including his best-known 1923 work, *The Prophet*. Gibran's seminal work is a series of 28 poems and short stories containing his heartfelt and poignant musings on such things as beauty, children, love, marriage, pleasure, religion and time, etc. It is a book which has been translated into dozens of languages, and the American edition alone has sold in excess of nine million copies, famed for its depth of feeling and almost mystical qualities. Following a lengthy battle with alcohol abuse, Gibran died on 10 April 1931 from cirrhosis of the liver and tuberculosis. Despite residing for much of his life outside Lebanon, in the US, he never forgot the beauty of his hometown landscape which had helped to inspire him, and his wish to be buried back in Lebanon was fulfilled and his body lies within the Khalil Gibran Museum, along with a number of his personal effects.

ascent and to take plenty of water. You can start the climb from a location within the Cedars ski resort or arrange a guided hike with one of the many organisations such as **SKILEB** (m *70 103 222*; e *info@skileb.com; www.skileb.com*), who offer a guided hike with lunch, and **Lebanese Adventure** (\ *03 360 027*; e *infos@lebanese-adventure.com; www.lebanese-adventure.com*) who also run day hikes from Beirut and come highly recommended (the cost in July 2011 was US$25 which included transport from and to Beirut, guides and insurance).

Other activities Paragliding has been gaining in popularity over the last few years, and it is now possible to chase the thermals high up over the Cedars. If gaining an aerial view of the surrounding landscape appeals, **Cedars Paragliding**

(m *03 544 449*; e *info@cedarsparagliding.com; www.cedarsparagliding.com*) offers flights with and without instructors for suitably qualified pilots as well as five-day courses for absolute beginners. One qualified pilot, who comes highly recommended and conducts flights over the Cedars, is Georges (m *03 544 449*).

BQAA KAFRA At an elevation of 1,750m above sea level, Bqaa Kafra, 4km south of Bcharré on the road to Hasroun, is the highest village in Lebanon. Located up a steep side road between Deir Mar Elisha and Deir Mar Semaan, this little village of traditional and well-preserved rural houses and slender streets is also famed as the birthplace of Lebanon's revered Maronite saint, St Charbel, whose house is now converted into a museum–art gallery, with his life story told in a series of paintings. On the third Sunday in July each year, a feast in the saint's honour is held in the village. A convent in honour of St Charbel has recently been built in the village, and there is also the Notre Dame Church near the museum.

Tale of a Century
A Unique Lebanese Landmark

For Family Vacations   *For Cultural Trips*

Grand Hotel
1911   KADRI   *2011*

For Leisure & Short Breaks   *For Business*

6

The Bekaa Valley

Telephone code 08

Geographically, the Bekaa Valley is the result of earthly forces residing outside Lebanon, a vast geological fault that extends from east Africa northwards to neighbouring Syria, known as the Great Rift Valley. Separated by the Mount Lebanon and Anti-Lebanon mountain ranges, the Bekaa is an elongated plateau but still reaches up to 1,000m above sea level in places. It stretches for some 120km and averages only 16km in width. With its favourable climate of warm, dry summers and cold, wet winters, the valley has been an important agricultural region since antiquity. Referred to as Coele-Syria (Hollow Syria) by Alexander the Great, it was also the 'breadbasket' of Rome during that empire's era. The Bekaa retains its agricultural importance to this day, comprising some 40% of Lebanon's arable farmland, thanks to its fertile soil, drained by the Orontes and Litani river systems. A variety of crops are grown including wheat, vegetables and fruits such as grapes and olives. Both wild and beautiful, the landscape is characterised by a patchwork of cultivated fields, grazing sheep and goats and a variety of Bedouin encampments. Nonetheless, despite the area's rural importance, the Bekaa remains a largely traditional, poor and underdeveloped part of Lebanon with none of the frenzied rebuilding and construction seen in the capital.

The region has perhaps become more familiar to many Western eyes as a Hezbollah area, and it suffered greatly during its 2006 war with Israel with an estimated one-fifth of its buildings destroyed. It also has long been, though a now much-diminished, centre for cannabis production, the famous (or infamous, depending on your point of view) 'Red Leb', which has no doubt seen many a visitor depart these lowlands on a high. It was also the main base for Syrian occupation troops until their withdrawal from Lebanon in 2005. The region as a whole nowadays has a much more sedate and less troubled feel. The archaeological evidence of the great Arab and Roman civilisations which have passed through here in history are reason enough to visit, with the glorious UNESCO World Heritage Sites at Aanjar and Baalbek demanding any visitor's time. Adding in a visit to a winery or two to appreciate Lebanon's tradition of viticulture can only serve to enhance a rich cultural visit to this region. While the Bekaa is easily reached by bus, taxi or organised tour on a day trip from Beirut, to get the most from a visit to the region, a few days' touring by car or van would be a more rewarding experience.

ZAHLÉ

The town of Zahlé, around 54km east from Beirut, is Lebanon's third-largest city and the only major town in Lebanon not located on the coast. As the capital of the Bekaa Governorate, it is quite different from other parts of the more conservative Bekaa Valley. The hometown of former president Elias Hrawi (1925–2006) and childhood residence of film star Omar Sharif, Zahlé is the country's largest Christian Greek

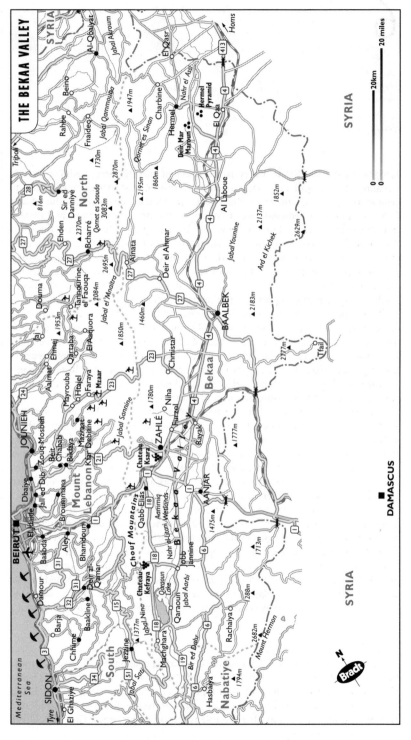

THE BEKAA VALLEY

Catholic town and is often referred to as the 'Bride of the Bekaa' by locals. This friendly, pleasant and picturesque town of Ottoman-era red-tiled dwellings sits on the eastern slopes of Mount Sannine and has the Bardouni River flowing through its centre. The town has, however, known darker days. Sectarian conflict between Christian and Druze militias in 1860 all but razed the town to the ground, with the latter's victory helping to initiate the migration *en masse* of the town's inhabitants to Brazil. During the civil war the 'Arab Deterrent Force' of the Syrian army in the Bekaa, with the aim of staving off Palestinian influence in the area, came into conflict with the Lebanese Forces of Bashir Gemayel. The Phalangist leader decided to construct a road link connecting Zahlé to Mount Sannine for the benefit of the Christian population. The Syrians, perceiving this as a threat by giving Israel a strategic advantage in allowing their forces access to the Bekaa and even Syria itself, decided to take military action against the Phalange. During the spring and summer of 1981, relentless Syrian bombardments not only left 300 dead and 3,000 wounded, according to Phalange estimates, but also set in motion the first stage of Syrian–Israeli conflict during the civil war.

No traces of note remain of Zahlé's bloody past and a good clue to the preoccupation and prosperity of the town today is found in the statue on the roundabout at the entrance to Zahlé of a slim, attractive woman, holding aloft a bunch of grapes; for the town's main preoccupation is with wine, food and *arak* (see box, page 216). Zahlé is the perfect place to sample some of the best *mezze*, wine and fine dining in Lebanon, especially around the cluster of eateries known as Cafés du Bardouni. With a varied selection of hotels to suit all budgets and good minivan and taxi links to the nearby ancient sites at Aanjar and Baalbek, Zahlé makes an excellent base for an extended tour of the Bekaa region. Be aware, however, that the main summer season is between June and mid-September, and outside this period the colder winter months in Zahlé can resemble a ghost town, and many of the town's eateries may well be shut. In June each year, the town holds the **Corpus Christi Festival** with an evening torchlight display followed the next day by a procession through the streets. During September each year, Zahlé also holds its annual week-long, carnival-like **Vine and Flower Festival**.

GETTING THERE

By bus Buses to Zahlé leave regularly from the southwest section of the Cola bus station in Beirut. The one-way bus fare costs between LBP4,000 and LBP5,000 for the 1¼-hour journey, though this can sometimes take slightly longer depending on traffic. The bus will drop you off at the highway turn-off around 1km from the centre of town. A service taxi from here to the centre should cost no more than LBP2,000 for the five-minute journey.

By taxi Taxis and service taxis from the capital also regularly ply this route with the latter costing around LBP5,000–10,000. Taxis will need to be negotiated; be prepared to be quoted anywhere between LBP75,000 and LBP90,000 to the centre of Zahlé from Beirut.

Self-drive If you have rented a car to visit the Bekaa, a popular route option is to take the Damascus Road in Beirut which travels through Hazmieh, Aley and Bhamdoun. Keep on this road as you descend Mount Lebanon into the Bekaa Valley travelling east towards Chtaura and finally Zahlé, a further 3km or so from Chtaura. Traffic permitting, the journey time to Zahlé should be around an hour from Beirut.

The Bekaa Valley ZAHLÉ

6

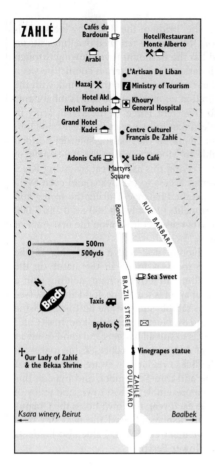

ZAHLÉ

Cafés du Bardouni
Hotel/Restaurant Monte Alberto
Arabi
L'Artisan Du Liban
Mazaj
Ministry of Tourism
Hotel Akl
Khoury General Hospital
Hotel Traboulsi
Grand Hotel Kadri
Centre Culturel Français De Zahlé
Adonis Café
Lido Café
Martyrs' Square

Bardouni
RUE BARBARA

0 — 500m
0 — 500yds

N
Bradt

Sea Sweet
Taxis
BRAZIL STREET
Byblos
Vinegrapes statue
Our Lady of Zahlé & the Bekaa Shrine
ZAHLÉ BOULEVARD
Ksara winery, Beirut
Baalbek

GETTING AROUND For the most part, the town of Zahlé is easily navigated on foot. All of the hotels (with the exception of the Monte Alberto), banks, eateries and post office are all easily reached on or nearby the main Brazil Street. Taxis are plentiful as are buses and minivans serving other areas of the Bekaa Valley and, of course, Beirut, with regular departures every day. Slightly more outlying areas such as the Our Lady of Zahlé shrine and vineyards such as Ksara, 2km outside Zahlé, may require a short service taxi ride (LBP2,000). As in many areas of the country, driving outside the main town at night whether in a hire car or taxi, is not something that is recommended owing to the often poorly or even unlit roads which can make travelling a somewhat hazardous undertaking, especially when combined with an often total lack of awareness of other drivers from locals. Caution and alertness is advised if you do decide to travel at night.

TOURIST INFORMATION

Ministry of Tourism Near Cafés du Bardouni & L'Artisan Du Liban; ℡ 08 802 566; ⊕ Jun–Sep 08.00–14.00 Mon–Fri, 08.00–13.00 Sat. This seasonally open office has leaflets & pamphlets on Zahlé & other regions of Lebanon.

WHERE TO STAY

Grand Hotel Kadri (105 rooms & suites) Brazil St; ℡ 08 813 920; e info@grandhotelkadri.com; www.grandhotelkadri.com. Zahlé's 5-star option, formerly home to an army hospital during the Ottoman period, it has all the business & leisure facilities you would expect for the price including outdoor swimming pool, tennis court, health club & spa, children's play area & a comprehensive business & conference centre with secretarial services & 24hr Wi-Fi. The rooms, however, look a little tired & dated & don't quite live up to the hotel's name. Internet access using the hotel's computer is available & charged at LBP10,000/hr. The hotel can also organise winery tours & cultural tourism packages. Buffet b/fast inc, but is a little disappointing. $$$$$

Arabi Hotel (10 rooms) Wadi Zahlé; ℡ 08 821 214, 08 800 144; m 03 276 545; e racharabi@hotmail.com. A very average hotel, though all rooms have AC & TV, but in a great location in the thick of the town's eateries next to the popular Cafés du Bardouni. There is a large outdoor seating area which is popular in summer for eating & drinking. $$

Hotel Akl (10 rooms) Brazil St; ℡ 08 820 701; m 03 820 701; e contact@aklhotel.com; www.aklhotel.com. Run by the delightful & friendly Nada, this excellent value option in a 100-year-old house, full of old-world charm, has good, clean rooms (6 en suite) with stove heating in winter & fan-cooled rooms in summer. At the time of research Wi-Fi access was free to guests. $$

⌂ **Hotel Monte Alberto** (20 rooms) Mountainside overlooking Wadi Zahlé; ☎ 08 810 912/3/4; e info@montealberto.com; www.montealberto.com. Zahlé's premier hotel in terms of location perched high up on the mountainside with superb views over the town & surrounding countryside – 'the hanging paradise' – according to the hotel's marketing literature. The en-suite rooms are clean & comfortable with AC, TV & fridge. Even if you are not staying here, it is worth a visit to dine in the hotel's top-floor revolving restaurant. Given the hotel's hillside location, for those unable to undertake the uphill walk to reach the hotel a *servees* taxi (LBP1,500–2,000) may be necessary. **$$**

⌂ **Hotel Traboulsi** (3 rooms) Brazil St; ☎ 08 812 661; m 03 727 400; e hotel_traboulsi@yahoo.com. Close to Hotel Akl, this is another character-filled house with dark-wood furniture & chandeliers complemented by good, clean rooms, all with AC & TV. **$**

✖ **WHERE TO EAT AND DRINK** As principally a resort town, Zahlé's eating and drinking options are both numerous and varied, catering to most budgets and ranging from a few fast-food places serving up the usual fare of chips and burgers, to more illustrious and formal feasts of *mezze*, wine and *arak*. The selections below are all good choices for either a quick snack or full-blown meal, but the group of eateries known as **Cafés du Bardouni**, nestled along the banks of the Bardouni River, make for the quintessential Zahlé dining experience in pleasant surroundings. Although many are called 'casinos' they are in fact restaurants, and only chips of the edible variety are served. Many eateries, such as Mazaj and Lido below, double as nightspots with discos and live music, as do those at the Cafés du Bardouni which also have dodgems and other fairground rides and entertainment for children and families.

✖ **Restaurant Monte Alberto** Mountainside overlooking Wadi Zahlé; ☎ 08 810 912/3/4; e info@montealberto.com; www.montealberto.com; ⊕ 08.00–late daily. The most eclectic restaurant in Zahlé with the best views in town has a small rotating restaurant, winter & summer terrace dining areas, the Al Ourzal Restaurant, with thatched ceiling & wooden beams, & the Alberto Café, serving Lebanese & international dishes. The Oriental Room, although a little kitsch, is the place to enjoy a nargileh & Arabic coffee in an 'authentic' setting. The service & food here are both of a good standard. **$$$$**

✖ **Lido Café** Brazil St; ☎ 08 818 656; ⊕ 10.00–midnight daily. Specialising in mainly international cuisine such as pasta, steaks & pizzas, this centrally located eatery offers great service & excellent food. They also serve a range of wines from the Domaine Wardy, Kefraya & Ksara vineyards. There is live music from 22.00 to midnight every Sat. The relatively new statue outside the café has replaced the former clock tower & has been renamed Martyrs' Square, in honour of those who died fighting the Syrians in 1981. **$$$**

✖ **Mazaj Restaurant & Pub** Wadi Zahlé (opposite the Ministry of Tourism office on the other side of the Bardouni River); ☎ 08 806 806; m 03 343 425; e info@zahlemazaj.com; www.zahlemazaj.com; ⊕ 12.00–late daily, except Good Friday. A one-stop shop for excellent Lebanese & international cuisine & serving a full range of alcohol including arak & wine. There is live Arabic & English music & DJ on Sat nights. **$$$**

▢ **Adonis Café** Brazil St (opposite Lido Café); ☎ 08 820 329; m 03 877 379; ⊕ summer 07.00–02.00 daily, winter 08.00–23.00 daily. A good place for fresh fruit juices, cocktails & snacks such as sandwiches. Also serves a decent breakfast menu including *mannouche* & *labneh*. **$**

▢ **Sea Sweet** Zahlé Bd; ☎ 08 822 379; e seasweet@lebanon.com; www.lebanon.com/seasweet; ⊕ 06.30–22.00 daily. This Lebanese chain of patisseries specialises in delicious varieties of take-away baklava, cakes, chocolates, ice cream & knefeh. **$**

SHOPPING There is no shortage of shopping options in Zahlé, including a couple of decent pharmacies, and you will be able to buy almost anything you could want for your day-to-day needs. But perhaps the best and most interesting retail experience is at the **L'Artisan Du Liban** (*08 809 229*; ⊕ *May–Nov 11.00–19.00 daily, Dec–Apr 11.00–16.00 Mon–Sat*), a couple of doors along from the Ministry of Tourism office near the Cafés du Bardouni, which has a wide selection of locally made products manufactured by Lebanese craftsmen and women. Items which you can buy here, in the knowledge that you are supporting Lebanese artisans and the local economy, are glass, purses, tablecloths, ornaments, jewellery, kaftans, *nargileh* (sheesha) pipes and postcards, all at reasonable prices.

OTHER PRACTICALITIES

$ **Byblos Bank** Zahlé Bd (opposite Libanpost); 08 818 330; ⊕ 08.30–17.30 Mon–Fri, 08.30–13.00 Sat. Has a 24/7 ATM, but doesn't change travellers' cheques.

Centre Culturel Français De Zahlé Brazil St (opposite Grand Hotel Kadri); 08 821 293; e zahle@ccf-liban.org; www.ccf-liban.org; ⊕ Jul/Aug 08.00–15.30 Mon–Fri, Sep–Jun 08.00–13.00 & 15.00–18.00 Mon–Fri, 09.00–14.00 Sat. This very active French Cultural Centre organises exhibitions, conferences, music concerts & an annual international theatre festival in May. It also houses a library with a small children's section.

✚ **Khoury General Hospital** Brazil St (opposite Hotel Akl & Hotel Traboulsi); 08 807 000/1/2; e info@khouryhospital.com; www.khouryhospital.com. Comprehensive range of medical services & facilities, including a 24/7 Accident & Emergency Department.

✉ **Post office** Ogero Bldg, Zahlé Bd; 08 822 127; ⊕ 08.00–17.00 Mon–Fri, 08.00–13.30 Sat

✚ **Red Cross** 140, 08 800 735, 08 808 145

WHAT TO SEE AND DO IN AND AROUND ZAHLÉ Apart from the surrounding vineyards, the main town of Zahlé is not overendowed with sights to visit and there is not much to distract you from the principal pursuits of eating and drinking. However, a short service taxi ride east of the main town is the **Our Lady of Zahlé and the Bekaa shrine** which yields, from atop the 54m-high structure, unparalleled and stunning views of the town, its trademark red-roof-tiled buildings, looking resplendent amid the surrounding valley and mountains. A lift (LBP1,000) takes you to the summit of the viewing platform, which is topped by the 9m-tall bronze statue of the Virgin Mary, a work by the Italian artist Pierroti. The small chapel at the base of the shrine can accommodate up to 100 worshippers. It's well worth the visit. A few kilometres northeast of Zahlé, just off the main road to Baalbek, are some interesting remains of caves, rock-cut tombs and Roman temples at **Furzol** and **Niha**, which could make for an interesting detour if *en route* to the temples at Baalbek from Zahlé.

LEBANON'S WINE INDUSTRY AND VINEYARDS

It may not be the first thing that springs to mind when one thinks of Lebanon, but the country produces some excellent wines which have won many international awards over the years. In fact, Lebanon has a viticulture tradition as old as the Lebanese themselves, making the country one of the most ancient wine producers in the world. The Bekaa Valley has always been the epicentre for viticulture – the predominantly chalky soil, wet winters and long, dry, hot summers with some 240 days of continuous sunshine, provide ideal growing and ripening conditions for the grape. The ancient Phoenicians were prolific producers and oceanographic and archaeological evidence from shipwrecks suggest that this entrepreneurial race produced and exported the drink throughout the Mediterranean region, ushering in a golden era for wine production from 3000BC to 350BC. The era of Roman rule continued the tradition with the Temple of Bacchus at Baalbek paying homage to their god of wine. Production declined somewhat with the onset of Islamic rule, but picked up again during the Ottoman period. The French Mandate era, following the end of World War I, was influential in popularising wine and this impact survives to this day.

Production was severely hampered during the 1975–90 civil war, though many producers continued to flourish. With Lebanon once again experiencing a period of stability, the industry is once more a prosperous one and the country is now starting to market itself as a boutique wine destination. The number of producers has risen from a mere five in 1995 to 33 in 2010, and this figure is expected to rise further. Lebanon now produces some six–seven million bottles annually with the industry worth US$25 million per annum. This figure is small by the standards of other major international producers with Lebanon producing less than 1% of the wine made by France, for example. Nonetheless, Lebanese wine is exported to over 30 countries, with the UK, followed by France and the US the largest importers amongst Lebanon's main Western markets. Amongst other Arab countries, Lebanese wines are bought by the UAE, Syria, Iraq, Jordan and Bahrain.

CHATEAU KSARA (*Caves of Ksara, entrance to Ksara village, near Zahlé;* ↘ *08 813 495, 08 801 662;* e *info@ksara.com.lb; www.ksara.com.lb;* ◷ *Jan/Feb 09.00–18.00 Mon–Sat, Mar, Nov & Dec 09.00–17.00 daily, Apr–Oct 09.00–18.00 daily*) If there is one winery which symbolises the tradition and importance of wine making in Lebanon it is the multi-award-winning Ksara label. The château celebrated its 150th anniversary in 2007, and is Lebanon and the Middle East's oldest winery and largest producer, exporting its current output of around 2.7 million bottles to over 30 countries. Ksara began life in 1857, when the religious order of the Jesuits inherited a 25ha parcel of land and began to produce wine for religious purposes, importing the vines from Algeria. In 1898, they discovered nearly 2km of labyrinthine Roman-era caves beneath the château which to this day, with their humidity and stable temperature of 11–13°C, provide optimum conditions for storage of the wine. By 1972, Ksara was producing 1.5 million bottles, accounting for 85% of Lebanon's total wine production. The Jesuits sold the winery to a consortium of local businessmen in 1973 under pressure from the Vatican who deemed their increasing commercial affairs incompatible with their religious calling. Today, the Ksara estate extends over some 300ha, embracing four vineyards. Without doubt, Ksara is the best of Lebanon's many vineyards to visit. Daily 45-minute tours commence with a short 15-minute film telling the history of the château and the process of wine making followed by a free tasting session in the purpose-built tasting rooms. The tour concludes with a fascinating guided visit to the cobwebbed and dusty cellars (caves), which hold some 700,000 bottles of the tipple. In the onsite shop you can purchase Ksara wine, including its *arak*, together with a range of Ksara memorabilia such as books and DVDs.

OTHER NOTABLE BEKAA VALLEY VINEYARDS Although opening hours are given where available, it is still advisable to call in advance to arrange an appointment before setting off for a tour of the following wineries.

Château Kefraya (*Kefraya;* ↘ *08 645 333/444, 01 485 207,* m *03 362 664/5;* e *admin@chateaukefraya.com; www.chateaukefraya.com;* ◷ *10.00–17.00 (cellar tours) daily, 12.00–22.00 (restaurant)*) One of Lebanon's newer wineries and after

Ksara the country's largest producer, Kefraya corks some two million bottles annually and exports to over 35 countries. With vineyards spread over more than 300ha, Kefraya began producing its own wine in 1979, and its mantra '*semper ultra*' (Latin for 'always better') has resulted in its label winning an array of national and international accolades, including numerous awards for its Chateâu Kefraya Celebration red wine. Located just over 20km south of Chtaura, the majority shareholder is Druze leader Walid Jumblatt. Set amid picturesque gardens named after famous people from the world of opera, the delightful 350-seat Le Relais Dionysos Restaurant serves fine *mezze* as well as international cuisine. The daily tours of the winery, including free tastings, consist of a train ride through the attractive vineyards of the château.

Château Khoury (*Overlooking Zahlé;* \ *08 801 160;* m *03 075 422;* e *info@ chateaukhoury.com; www.chateaukhoury.com;* ⏱ *by prior appointment*) Run by the Khoury family since 2004, this small, boutique winery produces only around 50,000 bottles annually with quality over quantity the prime concern. The chateâu is credited with introducing new grape varieties to Lebanon such as Pinot Noir, Pinot Gris and Reisling. Call a couple of days in advance to arrange your visit.

Château Massaya (*Relais de Tanail Property, near Chtaura;* \ *08 510 135/6;* m *03 735 795, 03 744 047;* e *services@massaya.com, coordinator@massaya.com; www.massaya.com;* ⏱ *summer 08.00–17.30 Mon–Sat, 10.00–17.30 Sun; winter 08.00–16.00 Mon–Fri, 10.00–12.00 Sat/Sun*) The chateâu is owned and run by brothers Sami and Ramzi Ghosn, who returned to Lebanon in 1992 after the civil war to kick-start the family's vineyard estate. Having respectively pursued careers as a LA architect and French-based restaurateur, they once again established the production of *arak* and, in 1998, red and white wine production was added to their viticulture portfolio. They now produce on average 200,000 bottles per year. Their Le Relais Restaurant, situated within the vineyard itself, serves food cooked by local women.

Château Musar (*Sopenco Bldg, Baroudy St, Achrafieh, Beirut;* \ *01 201 828, 01 328 111, 01 328 211;* e *info@chateaumusar.com.lb; www.chateaumusar.com.lb;* ⏱ *by prior appointment*) Probably Lebanon's most recognisable label internationally, Chateâu Musar began life back in the vault of a 17th-century castle in 1930 as a pastime of Gaston Hochar. Upon meeting the famous British viticulturalist Ronald Barton during his posting to Lebanon during World War II, Hochar's hobby quickly blossomed into a 'passion' and since 1962, the 180ha vineyards are run by Hochar's youngest son Ronald, producing 500,000 bottles annually, almost exclusively for the overseas market. Unlike the other Bekaa wineries, the château is located away from the valley in the village of Ghazir, above Jounieh, north of Beirut.

Clos St Thomas (*Qabb Elias, about 6km from Chtaura;* ❧ *08 500 812/3;* e *info@ closstthomas.com; www.closstthomas.com;* ⏰ *09.00–16.00 Mon–Sat*) Run by the Touma family, this 50ha vineyard has been a long-time major *arak* producer with wine production added in the 1990s. Daily tours, except on Sundays, take place in lovely surroundings which encompass picturesque gardens, a picnic site and a chapel devoted to St Thomas.

Domaine des Tourelles (*Main Rd, Chtaura;* ❧ *08 540 114;* m *03 775 943, 03 805 925;* e *info@domainedestourelles.com; www.domainedestourelles.com;* ⏰ *by prior appointment*) Founded in 1868, this is one of Lebanon's oldest wineries, producing 100,000 bottles per year. Originally renowned for its *arak*, which is aged for five years in clay jars, wine production has increased and its red Marquis de Beys has won a slew of awards. Guided tours of the delightful cellars, garden and winery are by appointment only.

Domaine Wardy (*Industrial Park, Zahlé;* ❧ *08 930 141/2/3;* e *info@domaine- wardy.com; www.domaine-wardy.com;* ⏰ *08.00–17.00 Mon–Fri, 08.00–12.00 Sat*) Another relatively new winery, Wardy was established in 1999, and in 2004 became the first winery in the country to donate a portion of sales to its Cedars Campaign, the winery's own initiative to help preserve Lebanon's natural heritage. The winery produces a variety of reds, a rosé, two varieties of *arak* and a selection of whites including a fruit-filled and aromatic Sauvignon Blanc.

AANJAR

With an area of only some 20km² Aanjar is more village-like than town. Around 58km from Beirut and just a few kilometres from the Syrian border, the area takes its name from a large spring, Ain Gerrha, a few kilometres northeast of Aanjar's main archaeological site. It is also often referred to locally as Haouch Moussa or Moses's Farm. Aanjar's population numbers only around 2,500, almost exclusively Armenian, settled by those fleeing the 1915 genocide in Turkey which is estimated to have cost the lives of 1.5 million Armenians under the Ottoman Turks, and their descendants. (Three centuries earlier the maverick Fakhreddine Maan II had managed to subdue Ottoman forces at the Battle of Aanjar in 1623.) During the more recent Lebanese civil war, Aanjar was the main base for Syrian occupation troops and *mukhabbarat* (security service) until their departure from the country in 2005. The area benefits from a very picturesque setting against the snowy backdrop of the Anti-Lebanon Mountains, and offers some fine waterside dining of *mezze*, Armenian food and the local speciality, farmed trout, at many of its restaurants and the town today evokes a splendid aura of peace and tranquillity. But the main draw of Aanjar is its much earlier historical settlement built during the Umayyad period, which has left a beautiful and unique architectural legacy from the earliest years of Islamic rule.

GETTING THERE Public transport to Aanjar is best taken from either Zahlé or Chtaura with a journey time of less than half an hour and costing between LBP3,000 and LBP4,000. If you are on a self-drive visit, Aanjar can be reached from Chtaura,

6

around 15km to the northwest, by taking the road to Damascus. If based in Zahlé, drive to Chtaura and follow the above road. Aanjar is also quite close to the border crossing point to Syria at Masnaa, a few kilometeres south of Aanjar.

🏠 WHERE TO STAY

🏠 **Challalat Anjar Hotel** (23 rooms & suites) Al Nabeh St; ☎ 08 620 753; m 03 620 753. A 10min walk from the Aanjar ruins, this ultra-modern & clean hotel has good en-suite rooms, AC, TV & fridge. There is a nice communal lounge area with TV & the large terrace hosts live music during the summer months. B/fast inc. $$

✕ WHERE TO EAT AND DRINK
Although there is a cluster of signposted eateries near the Aanjar ruins, the establishment below is definitely the pick of the bunch and a favourite of locals and visitors alike.

✕ **Shams Restaurant** Near the main entrance to Aanjar; ☎ 08 620 567, 08 620 775; m 03 640 947, 03 699 010; e info@shamsrestaurant.com; www.shamsrestaurant.com; ⊕ year-round 11.00–midnight daily. This large, sprawling restaurant can accommodate up to 2,000 diners & is a favourite with locals, serving superb mezze & fresh, locally farmed trout. It gets very busy in the summer months & there is a pleasant children's play area. $$$$

OTHER PRACTICALITIES Being a small rural town, Aanjar is not the best place for exchanging currency, making cash withdrawals or using the post office and you would be best advised to seek out the plentiful supply of banks and the post office in either Chtaura, or better still Zahlé.

WHAT TO SEE
Aanjar Umayyad Archaeological Site (⊕ *winter 08.00 until 30min before sunset daily, summer 08.00–19.00 daily; admission: adults & children over 10 years LBP6,000, children under 10 years free. The ticket office usually has free Ministry of Tourism brochures available on the Aanjar site in Arabic, English, French, Italian, Portuguese & Spanish*) Unlike at Lebanon's other archaeological sites there are no onion layers to peel away in order to reveal the seams of existence of successive civilisations. Aanjar is, uniquely, the product of only one historical period; the 8th-century Umayyad caliphate, the first and most short-lived of the Arab dynasties, which founded an Islamic empire extending from the Indus Valley to southern Spain. Strategically located at the intersection of important trade routes linking Damascus and Homs in Syria, and Baalbek and Sidon in the south, Aanjar is also Lebanon's sole example of an inland trading centre. It is believed that the city was built by Caliph Walid I somewhere between AD705 and AD715 and prospered for around half a century until the Umayyads were overthrown by the Abbasids.

Incorporated into UNESCO's list of World Heritage Sites in 1984, the site was only discovered by chance in 1949, when archaeologists from the General Directorate of Antiquities were searching for the old city of Chalcis but unearthed Aanjar instead. Today this historic city has been comprehensively excavated to reveal an important and hitherto missing part of the Lebanese architectural jigsaw puzzle making this a must-see, but often overlooked, site on any visit to the Bekaa Valley. Being compact and well organised, Aanjar makes for a pleasant couple of hours perambulating its delicate structures.

Comprising an area of some 114,000m², the site is rectangular in form with a length of 385m and a width of 310m, enclosed by walls which are 2m thick on all sides to help secure the town against the threat of invaders. Possessing a wonderful

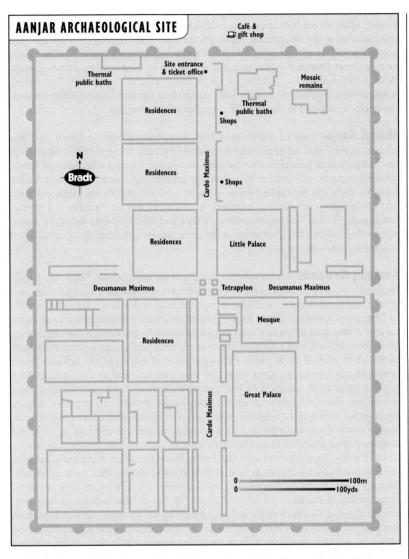

AANJAR ARCHAEOLOGICAL SITE

Café & gift shop

Thermal public baths

Site entrance & ticket office

Mosaic remains

Residences

Thermal public baths

Shops

N

Bradt

Cardo Maximus

Residences

Shops

Residences

Little Palace

Decumanus Maximus

Tetrapylon

Decumanus Maximus

Residences

Mosque

Cardo Maximus

Great Palace

0 ———————— 100m
0 ———————— 100yds

symmetry of design, two main north–south (Cardo Maximus) and east–west (Decumanus Maximus) 20m-wide streets divide the town into more or less four equal quarters, a design feature indicating the influence of Roman town planning. To your left as you enter from the main northern entrance are some very eroded but still discernible **mosaics** next to the **public baths**, and in front of these lies the **Little Palace** adorned with some nice little carvings of acanthus leaves, eagles and birds. But the main highlight is to walk from the main entrance up the principal north–south street, lined with shops and residential houses on either side to get an insight into the former life of the town. Some 600 shops have been uncovered, testifying to the importance of Aanjar's role as a hub of trade and retail activity. At the midway point is the restored **Tetrapylon**, a structure consisting of four columns which stands at the crossroads of the two main streets. With its alternating stonework, it once again shows how the Umayyads drew upon earlier architectural styles, in this case that of the Byzantines. Although there are scant remains of a mosque just across the east–west road from the Little Palace, Aanjar's undoubted highlight is the nearby **Great Palace**, the first part of the town to be excavated by archaeologists. With one of its walls and two tiers of fragile and slender arches beautifully restored, it doesn't take much imagination when standing in the 40m^2 courtyard to envisage the palace enveloped by the lithe-like structures in its heyday.

Majdal Aanjar Located a little over 1km south from the main Aanjar site, this seldom-visited small 1st-century Roman temple with a scattering of fallen entablature and subterranean passages, later fortified during the 7th and 8th centuries by the Abbasid dynasty, sits atop a hill affording superb views over the Bekaa Valley. Unfortunately, the area suffers from sporadic conflict between the Lebanese army and groups and individuals sympathetic to al-Qaeda, and on the author's last visit, two members of the Lebanese army were shot and killed. To find out if the area is safe to visit, ask at the ticket office at the main Aanjar site or at the small café just outside its main entrance.

Aammiq Wetlands An ecotourist's delight, these marshes are Lebanon's largest freshwater reserve and one of the few remaining in the Middle East. This elongated area of land consisting of over 250ha of marshes, lakes and swamps lies at the foothills of Jebel Barouk and the Litani River. This entire area is a delicate ecosystem and is on one of the most important migratory bird routes in the eastern Mediterranean. Over 250 species of bird have been identified here including endangered types such as the great spotted eagle (*Aquila clanga*), imperial eagle (*Aquila heliaca*), lesser kestrel (*Falco naumanni*), great snipe (*Gallinago media*), and the ferruginous duck (*Aythya nyroca*). In addition to our feathered friends, Aammiq is an important habitat for over 20 species of animal such as the swamp cat, otter, hedgehogs, foxes and a variety of lizards and snakes. In recognition of the area's importance, Aammiq was made an Important Bird Area by Birdlife International in 1994, and was designated a UNESCO Biosphere Reserve in 2005.

Until a few years ago, the area was under threat from the impact of a range of man's activities such as hunting, the dumping of waste and less than environmentally friendly agricultural practices. In 1996, however, a Christian environmental organisation, **A Rocha** (✆ *08 566 578;* m *03 139 614;* e *lebanon@arocha.org; www. arocha.org*) was founded, dedicated to conserving the marshes' flora and fauna. A Rocha have taken great strides in curtailing the threats to the marsh through a variety of practical measures such as restricting hunting, reducing vehicular access to the area and working with local farmers to protect the most vulnerable parts of the marsh by reducing the number of goats and putting in place a more environmentally friendly grazing management scheme. A Rocha's ongoing tasks include research, conservation and working with the local population. An important part of their remit is collaborating with schools and universities and organising group visits to the area to give schoolchildren and students hands-on experience of the importance of the wetland environment.

Getting there Aammiq is situated around 7km south of the town of Qab Elias between Zahlé and Lake Qaraoun. The area is not on a service taxi or main bus route and so unless you have your own car you will need to negotiate the fare with a taxi driver. If you are on a self-drive visit from Chtaura or Zahlé, take the road south which goes through the town of Qab Elias and Aammiq Wetlands is around

1km before the main village of Aammiq. It may be best to combine a visit to the marshes with a trip further south along this road to Lake Qaraoun and the Litani Dam.

Lake Qaraoun and the Litani River Dam Project
What its neighbours lack – water – Lebanon has been able to successfully capitalise on to great economic and social benefit. Located about 10km south of Aammiq, the 11km² Lake Qaraoun was created by the Litani River Dam Project in 1959. This is Lebanon's most ambitious hydro-electricity project to date, providing electricity and irrigation throughout the Bekaa Valley and the south of the country. The harnessing of the waters of the Litani – the country's largest river, flowing south some 160km from its source near Baalbek before emptying into the Mediterranean Sea north of Tyre – has also created an extremely scenic area to visit. Although the 6km-long lake is not suitable for swimming due to the water's bacterial contamination, in spring, when the water level reaches its zenith, boats are available to take visitors around the lake. There are also a few fish restaurants nearby serving locally farmed trout.

Where to stay and eat
Blue Lake Restaurant Saghbine, approx 500m from Macharef Saghbine Hotel; ☎ 08 670 146, 08 670 254; e bluelakerestaurant@hotmail. com; ⏰ summer 10.00–midnight daily, winter 10.00–20.00 daily. Serves a variety of Lebanese food, grills & arak with a nice terrace overlooking the Litani Dam & mountains. A new hotel was under construction above the restaurant at the time of research, due to open sometime in 2012. $$$$

Macharef Saghbine Hotel (40 rooms & suites) Saghbine, overlooking Lake Qaraoun; ☎ 08 671 200; m 03 423 307; e macharef@ destination.com.lb. An average hotel with quite ordinary, but clean & spacious rooms, with superb views over Lake Qaraoun. Dining in the 1st-floor restaurant is also a good opportunity for absorbing the picturesque vistas. The hotel also has a swimming pool which is open from Jun to Oct. B/fast US$7 extra. $$

BAALBEK

Located around 35km northeast of Zahlé and 85km northeast of Beirut, the modern town of Baalbek has little to interest visitors. Despite some recent regeneration, the area has a raw and rugged feel and retains its long-standing poor and traditional appearance. It does boast a mildly engaging souk, selling mainly standard tourist fare, but it is nowhere near as atmospheric as those in Sidon and Tripoli. A predominantly Shi'ite town, Baalbek has become all too familiar to Westerners in recent times in its capacity as a base for Palestinian and Syrian forces during the civil war. More recently it has been known for its association as the 'home' of many high-profile Western hostages and for being synonymous with Hezbollah; the latter's presence today remains in the form of placards adorned with images of the Party of God's Secretary General Hassan Nasrallah and martyrs killed fighting Israel. Whilst these associations endure, the town today is a friendly and perfectly safe place to visit with its main attraction on the outskirts of the town: a world-class archaeological and historical site, Heliopolis or 'Sun City', a short walk from the centre.

There are also innumerable local tour operators (see page 100) offering day trips to Baalbek, and if you are planning on seeing only this main site or perhaps combining it with Aanjar or the wineries, then an organised tour, which often includes lunch and a guide, could be worthwhile if time is short or you would prefer not to organise a schedule yourself.

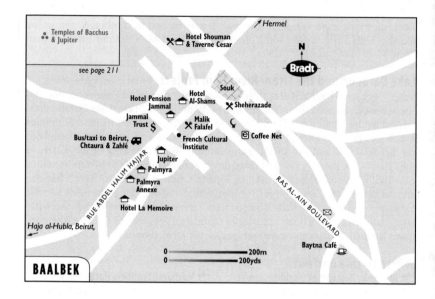

BAALBEK

GETTING THERE Baalbek is quite well served by both taxis and minivans from the southwest area of Beirut's Cola station. A bus or van will cost somewhere between LBP4,000 and LBP6,000 for the journey of just over an hour, depending on traffic, whilst a service taxi will set you back around LBP7,000, terminating almost opposite the Palmyra Hotel. If you are coming from Zahlé, a minivan will cost around LBP4,000–5,000 for the 45-minute journey.

If you have a rental car, Baalbek is around a two-hour drive from Beirut travelling east along the Damascus Road towards the Bekaa. When you reach Chtaura, take the road in the direction of Zahlé and continue north, following signs in the direction of Baalbek.

GETTING AROUND As a compact town, Baalbek is easily explored on foot. Its two main intersecting roads – Rue Abdel Halim Hajjar and Ras al-ain Boulevard – are home to most of its banks, eateries, hotels and post office, along with most other amenities useful to tourists and visitors.

TOURIST INFORMATION

🛈 **Ministry of Tourism** Baalbek archaeological site; ☎ 08 370 645; ⏰ 08.00–14.00 Mon–Fri, 08.00–13.00 Sat. The office should have free pamphlets available on the Baalbek site.

 WHERE TO STAY

🏠 **Hotel La Memoire** (10 rooms) approx 400m behind Jupiter & Palmyra hotels, next to Mar Jeorgous Church; ☎ 08 373 730/1; m 03 556 944; e info@hotel-lamemoire.com; www.hotel-lamemoire.com. The modern façade & facilities are well complemented by some nice dark wood furniture, stone walls, chandeliers & decorative doors, making this hotel a characterful, though not particularly cheap, boutique-style option. There is free Wi-Fi & a nice terrace area for summer dining. B/fast inc. **$$$**
🏠 **Hotel Pension Jammal** (30 rooms) Rue Abdel Halim Hajjar; ☎ 08 370 649; m 03 716 072. Housed within a 100-year-old building – with a selection of rooms also available across the street – this is a decent, clean hotel with

all rooms en suite. Rooms are charged per person & there are discounts of 50% for children under 10 years. According to their promotional literature, this hotel is 'favoured by the German archaeologists working at the archaeological site'. **$$**

🏠 **Jupiter Hotel** (20 rooms) Rue Abdel Halim Hajjar; ☎ 08 376 715, 08 370 151; **m** 70 269 079. As the name suggests, this hotel has terrific views of the ruins opposite (rooms 13, 14, 15, 16 & 17) & is clean & friendly, with all rooms *en suite* with TV. Only 2 rooms have AC but all are equipped with fan & oil heated in winter. The hotel also has free Wi-Fi & the courtyard below the rooms is a pleasant area for relaxing & refreshments. At the time of research the owner was in the process of adding a further 5 rooms. A good & popular choice. **$$**

🏠 **Palmyra Hotel** (32 rooms) Rue Abdel Halim Hajjar; ☎ 08 370 011, 08 370 230. Directly opposite the Baalbek ruins, this hotel is a tourist attraction in its own right & worth a look in even if you are not staying here. Those who have stayed here include General de Gaulle (room 30), Kaiser Wilhelm II, French Surrealist painter Jean Cocteau, whose works & a handwritten letter still adorn the walls near the hotel's restaurant, Brigitte Bardot, Rudolf Nureyev & the King of Belgium amongst many others. One of Lebanon's oldest hotels dating back to 1874, it has a slightly melancholic look & feel nowadays but still

manages to evoke its old-world charm; creaky floors, a warren of long, narrow corridors with a ghostly feel, dark wood furniture & chandeliers. The rooms, all with bathroom, have changed little over time & have a wonderful faded grandeur but are clean & cosy. The small, intimate bar on the ground floor is open from 18.00 to 23.00 & serves a range of spirits & beers. The Palmyra also has an annexe a few doors along from the main hotel whose 5 rooms all have character but with the addition of more modern bathroom facilities & AC. There is also a pleasant outdoor garden area for the summer months. B/fast US$7 extra. Annexe flat-rate US$100/room. **$$**

🏠 **Hotel Al-Shams** (5 rooms) Rue Abdel Halim Hajjar; ☎ 08 373 284; **m** 70 069 757, 03 770 990. Extremely basic & run down with shared bathrooms this place is best seen as a last resort. Avoid the hotel's only single room like the plague – unless you want to catch it! A dorm room is US$10/pp. **$**

🏠 **Hotel Shouman** (7 rooms) Ras al-Ain Bd; ☎ 08 372 685; **m** 03 796 077; **e** shouman-hotel@hotmail.com. Although this is a typical budget hotel with clean rooms which are stove-heated in winter & fan-cooled in summer, its main advantage is its great location opposite the Baalbek site. Not all rooms have bathrooms. A decent b/fast US$5 extra. Dorm room US$10pp. **$**

✕ **WHERE TO EAT AND DRINK** In comparison with Zahlé, Baalbek's eating and drinking options are nowhere near as varied or formal and veer more towards the informal and snacking variety, but the places reviewed below are excellent and representative of the town's eateries and watering holes.

✕ **Sheherazade Restaurant** 6th Fl, Yaghi & Sunbola Shopping Centre; ☎ 08 371 851; **m** 70 642 797; ⏱ 09.00–22.00 daily. A window onto the ruins, literally, this place is reached by lift (when working) or by stairs in a rather bizarre-looking shopping centre adjacent to the souk. It serves filling though unremarkable fish & meat dishes & desserts at very reasonable prices. **$$$**

✕ **Baytna Café** Ras al-Ain Bd, opposite Riviera Restaurant; ⏱ 08.00–00.00 daily. Nice little café serving tasty local & home-cooked food & a good Lebanese b/fast. Doesn't serve alcohol. **$$**

✕ **Taverne Cesar** Ras al-Ain Bd; ☎ 08 372 685; **m** 03 796 077, 70 854 352; ⏱ 08.00–01.00 daily. Located directly beneath Hotel Shouman & run by the hotel's friendly owner, Muhammad Shouman, this is an excellent choice for tasty & filling Lebanese snacks & fresh fruit juice. **$$**

✕ **Malik Falefel** Rue Abdel Halim Hajjar; **m** 70 735 526; ⏱ 08.00–22.00 Mon–Thu, 08.00–22.00 Sat/Sun. Malik means 'King' in Arabic & this small eatery certainly lives up to its name, with probably the best falafel in town at great prices. **$**

OTHER PRACTICALITIES

Centre Culturel Français Pl de L'Evêche, just off Rue Abdel Halim Hajjar near the Jupiter Hotel; ☎ 08 377 436; www.ccf-liban.org; ⏰ 10.00–13.00 & 15.00–18.00 Mon–Fri, 13.00–18.00 Sat. Has a well-stocked library & organises exhibitions & concerts.

🖥 **Coffee Net** Ras al-Ain Bd; ☎ 08 371 547; ⏰ 10.00–02.00 daily. Cosy little internet café with a small bar area selling a range of light refreshments. Internet access is charged at LBP1,500/hr.

$ **Jammal Trust Bank** Rue Abdel Halim Hajjar, opposite the taxi stand; ☎ 08 371 277, 08 371 198; ⏰ 08.00–14.00 Mon–Thu, 08.00–13.00 Fri/Sat. Has a 24/7 ATM.

✉ **Post office** Ras al-Ain Bd; ☎ 08 371 169; ⏰ 08.00–17.00 Mon–Fri, 08.00–13.30 Sat

WHAT TO SEE AND DO

Baalbek Roman archaeological site (☎ *08 370 520;* ⏰ *winter 08.30–16.00 daily, summer 08.30–19.00 daily; admission: adults LBP12,000, students LBP7,000, children under 10 years free. Available free of charge at the site entrance is a useful map from the German Archaeological Institute called* Heliopolis Baalbek 1898–1998: Rediscovering the Ruins, *& is highly recommended to accompany you on a tour of the site. Knowledgeable tour guides are also available at the entrance & you can expect to pay around US$20 for an approximately 1hr guided tour)* The Baalbek complex, a homage to the gods of the Heliopolitan Triad: Jupiter, Venus and Mercury, contains some of the largest and most impressive Roman remains in the world. Lebanon's most feted archaeological attraction, Baalbek was made a UNESCO World Heritage Site in 1984 with the comment that 'Baalbek, with its colossal structures, is one of the finest examples of imperial Roman architecture at its apogee'. On his journey through Asia in the 1930s, Robert Byron, in his acclaimed *The Road to Oxiana*, referred to Baalbek as a 'triumph of stone; of lapidary magnificence on a scale whose language, being still the language of the eye, dwarfs New York into a home of ants'. Despite a series of devastating earthquakes and a succession of conquering civilisations over the millennia, the Baalbek site is one of the most remarkably preserved complexes in the Middle East and a visit should be on every traveller's itinerary to Lebanon. Visiting the site early on in the day will ensure there are fewer crowds and coach parties and yield better, warmer photographs of the ruins. At present the main entrance was at the southeast corner of the site but a second, additional entrance, was planned to open sometime during 2011 by the parking area.

The history of settlement at Baalbek can be traced back to the ancient Phoenicians, when it was an important waypoint on their trade route from Tyre to Damascus, and they worshipped their god Baal, the sun god, here. By 333BC the Greeks, under Ptolemy who had been given Syria by Alexander the Great before he died, renamed the city Heliopolis or City of the Sun. This name was retained following the onset of Roman rule in 64BC but under Julius Caesar in 47BC, the city was incorporated into the Roman Empire as a colony and renamed after his daughter, Julia, as Julia Augusta Felix Heliopolis. Roman rule ushered in a period of remarkable prominence for Baalbek. It was most likely chosen as the location for construction of ancient Rome's largest-ever temples owing to the town's important location at the junction of important trade routes together with its sound agricultural base. The temples and structures which we see today, however, were constructed piecemeal over a period of some two centuries which gives new meaning to the expression that Rome wasn't built in a day. It is only relatively recently, however, following a series of devastating earthquakes, conquests, thefts and destruction over the years that we can finally experience the splendour of Rome's architectural wonders.

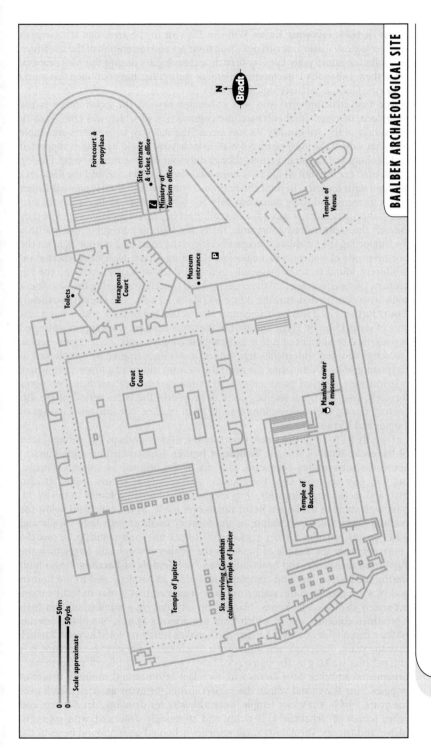

BAALBEK ARCHAEOLOGICAL SITE

N

Bradt

Forecourt & propylaea

Site entrance
& ticket office

Ministry of
Tourism office

Temple of Venus

Toilets

Hexagonal Court

Museum entrance

P

Great Court

Mamluk tower & museum

Temple of Jupiter

Six surviving Corinthian columns of Temple of Jupiter

Temple of Bacchus

50m
50yds

Scale approximate

0
0

It was in 1898, following Kaiser Wilhelm II's visit to the area, that the German Archaeological Mission carried out the first survey and restoration of the site which was followed some years later by French archaeologists during the Mandate era. Since then, Lebanon's Directorate General of Antiquities has continued this work, as has the German Archaeological Institute.

The first structure that you will encounter beyond the ticket office is the **propylaea**, or ceremonial entrance, the construction of which was completed in the middle of the 3rd century. As you ascend the stairway, large towers are visible on either side of the great portico which in its heyday would have been supported by 12 columns of Egyptian granite, though only four of these remain today. During the Roman era the roof would have been made from cedarwood and the floor area adorned with mosaics. Beyond the *propylaea* you pass into the **Hexagonal Court** which formerly had three doors but only one now survives. Built during the first half of the 3rd century, it was a place for pilgrims to prepare themselves before they entered the more sacred courtyard. Thirty 8m-high granite-columned porticos for supporting the entablature originally ringed the court and to your right on the northern side of the court is a bas-relief depicting Jupiter wearing a wheat-sheaf headdress, found in a nearby spring on the outskirts of Baalbek. Around the 5th century, Christians converted the courtyard to a church, and during the Islamic era walls were constructed, turning it into a Q'ala or fortress. The **Great (Sacrificial) Court** further along was built sometime during the 2nd century, and covers a vast area of some 134m by 112m. This part of the site was where worshippers witnessed the sacrifice of animals and it is extremely decorative, with a variety of *exedrae* (recesses) adorned with niches and statues. It was once fronted by 84 columns of Egyptian granite. Dominating the central area is the altar and a tower from where pilgrims were afforded panoramic views of the spectacle of sacrifice. Two pools formerly used for ritual washing were destroyed in the latter period of the 4th century during the construction of a Christian basilica, but intricate carvings of Cupids and Medusas remain.

Directly in front of the Great Court looms what is perhaps the defining icon of the entire Baalbek site: the **Temple of Jupiter**. Constructed on a podium 7m above the surrounding courtyard, only six of the original 54 columns remain, but they give no doubt as to the grandeur and artistry of ancient Rome. At 22m high and measuring 2.2m wide, they are the tallest Roman columns in the world, built with some of the largest hewn stones ever made. In the courtyard below the podium some fallen entablature in the form of cornices with lions' heads and water spouts provides further evidence of Rome's fine craftsmanship. Across the courtyard from the Temple of Jupiter is the smaller (though still larger than the Parthenon in Athens) and beautifully preserved **Temple of Bacchus**. It was built during the 2nd century and completed in AD150, and is dedicated to the Roman god of wine, though some authorities have suggested that it may in fact be more accurately dedicated to Venus. Flanked on all sides by a number of 19m-high Corinthian columns, one of which leans precariously against one of the exterior walls, a casualty of one of the many earthquakes which rumbled around Baalbek over the years, the temple was built over a much earlier Phoenician structure. It is entered after walking up the stairway's 33 steps where a magnificent and extremely ornamental entrance door awaits with its fallen keystone and stunning friezes of poppies, vine leaves and wheat; the subject matter for many an artist's work over the years. Inside, the inner temple, once a theatre for drinking, drug-taking and other scenes of debauchery, is richly and stunningly decorated with columns, niches and friezes. The nearby small museum is housed underground beneath the

STONE ME!

About 1km from the main Baalbek site, in a quarry which once supplied the stones for construction of the Baalbek complex on Sheikh Abdullah Hill, lies the biggest cut stone in the world. It is known as the Hajar al-Hubla or 'Stone of the Pregnant Woman', so called because according to local legend, any woman who touches it will experience an increase in fertility. This huge monolithic limestone block weighs more than 1,000 tonnes and measures some 21.5m x 4.8m x 4.2m, and would have required over 40,000 labourers to move it. Originally destined as the base rock for the Temple of Jupiter, it is an enigma why the stone was never used and it has remained *in situ* for over 2,000 years. If it wasn't for the efforts of 52-year-old local resident Abdul Nabi al-Afi, the stone would probably have disappeared into oblivion or, more accurately, under a pile of rubbish. In the early 1990s, Mr al-Afi, dismayed at the amount of household waste and other garbage that was filling the quarry, decided to undertake a one-man mission, to preserve the site for posterity. Since that time, he has managed to tidy up and prettify the quarry, construct a short footpath down to the structure, and open a small gift shop selling books and other memorabilia in order to support his charitable endeavours. Although the stone won't win any awards for its aesthetic qualities, it is free to visit and there is a certain caché for visitors in having someone take your picture whilst standing on top of the stone next to the Lebanese national flag.

Mamluk tower, and within its dark confines it houses some quite engaging Roman artefacts of sarcophagi from the 2nd and 3rd centuries, an eagle symbolising life and the basalt door of a tomb. The **main Baalbek museum**, however, is located in tunnels beneath the Temple of Jupiter. This elongated underground museum first opened in 1998 to commemorate the 100th anniversary of the visit to Baalbek of German emperor Wilhelm II, and is worth a look in to appreciate the history of the complex from the Bronze, Hellenistic and Roman eras, as well as learn details of the techniques used in construction of the temples. There is also a range of statues and other artefacts related to the site on display. A pictorial representation of life in Baalbek is provided in the form of excellent images in a permanent exhibition by the renowned German photographer Herman Burckhardt.

Although currently closed because of ongoing restoration works, the **Temple of Venus**, a few hundred metres southeast of the main ticket office, is definitely work a look from the roadside. Despite being dwarfed in size by Baalbek's other temples, its cupola roof with a series of columns and niches depicting doves and seashells make it a charming little feature. In the Byzantine era, the temple was turned into a church and dedicated to the Christian martyr Saint Barbara. Folklore has it that Barbara's father, angered at her Christian beliefs, murdered her but was struck by lightning, as if by divine intervention, and engulfed in flames for his treacherous act. In the English village of Stourhead in Wiltshire, a replica of the temple stands in the grounds of a country manor, built by its 19th-century owner.

Baalbeck International Festival (*Doursoumian Bldg, Osman Ben Affan St, Beirut;* 01 373 150/1/2; m 03 041 006/7; e *baalbeck@baalbeck.org.lb; www.baalbeck.org.lb; see the festival website for details of the current annual programme of events, transportation to & from the festival together with details of how to book*

The Bekaa Valley BAALBEK

6

tickets to the performances) Founded in 1955 and held annually during the months of July and August, the Baalbeck International Festival is the oldest and most prestigious festival in the entire Middle East. Held within the historic courtyards of Baalbek's Roman temples amidst atmospheric and dramatic lighting displays, the festival serves up a full gamut of performing arts – ballet, classical music, jazz, opera, pop and rock music together with a variety of theatrical productions. Since its inaugural season in 1956, the festival has played host to an eclectic range of national and international artists, including Lebanese icon Fairuz, Duke Ellington, Ella Fitzgerald, Joan Baez, Rudolf Nureyev and the Bolshoi Ballet, the Royal Ballet and Dame Margot Fonteyn, and the Berlin Philharmonic Orchestra, to name but a few. In 2010, pop sensation Mika performed at the festival.

HERMEL

At around 140km from Beirut and 50km north from Baalbek, the Shi'ite town of Hermel is the Bekaa Valley's most far-flung rural outpost, sitting at some 700m above sea level and only a few kilometres from the Syrian border. For the area's inhabitants, agriculture is the mainstay of the local economy, with the region having remained insulated from the conflicts and modernisation programmes which have engulfed many areas of the country. It therefore retains a rugged and wild appearance evinced in the landscape as well as in the traditional ways of life of its rural population, and remains perhaps Lebanon's poorest region in almost all of the indices used to measure development. This, coupled with its relative geographical isolation and lack of a well-developed transport infrastructure, means that the area is one of the least-visited places in the country.

Although not on the mainstream tourist trail, Hermel is still well worth a visit for a number of interesting monuments, including perhaps Lebanon's most puzzling, the Hermel Pyramid, whose origin remains the subject of scholarly debate to this day. Meandering past Hermel is the north-flowing Orontes River (Nahr al-Assi), making this area the country's premier location for water-based activities such as canoeing and kayaking. If you are intending to engage in any of these or the range of other outdoor adventure activities which are popular in the area, Hermel is a great place to stay for a night or two to sample an alternative slice of Lebanese life in authentic and traditional surroundings which are far removed from the urbane existence of the capital. Otherwise, Hermel makes for an interesting trip extension if visiting the archaeological sites at Aanjar and Baalbek. Combining a visit to this area with one of the activity- and ecotourism-based organisations listed below can also enhance the experience.

GETTING THERE The sights and activities below are somewhat remote from the main town of Baalbek, being in the far north of the region, but if you have your own vehicle they make an excellent addition to an extended tour of the Bekaa Valley region. If driving from Baalbek, take the main road north towards Hermel and when you reach Ras Baalbek, turn left and the Hermel Pyramid is around 10km further on. If you don't have your own car, minivans ply the route north for around LBP5,000–6,000, but expect to pay around US$50 for a return trip by taxi from Baalbek to Hermel, which takes around 1½–2 hours.

WHERE TO STAY The accommodation options below all offer a completely different lodging and travel experience from anywhere else in the country in an area well off the beaten tourist track. This area is remote and wild, inhabited by

Bedouin mountain dwellers and grazing sheep and goats, giving an insightful look at an alternative, relatively raw Lebanon, far removed from the ongoing urban development and sprawl of the city. These places can also organise a range of outdoor pursuits in the local and surrounding areas. In all cases it is best to phone ahead to book your accommodation in advance.

🏠 **Al Jord Eco-lodge** Hermel area; m 03 458 702; e aljord@aljord.org, info@aljord.org; www. aljord.org. Located about 27km from the town of Hermel & run by an NGO to promote ecotourism in the more remote & less-visited regions of the Bekaa, accommodation here is in simple, yet comfy cotton or goat-hair tents & stonewall bungalows with a capacity to sleep up to 100 people. All meals are made using local produce & are prepared by local people. Activities such as hiking, trekking, cycling, kite flying, rafting & donkey rides are also on offer here. **$**

🏠 **Al Kwakh Eco-lodge** Hermel; m 03 454 996, 03 529 419, 71 608 987; www. kwakhecolodge.org. Al Kwakh – which means 'huts' in English – is an eco-initiative by a collective of local women. Accommodation comprises 3 old traditional houses with mud chimneys & ceilings made out of juniper wood & the Bedouin-style bedding is made by the

women themselves out of goat hair. The lodge has a capacity for 20–30 people & all meals are prepared by the women's co-operative. A variety of local outdoor pursuits are also arranged such as hiking, rafting, rock climbing & even herb picking with the local women themselves. Hiking trips with a guide cost around US$7. **$**

🏠 **Lazzab Club & Lodge** Hermel; m 03 797 569, 71 146 915; e info@lazzab.net; www. lazzab.net. This eco-lodge is situated 20km from Hermel with mud-hut accommodation equipped with toilets & hot water. Meals are provided using ingredients from the local area. If you have your own tent camping is charged at US$5 for a pitch per night. Lazzab also arranges 1–3-day hiking trips in & around Hermel with knowledgeable guides. If you do not have your own transport, Lazzab also run a club bus which, for US$5, will collect you from Hermel Town & bring you back again after your stay. **$**

OTHER PRACTICALITIES

$ BLC Bank Shahine Centre, facing Seray Bldg, Main Rd; 📞 08 201 771; ⏰ 08.30–13.30 Mon–Fri, 08.30–12.00 Sat. Has a 24/7 ATM.

✚ **Hermel Governmental Hospital** Main Rd; 📞 08 225 312

$ Lebanese Canadian Bank Main Rd; tel/f 08

200 600; ⏰ 08.30–13.00 Mon–Fri, 08.30–12.00 Sat. Has a 24/7 ATM.

✉ **Post Office** Main Rd, c200m from BLC Bank; 📞 08 200 403; ⏰ 08.00–17.00 Mon–Fri, 08.00–13.00 Sat

✚ **Red Cross** 📞 140, 08 200 023, 08 200 098

WHAT TO SEE AND DO

Hermel Pyramid This isolated, but by no means forlorn-looking structure, also known as 'God's Pyramid' remains something of a mystery, though many legends and stories abound about just why it is here. The most likely explanation, given its similarity to tombs discovered in Palmyra in Syria, is that it is the tomb of a Syrian prince dating from the 1st or 2nd century BC. This 27m-high column has a black marble base with two distinct, cube-shaped stone blocks, topped by a pyramid. It is decorated with a range of friezes which show hunting scenes of deer, a wounded boar and wolves attacking a bull. Some fervent restoration carried out by the Department of Antiquities is clearly visible on the sides of the monument. Visible for miles around, this ancient remnant is some 50km north of Baalbek and 6km south of the town of Hermel.

Deir Mar Maroun About 6km southwest of the Hermel Pyramid 200m above the source of the Orontes River, are a series of caves interlinked by stone stairways and dominated by the Monastery of Mar Maroun or 'Caves of the Monks'. It was

Lebanon's national drink, *arak*, evokes that Marmite moment – you'll either love it or hate it. This aniseed-flavoured tipple has relatives all over the Mediterranean and beyond, and is known as *ouzo* in Greece, *raki* in Turkey, *ojen* in Spain and *pastis* in France. It is most often drunk to accompany a *mezze* meal, because it refreshes the taste buds when drunk after each dish, leaving the palate refreshed for the next course. It is usually mixed with two-thirds water and then some ice is added. The addition of water causes the *arak* to cloud over resembling a milky-white colour, because the aniseed oil is soluble in alcohol but not in water, resulting in an emulsion. Loosely translated, *arak* means a rather unpalatable 'sweat' or 'perspiration' in Arabic, a term referring to the series of distillation processes of heating, cooling and perspiring into vats of a near-pure form of alcohol. The ageing process of the final concoction can take between 12 and 18 months for the best varieties.

founded by St Maroun, founder of the Maronite sect and used as a place of sanctuary for Maronites fleeing from Emperor Justinian's war on heresy in the 7th century.

Activities

Assi Club Hermel   Al Zwaytineh, Hermel; administrative office: 2nd Fl, Makari Bldg, Makdissi St, Hamra, Beirut; m 03 445 051, 03 163 014; e info@assirafting.com; www.assirafting.com. For the adventurous, this club runs rafting trips along a 7km stretch of the Assi (Orontes) River, Lebanon's premier rafting area. Canoeing & kayaking, together with activities such as basketball, fishing & volleyball, are also offered along with overnight stays in the club's 24 rooms.

Vamos Todos   m 03 561 174; e info@vamos-todos.com, mark.aoun@gmail.com; www.vamos-todos.com. This ecotourism club (*Vamos todos* is Spanish for 'Let's all go!') also organises rafting activities in the area as well as a range of other eco-friendly activities all around the country.

7

The Chouf Mountains

Telephone code 05

The Chouf Mountains, around 40km southeast of Beirut, lie within the southern Muhafazah or district of southern Mount Lebanon. Although only an hour away from the capital, this region maintains a distinct geographical, cultural and ethnic identity quite unlike any other in the country. Its lush green vegetation, undulating terrain and cultivated fields of apples, grapes and olives is dotted with over 20 picturesque towns and villages, making the Chouf one of the most scenic places in Lebanon. This is also the heartland of both the Maronite Christian and Druze communities; breakaway religious groups who have long made the area their home, fleeing persecution and sectarian rivalry. They have held steadfast to their traditions and it is here, especially in the towns of Baakline and Moukhtara, that you will see the eccentric moustaches, white skullcaps and baggy *sherwal* trousers worn by Druze men together with the white veil worn by women.

During the Ottoman era the Chouf was the seat of power, given quasi-autonomous status by the Porte, first to the Maan family and later the Shihab dynasty who administered the feudal kingdom from their capitals at Deir al-Qamar and Beiteddine respectively on behalf of Istanbul. Rule by the two leaders – Fakhreddine II and Emir Bachir II – brought a veneer of unification to the Christians and Druze orders, for a time at least, and they are today widely regarded as nationalist icons in Lebanese history. Nowadays, the nearby town of Moukhtara serves as the base for Druze power under the leadership of the charismatic Walid Jumblatt (see box, page 229). Despite its present-day tranquility, the Chouf has seen its fair share of conflict over the years, most notably the 1860 clashes between Christians and Druze and more recently during the so-called War of the Mountain during Lebanon's civil war. Today, however, visitors to the area will be most struck by the well-preserved Ottoman-era architecture, the beautiful Beiteddine Palace and, of course, the opportunity to see Lebanon's largest reserve of remaining cedar trees.

Despite a sign indicating otherwise in Deir al-Qamar, there was no tourist office in the Chouf at the time of writing, but useful and informative brochures and pamphlets on the sites and towns covered in this chapter can be obtained from the Ministry of Tourism's Hamra office in Beirut (see page 99).

DAMOUR

This coastal Christian town, the first settlement of interest *en route* to the Chouf, is about 20km south from Beirut just before where the highway turns east towards the village of Kfarhim and its small grotto, and the towns of Deir al-Qamar and Beiteddine. Once known for its silk factories, olive groves, orange trees and sandy

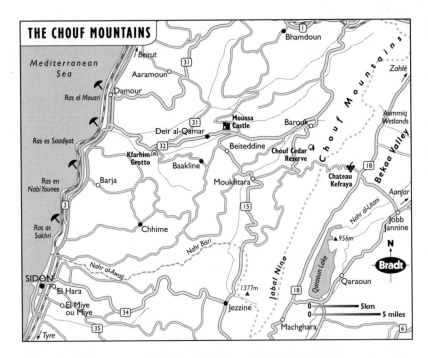

beach, Damour was the scene of fierce fighting in World War I during an Australian operation as part of its Syrian–Lebanese offensive in 1941. The town hit the headlines for even more notorious reasons in 1976, during the tit-for-tit killings between Christians and Muslims which ensued in the early stages of the civil war. Following a Christian Phalangist massacre of 1,500 Palestinians in the Beirut district of Karantina, Palestinians responded by executing 149 Christians in Damour, largely destroying the town itself and proceeding to install their own people, victims of another atrocity at the Tel al Za'atar refugee camp in Beirut, into the abandoned Christian homes. In 2009, the town was once again in the news for somewhat more palatable reasons for being selected as the site for the 'Cedar Island' project (*www.cedarsisland.com*), the biggest tree-shaped manmade island in the world. It is currently awaiting Lebanese government approval for work to commence on what is proposed to be a huge complex of a luxurious offshore hotel, leisure and residential development.

There are quite a few local tour operators who offer day trips to the area if you prefer a more organised visit (see page 100).

GETTING THERE Although the main areas of interest in the Chouf are clustered fairly close together, the absence of a plentiful supply of transport links between them, coupled with the fact that most buses and taxis become quite scarce from early evening, means that the most efficient way to travel to (and around) the region is by hiring a car, with or without a driver. The Chouf is quite well connected from Beirut and buses and vans travel quite frequently during the daytime, every 30–60 minutes, from the northern end of the capital's Cola station to the major towns in the area. At the time of writing buses from Cola to both Damour (c20–30 minutes) and Kfarhim (c45 minutes) cost LBP2,000, with many buses continuing their onward journey to Deir al-Qamar and Beiteddine. There is also a plentiful supply of both service taxis and taxis serving the Chouf from Cola. Expect to pay somewhere between LBP5,000 and LBP7,000 for the former, with the latter needing to be negotiated.

🏠 **WHERE TO STAY AND EAT** As principally a region for beach and watersport enthusiasts, Damour is best visited as a day trip for the beach and clubs such as the Oceana resort mentioned below. However, the town does have a handful of resort-type hotels and eateries offering standard fare, with food also available at the beach clubs which dot the area. But with Damour's proximity to Beirut and the main Chouf towns of Deir al-Qamar and Beiteddine your LBP would be better spent in those places which offer a much more authentic dining and sleeping experience compared to what is on offer in Damour.

OTHER PRACTICALITIES Damour is extremely limited as regards post offices, banks and other utilities and you would be advised to do your banking or send a postcard or letter from either Beirut or from one of the following Chouf towns prior to journeying here.

WHAT TO SEE AND DO Although Damour is an unremarkable town from a sightseeing perspective, this area is dotted with beach clubs and you will see their advertising hoardings as you travel south along the coast road towards the Chouf. One of the most popular of these for indulging in endless partying amid its setting amongst a banana orchard is the 25,000m² resort **Oceana** (m *03 998 080; www. oceana-resort.com; admission: adults LBP25,000 Mon–Fri, children 8–12 years LBP12,000 Mon–Fri, adults LBP30,000 Sat/Sun, children 8–12 years LBP15,000 Sat/ Sun, children under 7 years free daily*), which proclaims itself to be 'Lebanon's ultimate destination for beach lovers'. It can accommodate 2,500 sun worshippers, boasts five swimming pools, a number of fast-food outlets, coffee shops, walking trails and a children's nursery. For a comprehensive listing of other nearby and countrywide beach resorts, have a look at the website of LebBeach (*www.lebbeach.com*).

Kfarhim Grotto (*2km from Deir al-Qamar, Kfarhim Village;* ✆ *05 720 500;* m *03 388 048, 03 380 588;* e *info@kfarhimgrotto.com, kfarhimgrotto@hotmail.com; www. kfarhimgrotto.com;* ⊕ *winter 08.00–18.00 daily, summer 08.00–20.00 daily; admission: adults LBP10,000, children under 7 years LBP5,000*) At around 11km from Damour, this grotto was only discovered in 1974, and opened for the first time a year later. Small and intimate, the grotto doesn't have either the scale or jaw-dropping appeal of its far more impressive relative at Jeita, but Kfarhim's limestone stalactites and stalagmites are still worth a visit and are quite nicely lit in colourful hues, though the town itself possesses no other sites of note to detain the visitor. The grotto houses a souvenir shop upstairs selling a wide range of postcards, jewellery items, woodcarvings, glassware and other handicrafts. There is also a small café outside the grotto serving drinks and snacks together with another small shop selling ornamental souvenirs.

DEIR AL-QAMAR

This overwhelmingly Christian town of some 10,000 souls was where the ancient Phoenicians worshipped the moon, but it is Deir al-Qamar's more recent history which tells the story of modern Lebanon. With its red-roofed buildings, stone houses, cobbled walkways and serene atmosphere, the town became the capital of Mount Lebanon in 1590, following Fakhreddine II's decision to move it from Baakline owing to a chronic water shortage in his hometown. The well-watered

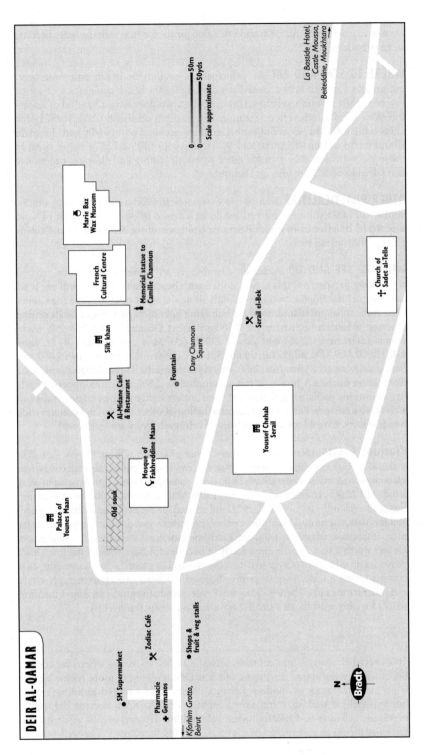

DEIR AL-QAMAR

SM Supermarket
Pharmacie Germanos
Zodiac Café
Shops & fruit & veg stalls

Kfarhim Grotto, Beirut

Palace of Younes Maan

Old souk

Mosque of Fakhreddine Maan

Al-Midane Café & Restaurant

Silk khan

French Cultural Centre

Marie Baz Wax Museum

Memorial statue to Camille Chamoun

Fountain
Dany Chamoun Square

Youssef Chehab Serail

Serail el-Bek

Church of Sadet al-Telle

La Bastide Hotel, Castle Moussa, Beiteddine, Moukhtara

0 — 50m
0 — 50yds
Scale approximate

N

Bradt

Deir al-Qamar, fed by innumerable springs, remained the capital until the 18th century, when the Shihab dynasty moved the capital to Beiteddine. Despite the decline in the town's political stature from the 19th century, Deir al-Qamar retains the rich legacy of its medieval architecture in one of the most charming and best-preserved areas in the whole country.

GETTING THERE Buses from the northern section of Beirut's Cola station cost around LBP2,500 and take about an hour. Service taxis and taxis also travel to Deir al-Qamar from Cola though they are not frequent or plentiful.

GETTING AROUND Deir al-Qamar is small, making the town easily (and best) explored on foot with all of its main sites and amenities such as cafés, restaurants and stores pretty much adjacent to each other.

WHERE TO STAY At the time of writing there was no hotel in the town of Deir al-Qamar itself, but the following accommodation option is only 1km on the outskirts of town on the road leading to Moussa Castle and Beiteddine.

La Bastide (15 rooms) Main Rd to Beiteddine; ☎ 05 505 320, 05 505 848; m 03 643 010; e bastideir@hotmail.com. In a good & picturesque location & with a very homely reception area. The rooms are all en suite, spacious & clean but feel a little sparse & don't quite match the character & cosy lobby area. B/fast inc. **$$**

WHERE TO EAT AND DRINK In addition to the eateries below there are a few shops selling take-away snacks, fruit and vegetables and such like, just across the road from the Zodiac Café.

Al-Midane Café & Restaurant Main Sq; ☎ 05 511 651; m 03 763 768; e rafatabet@ hotmail.com; ⏱ Jun–Sep 10.00–03.00 daily, Oct–May 10.00–midnight Tue–Sun. An excellent restaurant in a great setting overlooking the square, making for lovely Lebanese & European dining amidst the history & architecture of Deir al-Qamar. **$$$$**

Serail el-Bek Serail Bldg, Main Sq (opposite the Camille Chamoun memorial statue); ☎ 05 510 006; m 71 181 023; ⏱ Apr–Sep 10.00–22.00 Mon–Fri, 10.00–midnight Sat/Sun. A good-value eatery, specialising in tasty Lebanese *mezze*. **$$**

Zodiac Café Pl Nabeh al-Chalout; m 03 287 960; e zodiac_cafe@yahoo.com; ⏱ 07.00–02.00 daily. A small & pleasant café a short walk from the main square, this friendly little place serves a range of hot & cold drinks including beer, & snacks such as pizzas, pasta dishes, doughnuts & sandwiches; they also have nargileh. **$**

ENTERTAINMENT AND NIGHTLIFE Deir al-Qamar, like much of the Chouf, is not really a place for night owls with most of the town's few bars, cafés and restaurants all closing by midnight at the latest. The area really only springs into nocturnal *joie de vivre* during its annual summer festival (see pages 224–5).

SHOPPING The **SM Supermarket** (*entrance to Deir al-Qamar*; ☎ *05 505 166*; ⏱ *07.30–22.00 daily*) is a small store, selling a decent range of fruit and vegetables, cheese, and general household goods and toiletries.

OTHER PRACTICALITIES
$ Byblos Bank Main Rd, near Dany Chamoun Sq & the town's public school; ☎ 05 511 173/4; ⏱ 08.30–17.30 Mon–Fri, 08.30–13.00 Sat. Has a 24/7 ATM.

✚ **Pharmacie Germanos** Bd Camille
Chamoun, near the entrance to Deir al-Qamar;
☎ 05 505 196; ⏱ 08.00–21.00 Mon–Sat. Stocks
a good range of medicines & a small selection of cosmetics.

WHAT TO SEE AND DO The town is dominated by the large and central expanse of the **Dany Chamoun Square** (formerly known as the Midan), the namesake of which was born in the town and was the youngest son of former president Camille Chamoun. During the 16th century, the square played host to jousting and other equestrian events but today is an atmospheric and altogether more sedate meeting place. In the square's centre, the 19th-century fountain once provided weary travellers with an opportunity to satisfy their thirst. Just to the west of the fountain and square stands the **Mosque of Fakhreddine Maan** which dates from 1493, and was built over an earlier Mamluk-era structure. The slight displacement of its octagonal minaret is the result of a severe earthquake in 1630. On the western side of the mosque's exterior there are engravings of verses from the Koran and the date of construction. The interior of this still-working mosque has a high stone roof supported by a large pillar.

To the rear of the mosque the once-bustling souk formerly contained numerous shops and working artisans plying their trade, but is now home to only a handful of small stores. Behind the souk the **Palace of Younes Maan**, who was commander-in-chief of the army in Deir al-Qamar whilst his brother was exiled in Italy, was burnt to the ground by the Ottoman governor (*pasha*) Yusuf Sayfa, but later restored by Fakhreddine, and merits a look to see its fine and imposing façade. Opposite the fountain on the northern section of the square is the Silk Khan (Qaisariyah), constructed by Fakhreddine in 1595, and built in the traditional *khan* style with a central fountain, open-air courtyard and surrounding arches, formerly used by merchants to sell their wares. Today, part of the *khan* is home to an active **French Cultural Centre** (☎ 05 510 016; *www.ccf-liban.org*; ⏱ *08.30–13.00 & 15.00–18.00 Mon–Fri, 10.00–18.00 Sat*). Just behind the *khan* are the remains of a 16th-century synagogue testifying to Fakhreddine's cosmopolitan leadership.

The **Palace of Fakhreddine** lies just to the east of the Silk Khan. Constructed in 1620, once again in typical *khan* style, it is on the site of his former palace which in 1614 was burnt to the ground by the Ottoman *pasha* Yusuf Sayfa in an attempt to rein in Fakhreddine's authority and power. Vowing revenge on Yusuf upon hearing of its destruction whilst in self-imposed exile in Italy, Fakhreddine proceeded to dismantle the stones from Yusuf's own palace in Akkar, northeast of Tripoli, and used some 20,000 defeated soldiers to transport them to Deir al-Qamar to rebuild the palace which today is home to the **Marie Baz Wax Museum** (*Main Sq;* ☎ *05 512 777, 05 511 666;* 📱 *03 756 000;* ✉ *museemariebaz@gmail. com;* ⏱ *Mar–Oct 08.00–22.00 daily, Nov–Feb 09.00–17.00 daily; admission: adults LBP12,000, children under 11 years LBP8,000, children under 3 years free*). Spread over four rooms, this museum contains 93 waxwork figures giving a who's who of Lebanese history with most of the main players – both Lebanese and non-Lebanese – in the country's history lined up as if in readiness for a press photocall. From, appropriately, an elderly Fakhreddine Maan at the entrance, the collection ranges across religious, political and cultural figures such as singer Majida al Roumi, Egyptian presidents Mubarak and Sadat, Nabih Berri, Hezbollah Secretary General Sayed Hassan Nasrallah, former prime minister Rafiq Hariri and former president Camille Chamoun, looking like a rock star in his dark sunglasses. There is even a nonchalant-looking Lady Hester Stanhope gazing down in her medieval garb as if ruminating on her impending downfall. In the main square between the museum

The most prominent member of the Maan dynasty, a Druze family who first came to Lebanon in 1120 to assist in ousting the European Crusaders, the emir Fakhreddine II was born in Baakline and is regarded as Lebanon's first national hero for his direct challenge to Ottoman rule and for his unifying of the Christian and Druze faiths. Fakhreddine ascended to power in 1591 following the murder of his father during the formative years of Ottoman power in Lebanon, which was characterised by a considerable amount of autonomy granted to the often-competing fiefdoms by the Porte in Istanbul. Driven by the twin aims of avenging his father's death and achieving a free, independent Lebanon, relations between himself and Istanbul were initially cordial with the timely payment of taxes and deference to the Porte's authority. By 1607, however, Fakhreddine's progressive expansion of his domain had broadened to include Beirut, the Bekaa Valley, northern Mount Lebanon and the southern port city of Sidon. As an enlightened, visionary and unifying leader, Fakhreddine introduced silk production to the country and encouraged Christian migration to the Chouf from their Mount Lebanon heartlands to engage in its agricultural production. He built the Khan al-Franj or travellers' inn at Sidon to encourage foreign silk merchant traders and in 1608, entered into a series of alliances with the influential Medici family in Tuscany. Increasingly concerned at Fakhreddine's attempts to usurp their power, the Ottomans dispatched soldiers to hunt him down and ships to blockade ports to prevent his escape. The resourceful Fakhreddine proved as elusive as the Scarlet Pimpernel, and with a combination of incentives and cunning, managed to acquire French and Flemish vessels to embark on a two-month voyage from Sidon to Tuscany where he remained for the next five years. During his self-imposed exile in Italy, Fakhreddine observed the economic and cultural mores of post-Renaissance Florence, but upon his return to Lebanon in 1618, timed to coincide with Ottoman preoccupations with their Persian enemy, he found the country a very different animal from the one he had left. Divisions within the Druze community had come to the fore and the Ottomans had reclaimed former territory under his control. Fakhreddine's resolve strengthened and he built a formidable army which, in 1623, defeated the Turks at the Battle of Aanjar in the Bekaa Valley at which he captured the Governor of Damascus, Mustafa Pasha, whose release was only achieved after Fakhreddine had successfully negotiated the return of his former territories. With the Ottomans having finally defeated the Persians in 1629, the Ottomans focused their attention on ridding themselves of Fakhreddine's threat to their power. With internal schisms and rivalries rife, and his Druze followers refusing to bear arms against the massed Ottoman forces after a period of hiding, Fakhreddine was finally captured and taken to Istanbul in 1633 where he was executed, along with his three children, in 1635. Following his death, the Maan dynasty was led by his nephew and later by his grandson but, in the absence of a male heir, the family died out, to be succeeded by the Sunni Shihabs. The threat to Ottoman dominance was now over.

and the Silk Khan is a recently erected **statue** of former president Camille Chamoun (1900–87), who is probably best known for evoking the 1957 Eisenhower Doctrine in 1958, requesting US military assistance to quell a Muslim rebellion.

7

On the southern side of the main square is the site of the **Youssef Chehab Serail**, which dates from the 18th century, and in 1860 was the scene of a massacre, which cost the lives of 1,200 Christians in its courtyard. It now serves as the offices of the local municipality and from 08.00 to 14.00 Monday to Friday it can be visited to view its splendid rooms and courtyard and entered via its very decorative façade. Just behind and below the Serail and accessed by a flight of steps is the **Church of Sadet al-Telle,** which is built on the site of a much earlier Phoenician temple to Astarte. It is thought that the stone carving with a cross above an inverted crescent moon may explain why the town's name, Deir al-Qamar, may mean 'Monastery of the Moon'; and that this symbolises the transition from the cult of Astarte's paganism to that of Christianity.

Apart from those sites mentioned above the town is a pretty and charming place to go for a wander around the streets and alleyways to admire the traditional houses and architecture. There are also superb views over the town and surrounding mountains and valleys if you venture up the hillsides.

Moussa Castle (*Main Rd between Deir al-Qamar & Beiteddine;* ✆ *05 500 106;* m *03 273 750;* e *moussa@moussacastle.com; www.moussacastle.com;* ⊕ *May–Oct 08.00–20.00 daily, Nov–Apr 08.00–18.00 daily; admission: adults LBP10,000, children LBP5,000, children under 5 years free*) A pleasant and picturesque 2km walk or service taxi ride from Deir al-Qamar on the road east to Beiteddine, this is one of Lebanon's (and possibly the world's) most offbeat and odd attractions. Its history and existence tell the story, not of omnipotent foreign conquest and rule, but of one man's childhood dream and ambition which endured for some 60 years, and reads as a variation on the theme of all those children's fairytales from Cinderella to a Disney animation. The story goes, as every Lebanese knows, that Moussa Abdel Karim al-Maamari as a 14-year-old schoolboy had a dream that he would one day 'turn sand into gold' and live in a castle. His teacher at school, Anwar, caught him in class drawing his embryonic architect's plans for his future creation and proceeded to berate and beat him, telling him he would never live in a castle, whilst the rest of the class, including his first love, Saideh, mocked him. Undeterred by the humiliation, Moussa left school and set to work with his uncle on helping to restore the sea castle in Sidon which, he says, provided the 'yeast' from which his future edifice would rise. Further forays at Beirut's National Museum and the Beiteddine Museum followed. Eventually saving enough money to buy some land, work started on the present castle with the foundation stone laid by his supportive mother who had always told him that 'everyone holds billions in their brains'. Work was finally completed in 2005, with each brick in the wall, not just one of many as Pink Floyd would have us believe, telling its own story, having been cut and positioned by Moussa's own hands. Inside the castle a tableaux of plaster figures give snapshots of scenes from traditional Lebanese life such as silk making, grape picking, corn workers and sheep shearing. On the ground floor is a classroom scene depicting Moussa's teacher about to strike Moussa with a cane together with scenes of bread making, the Last Supper and *dabke* dancing.

Deir al-Qamar Festival (*Block B, Ivoire Centre, Moussa Nammour St, Horch Tabet;* m *70 225 007;* e *info@deqfestival.org; www.deirelqamarfestival.org*) This festival in the town is held annually between the months of July and August, and hosts a wide range of music, concerts, exhibitions and other cultural events and acts as a stage for promotion of the town itself and for emerging and young Lebanese artists and performers. The festival website has a comprehensive downloadable diary of events for each season, and tickets can be purchased from any Virgin Megastore or online from www.ticketingboxoffice.com.

BEITEDDINE

Located 5km from Deir al-Qamar on the opposite side of a deep gorge some 50km from Beirut, Beiteddine is best known as the home of one of Lebanon's must-see attractions, nestled 850m up on a hilltop with outstanding views of over the surrounding countryside, which blends Italian and Arabic architectural design and skills and testifying to the grandeur and power of an important legacy in the modern history of the country.

GETTING THERE Buses and vans from Cola station in Beirut travel to Beiteddine in around an hour and cost LBP2,500 with a journey time of just over an hour. The bus will drop you off at the roundabout on which stands a large Christian–Druze war memorial, and from there it is a five-minute service taxi (LBP2,000) ride to the entrance of Beiteddine Palace.

WHERE TO STAY
Mir Amin Palace Hotel (24 rooms & suites) On a hill overlooking Beiteddine Palace; ☎ 05 501 315; m 03 900 924/5; e miramin@ cyberia.net.lb; www.miraminpalace.com; closed annually for the winter season 25 Oct–1 Apr. Built by Emir Bachir II for his youngest son, Amin, this hotel is a smaller sibling of the palace itself with its rooms of some character every bit as luxurious & boasting all the 5-star facilities you would expect for the price. The terrace has outstanding views of the palace & surrounding countryside. **$$$$$**

WHERE TO EAT AND DRINK
Mir Amin Palace Hotel ☎ 05 501 315; m 03 900 924; ⏰ 12.00–23.00 daily. The hotel's 2 main restaurants, serving excellent Lebanese & Italian cuisine, are supplemented by lovely outdoor terrace & garden dining areas affording panoramas of the mountains & Beiteddine Palace below. **$$$$$**

ENTERTAINMENT AND NIGHTLIFE Beiteddine's principal offering is its world-class annual summer festival (see page 228), which has attracted audiences of more than 3,000 to the environs of the opulent palace (see below).

OTHER PRACTICALITIES
✉ **Post office** Ogero Bldg (opposite the police station, above the palace); ☎ 05 500 006; ⏰ 08.00–17.00 Mon–Fri, 08.00–13.30 Sat

WHAT TO SEE AND DO
Beiteddine Palace (☎ *05 500 077, 05 503 650;* ⏰ *Apr–Oct 09.00–18.00 Tue–Sun, Nov–Mar 09.00–16.00 Tue–Sun; admission: adults LBP7,500, students LBP5,000, children under 10 years LBP2,000. There is ample parking space for vehicles outside the main entrance to the palace & there are a couple of male/female public toilets to your right in the first courtyard*) Obliged to seek a safer haven away from Deir al-Qamar from opposition to his despotic rule, which had involved cutting the throats of his opponents and executions, Emir Bashir II's Beiteddine Palace or House of Faith became the charming and regal-like architectural legacy of Lebanon's final ruling prince. Built over a 30-year period, using Italian architects and highly skilled artisans

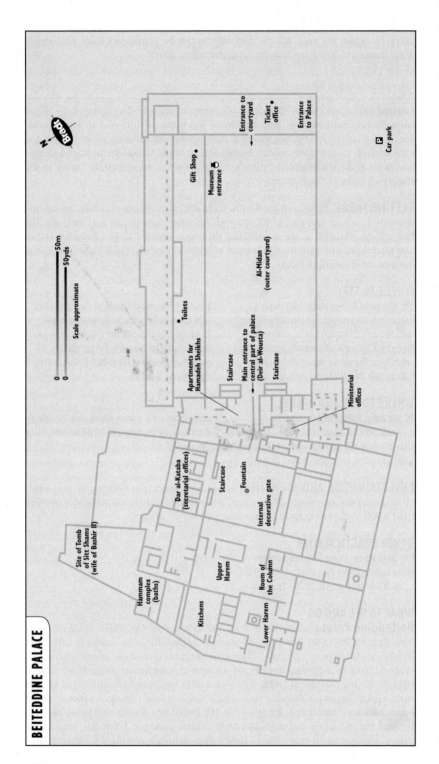

BEITEDDINE PALACE

N

Beit?

0   50yds
0   50m

Scale approximate

Entrance to courtyard

Ticket office

Entrance to Palace

Car park

Gift Shop

Museum entrance

Al-Midan (outer courtyard)

Toilets

Apartments for Hamadeh Sheikhs

Staircase

Main entrance to central part of palace (Deir al-Wousta)

Staircase

Ministerial offices

Dar al-Kataba (secretarial offices)

Staircase

Fountain

Internal decorative gate

Site of Tomb of Sitt Shams (wife of Bashir II)

Hammam complex (baths)

Kitchens

Upper Harem

Room of the Column

Lower Harem

from Damascus, construction commenced in 1788, and upon completion remained the emir's place of residence until 1840 when he was forced into exile to Turkey by the British and the Ottomans for forging an alliance with the Egyptian *pasha*, Muhammad Ali, against the Ottomans. Following Bashir's banishment to Turkey, the Ottomans utilised the palace for their own governmental purposes and during the French Mandate period it served a similar function. When Lebanon achieved independence in 1943, the country's first president, Becchara al-Khoury, used it as his summer residence, a tradition which continues to this day. In 1947, the remains of Bashir were returned to Lebanon from Istanbul, where he died in 1850, and were buried in a tomb with his first wife, Sitt Shams, in the northwest section of the palace. Designated a historic monument by Lebanon's General Directorate of Antiquities in 1934, the palace has undergone impressive restorations over the years, culminating in 1984 when Walid Jumblatt, the Druze leader, helped finance renovations and renamed it the 'Palace of the People'. Today it remains a fine example of both 19th-century Lebanese architecture and of one man's quest to create a grandiose and stunning architectural legacy to his rule and supremacy. Depending upon your interests it would be wise to allow at least a couple of hours to view the palace at a leisurely pace in order to appreciate its finely crafted design and luxurious contents.

The palace is organised into a number of sections: the first part you will come to from the main entrance is the Dar al-Baraniyyeh, a large, open main courtyard with a length of some 100m which was once used as a meeting place for guests and horsemen as well as for other public events. The Al Madafa on the right-hand side of the courtyard was formerly a two-storey accommodation block for visitors and, as was the custom of the time, a visitor could stay here and remain anonymous for three days before they were obliged to disclose their identity. One notable guest who did was the famous French poet Lamartine (1790–1869). On the upper level of the Madafa is the **Rashid Karami Archaeological and Ethnographic Museum**, containing a huge collection of Bronze, Iron-Age and Islamic pottery together with glass objects from the Roman era, gold jewellery, weaponry and costumes from the period. There is also an overview of the palace design in the form of a scale model. The tranquil and exquisite middle-court section, or Dar al-Wousta, is accessed via a dual stairway and was home to apartments and offices of the emir's ministers, secretaries and other dignitaries, richly decorated with mosaics, marquetry, oriental furnishings and some fine Arabic calligraphy.

As you enter the main courtyard, there is a delightful baby fountain at its centre with Lamartine's room ahead. As was traditional in Lebanese architecture, the arcades surrounding the courtyard were left open on one side to allow views of the surrounding countryside and nature's wonders. The third of the main sections of the palace is the Dar al-Harim, or private lodgings and apartments, and contains the most decorative elements in the entire complex. A major highlight is the huge façade of the richly decorated internal gate. Beyond here, the waiting room is known as the room of the column, on account of the single pillar which supports the ceiling. The adjacent reception rooms or *salamlik* comprise two levels with one of these having a fine mosaic floor and walls with marble carvings. Probably one of the most important areas in the palace, this is where Bashir carried out the day-to-day affairs of his administration and handed out justice. On one of the walls is one of his proverbs which says: 'The homage of a governor towards God is to observe justice, for an hour of justice is worth more than a thousand months of prayer.'

Although closed to visitors at the time of writing, the kitchens once fed over 500 people assembled in the reception area. The maze-like domed *hammams* (baths) complex, with ornate niches, marble floors, basins and fountains, comprised a series of cold and warm rooms for relaxation, massage and bathing whose impressive décor is enhanced when light shafts through the domed ceiling, giving an almost heavenly look and feel. A short walk north of the baths is the site of the final resting place of Bashir's first wife, the **tomb of Sitt Shams**, which also contains Bashir's ashes, which were transported here from Turkey in 1947. Beneath the main and central sections of the palace are the stables, which once kept 600 horses and accommodated 500 of the emir's soldiers, but are now home to a very impressive and eclectic array of Byzantine mosaics dating from the 5th and 6th centuries, discovered in the coastal town of Jiyyeh, a few kilometres north of Sidon.

Beiteddine Art Festival (*Block C, 4th Fl, Starco Centre, Downtown, Beirut;* ↘ *01 373 430;* e *info@beiteddine.org; www.beiteddine.org*) Held annually within the opulent courtyards of the Beiteddine Palace during July and August, the Beiteddine festival celebrated its 25th anniversary in 2010. Since its inception, the festival has played host to a wide range of Lebanese and international performing artists across a range of music genres. Log on to the festival website for information on the upcoming festival programme, together with full details of how to book tickets to the performances.

BAAKLINE

Located some 7km from Moukhtara and 4km south from Deir al-Qamar, this large town of some 30,000 people, the birthplace of the Maan leader Fakhreddine II, rises to 900m above sea level with superb views over the surrounding mountains and valleys. Compact and easy to walk around, this was the leafy tree-lined former Ottoman-era capital of the Chouf during the Maan dynasty, before it was moved to Deir al-Qamar owing to a shortage of water. It has an overwhelming Druze presence and the traditional costumes worn by Druze men are plentiful around the town which makes for a pleasant wander. Although there is a sign outside the library denoting 'Office de tourisme' there was at the time of research no tourist office presence in Baakline. The town has a few engaging architectural monuments including an ancient cemetery, but possibly the most interesting site to visit is the Baakline National Library (see opposite).

GETTING THERE Buses to Baakline go from the northern end of Cola station in Beirut, cost LBP2,500, and take around one hour.

 WHERE TO STAY AND EAT There is no hotel in Baakline itself but the town doesn't really warrant an overnight stay in any case and is best visited as part of a day trip or extended excursion to the other main sites and towns in the Chouf region. The town boasts a range of small cafes and restaurants catering to most budgets.

OTHER PRACTICALITIES

$ **BBAC Bank** ↘ 05 300 776; e baakline@bbac. com.lb; ⏱ 08.30–14.00 Mon–Fri, 08.30–12.00 Sat. 24/7 ATM for cash withdrawals.
$ **Fransabank** ↘ 05 303 005; m 03 650 711. Has an ATM.

🖥 **Garden Net Café** ↘ 05 305 338; m 03 818 949; ⏱ 14.00–01.00 Mon–Fri, 11.00–01.00 Sat/Sun. Towards the far end of town. Internet access is LBP1,500/hr.

The town also has a range of amenities such as small shops, a Western Union money transfer office and a couple of pharmacies, which should cater for most visitors' day to day needs.

WHAT TO SEE AND DO
Baakline National Library (\ *05 304 050/1, 05 302 901;* e *info@baakleenlibrary. com; www.baakleenlibrary.com;* ⊕ *08.00–18.00 Mon–Fri, 08.00–16.00 Sat*) This is one of the largest libraries in Lebanon, containing some 100,000 books in Arabic, English and French. Built in 1897, it functioned as the former Grand Serail (Municipality Building) during the Ottoman era, later becoming a police station and prison before finally becoming a library in 1987. It's well worth a look inside to examine its collection of new and dusty tomes and the building itself, which has an impressive façade and interior. Internet access is also available.

MOUKHTARA

Around 10km southeast of Beiteddine, this is an attractive town for a stroll amid picturesque buildings whilst on a day trip to the Chouf. The main reason for visiting is that this is overwhelmingly the Druze seat of power dominated by the **Walid**

THE JUMBLATT FAMILY

The Jumblatt family is one of the most enduring and iconic names in Lebanese history and politics. Originally descendants of the Kurdish Janbulad clan, the Druze Jumblatt dynasty have survived persecution by the Ottomans and a series of political assassinations and wars, yet remain at the forefront of Lebanese affairs and politics. Making the Chouf their home since the 16th century, the Jumblatt line has been a powerful force since Ottoman times. Following the murder of Fouad Jumblatt in 1921, it was left to his determined wife, Nazira, to assume the role of head of the family and lead the Druze community for the next 25 years; a challenging task for a woman during that period. When her son, Kamal, was old enough he assumed the helm and founded the Progressive Socialist Party (PSP) in 1949, seeking to challenge the sectarian nature of Lebanese politics: 'only a secular, progressive Lebanon freed of confessionalism could ever hope to survive,' he argued. Highly educated in law and philosophy in both Paris and Beirut, his socialist leadership made him a revered and key player in the early years of the Lebanese civil war. Along with Muslims, Pan-Arabic groups and other left-wing organisations, he forged a coalition known as the Lebanese National Movement (LNM) that was to become one of the strongest militias in the conflict. His assassination in 1977 was widely attributed to Syrian involvement, fearing a loss of Christian power in Lebanon. Nowadays, Kamal's son Walid Jumblatt leads the Druze cause and heads up the PSP. Known for his butterfly mentality of constantly shifting allegiances according to the prevailing political tastes and winds, he was a supporter of Syria after the civil war, but later began to question their dominance in Lebanese political affairs. He praised Hezbollah for ousting Israel from south Lebanon, but became concerned that in the aftermath of war they had an Iranian and Syrian agenda for Lebanon. Walid Jumblatt has been called a 'rebel with a cause', and has often commented that he is fearful of assassination for his views. Married to his second wife Nora, daughter of a former Syrian defence minister, his son Taymour is earmarked to eventually succeed him. Responsible for the founding of the annual Beiteddine Festival and a staunch advocate of preserving the Chouf's natural environment, he returns to his home in Moukhtara weekly to receive his fellow Druze followers and discuss their grievances.

7

Jumblatt house and palace (✆ *05 310 555;* ⊕ *10.00–17.00 Mon–Wed; admission free*), an imposing fusion of Italian and oriental architectural influences comprising a lovely curved staircase entrance, Roman sarcophagi, *hammam* and lush gardens complete with waterfall. Every Saturday, between 09.00 and 12.00, the Druze leader holds his weekly surgery here and residents and visitors alike are welcome to attend. Even if your visit doesn't coincide with Mr Jumblatt's weekly surgeries, it is still possible to tour the public areas of this imposing house during the week and guards at the entrance will happily show you around for free.

GETTING THERE There are buses and taxis from Cola station in Beirut to Moukhtara and buses from outside Baakline National Library which also serve the town, costing LBP1,000 for the 20-minute journey and stopping just across the road from the Walid Jumblatt house.

CHOUF CEDAR RESERVE

(*Chouf Cedar Society Office: Park House, Masser El Shouf, Village Sq, opposite the public gardens;* ✆ *05 350 250/150;* m *03 964 495;* e *info@shoufcedar.org; www. shoufcedar.org; office opening hours: 08.30–16.30 Mon–Sat; Cedar reserve* ⊕ *10.00– 18.00 daily; admission: adults LBP5,000, children over 10 years & students LBP3,000, children under 10 years free. From the main hut at the entrance to the reserve it is a further 6km walk to the cedars & walking trails themselves. There is a vehicle on hand*

CEDAR OF LEBANON (*CEDRUS LIBANI*)

The legendary cedar tree symbolically percolates through Lebanon; it forms part of the national flag, the livery of the national carrier Middle East Airlines, and it is the emblem of choice among political parties such as the Phalangist Kataeb, the Lebanese Forces and the Future Movement. As a figure of longevity and strength, it has numerous references in the Bible with Psalm 92 proclaiming that: 'the righteous shall flourish like the palm tree: he shall grow like a cedar of Lebanon.' In the ancient Sumerian tale of the *Epic of Gilgamesh*, the King of Uruk raids the cedar forests to build his city, infuriating the gods. The Lebanese cedar is part of the tripartite pine family of trees (Pinaceae) also native to Syria and southern Turkey, with the Atlas cedar (*Cedrus atlantica*) growing in the Tell Atlas Mountains of Algeria and Morocco, and the Deodar cedar (*Cedrus deodara*) in the western Himalayas. Characterised by their broad trunks and dense, needle-like leaves, these evergreen coniferous trees can attain heights of up to 130ft although they are slow growing, and it can take up to 40 years just to produce seedlings. Since ancient times the cedar tree in Lebanon has been the source of many a utilitarian and ornamental usage. This strong and durable tree was vital to the economic prosperity of the Phoenicians, who used it to build their trading vessels, homes and palaces; the Egyptians used the resin from the cedar tree to embalm their pharaohs, and the wood was also utilised for the construction of King Solomon's Temple in Jerusalem. The Romans, under Emperor Hadrian, practiced an early form of conservation, restricting the use of the tree for military purposes. But progressive deforestation over the years has severely depleted the number of cedars in existence with a few remaining near Bcharré, in addition to those standing in the Chouf Cedar Reserve.

to take visitors but may not always be available so it is best to call in advance) To get up close and personal with Lebanon's iconic national symbol, a visit to this extremely scenic protectorate should be high on your list of things to see and do in the Chouf, and is a good example of Lebanon's burgeoning ecotourism potential. As Lebanon's largest nature reserve, covering some 5% (around 500km²) of the country's landmass, it represents the most southerly point of Lebanese cedar growth and is home to a quarter of the last remaining stands of cedar, with some thought to be 2,000 years old. Spread over three forests – Masser Al-Chouf, Barouk, and Ain Zhalta-Bmohary – the area was made a protected Biosphere Reserve by UNESCO in June 2005.

This delicate ecosystem contains more than 20 species of other trees, numerous types of reptiles, 500 varieties of plants and 250 species of birds, and was designated an Important Bird Area by BirdLife International. Wild mammals such as the gazelle, hyena, Lebanese jungle cat and the wolf continue to roam the undulating landscape which varies from 1,000m to 2,000m above sea level. The Chouf Cedar Society, who have administered and run the reserve since 1996 with Druze leader Walid Jumblatt as its president, operate a number of activities including animal spotting, guided walks and hikes, trekking, birdwatching, mountain biking and snow-shoeing during the winter months. Ecotourism trips of between one and five days are also offered by the society. The society aim to foster rural development and local economies and have an active engagement programme with local communities. You can purchase locally made foodstuffs such as jams and herbs, together with a range of handicrafts at the hut at the reserve's entrance. Although there are four entrances to the reserve at Masser Al-Chouf, Barouk, Ain Zhalta-Bmohary and Niha by far the best and most accessible is at Barouk, about 15km from Beiteddine, which can best be reached by service taxi.

GETTING THERE Although not quite as frequent as buses to Beiteddine or Deir al-Qamar, buses from Cola station in Beirut travel to the nearby town of Barouk (LBP2,500), where you can get a taxi to the reserve. You can also catch a bus from outside the library in Baakline to Barouk for the Cedars which takes around half an hour and costs LBP1,000. The bus will drop you off in the town from where you can take a taxi to the reserve, though they are not frequent. The reserve itself can also arrange transport if you call ahead, though this is one place where having your own transport is definitely an advantage. If you do have your own car the following three routes from Beirut, Aley and the Bekaa Valley will all take you to Masser Al-Chouf, the location for the Chouf Cedar Society main office. To reach the Barouk entrance from Masser Al-Chouf just continue heading north on the snaking main road.

From Beirut Take the coast road south from the capital and follow the road and signs to Damour, turning inland shortly after Damour and follow the roads to Deir al-Qamar, Beiteddine, Semkanieh, Moukhtara, Boutmeh and finally Masser.

From Aley Head towards Dahr El Baidar, Ain Zhalta, Barouk and Masser.

From the Bekaa Valley Start from Chtaura and drive south towards Aammiq then shortly after turning east towards Kefraya and follow this road, which will bring you to Masser.

TOUR OPERATORS
Esprit-Nomade 09 933 552; m 03 223 552; e coord@esprit-nomade.com; www.esprit-nomade.com. Specialising in ecotours, this

organisation often runs day trips to the Chouf as well as to other parts of the country.

Liban Trek ☎ 01 329 975; f 01 329 956; m 03 291 616; e info@libantrek.com; www. libantrek.com. This well established, & Lebanon's first ecotourism company, operates scheduled hikes every Sun & they can also customise trips according to your needs. In Sep 2011 the cost of a day's hiking through all 3 cedar forests was LBP42,000, including return transport from Beirut, entrance fees, guide & insurance.

WHERE TO STAY The following places are all in or around the cedar reserve, and make an ideal stopover if you are planning an extended tour of the Chouf and want to combine the attractions at Deir al-Qamar and Beiteddine with an ecotourism experience.

Barouk Palace Hotel (25 rooms & suites) Main Rd, Barouk, Chouf; ☎ 05 240 251/2; m 03 630 056; e info@baroukpalace.com; www.baroukpalace.com. Although the rooms are quite ordinary, the location is not, with stunning views over the mountains. There are also 4 restaurants, a swimming pool & the hotel can also organise excursions. **$$$**

Association for Forests, Development & Conservation (AFDC) (22 rooms) Ramlieh, Aley; ☎ 05 280 430; e afdc@afdc.org.lb; www. afdc.org.lb. A youth hostel 7km from the Chouf Cedar Reserve, offering clean, basic accommodation together with a range of educational & ecotourism activities. **$$**

Auberge St Michel (7 rooms) Masser Al-Chouf; ☎ 05 350 451/2; e auberge@arcenciel. org; www.arcenciel.org (website in French); ☾ May–Oct only. A former convent, this friendly & clean budget option also organises activities such as hiking & cycling & there is a playground for children. Internet & laundry facilities are also available. B/fast inc. **$**

Ecovillage Dmit Valley, Chouf; ☎ 01 369 488; m 03 211 463, 03 381 733; e ecovillagelebanon@gmail.com; www.ecoecovillage.com. Basic lodgings in huts & tents with a real back-to-nature feel. A range of activities is also on offer at this sustainable village, including donkey rides, hiking, rock climbing & yoga, etc. B/fast inc. **$**

8

South Lebanon

Telephone code 07

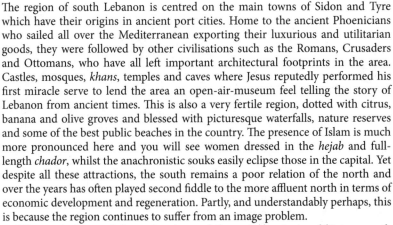

The region of south Lebanon is centred on the main towns of Sidon and Tyre which have their origins in ancient port cities. Home to the ancient Phoenicians who sailed all over the Mediterranean exporting their luxurious and utilitarian goods, they were followed by other civilisations such as the Romans, Crusaders and Ottomans, who have all left important architectural footprints in the area. Castles, mosques, *khans*, temples and caves where Jesus reputedly performed his first miracle serve to lend the area an open-air-museum feel telling the story of Lebanon from ancient times. This is also a very fertile region, dotted with citrus, banana and olive groves and blessed with picturesque waterfalls, nature reserves and some of the best public beaches in the country. The presence of Islam is much more pronounced here and you will see women dressed in the *hejab* and full-length *chador*, whilst the anachronistic souks easily eclipse those in the capital. Yet despite all these attractions, the south remains a poor relation of the north and over the years has often played second fiddle to the more affluent north in terms of economic development and regeneration. Partly, and understandably perhaps, this is because the region continues to suffer from an image problem.

Often at the heart of the country's – and the region's – tortured history, south Lebanon suffered greatly during the civil war years, especially during the 1982 Israeli invasion of the country. The 22-year Israeli occupation from 1978 to 2000 effectively severed any link with tourism and the region also became off-limits for most Lebanese. The 2006 July War between Israel and Hezbollah, with its large loss of life and huge infrastructure damage, merely accentuated the image of the south as a virtual no-go area for locals and visitors alike. The continued presence of UN peacekeeping forces in the region, which numbered some 11,733 UNIFIL troops from 35 countries in March 2011, testifies to the area's ongoing potential volatility, but a visit to the south is also an essential part of the historical Lebanese jigsaw. The region possesses the same ingredients which characterise the north, such as friendly and hospitable people, world-class archaeological sites, and great food which combine to offer the traveller an authentic and much more raw experience.

SIDON (SAIDA)

Lebanon's third-largest city after Beirut and Tripoli and the largest town in the south, the old Phoenician port city of Sidon is only 45km south from Beirut along the coastal highway. As a conservative, predominantly Sunni Muslim town, surrounded by banana and citrus groves, it evokes a much more traditional and relaxed way of life compared with the capital, lacking the frenetic construction and nightlife of Beirut. Sidon is also the birthplace of former prime minister Rafiq Hariri as well as the childhood home of Lebanon's first prime minister, Riad al–Solh, but its claim to fame over the last few decades has, unfortunately, come to be for wars and

233

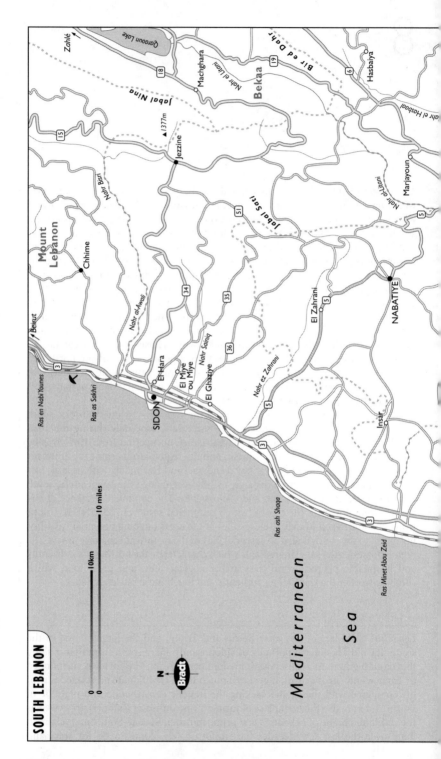

Mediterranean

Sea

Mount
Lebanon

Bekaa

Jabal Niha

Jabal Safi

Beirut

Chhime

SIDON

El Hara

El Miye
ou Miye

El Ghaziye

Jezzine

▲1377m

Machghara

Bir ed Dahr

Hasbaiya

Zahlé

Qaraoun Lake

El Zahrani

NABATIYE

Insar

Marjayoun

Nahr el Bisri

Nahr al-Awali

Nahr Sainiq

Nahr ez Zahrani

Nahr el Litani

Nahr el-Litani

Nahr el Hasbani

Ras en Nabi Younes

Ras as Sakhri

Ras ash Shaqa

Ras Minet Abou Zeid

18

19

6

15

51

34

35

36

5

5

5

3

3

3

10km

10 miles

0

0

N

Bradt

234

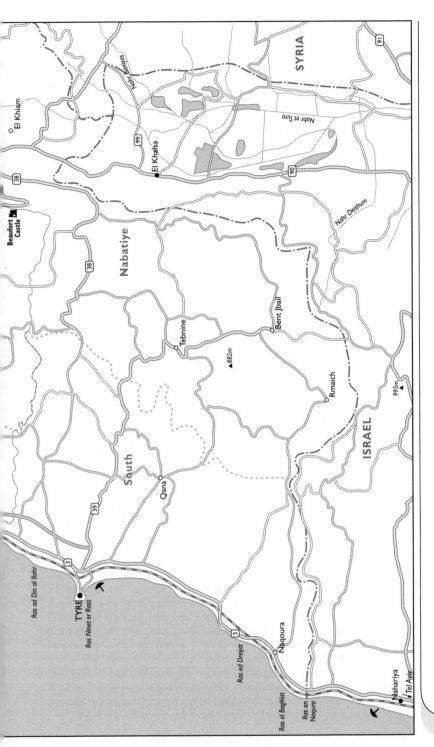

SYRIA

91

Nahr Baniyas

El Khiam

99

Nahr et Tura

El Khalsa

38

90

Beaufort
Castle

Nahr Deishum

Nabatiye

38

Tebnine

Bent Jbail

▲882m

Rmaich

995m ▲

ISRAEL

South

Qana

39

3

Ras ad Din el Bahr

TYRE

Ras Ninet er Rass

Naqoura

3

Ras ed Dreijat

Nahariya

Tel Aviv

Ras el Baghlat

Ras an
Naqura

occupation. Heavily damaged during the Lebanese civil war, it was also hard-hit by the Israeli military machine during their occupation of the south. If visiting straight from the capital, the city's much more laid-back atmosphere will prove quite a contrast. But while Sidon may lack the eclectic entertainment and nightlife of the capital – alcohol is served in only one restaurant in the city at present – it more than makes up for this in being a largely authentic and traditional Arab city with anachronistic souks and artisans plying their trade like they have done for centuries. A famous sea castle, *khans*, a couple of excellent museums and a busy, picturesque fishing port make Sidon a very pleasant place for a day or two, and it is a good base for an extended stay if you are intending to make a comprehensive tour of the south.

TRAVEL ADVICE

Although south Lebanon is a basically safe and rewarding region to visit, it needs to be borne in mind that the area has been the front line in the on/off war between Israel and Hezbollah for many years, despite the former's withdrawal from the country in May 2000. The area also saw intense fighting during the civil war, which again embroiled Israel. At the time of writing the area was relatively calm, with just the odd minor skirmish on the border zone. But tensions are high between these implacable foes and remain, like Israel and Lebanon, technically in a state of war and things can change very rapidly in this part of the world. Keep abreast of developments by tuning into television stations or perusing the English-language *The Daily Star* newspaper. It would also be a good idea to check on the current security situation at the Ein el Helwe Palestinian refugee camp in Sidon if you intend visiting.

Given the continued tensions between Israel and Hezbollah, at the time of research any non-Lebanese citizen intending to visit areas south of Tyre must obtain a security pass number from the army security service in Sidon prior to travelling south of Tyre, and which must be presented at the army checkpoints. There is no charge for this and the relevant document is usually issued while you wait, but it can take up to 24 hours. In practical terms, any visitors intending to travel to the Orange House in Naqoura (see page 253) and those wishing to hike the southern sections, 22–26, of the Lebanon Mountain Trail (see *Chapter 5*, page 181) must have this numbered security pass. When in Sidon take a service taxi (LBP2,000) and ask for the *'mukhabbarat al-jeish'* (*Army St;* ↘ *07 725 800 ext 221, 07 724 912;* ⏰ *08.00–14.00 Mon–Fri, 08.00–13.00 Sat*), which is the headquarters of the army intelligence service in Sidon. It would be a good idea to bring a photocopy of your passport's main pages in addition to the passport itself and you may be asked to deposit your mobile phone and/or camera prior to being admitted through the security gate. It is also worth bearing in mind that since the end of the 2006 Israel–Hezbollah conflict, a large amount of cluster bombs and other unexploded devices remain in the region, which have subsequently killed over 30 civilians and wounded more than 200. Further fatalities and injuries have occurred to those responsible for de-mining the area. Operations are ongoing to rid the land of unexploded munitions but there is still much work to do, and until complete it is best to stick to well-trodden paths and highways. You can keep up to date with these issues by logging onto www.unifil.unmissions.org, the official website of the United Nations Interim Force in Lebanon (UNIFIL).

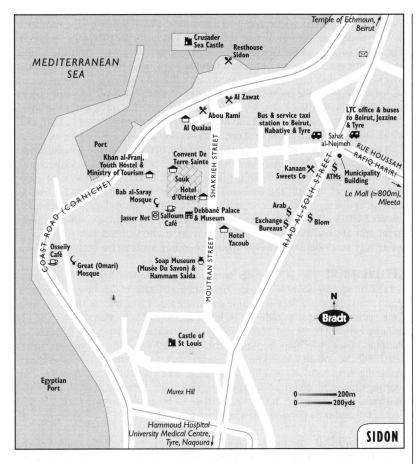

SIDON

HISTORY As one of Lebanon's main coastal cites, Sidon's illustrious past is intimately bound up with the earliest civilisations that took advantage of its favourable geography to carve out successive empires. In the Book of Genesis in the Old Testament, Sidon is referred to as the 'first born' of Canaan, making the city the earliest of the Phoenician city-states and, along with Tyre, one of its most important. During the Phoenician era the economy of Sidon prospered, with Phoenician artisans producing glass items and the famed purple dye which adorned many a royal and well-heeled citizen of the day, and who were praised in the writings of Homer for their artistry and skill. At the peak of their empire, around 550–330BC, the Phoenicians equipped the Persians with vessels and sailors to stave off the Egyptians and Greeks. Sidon was also one of the Phoenician state's most important religious cities and around this time the Temple of Echmoun was constructed. Following the end of the Persian period, Sidon experienced wave after wave of invaders with its most famous being Alexander the Great in 333BC who ushered in the Hellenistic period, with Greek becoming the lingua franca of the area.

The city's comparative autonomy and freedom continued into the Roman epoch which saw the Pax Romana with Sidon's citizens having a degree of parity of rights with their Roman occupiers. During the Byzantine era, the city continued to enjoy a relatively quiet period in its long history with many achievements in areas such as literature, the arts and science, etc, and it became the ideal choice for the relocation of Beirut's famous School of Law following a devastating earthquake in AD551. The Arabs conquered the city around AD636, and the city came under the banner of Islam for over 500 years until the advent of the Crusaders who, in 1111 under Baldwin, included Sidon alongside Jerusalem amongst its successes. The imposing sea castle remains the most salient reminder of this period of Sidonian history along with the Castle of St Louis. The Crusader presence was quite short-lived, however, and they were defeated and forced out by the Mamluk forces in 1291, after which the city enjoyed a couple of centuries of relative calm.

It wasn't until the 17th century, during the reign of the Ottomans, that Sidon was to once again achieve a degree of illustrious existence not enjoyed since antiquity. Under the enlightened rule of Emir Fakhreddine II, Sidon's port underwent major restoration and he built the famous Khan al-Franj or travellers' inn for foreign merchants trading in silk and cotton. During the 20th century, the town was heavily involved in the civil war and was also embroiled in the ongoing conflict between Israel and Hezbollah. Today, Sidon retains its traditional feel but trappings of modernity are evident in its newly opened shopping malls on the outskirts of town.

GETTING THERE The LCC's sister company, the Lebanese Transport Company (*LTC; Zantout Bldg, Sahat al-Nejmeh;* 07 720 566, 07 722 783; e *lebanesetransportco@ gmail.com*) operates a fleet of 70 blue and white buses which serve the route from Cola station in Beirut to Sidon with buses departing daily roughly every 15–20 minutes between 05.00 and 22.00. You have two choices of bus: the air-conditioned Pullman buses travel non-stop along the main highway and the one-way fare is LBP2,500; the non air-conditioned or 'normal' bus is a stopping service and travels along the *tariq bahriyeh* or 'old seaside route' and costs LBP1,500 one way. The journey time is 30–45 minutes, depending on traffic. A variety of other buses and minivans also serve the route south from Cola, as do service taxis (around LBP2,500) and taxis (around LBP45,000–55,000).

GETTING AROUND Like most of Lebanon's towns and cities, Sidon is easily explored on foot with all the main sights (and sites) in the city mentioned below quite close together. The slightly more outlying Temple of Echmoun can easily be reached by taxi (around LBP8,000) from Sidon's Sahat al-Nejmeh Roundabout or by hailing a taxi on the street. Buses and minivans travelling north from here can also drop you off by the Stade De Saida (Sports Stadium), where you can flag down a taxi or walk the remaining 1km to the temple, which is signposted. This is a very picturesque route, as dotted along the riverbanks are a few outdoor cafés which make for a pleasant detour.

TOURIST INFORMATION

Ministry of Tourism Khan al-Franj; 07 727 344; 08.00–14.00 Mon–Thu, 08.00–11.00 Fri, 08.00–13.00 Sat. Located at the far end of the main entrance to the khan, this tiny office has a range of free brochures & pamphlets in English, French, German, Italian & Spanish about south Lebanon, as well as other areas of the country. Be advised, however, that opening hours can sometimes be erratic!

Najwa Harb m 03 262 653; e najwa_ harb@hotmail.com. Excellent & knowledgeable trilingual tourist guide offering guided visits around the city in Arabic, French & Italian.

WHERE TO STAY

Al Qualaa Hotel (10 rooms) Seaside Rd; 07 734 777; m 03 759 395; e info@alqualaa. com; www.alqualaa.com. Excellent location right opposite the sea castle, this is Sidon's premier address housed inside a lovely old medieval building. Exceptionally clean rooms with character, ethnic décor. Recommended for those not on a tight budget. B/fast inc. **$$$**

🏠 **Hotel Yacoub** (8 rooms) Moutran St, near the old souk; 📞 07 737 733; **m** 03 327 034; **e** contact@yacoubhotel.com; www.yacoubhotel. com. The building dates from Ottoman times & the present hotel is converted from an old family house. Very clean with comfortable beds, AC, TV & en-suite rooms, this is a great place to base yourself for a few nights if exploring the south of the country. A very basic breakfast consisting of manaoushe & coffee is included. **$$**

🏠 **Convent De Terre Sainte** (8 rooms) Behind the Khan al-Franj (look for the sign 'Latin Church – Our Lady of the Annunciation'); **m** 03 442 141, 70 668 398. Basic, but clean, all rooms have fan, toilet & shower & there is a pleasant courtyard area for relaxing & dining. A characterful place & the delightful manager, Katia, will prepare evening meals on request (US$10–15). Sidon's best budget option

right in the heart of the souk. B/fast US$5 extra. **$**

🏠 **Hotel d'Orient** (7 rooms) Shakrieh St (near Debbané Palace & Museum); 📞 07 720 364. This place takes budget accommodation to new lows. It is downright bleak, depressing & not very welcoming. There is no AC & not all rooms have fans. Best seen as a last resort. **$**

🏠 **Khan al-Franj Youth Hostel** (7 rooms) Khan al-Franj; **m** 03 980 603; **e** tarek_abouzeinab@yahoo.com; www.hariri-foundation. org. An excellent initiative by the charitable Hariri Foundation, set up by former prime minister Rafiq Hariri, which from Mar 2010 began to offer hostel-style accommodation on the top floor of the khan. The accommodation has clean, modern facilities with high vaulted ceilings in an authentic 17th-century style. Plans are afoot to expand the number of rooms to 12 within the next 2 years. Highly recommended for the budget-conscious traveller, with a certain caché in staying in a delightful heritage building once again serving its originally intended purpose. B/fast inc, in the downstairs lecture room. **$**

✗ **WHERE TO EAT AND DRINK** In addition to the places below, there are a number of other eateries thronging the road opposite the sea castle which offer good value, filling meals and snacks in a nice location opposite the Corniche, though none of these places serve alcohol. There is also a range of cafés and snack bars in Sidon's souks.

✗ **Resthouse Sidon** Seaside Rd, next to the sea castle; 📞 07 722 469; ⏰ 12.00–midnight daily. At the time of writing this government-run restaurant is the only place in the city serving alcohol including arak, wine, beers & spirits. It is housed within a converted Ottoman era khan & has 2 restaurants: the smaller 'Italian Room', serving excellent Italian cuisine, whilst the much larger room specialises in delicious Lebanese food. It also has a nice outdoor area with in-your-face views of the sea castle. There is also a daily menu of fresh fish from the market. **$$$$$**

✗ **Al Qualaa Hotel** Seaside Rd; 📞 07 734 777; **m** 03 759 395; **e** info@alqualaa.com; www. alqualaa.com; ⏰ 08.00–midnight daily. A good choice for mezze & international French & Italian cuisine. **$$$$**

✗ **Al Zawat** Seaside Rd, opposite the sea castle; 📞 07 723 724; **m** 03 350 050; **e** info@ zawat.com; www.zawat.com; ⏰ 09.00–01.00

daily. A lovely terrace restaurant overlooking the Corniche, serving delicious mezze, locally caught fish dishes & variety of grilled meats. A very atmospheric place for puffing on a nargileh (US$6). **$$$$**

✗ **Abou Rami** Seaside Rd, directly opposite the sea castle; 📞 07 721 907; ⏰ 08.00–20.00 Mon–Thu, 08.00–20.00 Sat/Sun. Specialising in tasty falafel, this is a delightful little informal eatery with nice outdoor-only seating. A popular haunt for locals. **$**

💻 **Osseily Café** Corniche, just west of Omari Mosque; **m** 03 495 459; ⏰ 07.00–midnight daily. Although there is nothing special about this café it does offer free Wi-Fi & on Sat & Sun nights there is a disco. Only serves drinks. **$**

✗ **Kanaan Sweets Co** Riad al-Solh St, near Sahat al-Nejmeh; 📞 07 720 271; **e** kanaan@ kanaansweets.com; www.kanaansweets.com; ⏰ 05.30–22.00 daily. The place to try Sidon's local speciality, the *sanioura*, an oval–shaped, deliciously sweet, crumbly biscuit. A good place for a sit-down coffee & they also serve a range of other sweets & cakes, including baklava. This is a rare non-smoking eatery in Lebanon. $

🖵 **Salloum Café** Next to Bab al-Saray Mosque; m 70 600 348; ⏰ 07.00–midnight daily. Nice little indoor & outdoor café for a drink overlooking the square for people watching & kids playing football. $

ENTERTAINMENT AND NIGHTLIFE Like other conservative towns in the country, Sidon's nightlife is not especially sophisticated or vibrant, and at the time of writing only the Osseily Café above offered anything approaching a lively night out. Evenings tend to be dominated by a more restrained café culture with couples and families eating and drinking whilst puffing on a *nargileh*. As a predominantly 'dry' city, your only possibility for drinking alcohol is at the Resthouse Sidon, beside the sea castle.

SHOPPING In addition to those places listed below, some of the best shopping in the city, whether for foodstuffs like fruit and vegetables or souvenirs, is undertaken in Sidon's atmospheric souks which offer a range of traditionally crafted products that can make great gifts. Away from the souks, the streets radiating off Sahat al-Nejmeh offer more modern retail outlets selling a whole range of items to meet day-to-day needs.

Hammam Saida Moutran St; ☏ 07 733 353; e ilaudi@inco.com.lb; www.fondationaudi.org; ⏰ 08.30–18.00 Sat–Thu. Housed inside the Soap Museum, this small boutique shop sells an assortment of kaftans, jewellery, a range of different soaps together with books about Lebanon, postcards, coasters & ornamental glass items, though prices are not particularly cheap.

Le Mall Rue Houssam Rafiq Hariri, 800m from Sahat al-Nejmeh; ☏ 07 732 999; e info@lemall. com; www.lemall.com; ⏰ 10.00–22.00 daily. A new, ultra-modern complex for everything from designer fashion wear to Dunkin' Doughnuts. In fact, everything you can buy back home! A variety of cafés are housed on the top floor.

OTHER PRACTICALITIES The area around Sahat al-Nejmeh, besides being the main hub for the city's transport network of buses and taxis, is where most of the banks, ATMs, larger stores and travel companies are located. The area also has numerous cafés and houses the municipality building. Good and reliable internet cafés were not exactly widespread at the time of writing, but there was talk of Sidon's public library reopening in the near future which would offer the service. It may be worth asking around to see if this has become a reality.

➕ **Hammoud Hospital University Medical Centre** Dr Ghassan Hammoud St; ☏ 07 723 111, 07 723 888; e info@hammoudhospital.com; www.hammoudhospital.com. A high-quality, 325-bed teaching hospital with Accident & Emergency Department.
📧 **Jasser Net** Near Bab al-Saray Mosque in the souk; m 70 318 150; e abed.jasser@live.com;

⏰ 09.00–late daily. Good, friendly internet café for checking your mail with plenty of computers charging LBP1,000/hr.
✉ **Post office** Bizri Bldg, Riad al-Solh St; ☏ 07 721 604; ⏰ 08.00–17.00 Mon–Fri, 08.00–13.00 Sat. Provides the full range of postal services, including Western Union money transfer.

WHAT TO SEE AND DO
Crusader Sea Castle (*Seafront;* m *03 433 287;* ⏰ *summer 09.00–18.00 daily, winter 09.00–16.00 daily; admission: adults LBP4,000, students LBP1,000, children under 10 free*) This is Sidon's most recognisable and popular visitor site. Known as

Qala al-Bahr in Arabic, the castle is located offshore but connected to the mainland by an 80m causeway constructed by the Arabs. Built by the Crusaders in 1228, using the foundations of a much earlier Phoenician temple dedicated to their god Melqart, the rise to power of the Mamluks led to the destruction of the castle in order to deter future incursions by the medieval knights. The castle comprises a west and an east tower either side of the main entrance; the former is in the better condition of the two. Following their defeat of the Mamluks, the Ottomans built a compact domed mosque on the castle's west side. The exterior walls of the castle show evidence of the use of Roman stonework used to strengthen the structure indicating that the Crusaders were great early recyclers. Both towers are easily accessed on foot via staircases and from aloft yield great views over the town and the old fishing port.

Khan al-Franj (Inn of the Foreigners) (\ 07 727 344; ⊕ 08.00–22.00 daily; admission free) A few minutes walk south of the sea castle is this inland *khan* built by Fakhreddine II in the early 17th century, as a one-stop shop for cotton and silk merchants trading locally and with overseas markets as part of his cosmopolitan philosophy to stimulate economic activity and assert his independence from the Ottomans. Architecturally, the *khan* follows the design of other *khans* attributed to Fakhreddine. It consists of a large central courtyard dominated by arches and vaulted ceilings. The ground floor would have been used for storing goods, as stables for animals such as camels and horses, hostelries and a marketplace. The upper floor was reserved for traveller accommodation. This was Sidon's hub of economic prosperity during the 19th century, and which also housed the French consulate, to which Fakhreddine donated the *khan*. Nowadays it remains an icon of its time and has been thoughtfully restored by the Hariri Foundation, now home to a crafts complex and a small office of the Ministry of Tourism. Events and activities are also staged here, including in late 2010 Sidon's first ever Career Days for jobseekers when the entire ground floor was covered with white marquees. The first floor once again serves its original function of providing accommodation and there is a certain caché in staying in its superbly renovated and character rooms (see page 239). The *khan* should certainly be on your list of places to visit in Sidon.

Great (Omari) Mosque Dating from 1291, the mosque was originally a Church of St John of the Hospitallers Order (Knights of St John) during the latter period of the Crusader era, housing a chapel and stables. The onset of Mamluk rule saw the fortress converted into a mosque but retaining its original walls. The structure had suffered immense damage over the years from earthquakes, storms and war, especially the 1982 Israeli invasion that left the mosque in a perilous state. Between 1983 and 1986, the mosque underwent extensive renovations, funded by Rafiq Hariri, and in 1989 received the coveted Aga Khan Award for Architecture (see www.akdn.org/architecture, which has interesting and extensive background notes on the architectural details and history of this building). The mosque today, entered via its main northern gate in the souk, is an impressive site, with its large courtyard surrounded by archways and impressive 10m-high vaulted ceilings. The elongated prayer hall, with its customary niche pointing towards Mecca, stained-glass windows and imposing domes make this mosque a highly recommended site.

Bab al-Saray Mosque Built in 1201, the Bab al-Saray or Gate of the Palace is Sidon's oldest mosque. With its imposing dome supported by a series of large pillars, it has some newly renovated and beautiful medieval stonework with vaulted ceiling and large arches.

Port Just a couple of minutes walk south from the sea castle, this still traditional and working fishermen's port has an early morning daily fish market from around 06.00 to 11.00 and is well worth getting up early for to watch the fishermen bring back the product of their nighttime scaly labours and to observe the frenetic trading activity.

Souks Whilst not as extensive as Tripoli's souks, Sidon's labyrinthine streets still make for a few hours of happy wandering to appreciate this atmospheric slice of traditional Arab and Sidonian life. This remains a living museum of tradition with artisans plying their trade as cobblers, furniture-makers and metalworkers tapping and hammering away at their tasks, as they have done for generations. It's probably best not to take a set route; just head straight across the road from the sea castle and begin your meanderings at the innumerable fruit and vegetable stalls and get lost amongst them and the crowded alleyways to soak up the medieval atmosphere, stopping *en route* at one of the many cafés to drink tea, smoke a *nargileh* and watch young and old play backgammon and cards. The souk is also a good place to try Sidon's very own *sanioura* crumbly biscuit in authentic surroundings.

The Soap Museum (Musée Du Savon) (*Moutran St;* ℡ *07 753 599;* e *ilaudi@ inco.com.lb; www.fondationaudi.org;* ◷ *09.00–17.00 Mon–Thu, 09.00–17.00 Sat/ Sun; admission free*) Sidon's tradition of soap manufacture dates back to the 17th century, when the city was a hub for exports to France. Although production has all but ceased today, Lebanon's first museum dedicated to the art and craft of this once-flourishing industry is absorbing and definitely worth a look. The museum's building dates from the Middle Ages, but it wasn't until the mid 19th century that it became a soap factory supplying local markets such as the bathhouses or *hammams* which once proliferated in the city. Towards the end of the 19th century, the building was purchased by the affluent Audi family who continued soap making under their own brand label. Production finally came to a halt in 1975 with the onset of the civil war, and the ground floor of the building became a safe haven for refugees from the conflict. In 1996, the Audis began renovating the factory and it finally opened to the public as a museum in November 2000. The end result is a very well-designed and organised shrine over two floors with clear labelling of the exhibits in Arabic, English and French. The museum takes you on a journey through the history, raw materials and processes involved in soap manufacture in the countries of the Levant and includes the fascinating 'Saponification' process; a two-stage and week-long procedure of fermentation and heating of the raw materials.

Debbané Palace and Museum (*Moutran St;* ℡ *07 720 110;* e *museedebbane@ debbane.com; www.museumsaida.org;* ◷ *09.00–18.00 Sat–Thu; admission free*) This little gem of a palace is hidden away inside the souk, though very close to the Hotel Yacoub, and is a must-see site in the city. Built by prominent local Ali Agha Hammoud as his private place of residence in 1721, it was later purchased by the affluent Debbané family c1800, who proceeded to renovate and extend the property to the one you see today. It remained the family home until 1978, when the civil war forced them out to make way for hundreds of refugees who sought sanctuary there from the horrors of war. The building and house itself is an archetypal example of Ottoman-era architecture – a main courtyard as the centrepiece of the building and the very private layout of the entrance. Inside the house there are numerous exquisite decorative items, including a ceiling of cedarwood, paintings, a fountain and a variety of motifs. More recent renovations show the influence of the French presence with the addition of two extra storeys in the 1920s. The Debbané Foundation, inaugurated in 1999, was established to restore and showcase Ottoman-era architecture and, more widely, the history of the town of Sidon itself, and the building first opened to the public in 2001.

Castle of St Louis Like many archaeological ruins throughout Lebanon, this Crusader-era fortress, dating from 1254 and built by King Louis IX, occupies the site of an earlier 10th-century fortification built during the Fatimid dynasty and restored during the Mamluk epoch. The castle was the first ever built in the city, and sits atop a large mound. At the base of the castle are numerous Roman columns dotted around. The castle is in a poor state of repair and enclosed by wire fencing; the site is unattended so you can just walk around the perimeter to view it or enter via a gap in the fence for a closer peek, though it would be unwise to walk up to the top because of the possibility of falling masonry.

Murex Hill Located a few metres southeast and across the road from the Castle of St Louis is Sidon's 100m-long and 50m-high hill, the most 'invisible' evidence of its once-great importance during the Phoenician era. It was here that archaeologists discovered some 40m-high piles of discarded murex shells from the purple dye-manufacturing process, which hints at the once-massive scale of production. Alas, ongoing residential development and the advent of a Muslim cemetery now mark this spot, and you are likely to have more luck locating a murex shell on eBay.

Temple of Echmoun (⏲ *08.00–18.00 daily; admission free; a small manned office which at the time of writing didn't have any brochures on the site; there are toilet facilities just inside the entrance*) Located just over 1km north of Sidon, the Temple of Echmoun, or Bustan al-Sheikh as it is known locally in Arabic, is located in a picturesque location along the banks of the Awali River lined with lush green vegetation and citrus plantations. More importantly from an archaeological viewpoint is that this ancient site, which dates from the 7th century BC, is the sole Phoenician site which preserves more than its stone foundations. Like many of Lebanon's archaeological ruins it has seen numerous additions over the centuries, illustrating how it has been revered by subsequent civilisations. The legend of Echmoun tells the tale of a handsome Beiruti hunter who attracted the romantic attentions of the goddess Astarte, who subsequently fell in love with him. He rebuked her affections and Echmoun proceeded to mutilate himself which resulted in his death. Astarte, venerating the young man even more, brought him back to life and transformed him into a god and as one who dies and is perennially reborn.

He subsequently became known as the god of fertility and healing and the site's location, adjacent to an abundant water supply, was most likely chosen to facilitate in ritual ablutions. The custom of the times was to offer the god engraved statues of the names of the sick, and as many of these depict children it is possible that Echmoun was known as the local paediatrician during this period. Many of these marble statues of children are now housed in the National Museum in Beirut. The Greeks later identified Echmoun with the medical arts and the Greek god Asklepios, and a gold plaque uncovered at the temple of a snake curled around a staff survives to this day as a symbol of the medical profession. Although work had commenced at the original temple some three centuries previously, beginning with the rule of King Eshmounazar II, successive civilisations (64BC–AD330) further embellished the complex, with the Romans building a colonnade, ritual basins and a nymphaeum complete with mosaics and with the fountain containing three now weathered

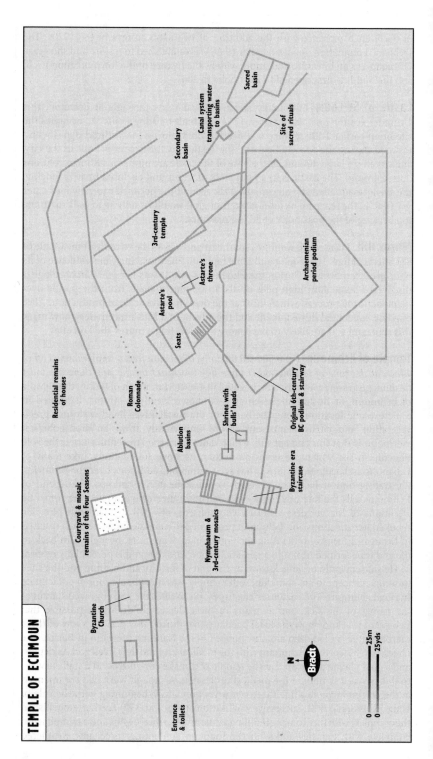

TEMPLE OF ECHMOUN

Sacred basin

Canal system transporting water to basins

Site of sacred rituals

Secondary basin

3rd-century temple

Archaemenian period podium

Astarte's throne

Astarte's pool

Residential remains of houses

Seats

Roman Colonnade

Original 6th-century BC podium & stairway

Shrines with bulls' heads

Ablution basins

Byzantine era staircase

Courtyard & mosaic remains of the Four Seasons

Nymphaeum & 3rd-century mosaics

Byzantine Church

Entrance & toilets

N

Bradt

0 25m
0 25yds

Lebanon has seen a few eccentric visitors to its shores throughout its history, but Lady Hester Stanhope, both as a woman of her time and as a person possessing a charismatic and strong personality, must rank as one of the more unorthodox of travellers. Born into a wealthy aristocratic background to the Earl of Stanhope, she was also the niece of the long-serving British prime minister William Pitt the Younger. Lacking a wife to fulfil the function of social hostess, she resided at 10 Downing Street, performing the duties which would be carried out today by the PM's wife. Lady Hester soon gained a reputation for her social, and sometimes unorthodox, social skills, and became well known in the upper echelons of politics. Shortly after the death of Pitt in 1806, the state granted her a lifetime pension of £1,200 per annum, a tidy sum and equivalent to c£100,000 in today's money. Unable to settle in the now less eccentric and social circles of the PM's residence, she moved briefly to Montagu Square in London, then on to Wales. After her brother died she departed England in 1810, where she embarked on a peripatetic lifestyle. She set off on a long sea voyage with a small entourage of physician, maid and a lover. They travelled to Greece, then Constantinople (then the capital of the Ottoman Empire), and planned to visit Cairo but owing to a shipwreck *en route* they lost all their clothes and were forced to wear Turkish costumes. Hester steadfastly refused to wear a veil and instead donned male clothing. She visited Palmyra in Syria on an Arabian horse and the local Bedouin revered her as the famous Queen Zenobia. By 1818, she had settled in Joun, near Sidon, into a disused monastery with an array of servants. With delusions of grandeur, she reputedly consulted the stars and believed that one day she would be married to a messiah. Yet she could also be a very generous person, ensuring she bought local produce, gave money and clothes to pregnant women and gave generously to the frail and elderly. But she could also spend money like it grew on trees, and eventually the British government stopped her pension to pay off what she owed to her range of debtors; even her servants stole everything she wasn't owing as soon as they knew she couldn't pay them. Hester died a lonely, very poor and disgruntled woman. Her now-dilapidated house is now just a ruinous bundle of rocks and her grave nearby has been plundered so now only the shell of it remains, meaning this site is only for devotees of Lady Hester.

examples of nymphs in the niches. Just in front of the main entrance on the left-hand side are the foundations of a Byzantine church, and a little further along on the same side of the road are some very eroded but still discernible Four Seasons Mosaics which also date from the 3rd century AD. The throne of the heroine herself, Astarte, dates from the later Hellenistic period and is built in Egyptian style. A fine panoramic view of the temple complex can be gained by walking up the Roman stairway opposite the Four Seasons Mosaics to the podium, the largest of the temples on the site built by King Echmounazzar II in the 5th century.

Beaufort Castle (⏱ 24/7) This fortress, known as Qala al-Shakif in Arabic, must rank as the most iconic and lofty structure (over 700m) to Lebanon's turbulent past. Although there is some uncertainty surrounding its history, it was definitely of paramount importance to the Crusaders for halting Arab incursions and during the

17th century, Fakhreddine renovated the castle and occupied it for a while until the Ottomans reclaimed it. More recently, its commanding hilltop position above the Litani River was used by Palestinian *fedayeen* fighters during the early stages of the Lebanese civil war before the Israelis and its proxy militia the South Lebanon Army (SLA) took it over until their withdrawal in May 2000. Today, the castle is empty and at the time of writing history's war machines have been replaced by a gigantic yellow crane and worker portakabins as the fort is undergoing extensive renovation, which is due to be completed towards the latter stages of 2012. At the time of writing the castle is free to visit and the views from its summit are amazing, affording panoramic vistas towards northern Israel, the Golan Heights and the Lebanese town of Arnun below. Be advised, however, that the structure is not, perhaps unsurprisingly given its history, in the best of shape and you need to take extra care when walking around, which is frequently made more precarious by the often high winds felt when walking atop the structure. Just below Beaufort is the **Kalaa Rest House** (*Arnun;* m *03 650 793;* ☼ *12.00–midnight daily*), a pleasant café and eatery which has a nice outdoor seating area with great views for indulging in its menu of *mezze*, fish and burgers. A meal for two should set you back around LBP30,000 with a *nargileh* costing LBP6,000–10,000. It gets very busy in the summer and has a children's play area.

Getting there Beaufort castle is around 9km southeast of the town of Nabatiye, which is easily reached by bus (LBP2,000) or service taxi (LBP5,000) from the bus and taxi station in Sidon. The journey time from Sidon is around 30–45 minutes to Nabatiye, from where you can catch a taxi for the remaining leg of the journey which should set you back between LBP10,000 and LBP20,000 for the return trip, depending upon how long you ask the driver to wait whilst you view the castle, but be prepared for taxi drivers to quote you a return fare of LBP30,000+!

JEZZINE

The predominantly Christian Maronite town of Jezzine, 22km east of Sidon and 40km south from Beirut, takes its name from the Syriac word meaning 'store', suggesting that in antiquity, Jezzine's strategic location functioned as a depot for traders peddling their wares eastwards from the port of Sidon to the Chouf region, the Bekaa Valley, and beyond to Damascus in Syria. Today, Jezzine's 950m altitude and milder climate in an extremely picturesque location overlooking mountains, valleys and pine forests serves as the south's principal summer resort town attracting scores of families to its cooler air, famous 40m-high waterfalls and the quality of its handicrafts. For the foreign visitor, too, Jezzine makes for a very laid-back and pleasant place to visit on either a day trip or as an overnight stay.

GETTING THERE Jezzine is easily reached by the LTC bus which departs daily approximately every 30 minutes from the garage just behind the company's office on Sahat al-Nejmeh. The 50-minute journey costs LBP2,000, and the route is a very pleasant and scenic one. The one-way taxi fare will set you back around LBP30,000 and a service taxi around LBP7,500–9,000. The bus can drop you off at the entrance to the town near the town hall (Serail Building). At the time of writing the last bus back to Sidon was at 20.00, so factor this into your visit if you don't want the extra expense of a taxi.

GETTING AROUND Jezzine is a straightforward town to navigate around. Walking is by far the best and most pleasant method of transport as the main town is really just one long street. Start a tour from the Municipality Building (near Infinity Blue Nightclub and Al-Shallal Restaurant) and continue ahead, which will bring you to the town's other main eateries, shops, the souk and handicraft area:

WHERE TO STAY

Auberge Wehbé (30 rooms) Off the main street (behind Mar Antonios Monastery); 07 780 217, 07 781 009; Mar–Oct only. A spotlessly clean, bright & airy hotel dating back to 1872 & full of character, with comfortable & homely reception area, & a nice terrace with good views over the town. The swimming pool is a nice addition for the summer months. B/fast US$5 extra. **$$**

Rizk Plaza Motel (5 rooms & 4 apartments) General de Gaulle St (close to Jezzine Spring); 07 781 066; m 03 901 990; e contact@rizkplazamotel.com; www.rizkplazamotel.com. Although the décor is a bit dated, this is nonetheless a good, clean hotel representing excellent value for money with all rooms en suite with TV, AC & heating. **$**

WHERE TO EAT AND DRINK, ENTERTAINMENT AND NIGHTLIFE

There is no shortage of options in the town, from fast-food places to more formal dining, but the pick of the crop is undoubtedly those venues overlooking the waterfalls. The following are just a selection of the possibilities.

Al-Shallal Restaurant Opposite Infinity Blue, overlooking the waterfalls; 07 780 067; m 03 513 497, 70 442 444; 11.00–02.00 daily. In a prime location for terrific views of the waterfalls & surrounding mountain vistas, this venue serves decent enough *mezze*, fried & grilled meats & *arak*. **$$$$**

Coin Rouge Town centre, near Rizk Plaza Motel; m 03 120 856; www.coinrougeclub.com; 15.00–late daily; admission US$10 'disco charge', Sat inc free drink. Jezzine's liveliest

venue combines a cosy downstairs pub with live music & DJ on Sat nights in a wonderfully intimate upstairs setting with compact dance floor. **$$**

Infinity Blue Entrance to Jezzine, next to the Municipality Bldg; m 70 587 090, 71 208 092; 22.00–late Thu–Sun; admission US$10, inc free drink. A lively nightclub venue offering karaoke during weekday nights with Arabic pop music, Latin tunes & a Sat-night English & Arabic DJ spinning the discs. **$$**

SHOPPING There are a number of everyday general stores catering to most needs of the visitor, including pharmacies, but by far the best shopping in Jezzine is in the town's small souk; only one street perhaps, but here skilled craftsmen continue to decorate distinctive decorative and utilitarian household items. The two shops reviewed below are something of an institution and turn out quality products a cut above the rest and are definitely worth a look in, even if you have no intention of buying, to see the exquisitely crafted items. However, if ever there was a place to pick up authentic local souvenirs then this is it, and so much more useful than an 'I love Beirut' T-shirt.

Abou Rached Old souk; 07 780 082, 07 780 839; m 03 227 550; 09.00–20.00 daily. A family-run business for over 50 years, Rached fashions handmade daggers, swords & cutlery out of horn & ivory in a variety of colourful designs & will custom-make items on request.
S & S Haddad Manufacturers Old souk; 01 280 353; m 03 683 369; e haddadf@

thisiscyberia.com; 09.00–20.30 daily. Established since 1770, Jezzine's most famous cutlery makers have supplied politicians, popes, ex-French president Jacques Chirac & other world dignitaries with their brightly coloured, handmade cutlery sets adorned with a Phoenix head in a range of colours. A 22-piece cutlery set will set you back from US$443.

OTHER PRACTICALITIES Banks and ATMs proliferate in Jezzine, therefore you will have no problem obtaining cash and changing currency. The town also boasts a couple of decent pharmacies.

✉ **Post office** Ogero Bldg, towards the far end of town just after the Aoun Tex bed linen store; ℡ 07 780 003; ⏰ 08.00–17.00 Mon–Fri, 08.00–13.30 Sat

WHAT TO SEE AND DO Jezzine's biggest pull is its more palatable climate in summer and its attractive 40m-high waterfalls which cascade down the mountainside, lending the area a very picturesque air following the winter rains. Although at the time of writing it was closed, the Arab–oriental-style **Farid Serhal Palace** has a very ornamental interior and will be well worth a visit when it once again opens to the public. The **Old Serail** or Municipality Building at the entrance to the town is also worth a look. The building dates from 1898 and has an interesting façade with arched doorways and wooden shuttered windows. Nestled deep in the valley beneath the town is **Fakhreddine's Cave**, a place of domed refuge for Fakhreddine's father Qurquma, who died there, and Fakhreddine himself who was eventually discovered and executed in Istanbul. This is not an easy site to visit, however, and really requires elementary climbing equipment and the services of a local guide. Try contacting the **Speleo Club of Lebanon** (*Speleo Club Du Liban;* m *71 727 929;* e *info@speleoliban. org; www.speleoliban.org*), who should be able to help with putting you in touch with a local guide. If all that sounds like too much hard work you could always seek out the **Karam Winery** (*Jezzine;* m *03 373 703;* e *info@karamwinery.com; www.karamwinery. com;* ⏰ *spring/summer 10.00–17.00 daily; call in advance for lunch & tasting sessions*), south Lebanon's first commercial vineyard producing some 55,000 bottles of red and white wine annually, 50% of which is destined for export. The tipple is also available all over Jezzine, with the Coin Rouge club above stocking a large range.

MLEETA

Located 82km from Beirut and around 27km southeast of Sidon, Mleeta was formerly just one of many remote and scenic, but strategically important, hilltop positions fought over by Israel and Hezbollah. Since 2010, however, this former stronghold of the resistance and theatre of conflict has hit the media headlines after being transformed into what some have called Hezbollah's Disneyland.

GETTING THERE At the time of writing, Mleeta was not the easiest of places to visit from a public transportation point of view, as it was not on any main bus or taxi route. The Mleeta website www.mleeta.com has a couple of suggested routes from Beirut and Sidon and another if coming from the Syrian border crossing at Masnaa which you could follow. From Sidon the journey time is a little over 45 minutes by taxi and expect to be quoted somewhere between LBP30,000 and LBP50,000 by drivers for a return trip. If travelling from Beirut by taxi, don't be surprised to be quoted a return fare of at least LBP150,000.

WHAT TO SEE
Where the Land Speaks to the Heavens: A Tourist Landmark about the Resistance (*Iklim al Tuffah, Jarjou-Ayn-Boswar Rd;* m *70 076 060;* e *info@mleeta. com; www.mleeta.com;* ⏰ *10.00–20.00 daily; admission LBP2,000. Informative free maps, containing a suggested walking route around the complex with background information on the reverse side, are available at the entrance*) As an in-situ open-air

and subterranean museum of war, the 60,000m² complex at Mleeta, which opened in May 2010 to coincide with the tenth anniversary of Israel's military withdrawal from Lebanon, must rank as one of the most unique and extraordinary shrines to military endeavour in the world. Some two years in the making, using the skills of 50 engineers and at an estimated cost of US$4 million, the site is a very graphic account of the conflicts between Israel and Hezbollah from 1982 to 2006. Although the site already has a large cafeteria, parking for over 200 vehicles and a gift shop selling Hezbollah DVDs, T-shirts and books, further expansion is planned including a Téléférique linking Mleeta with the former Israeli outpost of Sujud, along with hotels and restaurants to put this site firmly on the theme park map. The site has proved very popular so far, and within the first six months of opening some 700,000 visitors have viewed the complex, both Lebanese and foreign. Except for the red-coloured Mleeta emblem of a sparrowhawk in flight, a bird which refuses to accept defeat, there are few insights into the defining ideology and philosophy of the resistance with the site's principal aim of showcasing the spoils of war.

The ideal starting point for the visitor is to view the two short films which document the site's construction, followed by a short history of the conflict between Israel and Hezbollah, before proceeding to the 350m² Exhibition Hall to view captured Israeli war relics from 1982 to 2006, which includes uniforms, aircraft drones, medical supplies and an interesting breakdown of the Israeli military command structure. Outside the hall is the crater-like 3,000m² The Abyss, which showcases the 'Zionist enemy defeat' in the form of a captured Israeli Merkava tank with its gun turret in a twist, together with all manner of shells and rockets imbued with geometric and symbolic meanings. Following The Pathway from The Abyss takes you through a maze of former resistance positions; lifelike mannequins of Hezbollah fighters in battle readiness, together with the different fighting units and roles of the resistance including a field hospital and rocket launch sites. The 200m-long The Cave, built over a three-year period with a careful disposal of debris to avoid the attentions of Israeli surveillance, finally became home to over 7,000 resistance guerillas. Above ground, the final landmark, The Hill, at over 1,000m above sea level, gives commanding views over the mountains and valleys and former Israeli positions.

TYRE (SOUR)

Once dubbed the 'Queen of the Seas' for its mercantile and seafaring activities, Tyre was previously a flourishing commercial centre for international trade and appears in the classical writings of Herodotus and Homer. Some 80km from Beirut, and a little over 40km from Sidon, Tyre today evokes a battered and slightly melancholic feel with very few traces left of its once illustrious past. As the last major town before the Israeli border, Tyre's more recent and less salubrious past has tended to be dominated, like Sidon, by the intermittent Israel–Hezbollah conflict, but the city also suffered greatly during the civil war years. As an overwhelmingly Shi'ite town Tyre wears its heart on its sleeve, with effigies of the resistance movement and shops selling Hezbollah souvenirs and photos of its leader Hassan Nasrallah ubiquitous. Although economically less developed and visited than other areas of the country, Tyre's wealth for the visitor today lies in its still traditional and functioning fishing port, its lively and engaging souk area and its 1984 UNESCO-designated World Heritage Site of Roman-era architecture. During the summer months, an international arts and music festival is held within the environs of these Roman ruins (see page 256).

8

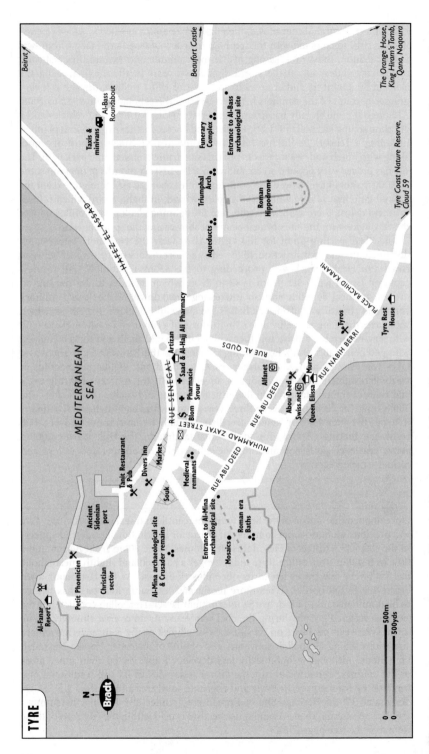

TYRE

MEDITERRANEAN
SEA

N
Bradt

Beirut

Beaufort Castle

Al-Bass
Roundabout

Taxis &
minivans

HAFEZ-EL-ASSAD

Funerary
Complex

Entrance to Al-Bass
archaeological site

Triumphal
Arch

Roman
Hippodrome

Aqueducts

The Orange House,
King Hiram's Tomb,
Qana, Naqoura

Tyre Coast Nature Reserve,
Cloud 59

Artizan

Saad & Al-Hajj Ali Pharmacy

RUE SENEGAL

Pharmacie
Srour

Blom

Tanit Restaurant
& Pub

Divers Inn

Market

MUHAMMAD ZAYAT STREET

Souk

Medieval
remnants

RUE AL QUDS

RUE ABU DEED

Alfanet

Abou Deed

Swiss.net

Queen Elissa

Murex

RUE NABIH BERRI

Tyros

PLACE RACHID KARAMI

Tyre Rest
House

RUE ABU DEED

Entrance to Al-Mina
archaeological site

Mosaics

Roman era
Baths

Al-Mina archaeological site
& Crusader remains

Christian
sector

Ancient
Sidonian port

Petit Phoenicien

Al-Fanar
Resort

0   500m
0   500yds

250

HISTORY Although the Greek historian Herodotus dates settlement at Tyre back to 2750BC, with further evidence of Neolithic-era occupation from 5000BC, it wasn't until the 10th century BC that the city began to experience the zenith of its power and wealth. Tyre was the largest and most successful city during the Phoenician era and under its most important leader, King Hiram, the city expanded both geographically and economically. Formerly consisting of an island and mainland settlement, Hiram connected the two areas and added a second port to take advantage of changing wind conditions. But it would take a chance discovery, according to legend, to usher in the golden age of Tyrian prosperity. According to mythology, Tyre's god Melqart was walking along the beach one day with Tyrus, a nymph, whose affections he coveted, when her dog chewed on a mollusc, turning the mutt's mouth purple. Desiring a dress of the same colour, Tyrus requested the garment be made for her or she would not see Melqart again. Thus the high-maintenance nymph's request was granted and so was born the manufacture of Tyre's greatest product, which became revered by rich and royal alike. But economic prosperity had a flip side, and as the ancient Greek geographer Strabo pointed out: 'the great number of dye works renders the city unpleasant as a place of residence, but the superior skill of these people in the practice of this art is the source of its wealth.'

Tyrian trade of luxury and utilitarian goods, in line with their skills in shipbuilding, expanded throughout the Mediterranean and in 814BC, Phoenician princess Dido sailed west and founded Carthage. Towards the end of the 7th century BC, the Babylonian king Nebuchadnezzar besieged the city for 13 years, but was unable to conquer it on account of its strong fortifications. With the fall of the Babylonians the Persians ushered in a period of stability and co-operation from around 539BC, with the Tyrians assisting the Persian navy with ships and personnel during their wars with the Greeks. But the city suffered a major setback to its commercial strength in 332BC when Alexander the Great, fresh from his success over Darius at the Battle of Issus, laid siege to the city for seven months, the most protracted battle in his short but illustrious military career, finally breaking the city's staunch resistance and massacring and enslaving Tyre's 30,000 inhabitants as the city came under Hellenistic rule, absorbing and adopting Greek culture and influences. The onset of Roman rule in 64BC was a period of remarkable peace and prosperity for Tyre, the so-called Pax Romana, with Tyre's citizens granted parity with Rome's own subjects under the law, whilst the Byzantine era saw Tyre become one of the first cities to welcome Christianity to its shores. A change of master doesn't necessarily mean a change in fortune, and when the Arab dynasties arrived around AD634, they met with no resistance from Tyre's citizens and the port was transformed into a naval base for the Arab fleet. The Middle Ages, however, did bring a marked change of fortune to the city, as the Crusader knights from Europe forced Tyre's leaders to pay heavy tributes and besieged the city for months until ousted by the Mamluks in 1291, who proceeded to destroy the city to prevent the Franks' return. Tyre then sunk into relative obscurity and came under the banner of the Ottoman Empire from the 16th century, before finally becoming part of the newly formed Lebanese Republic after the end of World War I.

GETTING THERE From Beirut's Cola station you can catch a bus or minivan to Tyre for LBP4,000–5,000 which, depending on traffic, will take on average 1½ hours. Expect to pay about LBP10,000 for a service taxi and LBP50,000 for a taxi from Cola. If coming from Sidon, an LTC bus leaves from near Sahat al-Nejmeh every 20 minutes and will cost LBP2,000 for a journey time of up to 1½ hours, arriving at the Al-Bass Roundabout and transport hub, which is a five–ten-minute walk from the Al-Bass archaeological site. Taxis (around LBP25,000) and service taxis (around LBP5,000) also serve the route south from Sidon to Tyre. If you are considering making the journey north to Tripoli from Tyre after visiting the south there were no service taxis or direct buses at the time of research but taxis do ply this route and the cost at the time of research was in the region of LBP150,000 for the one way fare.

GETTING AROUND Tyre is eminently walkable with the main sites, souks, port and utilities all quite close together, though some may want to take a short service taxi (LBP2,000) to the inland Al-Bass archaeological site if coming from the coast. Otherwise, it's about a 20–30-minute walk to the ruins.

⌂ WHERE TO STAY

⌂ **Murex Hotel** (29 rooms & 10 apartments) Nabih Berri Bd; ✆ 07 347 111; e info@murex-hotel.com; www.murex-hotel.com. Recently renovated to a high standard, this is an ultra-modern hotel situated right on the Corniche with great sea views & boasting all the comforts of home. Also has good business & conference facilities. **$$$$**

⌂ **Tyre Rest House Hotel & Resort** (62 rooms & suites) Sea Rd; ✆ 07 742 000, 07 740 677/8; m 03 356 663; e info@resthouse-tyr.com.lb; www.resthouse-tyr.com.lb. Although character is largely absent from this establishment, it is nevertheless Tyre's most salubrious option with the majority of rooms having sea views together with all the refinements you would expect from a top-end hotel. The hotel also benefits from its own exclusive beach, swimming pool, health & massage facilities. **$$$$**

⌂ **Queen Elissa** (28 rooms & suites) Nabih Berri Bd; ✆ 07 344 443/4, m 70 111 407; e info@queenelissahotel.com; www.queenelissahotel.com. Nice seafront location with fine, clean rooms with all the modern refinements you would expect for the price. **$$$**

⌂ **Al-Fanar Resort** (12 rooms) Rachid Nakhle St (next to the lighthouse); ✆ 07 741 111;

m 03 665 016; e info@alfanarresort.com; www.alfanarresort.com. Great seafront location in a lovely, character-filled & centuries-old building. Rooms are fairly basic, but clean, & the feeling is one of a cosy, cottage-like atmosphere. There is a large open-plan lounge area, outdoor space over the sea for relaxing & dining. All rooms have AC & en-suite bathrooms. 10 of the 12 rooms have sea views. The hotel's Cave Club downstairs is regularly open for drinking & dance nights enlivening an otherwise quiet, but excellent hotel. B/fast inc. **$$**

⌂ **Artizan Hotel** (17 rooms) Senegal St; ✆ 07 346 739; m 03 964 927; e info@artizanhotel.com; www.artizanhotel.com. A clean, but unremarkable hotel, with AC & TV in all rooms. Decently located for shops & amenities but really only a place if there is no room at the inn elsewhere. B/fast is an extra US$5. **$**

⌂ **The Orange House** (3 rooms) Mansoureh Village, Tyre-Naqoura Main Rd; ✆ 07 320 063; m 03 383 080; e orangehouseproject@gmail.com; www.orangehouseproject.com. They may only have 3 rooms, but this is a delightful little place for those interested in ecotourism & conservation or just looking for something a little different from more mainstream lodging options (see box opposite). **$**

✕ WHERE TO EAT AND DRINK

✕ **Al-Fanar Restaurant** Rachid Nakhleh St (next to the lighthouse); ✆ 07 740 111; ⏲ 12.00–late daily. Has a decent enough fresh fish & mezze menu but the prices are a little steep. The beach location of this hotel & restaurant is its greatest asset. **$$$$$**

✕ **Tyros Restaurant** Nabbi Berri Bd; ✆ 07 741 027; m 03 048 954; ⏲ 12.00–midnight daily. A very roomy restaurant with a varied fish & mezze menu which is very popular with local families. Live Arabic music every Sat night. It's hard to miss its wood-panelled exterior. A nice, friendly eatery. **$$$$$**

THE ORANGE HOUSE PROJECT

'My little peace of heaven' is how Mona Khalil describes her restored family home and ecotourism venture. Having left Lebanon for the Netherlands in 1975 after the onset of the country's civil war, she returned in 1999, with the aim of resettling in the abandoned family beach home. In memory of the country where she had spent over 20 years, the house was repainted orange and called, unsurprisingly, The Orange House. Located in the village of Mansoureh, 14km south of Tyre at Naqoura, close to the border with Israel, the renovated solar-powered residence, surrounded by banana groves, citrus plantations and a garden brimming over with orange trees and pretty flowers in beds and pots, is shared with Mona's friend and fellow environmental enthusiast Habiba Fayed, five goats, a black cat, two dogs and an African grey parrot. Whilst out walking one evening on the beach, a chance sighting of a turtle *en route* to lay her eggs also gave birth to Mona's passion and 'dream' to preserve and protect the turtles, their eggs and new hatchlings, which was put into action in 2000. There are two species of sea turtle which lay their eggs on Lebanon's coastline: the green turtle (*Chelonia mydas*) and the loggerhead (*Caretta caretta*), both of which are endangered species but can have a lifespan up to 100 years and typically take between 30 and 50 years to reach maturity. Fortunately, the female leaves traces of her tracks in the sand, so it is relatively easy to locate where the eggs have been laid and camouflaged. Together, Mona and Habiba cordon off the area with 1m² wire mesh to protect them from marauding predators such as crabs, dogs and foxes. Following some 45–55 days of incubation, depending on the warmth of the sand, the eggs hatch and the young make their way down the beach to the sea to begin their orphan life. Mona and Habiba's tasks also include ensuring the beaches are kept clean and educating the local people about the turtles and the importance of correct waste disposal, so vital to the environment and the turtles themselves. In order to continue funding the project, the women decided to provide bed-and-breakfast accommodation where guests can not only enjoy the beauty and tranquillity of the house, including a homemade breakfast made from their own garden produce, and beach area, but can also help out with keeping the beach clean and assisting with new hatchlings.

✗ **Petit Phoenician** Port; ☏ 07 741 562; ⏰ 12.00–midnight daily. The best location in the city for fish meals. This well-established & intimate, no-frills restaurant is located right on the port where you can watch fishermen bringing in their catch & mending their nets. Delicious fish *kibbeh*, crab, shrimps & a host of the day's catches are served along with wine from the Bekaa Valley, Almaza beer & spirits. $$$$
✗ **Tanit Restaurant & Pub** Port; ☏ 07 347 539; m 03 308 928; ⏰ 10.00–midnight daily. Small, intimate eatery with only 4 tables & well-stocked bar area, with vaulted ceiling & the walls adorned with old black-&-white photos of

Tyre & guns & swords. This atmospheric restaurant serves an eclectic range of seafood, mixed grills & stir-fry dishes. Gets quite lively in the evenings & at weekends. Many off-duty UNIFIL staff patronise this restaurant & are a useful source of information on travel south of Tyre & the overall security situation in this region. $$$$
✗ **Divers Inn Restaurant & Pub** port; m 03 359 687, 03 740 987; ⏰ 10.00–late daily. Run by active diver Nazih, this is a great place for delicious, locally caught fish dishes, *mezze* & paella. Its cellar-like appearance with vaulted stone roof & walls has a great atmosphere & screens live football matches. Serves beer,

whisky & wine. A *nargileh* costs around LBP7,000. **$$$**

✗ Abou Deed Abou Deed St; ☎ 07 349 808, 07 740 808; m 03 234 630; ⏱ 08.00–midnight

daily. Family-run & friendly Lebanese restaurant & take–away, serving tasty food in cheerful & pleasant surroundings. **$$**

ENTERTAINMENT AND NIGHTLIFE Despite its predominantly Shi'ite population, alcohol is readily available in the city and during the summer months Tyre's beaches come alive with late-night beach parties, with many also serving delicious food. The pick of the current crop is **Cloud 59** (m *03 517 996, 03 238 837;* ⏱ *09.00–late daily*). The bar of the **Al-Fanar Hotel** (☎ *07 740 111;* ⏱ *12.00–late daily*) is also a popular nightspot, with its cellar-like vaulted pub serving alcohol until the early hours.

SHOPPING Despite its once illustrious trade in purple-dyed garments worn by the rich and royal alike, Tyre's shopping options are today much more anodyne and this is not really the place to undertake any serious souvenir hunting. The city's numerous shops and stores, however, do cater for most visitors' day-to-day needs and you will have no problem buying food, cosmetics and other toiletries or any additional or replacement items of clothing you may require. The busy souk area is well worth a browse for handicrafts but can't compete with the offerings, or atmosphere, of the souks at Sidon and Tripoli. Tyre is, however, one of the best town's in Lebanon to purchase Hezbollah souvenirs (the other is Mleeta, see page 248). Whether you want a yellow T-shirt emblazoned with the Party of God's logo, a DVD, framed portraits of Secretary General Sayyed Hassan Nasrallah or other ornamental items, you are in the right place.

OTHER PRACTICALITIES

🖥 Alfanet Al-Quds St (2min walk from Abou Deed Restaurant); ☎ 07 347 047; e awad54@ hotmail.com; ⏱ 10.00–midnight daily. Internet access LBP1,500/hr.

$ Blom Bank Senegal St; ☎ 07 740 900; ⏱ 08.00–17.00 Mon–Fri, 08.00–12.00 Sat. Has 2 24/7 ATMs.

✉ Post office Senegal St; ☎ 07 740 565; ⏱ 08.00–17.00 Mon–Fri, 08.00–13.30 Sat

✚ Saad & Al-Hajj Ali Pharmacy Senegal St; ☎ 07 344 227; m 03 165 653; ⏱ 08.00–23.00 daily. A friendly & well-stocked pharmacy.

🖥 Swiss.net Al Quds St (behind Abou Deed Restaurant); m 03 256 978, 70 122 720; ⏱ 09.00–midnight daily. A good place to log on & check your email. Internet access LBP1,000/30mins, LBP1,500/hr.

WHAT TO SEE AND DO Tyre's port, like Sidon's, remains a hive of activity and is even more atmospheric with colourful boats, mounds of nets dotting the harbourside and plenty of seafood dining right on the edge of the harbour. Here you can watch fishermen mending their nets, fashioning a new craft and repairing an old one, drinking tea, playing cards and smoking a *nargileh*, lending the whole area a lovely old-world charm. The city's souks, however, although busy and bustling and engaging enough, don't quite evoke the same anachronistic feel of those in Sidon though the maze of alleyways of the Christian district with their old traditional houses and churches are certainly worth a look. Lebanon's southernmost city's main draw is in its excellent collection of Roman-era artefacts and ruins at the Al-Mina and Al-Bass sites.

Roman archaeological sites Tyre's UNESCO-listed Roman archaeological legacy is spread over a couple of different sites which have been extensively excavated over the course of half a century by Lebanon's Directorate of Antiquities. They are generally remarkably well preserved and give an excellent insight into the Roman and Byzantine period of Tyre's history. The Al-Bass ruins are the most extensive and imposing of the two main sites. At the time of writing the sites didn't have any detailed Ministry of Tourism pamphlets and like at many other of Lebanon's sites it is often best to pick up everything you will need for your visit from their main Hamra office in Beirut (see page 99).

Al-Mina site (✎ *07 740 115;* ⏱ *summer 08.00–20.00 daily, winter 08.00–17.00 daily; admission: adults LBP6,000, children over 10 years LBP3,000, children under 10 years free*) Also known as the Al-Medina or city ruins to locals, this site occupies a picturesque location leading onto the coastline on what was once the Phoenician island settlement. A pleasant ten-minute walk along the Corniche if coming from the Al-Fanar Hotel, the main entrance is dominated by the 170m-long Mosaic Road flanked by columns and once covered in Byzantine mosaic paving, some of which can still be seen. The smaller road to the right, containing some 26 columns tapering away to the coastline, sits adjacent to the 1st-century sporting arena, a large rectangular space with rows of stepped seating able to accommodate 2,000 spectators who would once have enjoyed the spectacles of boxing and wrestling. Across the main Mosaic Road towards the coast is a series of nine columns denoting the Palestra, a 30m^2 area dating back to the 2nd century AD, which appears to have had a number of functions over the years, ranging from a sporting venue, a marketplace and, following the 6th century AD earthquake, may have been used as a purple-dye factory. As was customary, the bathing areas are adjacent to the Palestra with extensive remains of these 2nd- and 3rd-century AD Roman baths and their hypocaust clay discs, which supported the marble floor, allowing hot air to circulate and provide underfloor heating. A couple of minutes' walk to the north of Al-Mina is the Crusader Cathedral. More than a little imagination is required to imagine this site in its heyday. This 12th-century cathedral offers up little of its history, save for a wall and a few fallen granite columns strewn around the site, which in parts is often eclipsed by the amount of domestic rubbish dumped around the area. Built on a much earlier site dedicated to Tyre's Phoenician god Melqart, during the Crusader period the cathedral was the setting for the coronation of the Kings of Jerusalem and archaeological digging here has revealed a system of earlier Roman and Byzantine roads beneath the shrine.

Al-Bass site (✎ *07 740 530;* ⏱ *summer 08.00–19.00 daily, winter 08-00–18.00 daily; admission: adults LBP6,000, children over 10 years LBP3,500, children under 10 years free*) The most grandiose of Tyre's Roman past, this second site covers a much larger area than the Al-Mina ruins with a cornucopia of archaeological finds spanning the 2nd to 4th centuries AD. Entering the site from the east–west Byzantine Road is a vast necropolis revealing an array of ornately decorated sarcophagi in marble and stone, followed further ahead by a 6th-century funerary chapel with patterned marble flooring within its compact courtyard. Undoubtedly one of the two main highlights of the Al-Bass site is the 2nd-century Triumphal Arch, probably built during the reign of the emperor Hadrian and marking the point at which the Byzantine Road becomes the older, Roman Road. At 20m high, the arch has been beautifully restored by the Directorate of Antiquities, which had suffered almost total destruction during the devastating earthquake of AD551. Just along the Roman Road beyond the arch are the remains of an aqueduct, which once supplied water from the Ras al-Ain Springs, 6km away to the south.

To the left of the aqueduct is Al-Bass's other key highlight, the unmissable U-shaped Hippodrome. Built during the 2nd century AD and measuring 480m by 160m, it is the largest and best preserved in the world, having once staged spectacular chariot races and other sporting events with the grandstand able to seat more than 30,000 spectators. Beneath the grandstand, still walkable, was a marketplace and shops. Today, the Hippodrome plays host to less death-defying activities in the form of a summer festival (see page 256).

Tyre Coast Nature Reserve (↘ *07 351 341;* m *03 483 331;* e *tcnr98@hotmail. com; www.moe.gov.lb;* ⊕ *08.00–17.00 Mon–Sat, closed Sun unless visitors call ahead; admission free, though voluntary donations to the reserve of around LBP10,000 per group of 3 people*) Covering an area of some 380ha and containing the largest sandy beach in the country, the reserve was founded in 1998, and contains a whole gamut of flora and fauna including birdlife and turtles. The activities on offer here include birdwatching, cycling, swimming and snorkelling, turtle watching and kayaking. The area also comprises the Ras al-Ain Springs, about 6km south of the city, which have provided irrigation and drinking water for the city since Phoenician times.

Festivals in the south

Ashura This annual Shi'ite festival of remembrance in Nabatiye is of overriding religious importance to this sect, which commemorates the martyrdom of the Prophet Muhammad's grandson Hussein who was slain at the Battle of Karbala, southern Iraq, in AD680. Spread over nine days, it is quite unlike any 'festival' you will experience anywhere in Lebanon (perhaps the world), with processions of sadness which build to a crescendo on the tenth day of Muharram, the actual date Hussein died, accompanied by women screaming and men and children chanting whilst lacerating themselves with razors, knives and swords drawing blood, re-enacting the pain and suffering of the Third *imam* Hussein. The best place to see this is in Nabatiye, an unremarkable, sprawling and nondescript town which is overwhelmingly Shi'ite. As the date is calculated according to the Muslim lunar calendar based on an actual sighting of the New Moon, it is a moveable feast, so to speak, but in 2011 was due on or around 5 December and in 2012, around 10–11 days earlier. Given the passion and grief attached to the occasion, it may be sensible to seek out the services of a trusted guide if you wish to attend, and to be sensitive by wearing conservative attire. From Sidon's transport hub at Sahat al-Nejmeh, buses travel regularly to Nabitiye and cost LBP2,000, taking around 30–45 minutes while the taxi fare is around LBP5,000.

Tyre and South Festival (↘ *01 791 140, 01 791 252; www.tyrefestival.com*) First held in 1996, this annual festival of performing arts takes place during July and August within the environs of the spectacular Hippodrome at the Al-Bass site, and showcases a range of local and international artists, dancers, musicians, singers, poets, puppetry and theatrical performances. The festival's 2010 lineup included a colourful collection of 46 dancers, poetry readings and singers from the Gulf. Tickets can be obtained locally from the Tyre Rest House Hotel and Resort (see page 252), or from any branch of Virgin Megastore (see page 115). See the festival website for details of the year's upcoming performances.

AROUND TYRE

KING HIRAM'S TOMB Although not one of Lebanon's most illustrious sites, King Hiram's Tomb or Qabr Hiram in Arabic, is still worth a quick look. Located 6km southeast of Tyre on the road to Qana, the limestone sarcophagus, unfortunately a little daubed with some 20th-century graffiti additions, is subject to some academic debate but often attributed to Hiram, Tyre's most prominent king, famous for his assistance in building King Solomon's Temple in Jerusalem during his 34-year reign. The tomb itself is not much more than a series of stone blocks, reaching a height of 6m, and is part of a larger excavated area which has unearthed Roman and Byzantine tombs. During his excavations in the 19th century, the French philosopher and writer Ernest Renan (1823–92) discovered the remains of an earlier stairway and chamber beneath the tomb (inaccessible), but its presence continues to remain a mystery. The tomb is about 20 minutes by car on the right-hand side of the road *en route* to Qana from Tyre, and there is a Ministry of Tourism sign for 'Tombe de Hiram' just before the structure.

QANA This small, mainly Shi'ite town of around 10,000 people is a further 8km along the road from the King Hiram's Tomb and is where, according to the Gospel of St John, Jesus reputedly performed his first miracle, turning water into wine at a local wedding ceremony. Although the authenticity of the claim has been the subject of ongoing debate (some scholars have advocated that in fact it was in the town of Kafar Qana near Nazareth in Israel), Lebanon's claim appears to be reinforced by the ecclesiastical 4th-century historian Eusebius, which in turn is backed up by the 3rd-century writings of St Jerome. The site of the alleged miracle, recently restored by the Ministry of Tourism, is well worth a visit (*Qana Grotto, 1km from the town of Qana;* ⊕ *08.00–19.00 daily; admission: adults LBP4,000, children LBP2,000, children under 10 years free; a small gift shop sells postcards & souvenirs & there is ample free parking outside the entrance*), and contains a bas-relief of Jesus and the Apostles and other carvings, ancient stone water basins and a cave with a wooden cross leaning beside the entrance which is still visited by Christian pilgrims each Christmas. More recently, Qana has come to be associated with a couple of less palatable religious associations, specifically the conflicts between Israel and Hezbollah. During the former's Operation Grapes of Wrath in 1996 against the Shi'ite resistance, Israel launched relentless shelling on the Fujian UNIFIL compound where refugees were sheltering from the conflict. The continuous 17-minute bombardment killed 106 civilians and wounded many others. Subsequent investigations revealed that the attack was most likely a deliberate one. The date of the genocide, 18 April, is now an annual day of mourning and remembrance in Lebanon. There is a monument and a series of photographs near the UN base that can be viewed. A decade later, during the 2006 July War between Israel and Hezbollah, 28 civilians were killed, mostly children, in nighttime air attacks by the Jewish state and a small and very poignant graveyard is a shrine to those who died.

Bradt Travel Guides

www.bradtguides.com

Africa

Access Africa: Safaris for People	
with Limited Mobility	£16.99
Africa Overland	£16.99
Algeria	£15.99
Angola	£17.99
Botswana	£16.99
Burkina Faso	£17.99
Cameroon	£15.99
Cape Verde	£15.99
Congo	£15.99
Eritrea	£15.99
Ethiopia	£16.99
Ghana	£15.99
Kenya Highlights	£15.99
Madagascar	£16.99
Malawi	£15.99
Mali	£14.99
Mauritius, Rodrigues &	
Réunion	£15.99
Mozambique	£15.99
Namibia	£15.99
Niger	£14.99
Nigeria	£17.99
North Africa: Roman Coast	£15.99
Rwanda	£15.99
São Tomé & Príncipe	£14.99
Seychelles	£14.99
Sierra Leone	£16.99
South Africa Highlights	£15.99
Sudan	£15.99
Tanzania, Northern	£14.99
Tanzania	£17.99
Uganda	£16.99
Zambia	£18.99
Zanzibar	£14.99
Zimbabwe	£15.99

The Americas and the Caribbean

Alaska	£15.99
Amazon Highlights	£15.99
Argentina	£16.99
Bahia	£14.99
Cayman Islands	£14.99
Colombia	£17.99
Dominica	£15.99
Grenada, Carriacou &	
Petite Martinique	£14.99
Guyana	£15.99
Nova Scotia	£14.99
Panama	£14.99
Paraguay	£15.99
Turks & Caicos Islands	£14.99
Uruguay	£15.99
USA by Rail	£14.99
Venezuela	£16.99
Yukon	£14.99

British Isles

Britain from the Rails	£14.99
Bus-Pass Britain	£15.99

Eccentric Britain	£15.99
Eccentric Cambrige	£9.99
Eccentric London	£13.99
Eccentric Oxford	£9.99
Sacred Britain	£16.99
Slow: Cotswolds	£14.99
Slow: Devon & Exmoor	£14.99
Slow: Norfolk & Suffolk	£14.99
Slow: North Yorkshire	£14.99
Slow: Sussex & South	
Downs National Park	£14.99

Europe

Abruzzo	£14.99
Albania	£15.99
Azores	£14.99
Baltic Cities	£14.99
Belarus	£15.99
Bosnia & Herzegovina	£14.99
Bratislava	£9.99
Budapest	£9.99
Cork	£6.99
Croatia	£13.99
Cross-Channel France:	
Nord-Pas de Calais	£13.99
Cyprus see North Cyprus	
Dresden	£7.99
Estonia	£14.99
Faroe Islands	£15.99
Georgia	£15.99
Greece: The Peloponnese	£14.99
Helsinki	£7.99
Hungary	£15.99
Iceland	£15.99
Kosovo	£15.99
Lapland	£15.99
Latvia	£13.99
Lille	£9.99
Lithuania	£14.99
Luxembourg	£13.99
Macedonia	£15.99
Malta & Gozo	£12.99
Montenegro	£14.99
North Cyprus	£13.99
Riga	£6.99
Serbia	£15.99
Slovakia	£14.99
Slovenia	£13.99
Spitsbergen	£16.99
Switzerland Without	
a Car	£14.99
Transylvania	£14.99
Ukraine	£15.99
Zagreb	£6.99

Middle East, Asia and Australasia

Armenia	£15.99
Bangladesh	£15.99
Borneo	£17.99
Eastern Turkey	£16.99
Georgia	£15.99
Iran	£15.99
Iraq: Then & Now	£15.99
Israel	£15.99
Kazakhstan	£16.99
Kyrgyzstan	£16.99
Lake Baikal	£15.99
Lebanon	£15.99
Maldives	£15.99
Mongolia	£16.99
North Korea	£14.99
Oman	£15.99
Palestine	£15.99
Shangri-La:	
A Travel Guide to the	
Himalayan Dream	£14.99
Sri Lanka	£15.99
Syria	£15.99
Taiwan	£16.99
Tibet	£13.99
Yemen	£14.99

Wildlife

Antarctica: Guide to the	
Wildlife	£15.99
Arctic: Guide to Coastal	
Wildlife	£15.99
Australian Wildlife	£14.99
Central & Eastern	
European Wildlife	£15.99
Chinese Wildlife	£16.99
East African Wildlife	£19.99
Galápagos Wildlife	£16.99
Madagascar Wildlife	£16.99
New Zealand Wildlife	£14.99
North Atlantic Wildlife	£16.99
Pantanal Wildlife	£16.99
Peruvian Wildlife	£15.99
Southern African Wildlife	£19.99
Sri Lankan Wildlife	£15.99

Pictorials and other guides

100 Alien Invaders	£16.99
100 Animals to See	
Before They Die	£16.99
100 Bizarre Animals	£16.99
Eccentric Australia	£12.99
Northern Lights	£6.99
Tips on Tipping	£6.99
Wildlife and Conservation	
Volunteering: The	
Complete Guide	£13.99

Wanderlust
READERS'
TRAVEL
AWARDS
2011
TOP GUIDEBOOK SERIES

Appendix 1

LANGUAGE

Arabic is the official language in Lebanon but the amount you will need to speak whilst in the country will very much depend on the type of trip you are taking. If you are spending just a few days in Beirut or on a week-long organised tour, then you will most likely be able to get by with just a few words such as those in *Lebanon Essentials* printed on the inside front cover of this book as many people speak English in the capital. If you are planning on more extensive or independent travel to Lebanon which will bring you into closer contact with the locals, then a more extensive vocabulary will be both practically beneficial and will win you many friends along the way, as it is a well-known and true cliché that Arabs really do appreciate foreigners' attempts to communicate in their language. If arriving on business English is widely spoken in commercial circles, but once again a pidgin command of Arabic will do you no harm in establishing a rapport. French is also widely utilised, especially in east Beirut and in many parts of the Mount Lebanon region, a hangover from colonial rule, and in the sections below is included alongside the Arabic words and phrases for a more comprehensive vocabulary and to help you negotiate your way in most linguistic situations. In some cases there is more than one way to say the same thing, and this is indicated by the forward slash in the relevant entry. For those with a desire or need to go beyond the basics, the Arabic alphabet is given below with a rough guide to pronunciation. *Appendix 3* details some further reading on the Arabic language and I would recommend the Levantine Arabic book and CD package for anyone wanting to delve more deeply into the details of the spoken Arabic in the region.

THE ARABIC ALPHABET

Final	Medial	Initial	Alone	Transliteration	Pronunciation
ـا	ـا	ا	ا	aa	as in 'after'
ـب	ـبـ	بـ	ب	b	as in 'bus'
ـت	ـتـ	تـ	ت	t	as in 'till'
ـث	ـثـ	ثـ	ث	th	as in 'thin', sometimes 't' or 's'
ـج	ـجـ	جـ	ج	j	as in 'John'
ـح	ـحـ	حـ	ح	H	strong heavy sigh
ـخ	ـخـ	خـ	خ	kh	similar to 'ch' in Scottish 'loch'
ـد	ـد	د	د	d	as in 'den'
ـذ	ـذ	ذ	ذ	dh	as in 'that'
ـر	ـر	ر	ر	r	as in a trilled or rolled 'red'
ـز	ـز	ز	ز	z	as in 'zero'
ـس	ـسـ	سـ	س	s	as in a hard 'sit'
ـش	ـشـ	شـ	ش	sh	as in a strong 'shut'
ـص	ـصـ	صـ	ص	S	deep guttural 's'
ـض	ـضـ	ضـ	ض	D	deep guttural 'd'

ط	ـطـ	ـطـ	ط	T	deep guttural 't'
ظ	ـظـ	ـظـ	ظ	Z	deep guttural 'dh'
ـع	ـعـ	عـ	ع	a'a	close to a dog growl
ـغ	ـغـ	غـ	غ	gh	emphasised gargling sound
ـف	ـفـ	فـ	ف	f	as in 'for'
ـق	ـقـ	قـ	ق	q	deep guttural 'k'
ـك	ـكـ	كـ	ك	k	as in 'kind'
ـل	ـلـ	لـ	ل	l	as in 'lad'
ـم	ـمـ	مـ	م	m	as in 'map'
ـن	ـنـ	نـ	ن	n	as in 'no'
ـه	ـهـ	هـ	ه	h	as in 'hear'
ـو	ـو	و	و	w	as in 'wall' or the 'o' in food
ـي	ـيـ	يـ	ي	y	as in 'yen' or the 'e' in 'lean'

ESSENTIALS

English	Arabic	French
Good morning	SabaaH el-khayr	Bonjour
Good evening	masaa' el-khayr	Bonsoir
Hello	marHaba	Salut
Goodbye (one leaving)	bkhaaTrak	Au revoir
Goodbye (one staying)	ma' es-salaameh	Au revoir
My name is…	ismee…	Je m'appelle…
What is your name?	shoo ismak? (m), shoo ismik? (f)	Comment vous appelez-vous?
I am from England	ana min ingleterra	Je viens d'Angleterre
I am from America	ana min amerika	Je viens des Etats-Unis
I am from Australia	ana min australia	Je viens d'Australie
How are you?	keefak? (m), keefik? (f)	Comment allez-vous?
Pleased to meet you	tcharrafna/ahlan	Enchanté
Thank you	shukran	Merçi
Don't mention it	ahlan	De rien/je vous en prie
Please	min faDlak (m), faDlik (f)	S'il vous plaît
Yes	na'am/aiwa	Oui
No	laa'	Non
I don't understand	ma fhemet	Je n'ai pas compris
Please would you speak more slowly?	mumkin tiHki 'ala mahlak (m), mahlik (f)?	Pourriez-vous parler plus lentement?

QUESTIONS

English	Arabic	French
Do you understand?	'aam tefham? (m), tefhami? (f)	Comprenez-vous?
How?	keef?	Comment?
What?	shoo?	Quoi?
Where?	wayn?	Où?
What is it?	shoo hayda?	Qu'est-ce que c'est?
Which?	aya…?/ayahoo?/ayeh?	Quel…?/Lequel?
When?	aymta?	Quand?
Why?	laysh?	Pourquoi?
Who?	meen?	Qui?
How much?	adeish?	Combien?

NUMBERS

1	*waHad*	*un*
2	*tnain*	*deux*
3	*tleteh*	*trois*
4	*arba'a*	*quatre*
5	*khamseh*	*cinq*
6	*sitteh*	*six*
7	*sab'aa*	*sept*
8	*tmeneh*	*huit*
9	*tis'aa*	*neuf*
10	*'aashra*	*dix*
11	*hda'ash*	*onze*
12	*tna'ash*	*douze*
13	*tleta'ash*	*treize*
14	*arba'ata'ash*	*quatorze*
15	*khamsta'ash*	*quinze*
16	*sitta'ash*	*seize*
17	*saba'ata'ash*	*dix-sept*
18	*tmenta'ash*	*dix-huit*
19	*tisi'ta'ash*	*dix-neuf*
20	*'eshreen*	*vingt*
30	*tleteen*	*trente*
40	*arba'iin*	*quarante*
50	*khamseen*	*cinquante*
60	*sitteen*	*soixante*
70	*sab'een*	*soixante-dix*
80	*tmeneen*	*quatre-vingts*
90	*tes'een*	*quatre-vingt-dix*
100	*meeyeh*	*cent*
1,000	*alf*	*mille*

TIME

What time is it?	*adeish es-sa'a?*	*Quelle heure est-il?*
It's…am	*es-sa'a…eS-SoboH*	*Il est…du matin*
It's…pm (afternoon)	*es-sa'a…ba'ed eD-Dohr*	*Il est…de l'après-midi*
It's…pm (evening and night)	*es-sa'a…el-masa*	*Il est…du soir*
today	*el-yom*	*aujourd'hui*
tonight	*el-layleh/el-yom el-masa*	*cette nuit/ce soir*
tomorrow	*bookra*	*demain*
yesterday	*mbareH*	*hier*
morning	*eS-SoboH*	*le matin*
evening	*el-masa*	*le soir*

DAYS

Monday	*et-tanain*	*lundi*
Tuesday	*et-taleta*	*mardi*
Wednesday	*el-ourba'a*	*mercredi*
Thursday	*el-khamees*	*jeudi*
Friday	*el-juma'a*	*vendredi*

Saturday	es- sabt	samedi
Sunday	el-aHad	dimanche

MONTHS

January	kanun et-tani	janvier
February	shbaT	février
March	adhar	mars
April	neesan	avril
May	ayar	mai
June	Hzayran	juin
July	tammooz	juillet
August	'aab	août
September	aylool	septembre
October	techreen el-awal	octobre
November	techreen et-tani	novembre
December	kanun el-awal	décembre

GETTING AROUND
Public transport

I'd like…	baddee…	Je voudrais…
…a one-way ticket	…tadhkara rowHa/ tadhkarat zahab	…un billet aller simple
…a return ticket	…tadhkara rowha raj'aa/ tadhkarat zahab wa owda	un billet retour/un aller retour
I want to go to…	baddee rooH 'aala…	Je veux aller à…
How much is it?	adeish Haqo?	Combien ça coûte?
What time does it leave?	aya sa'a biemshi/birooH?	A quelle heure part-il?
What time is it?	adeish es-sa'a?	Quelle heure est-il?
The bus has been delayed	ta'akhar maw 'aad el-baaS	Le bus a été retardé
The bus has been cancelled	eltagha maw 'aad el-baaS	Le bus a été annulé
first class	darajeh oola	…de première classe
second class	darajeh taniyeh	…de seconde classe
ticket office	maktab bay' et-tadhaker	guichet/bureau de vente des billets
timetable	jadwal el-mawa'eed	horaire
map	kharita	carte
from	min	de
to	ila	à
bus station	maHaTat otobees	gare d'autobus/gare routière
airport	maTaar	aéroport
port	marfaa'	port
bus	baaS	autobus/autocar
plane	Tayaara	avion
boat	markab/safeena	bateau
ferry	ferry	ferry / traversier
car	sayaara	voiture
4x4	four by four	quatre quatre

taxi	taxi	taxi
minibus	minibaaS	minibus
motorbike	motoceecle/darrajeh nariyeeh	moto
moped	mobilette	cyclomoteur/vélomoteur
arrival	el-wussool	arrivée
departure	el-inTilaaq	départ
here	hawn	ici
there	honik	là-bas
Safe journey!	safra muwaffaqa/bis-salaameh!	Bon voyage!

Private transport

Is this the road to...?	min hawn Tareeq...?	C'est par là la route de...?
Where is the service station?	wayn maHaTet el-benzine?	Où se trouve la station-service?
Please fill it up	faowilha please/'aabiha law samaHt	Faites-le plein, s'il vous plaît
I'd like...litres	baddee...litre	e voudrais ...litres
diesel	deesel	diesel
leaded petrol	benzine bi-raSaSS	essence au plomb
unleaded petrol	benzine bala raSaSS	essence sans plomb
I have broken down	ta'aTalet sayartee	Je suis en panne

Road signs

give way	afseH eT-Tareeq	céder le passage
danger	khaTar	danger
entry	madkhal	entrée
detour	taHwila	déviation
one way	Tareeq fee ettejah waHed	voie à sens unique
toll	rasem muroor	péage
no entry	mamnoo' ed-dukhool/ 'itijah mamnoo	entrée interdite/ sens interdit
exit	makhraj	sortie
keep clear	ibqa ba' eed	défense d'entrer/ dégager la voie

Directions

Where is...?	Wayn...?	Où se trouve...?
Go straight ahead	rooH deghree (m), rooHee deghree (f)	Allez tout droit
Turn left	brom (m), bremee (f) 'alash-shmel/'alal-yassar	Tournez à gauche
Turn right	brom (m), bremee (f) 'alal-yameen	Tournez à droite
...at the traffic lights	...'ala isharet el-muroor	...aux feux de signalisation
...at the roundabout	...'alal-mustadira	...au rond-point
north	shmel	nord
south	jnoob	sud
east	sharq	est
west	gharb	ouest
behind	wara	derrière

in front of	*edam*	*devant*
near	*janb/Had/qorb*	*près*
opposite	*muqaabil*	*en face de/opposé*

Street signs

entrance	*madkhal*	*entrée*
exit	*makhraj*	*sortie*
open	*maftooH*	*ouvert*
closed	*muqfal/mughlak*	*fermé*
toilets – men	*Hammam rijal*	*toilettes des hommes*
toilets – women	*Hammam sayidat*	*toilettes des dames*
information (desk)	*iste'alamat*	*accueil*
information	*ma'aloomat*	*renseignements/*
informations		

ACCOMMODATION

hotel	*funduq*	*hôtel*
Where is a cheap hotel?	*wayn fee funduq rkhiSS?*	*Où trouver un hôtel bon marché?*
Where is a good hotel?	*wayn fee funduq mneeH?*	*Où trouver un bon hôtel?*
Could you please write the address?	*mumkin tekteblee el-'iinwan?*	*Pourriez-vous m' écrire l'adresse s'il vous plaît?*
Do you have any rooms available?	*'iindak ghoraf faDyee?*	*Avez-vous des chambres libres?*
I'd like…	*baddee…*	*Je voudrais…*
…a single room	*…ghorfee la-shakheSS waHed*	*…une chambre simple*
…a double room	*…ghorfee la-shakhSeiyn/double*	*…une chambre double*
…a room with two beds	*…ghorfee fiha sarirayn*	*…une chambre à deux lits*
…a room with a bathroom	*…ghorfee ma'a Hammam*	*…une chambre avec salle de bains*
…to share a dorm	*…manameh mushtarakeh fi marqad*	*…partager un dortoir*
How much is it per night?	*adeish el-layleh?*	*C'est combien la nuit?*
How much is it per person?	*adeish la-shakheSS waHed?*	*C'est combien par personne?*
Where is the toilet?	*wayn el-Hammam?/ et-twaleet?/el-mirHaaD?*	*Où sont les toilettes?*
Where is the bathroom?	*wayn el-Hammam?*	*Où est la salle de bains?*
Is there hot water?	*fee mai sokhneh?*	*Y a-t-il de l'eau chaude?*
Is there electricity?	*fee kahraba?*	*Y a-t-il de l'électricité*
Is breakfast included?	*fee terwiqa/fee fuToor ma' el-ghorfee?*	*Petit déjeuner compris?*
I am leaving today	*raH etrok el-funduq el-yom*	*Je quitte l'hôtel/je pars aujourd'hui*

FOOD

Do you have a table for…people?	*'iindak Towlee la…ashkhaSS?*	*Avez-vous une table pour… personnes?*

…a children's menu?	*…menu lel-owlad?*	*…un menu pour enfants?*
I am a vegetarian	*ana nabatee*	*Je suis végétarien*
Do you have any vegetarian dishes?	*'iindak aSnaaf lel-nabateyeen?*	*Auriez-vous des plats pour végétariens?*
Please bring me…	*jiblee min faDlak… (m), jibeelee min faDlik… (f)*	*Apportez-moi, s'il vous plaît…*
a fork	*showkeh*	*une fourchette*
a knife	*sekkeen*	*un couteau*
a spoon	*mal 'aaqa*	*une cuillère*
Please may I have the bill?	*mumkin el-Hissab min faDlak?*	*Puis-je avoir l'addition, s'il vous plaît?*

Basics

bread	*khebez*	*pain*
butter	*zebdeh*	*beurre*
cheese	*jebneh*	*fromage*
oil	*zeyt*	*huile*
pepper	*bahar*	*poivre*
salt	*meleH*	*sel*
sugar	*sukkar*	*sucre*

Fruits

apples	*teffaH*	*pommes*
bananas	*mawz*	*bananes*
grapes	*'iinab*	*raisins*
mango	*manga*	*mangues*
oranges	*burtuqal*	*oranges*
pears	*njass*	*poires*

Vegetables

broccoli	*broccoli*	*brocolis*
carrots	*jazar*	*carottes*
garlic	*toom*	*ail*
onion	*baSSal*	*oignon*
peppers	*flayflee*	*poivrons*
potato	*baTaTa*	*pomme de terre*

Fish

mackerel	*samak makreel*	*maquereau*
mussels	*balaH el-baHer*	*moules*
salmon	*salamoon*	*saumon*
tuna	*tuna*	*thon*

Meat

beef	*laHem baqar*	*boeuf*
chicken	*dajaj*	*poulet*
goat	*laHem ma'ez*	*chèvre*
pork	*laHem khanzeer*	*porc*
lamb	*laHem 'ejel*	*agneau*
sausage	*maqaaneq*	*saucisse*

DRINKS

beer	*beera*	*bière*
coffee	*ahweh*	*café*
fruit juice	*'aSSeer fakiha*	*jus de fruit*
milk	*Haleeb*	*lait*
tea	*shai*	*thé*
water	*mai*	*eau*
wine	*nabeedh*	*vin*

SHOPPING

I'd like to buy…	*baddee ishtiree…*	*Je voudrais acheter…*
How much is it?	*adeish Haqo?*	*Combien coûte?*
I don't like it	*ma Habbayto (m), ma Habbayta (f)*	*Je ne l'ai pas aimé (m), aimée (f)*
I'm just looking	*aam betfarraj bass*	*Je voudrais juste regarder/ je regarde seulement*
It's too expensive	*ghalee kteer*	*C'est trop cher*
I'll take it	*raH bekhdo (m), raH bekheda (f)*	*Je le prends (m), je la prends (f)*
Please may I have…?	*mumkin akhod…?*	*Puis-je avoir…?*
Do you accept…	*btiqbal (m)…, btiqbali (f)…*	*Acceptez-vous…*
…credit cards?	*…biTaqat i'itimad?*	*…des cartes de crédits?*
…travellers' cheques?	*…chiccat el-musafer?*	*…des chèques de voyage?*
more	*aktar*	*plus*
less	*aqal*	*moins*
smaller	*aSghar*	*plus petit*
bigger	*akbar*	*plus grand*

COMMUNICATIONS

I am looking for…	*'aam fatesh 'aala…*	*Je cherche…*
bank	*bank*	*banque*
post office	*markaz bareed*	*bureau de poste*
church	*kaneesa*	*église*
embassy	*safaara*	*ambassade*
exchange office	*maktab Sayrafa/Sarraf*	*bureau de change*
telephone centre	*markaz hawatef*	*centre téléphonique*
museum	*matHaf*	*musée*
tourist office	*maktab siyaHa*	*office de tourisme*

HEALTH

diarrhoea	*isshal*	*diarrhée*
nausea	*ghathayan/la'ayan nafess*	*nausée*
doctor	*Tabeeb/Hakeem*	*médecin*
prescription	*waSfeh Tibbeyeh*	*ordonnance*
pharmacy	*Saydaliyeh*	*pharmacie*
paracetamol	*paracetamol*	*paracétamol*
antibiotics	*muDadat Hayaweeyeh*	*antibiotiques*
antiseptic	*muTahher*	*antiseptique*
tampons	*fatila tampon*	*tampon hygiénique*
condoms	*waqee dhakaree*	*préservatif*

Help!	sa'idoonee!/an-najdeh!	Au secours!
Call a doctor!	talfen lal-Hakeem!/laT-Tabeeb!	Appelez le médecin!
There's been an accident	Sar Haadeth	Il y a eu un accident
I'm lost	ana Diy'eh (m), Diy'aa (f)	Je suis perdu (m), perdue (f)
Go away!	rooH min hawn! (m), rooHi min hawn! (f)/imshi!	Allez-vous-en!
police	shorTa	police
fire	Hareeq	incendie
ambulance	is'aaf	ambulance
thief	Haramee	voleur
hospital	mustashfa	hôpital
I am ill	ana mareeD (m), mareeDa (f)	Je suis malade

contraceptive (pills)	huboob mana'a el-haml	pilules contraceptives
sun block	waqi min esh-shams	écran solaire
I am…	ma'ii…	Je suis…
…asthmatic	…raboo	…asthmatique
…epileptic	…daa' eS-Saraa'/epilepsiya	…épileptique
…diabetic	…sukkaree	…diabétique
I'm allergic to…	ma'ii Hassassiya 'ala…	Je suis allergique…
…penicillin	…el-penicillin	…à la pénicilline
…nuts	…el-mukassarat	…aux fruits secs à coque
…bees	…el-naHel	…aux abeilles

TRAVEL WITH CHILDREN

Is there a…	fee…	Y a-t-il…
…baby changing room?	…ghorfee lataghyier el-HifaDat?	…une salle à langer?/ pour changer les couches?
…children's menu?	…menu lel-owlad?	…un menu pour enfants?
Do you have…	'iindak… (m), 'iindik… (f)	Avez-vous…
…infant milk formula?	…Haleeb lel-aTfal?	…du lait maternisé?/ pour enfants ?
nappies	HifaDat	couches
potty	asriyeh/nooneyeh lel-aTfal/ pot lel-aTfal	pot
babysitter	babysitter/jaleesat aTfal	baby-sitter
highchair	kirsi akl lel-aTfal	chaise haute
Are children allowed?	masmooH lel-owlad?	Acceptez-vous les enfants?

OTHER

My/mine	zaherti	mon/le mien (m), ma/la mienne (f)
Your/yours (s)	zahertak (m), zahertik (f)	ton/le tien (m), ta/la tienne (f)
Your/yours (p)	zahretkom	votre/le vôtre (m), la vôtre (f)

Our/ours	zahretna	notre/le nôtre (m), la nôtre (f)
and	wa	et
some	shwayee/kam	un peu de/quelques
but	laken/bass	mais
this	hayda (m), haydee (f)	ceci/celui-ci (m), celle-ci (f)
that	haydaak (m), haydeek (f)	cela/celui-là (m), celle-là (f)
expensive	ghalee (m), ghaliyeh (f	cher (m), chère (f)
cheap	rkhiSS (m), rkhiSa (f)	bon marché/pas cher
beautiful	Helu (m), Helueh (f)	beau (m), belle (f)
ugly	bashe'a/mush Helu	laid (m), laide (f)
old	adeem (m), adeemeh (f)	vieux (m), vieille (f)
new	jdeed (m), jdeedeh (f)	nouveau (m), nouvelle (f)
good	mneeH (m), mneeHa (f)	bon (m), bonne (f)
good (food)	Tayyeb (m), Tayybeh (f)	bon (m), bonne (f)
bad	mush mneeH/'aaTel (m), 'aaTleh (f)	mauvais (m), mauvaise (f)
bad (food)	mush Tayyeb	mauvais/pas bon
early	bakkeer	tôt/en avance
late	muta'akhe	tard/en retard
hot	sokhn (m), sokhneh (f)	chaud (m), chaude (f)
cold	baared (m), baardeh (f)	roid (m), froide (f)
difficult	Sa'eb (m), Sa'abeh (f)	difficile
easy	sahel (m), sahleh (f)	facile
boring	mumel (m), mumelleh (f)	ennuyant (m), ennuyante (f)
interesting	mutheer (m), mutheera (f) lel-ihtimam	intéressant (m), intéressante (f)

Appendix 2

GLOSSARY

Abbasids (750–1258)	The second of the Islamic dynasties who ruled from their capital, Baghdad, until overthrown by the Mongol Empire
Ablaq	Architectural term referring to the technique of using patterns of alternating black and white stonework in a mosque or other building
Allah	God
Amal	Arabic acronym for 'Hope'. Founded in 1975 by Imam Musa al Sadr Amal, is an anti-Israeli, Shi'ite military and political organisation
Arab League	Association of 22 Arab countries established in 1945 by Egypt, Iraq, Lebanon, Saudi Arabia, Syria, Transjordan and Yemen to foster ties and unity across economic, social, military and political fronts
Ashura	Annual sacred Shi'ite festival. It commemorates the Battle of Karbala in AD680 and the martyrdom of Imam Hussein, grandson of the Prophet Muhammad on the tenth day of Muharram (Islamic New Year)
AUB	American University of Beirut
Ayyubids (1183–1250)	Founded by Saladin, they succeeded the Fatimid caliph and ruled from Cairo until superseded by the Mamluk dynasty
Beit	House, also spelt *bait*
Belt of Misery	Generic name for the southern suburbs of Beirut inhabited by Shi'ite refugees from south Lebanon and the Palestinian diaspora in the Sabra and Shatila refugee camps
Black September	Palestinian name for the defeat and expulsion of the Palestine Liberation Organisation by the Jordanian forces of King Hussein in 1970 and the relocating of the organisation's headquarters to Beirut
BMI	British Midland International, UK airline with daily direct flights to Beirut from London (Heathrow) Airport
Caliph	Generic title for all Islamic civil and religious leaders who ruled after the Prophet Muhammad

Cardo Maximus	The principal north–south-oriented street in a typical Roman city
Cedar Revolution	A series of peaceful demonstrations in Lebanon following the assassination of former Prime Minister Rafiq Hariri in 2005, calling for an end to 30 years of Syrian military and political involvement in Lebanese affairs. Under international pressure Syria, withdrew its forces on 14 April 2005.
Chador	A full-length, usually black garment, worn by some Muslim women
Corniche	Coast road or promenade
Cuneiform	A Sumerian invention composed of wedge-like inscriptions etched onto clay tablets and often regarded as the earliest known form of writing
Dabke	Lebanon's lively national folk dance
Decumanus Maximus	The principal east–west street in a typical Roman city
Deir	Convent or monastery
Diaspora	General term for the 'dispersion' of the Arab, Jewish and Palestinian peoples
Druze	Unique religious sect, derived from Islamic philosophy. The Druze comprise around 5% of Lebanon's population with additional communities in Israel and the Palestinian Territories, Syria and Jordan.
Eid	Feast or festival
Eid Al-Adha	Muslim festival and feast following the annual pilgrimage to Mecca
Eid Al-Fitr	Muslim festival and feast at the end of the fast of Ramadan
Eisenhower Doctrine	Formulated by President Eisenhower in 1957, it stated that any country could request military assistance from the US if threatened by aggression. First used at request of pro-Western Maronite president Camille Chamoun in 1958, when 15,000 US marines landed in Beirut to quell Arab nationalism.
Emir	Islamic leader or other high-ranking official, also spelt *amir*
Fakhr al-Din II (c1572–1635)	Widely seen as Lebanon's first national hero for uniting the nation during the Ottoman era. His expansionist ideology was eventually seen as a threat to Ottoman dominance and he was executed in Istanbul in 1635.
Fatimids (909–1171)	Cairo-based Shi'ite dynasty whose founder, Abdullah al-Mahdi Billah, claimed descent from the Prophet Muhammad's daughter, Fatima, and her husband Ali ibn-Abi Talib
Fertile Crescent	Arc of fertile agricultural land extending from Egypt to Iraq

Funduq	Hotel
Green Line	The border in Beirut which divided the Muslim western portion and Christian eastern section of the city during the civil war of 1975–90
Hajj	Muslim pilgrimage to Mecca
Hammam	Traditional Turkish steam bathhouse usually offering a sauna followed by a massage
Hezbollah	Party of God. A Shi'ite Muslim resistance movement and political party formed in 1982.
Hijab	Headscarf worn by some Muslim women
Hijra	Arabic word for 'migration' referring to the Prophet Muhammad's journey from Mecca to Medina in AD622, which heralded the start of the Islamic calendar
Hyksos	Nomadic Semitic tribe from west Asia who conquered Egypt, interrupting Phoenician– Egyptian trade relations for about three decades from 1600BC to 1570BC. They introduced new weapons and tools of warfare such as the composite bow and the horse-drawn chariot.
Hypocaust	a system of under-floor heating devised by the Romans to heat their public baths and houses by means of a raised floor held up by ceramic tiles through which hot air would freely circulate
IDF	Israel Defence Force
Iftar	Evening meal following the breaking of the Ramadan fast
Imam	Islamic religious leader
Islam	The religion practised by Muslims; literally, 'submission' or 'surrender' to God
Islamic Jihad	Muslim fundamentalist group, sometimes referring to the military wing of Hezbollah
Jebel	Mountain
Jihad	Ambiguous word which is Arabic for 'struggle' or 'striving in the way of Allah'. It commonly refers to a Muslim Holy War against non-Muslims, but also has a more personal or spiritual dimension that can be expressed by the tongue and the hand in the sense of attaining perfect faith and living a moral and virtuous life.
Kaaba	Black cube-shaped building within the Masjid al-Haram or Great Mosque in Mecca which is circumnavigated anti-clockwise many times by *hajj* pilgrims
Khalwat	Druze place of retreat and worship
Khan	Generic name for a travellers' inn in the Middle East, consisting of a central courtyard usually surrounded by the upper level living quarters, a ground floor for stables and a storage area and marketplace (eg: Khan al-Franj in Sidon)
Koran	Islam's Holy Book

LCC	Lebanese Commuting Company, providing private bus services throughout Greater Beirut and parts of Mount Lebanon
Levant	Eastern Mediterranean landmasses including Egypt, Israel and the Palestinian Territories, Jordan, Lebanon, Syria and the island of Cyprus. Literally, the land of the 'rising sun'.
Madrasa	Arabic for 'school' and usually associated with educational institutions offering instruction in the Koran and theology
Mamluks (1260–1516)	Islamic dynasty comprising former Turkish slaves who ruled over large parts of Lebanon and Syria from their capital in Cairo until overthrown by the Ottoman Empire
Maronite Christians	Breakaway Monothelite Lebanese Christians whose origins date back to Saint Maroun in AD400 and whose doctrinal faith holds that Christ had two natures but operated with a divine will
MEA	Middle East Airlines–Air Liban, Lebanon's national airline
Mihrab	Prayer niche in a mosque indicating the direction of Mecca
Millet System	Hierarchical system of governing during the Ottoman Empire in Mount Lebanon according to religion and sect
Minaret	The slender and tallest architectural feature of a mosque comprising the base, shaft and gallery from which the *muezzin* announces the call to prayer
Muezzin	Muslim cleric who calls the faithful to prayer from the minaret of a mosque
Murex	Shellfish or mollusc from which the ancient Phoenicians extracted the prized purple dye of Tyre
Mutasariffa	Administrative unit of the Ottoman Empire, for example, Mount Lebanon
Nahr	River
Nargileh	Water-pipe, *sheesha* or hubble-bubble for smoking fragrant tobacco
National Pact	Unwritten constitution agreed in 1943 designed to equalise power between Lebanon's various religious groups
Necropolis	An ancient burial site
Pasha	Governor, general or other high-ranking official of the Ottoman Empire
Phalange	Lebanese Christian political party and militia founded in 1936 by Pierre Gemayel; instrumental in the onset of the Lebanese civil war
PLO	Palestine Liberation Organisation

Qalaa	Castle or fort
Qibla	Direction to which Muslims turn during prayer, ie: towards Mecca
Ramadan	Ninth month of the Islamic calendar during which practising Muslims abstain from eating, drinking, smoking and sexual activity from sunrise until sunset
Ras	Headland
Sahat	Square
Saladin (1174–93)	Kurdish military leader who founded the Ayyubid dynasty and recaptured Jerusalem, Aleppo and Sidon from the Crusaders
Saray	Palace
Seleucids (312–63BC)	Monarchical dynasty founded by Seleucus Nicator following the death of Alexander the Great and the partition of his Macedonian Empire among his generals. At its height, the dynasty ruled over Lebanon and a vast area of west Asia.
Serail	Ottoman-era palace
Servees	service (shared) taxi
Sharia	Islamic law which informs the everyday life and conduct of Muslims
Shi'ite	Islamic sect who believe that only the Prophet Muhammad's son-in-law and cousin Ali and his successors – the 'partisans' of Ali – can be rightful *caliphs*
Solidere	The Lebanese Company for the Development and Reconstruction of Beirut Central District (BCD)
Souk	Arabic market
Special Tribunal for Lebanon	International court which began its work in 2009, at the request of the Lebanese government and under the auspices of the UN, to bring to justice those responsible for the killing of former prime minister Rafiq Hariri and others in 2005
Stela (pl *Stelae*)	stone slab(s) usually containing carvings or inscriptions such as those at Nahr al-Kalb (Dog River)
Sunni	The larger of the two main Islamic sects. Sunnis follow the tradition of *sunna* or life of the Prophet Muhammad and the Koran. They believe that successive *caliphs* unrelated to the prophet can succeed him. Sunnis represent some 90% of the world's Muslims.
Sykes–Picot Agreement (1916)	Agreement between Britain and France which gave the latter control over Mount Lebanon and Syria following the anticipated Allied victory over Germany and the Ottoman Empire at the end of World War I

Taif Accord (1989)	The agreement reached at Taif, in Saudi Arabia, which balanced confessional power between Muslims and Christians and ended the Lebanese civil war
Tell	artificial archaeological hill or mound resulting from successive generations of earlier human settlement
Tetrapylon	A typically Roman-style structure consisting of four pillars, often built at a crossroads or junction in a town. The term derives from the Greek word *tetra* meaning four
Umayyads (661–750)	First Arab dynasty of Sunni Muslims who ruled from Damascus
UN	United Nations
UNESCO	United Nations Economic, Social and Cultural Organisation
UNIFIL	United Nations Interim Force in Lebanon, established in 1978 as a multi-national peacekeeping force in the south of the country
UNRWA	United Nations Relief Works Agency
Wadi	Seasonal valley or riverbed
Waqf	Islamic religious (charitable) endowment

FOOD AND BEVERAGES

Almaza	Lebanon's local bottled and draught lager beer, available in alcoholic and non-alcoholic versions
Arak	The national drink of Lebanon, this highly alcoholic aniseed beverage is often drunk to accompany *mezze*
Baklava	Very sweet dessert made from filo pastry stuffed with nuts, syrup or honey and pistachios
Falafel	Round balls of fried chickpeas or fava beans often served in a pitta bread wrap or as part of a *mezze* dish
Fattoush	Crisp textured mixed salad comprising cucumber, garlic, lemon, mint, onions, parsley, tomatoes and toasted bread
Hummus	Creamy dip dish made from mashed chickpeas, lemon juice, olive oil and garlic and eaten with pitta bread
Ka'ik	Large, ring-shaped bread, often eaten as a snack, and garnished with sesame seeds
Kibbeh	The national dish comprising *burghol* (crushed wheat), chopped beef or lamb and fried in olive oil. They resemble a cross between Scotch eggs and a torpedo. Sometimes eaten raw.
Knefeh	A warm pastry dessert filled with cheese and topped with cream or syrup and nuts. Often eaten for breakfast and the preferred sweet after the *iftar* meal which breaks the Ramadan fast.

Labneh	A delicate creamy cheese made from yoghurt (similar to fromage frais) and garnished with olive oil and garlic
Man'oushe	A kind of pizza topped with cheese or thyme and a popular breakfast dish
Mezze	Hors d'oeuvres. An assortment of hot and/or cold dishes which comprise a Lebanese meal, eg: *tabbouleh, hummus, fattoush, labneh*
Moutabel	Slices of grilled aubergine with lemon juice and olive oil
Qamareddine	A thirst-quenching apricot drink, consumed after the Ramadan fast
Sanioura	A sweet and sugary crumbly biscuit from the southern city of Sidon
Shawarma	Chicken or lamb döner kebab
Shish Tawouk	Grilled boneless chicken flavoured with olive oil, garlic and lemon juice
Tabbouleh	Mixed salad consisting of parsley, onions, chopped tomatoes and cracked wheat with lemon juice and olive oil

Appendix 3

FURTHER INFORMATION

BOOKSHOPS In London, Foyles (*www.foyles.co.uk*) and Stanfords (*www.stanfords. co.uk*) both have a good range of travel and Middle Eastern literary sources. The bookshops below, however, are more specialised and offer a greater range of works devoted to Lebanon and the wider Middle East.

UK

Al Saqi Bookshop 26 Westbourne Grove, London W2 5RH; ☎ 020 7229 8543; e enquiries@ alsaqibookshop.com; www.alsaqibookshop.com. This is the largest Middle Eastern bookseller in the UK.

Arthur Probsthain 41 Great Russell St, London WC1B 3PE; ☎ 020 7636 1096; e ap@oriental-african-books.com, arthurprobsthain@hotmail. com; www.apandtea.co.uk. A long established bookshop since 1903 specialising in antiquarian & hard to find books by publishers worldwide.

Daunt Books 83 Marylebone High St, London W1U 4QW; ☎ 020 7224 2295; e Marylebone@ dauntbooks.co.uk; www.dauntbooks.co.uk. Also

has 5 other London branches at Belsize Park, Cheapside, Chelsea, Hampstead & Holland Park.

The Maghreb Bookshop 45 Burton St, London WC1H 9AL; ☎ 020 7388 1840; e Maghreb@ maghrebreview.com; www.maghreb-studies-association.co.uk. Stocks new, rare & out of print works on the Middle East & Islam.

SOAS Bookshop Brunei Gallery Bldg, School of Oriental & African Studies, Thornhaugh St, Russell Sq, London WC1H 0XG; ☎ 020 7898 4470; e bookshop@soas.ac.uk; www.soas.ac.uk/ visitors/bookshop. Academic, historical & cultural books on the Middle East region.

The following specialist independent book publisher is also worth keeping an eye on, as they produce around 300 titles annually on a variety of Middle Eastern countries and topics.

I B Tauris & Co Ltd 6 Salem Rd, London W2 4BU; ☎ 020 7243 1225; www.ibtauris.com

Republic of Ireland
Easons 40 Lower O'Connell St, Dublin 1, Ireland; ☎ 1 858 3800; e sales@easons.com; www. easons.ie

USA
The Globe Corner Bookstore 90 Mt Auburn St, Harvard Sq, Cambridge, MA 02138;

☎ 617 497 6277; e info@gcb.com; www.globecorner.com

BOOKS The literature on Lebanon is quite extensive and growing and dates back to the time of antiquity with Strabo, Homer and Herodotus among the classical scholars who have written about the country. The selections below are those which should give the reader further illuminating insights into Lebanon and the wider Middle East region. All the books listed should be available at the outlets mentioned above, secondhand bookshops or at the very least online at www.amazon.com. Failing that, try www.usedbooksearch.co.uk which at the last count had a worldwide database of 100 million used books, giving details of suppliers and prices.

Civil war

Fisk, Robert *Pity the Nation: Lebanon at War* Oxford: Oxford University Press, 1992. First published 1990. Thorough and poignant analysis of Lebanon's civil strife by the *The Independent* newspaper's veteran Middle East correspondent.

Folman, Ari *Waltz with Bashir: A Lebanon War Story* New York: Metropolitan Books, 2009. One man's recurring and disturbing dream and consequent psychoanalytic journey to uncover his role in the 1982 massacres at the Palestinian camps of Sabra and Shatila. This graphic book was also made into an award winning animated film.

Gilmour, David *Lebanon: The Fractured Country* Basingstoke: Palgrave Macmillan, 1983. A good account of the history of the country's civil unrest from 1975.

Haugbolle, Sune *War and Memory in Lebanon* Cambridge: Cambridge University Press, 2010. An intriguing and insightful analysis of the ways in which intellectuals and activists used cultural mores such as media, art, literature, film, and architecture, in an attempt to make sense of Lebanon's protracted 1975–90 civil war, in opposition to a state which was more interested in engendering a collective amnesia of the events.

Hiro, Dilip *Lebanon: Fire and Embers – A History of the Lebanese Civil War* London: Weidenfeld and Nicolson, 1993. An account of the minutiae of internal and external events leading to the 1975–90 civil war.

Keenan, Brian *An Evil Cradling* London: Vintage Books, 1993. First published 1992. A now classic and poignant account of this former hostage's time in captivity in Lebanon during the civil war, focusing on both his own and his peers' experiences.

McCarthy, John and Morrell, Jill *Their own Story: Some Other Rainbow* London: Transworld Publishers Ltd, 1994. John McCarthy's experiences as a hostage for five years in Lebanon, his friendship with Brian Keenan and the tireless endeavours of partner Jill Morrell to secure his release, together with her own psychological deprivation.

Reed, Eli and Ajami, Fouad *Beirut: City of Regrets* New York: W W Norton, 1988. Penetrating and insightful photojournalism of the 1975–90 civil war from Magnum photographer Reed.

Cookery

Dekmak, Hussein *The Lebanese Cookbook* London: Kyle Cathie Ltd, 2006

Hamady, Mary Laird *Lebanese Mountain Cookery* Massachusetts: David R Godine, 1995

Helou, Anissa *Lebanese Cuisine: More than 250 Authentic Recipes from the Most Elegant Middle Eastern Cuisine* New York: Grub Street, 1994

Karam, Michael *Arak and Mezze: The Taste of Lebanon* London: Saqi Books, 2008

Karam, Michael *Wines of Lebanon* London: Saqi Books, 2005

Khalife, Maria *The Mezze Cookbook: Over 90 Delicious Appetizers from Greece, Lebanon and Turkey* London: New Holland Publishers Ltd, 2008

Saleh, Nada *Fragrance of the Earth: Lebanese Home Cooking* London: Saqi Books, 1996

Salloum, Mary *A Taste of Lebanon: Cooking Today the Lebanese Way* New York: Interlink Books, 2001. First published 1988.

Flora

Haber, Ricardus M and Haber, Semaan Myrna *Floral Enchantment to Lebanon* Beirut: Edition Terre du Liban, 2009. Large format book with lovely colour photos of Lebanon's wide-ranging flora.

Haber, Ricardus M and Haber, Semaan Myrna *Orchids of Lebanon* Beirut: 2009. Another coffee-table book with beautiful colour photos.

Houri, Ahmad and Houri, Machaka Nisrine *Photographic Guide to Wild Flowers of Lebanon (Vol 2)* Beirut: AFDC, 2008. Pocket-size guide, with colour photos, giving detailed Latin and English names of Lebanon's flora.

Tohme, Georges and Tohme, Henriette *Illustrated Flora of Lebanon: 2600 Wild Flowers* National Council for Scientific Research, 2007

Health

Ellis, Matthew and Wilson-Howarth, Jane *Your Child Abroad: A Travel Health Guide* Bradt Travel Guides, 2005. An invaluable guide for those travelling or resident overseas with babies and children of all ages.

History and politics

Abulafia, David *The Great Sea: A Human History of the Mediterranean* London: Allen Lane 2011. Although not dealing with Lebanon specifically, this is an excellent and vivid approach to the subject, which brings to life the eclectic characters and individuals who have sailed the Mediterranean and Levant from antiquity to the present day. An excellent read for an overview of the region.

Barr, James *A Line in the Sand: Britain, France and the Struggle That Shaped the Middle East* London: Simon & Schuster, 2011. A thorough account which focusses on the 1916 Sykes-Picot Agreement together with the internal conflicts which ensued between Anglo-French interests.

Blanford, Nicholas *Killing Mr Lebanon: The Assassination of Rafiq Hariri and its impact on the Middle East* London: I B Tauris, 2006. An absorbing and highly detailed account drawing on interviews with many of Lebanon's key political figures and main players in the country's affairs together with background information on Hariri himself to elucidate the dynamics at work in his killing and why it continues to resonate throughout the region and beyond.

Bregman, Ahron and El-Tahri, Jihan *The Fifty Years War: Israel and the Arabs* London: Penguin and BBC Books, 1998. A good general overview of the Arab–Israeli conflict for the lay reader.

Catherwood, Christopher *A Brief History of The Middle East* London: Constable and Robinson, 2006. A good introduction and basis for further reading.

Fawaz, Tarazi Leila *An Occasion for War: Civil Conflict in Lebanon and Damascus in 1860* California: University of California Press, 1994. An excellent account of the Druze/Christian Mountain War of 1860.

Fisk, Robert *The Great War for Civilisation: The Conquest of the Middle East* London: Harper Perennial, 2006. A mighty paperback tome but worth the effort for its insightful analysis and regional sweep of events.

Friedman, Thomas *From Beirut to Jerusalem* London: HarperCollins, 1995. Journalistic account of two cities at the epicentre of the Middle East conflict.

Hirst, David *Beware of Small States: Lebanon, Battleground of the Middle East* London: Faber and Faber, 2010. A book which places Lebanon's past woes in the context of the wider international scene.

Hourani, Albert *A History of the Arab Peoples* London: Faber and Faber, 2005. First published 1991. A seminal work on the subject from the late renowned Arab historian. Highly recommended reading.

Jaber, Hala *Hezbollah: Born with a Vengeance* New York: Columbia University Press, 1997. Excellent account of the foundation and philosophy of this organisation with illuminating insights, which go beyond the media stereotypes.

Llewellyn, Tim *Spirit of the Phoenix: Beirut and the Story of Lebanon* London: I B Tauris, 2010. Interesting attempt by a former BBC correspondent to get under the skin of the country to explain the country's conflicts and divisions and the resilience of the Lebanese people.

Mackey, Sandra *Mirror of the Arab World: Lebanon in Conflict* New York: W W Norton, 2009. Another book which places Lebanon's crises and problems in a wider Middle East context.

Mansfield, Peter *A History of the Middle East* London: Penguin, 2010. Third edition. First published 2003. Historical and political overview of the region over the past 200 years.

Miles, Richard *Carthage Must Be Destroyed: The Rise and Fall of an Ancient Civilisation* London: Allen Lane, 2010. Although dealing with Carthage, this book is interesting reading for its historical sweep of the Levant in general and the ancient Phoenicians' presence in Lebanon.

Rawlinson, George *Phoenicia: History of a Civilisation* London: I B Tauris, 2005. Good account of this enterprising and innovative civilisation.

Rogan, Eugene *The Arabs: A History* London: Allen Lane, 2009. Highly readable, vivid and scholarly account of Arab history ranging widely across the Arab world from the Ottoman Empire to the present day with insightful analysis of Arab antipathy towards the West today.

Salibi, Kamal *A House of Many Mansions: The History of Lebanon Reconsidered*

London: I B Tauris, 2009. First published 1998. The author eschews a linear interpretation of Lebanese history in favour of a more analytical and critical approach to his country's conflicts and divisions.

Traboulsi, Fawwaz *A History of Modern Lebanon* London: Pluto Press, 2007. A classic and scholarly history of Lebanon since Ottoman times.

Language

Arnander, Primrose and Skipwith, Ashkhain *Upload Your Own Donkey* London: Stacey International, 2002. Although not a conventional language guide, this book is full of Arabic proverbs and sayings with their English translations and makes for an edifying and humorous read.

In-Flight Arabic: Learn Before You Land New York: Living Language, 2001. A crash course (so to speak).

McLoughlin, Leslie *Colloquial Arabic (Levantine): The Complete Course for Beginners* Oxon: Routledge, 2009. Second edition. First published 1982. Available as a book and CD package or separately, this is highly recommended if you want a good grasp of Arabic including the linguistic nuances which make up everyday life in Lebanon and the Levant.

Travel writing, novels and biographies

Al-Shaykh, Hanan *The Locust and the Bird: My Mother's Story* London: Bloomsbury, 2009. The themes of forced marriage, infidelity, resilience and survival are explored in this account of Lebanese author Al-Shaykh's mother and her home life.

Dalrymple, William *From the Holy Mountain: A Journey in the Shadow of Byzantium* London: Harper Perennial, 2005. First published 1997. Much-acclaimed book in which the author retraces the steps of two Byzantine monks which takes him from Greece through Turkey, Syria, Lebanon, Israel, Jordan and Egypt, and analysing the legacy of Christianity.

Ellis, Kirsten *Star of the Morning: The Extraordinary Life of Lady Hester Stanhope* London: Harper Collins, 2008. A meticulously researched, comprehensive and evocative account of this adventurous and independent woman traveller.

Gibb, Lorna *Lady Hester: Queen of the East* London: Faber and Faber, 2006. A very vivid account exploring the eccentricities of the life of the nonconformist Lady Hester.

Gibran, Khalil *The Prophet* New York: Alfred A Knopf, 1992. First published 1923. Gibran's seminal work ranges deeply across the whole gamut of human life from clothes to love, pain and pleasure.

Gorton, Andree Féghali and Gorton, Ted *Lebanon: Through Writers' Eyes* London: Eland, 2009. Collection of writings from antiquity to the modern era vividly illustrating the diversity and complexity of the country often neglected by the media headlines.

Khalaf, Roseanne Saad (Ed) *Hikayat: Short Stories by Lebanese Women* London: Telegram Books, 2006. An anthology of writings from Lebanese authors exploring such issues as identity, love, marriage and sex.

Khoury, Elias *Yalo* London: Quercus, 2009. Psycho-social novel in which the crimes, confusions and contradictions of a young man, Yalo, are set against the similarly chaotic background of Lebanon's civil war.

Najjar, Alexandre *Kahlil Gibran: A Biography* London: Saqi Books, 2008. Good book on Lebanon's well loved writer and philosopher.

Shimon, Samuel (Ed) *Beirut39: New Writing from the Arab World* London:

Bloomsbury, 2010. Poems and short stories across a range of subject areas from 39 emerging writers, all aged under 40, from across the Arab world.

Thubron, Colin *The Hills of Adonis: A Quest in Lebanon* London: Vintage Books, 2008. First published 1968. A now classic account of the author's four-month journey in 1967 of a bygone age in Lebanon. His descriptions of his encounters with the Druze, Maronites and Shi'ites *en route* make for fascinating reading.

Wildlife

Christensen, S, Porter, R and Schiermacker-Hansen, P *Field Guide to the Birds of the Middle East* London: Christopher Helm, 2010. First published 2004.

Larsen, T B *Butterflies of Lebanon* Beirut: Librairie du Liban, 1974. Nicely illustrated book on the subject.

FILMS There are a number of cinematic offerings which deal, not surprisingly perhaps, with various aspects of Lebanon's bloody past and include *Beirut Oh Beirut* (1975), directed by Cannes award winner Maroun Baghdadi, and B*eirut: The Last Home Movie* (1988), directed by Jennifer Cox and examining the attempts of a privileged Beirut family to maintain their lifestyle amid the carnage of war. Palestinian director Mai Masri's *Children of Shatila* (1998) looks at this infamous camp through the video narratives of the children who live there. Ziad Doueiri's *West Beirut* (1998) tells the often funny and touching rites of passage tale of two young boys growing up during the initial phase of the Lebanese civil war.

A unique perspective on the 1982 Lebanon War – shot from inside an Israeli tank – is the autobiographical and cathartic *Lebanon* (2009) which charts the catastrophic journey, geographically and psychologically, of the film's writer and director Samuel Maoz and his cohorts, as the young recruits negotiate the raw realities of war. The film won the Golden Lion Award for Best Film at the 2009 Venice Film Festival, and also the Satyajit Ray Award.

A couple of recent films worth tracking down, and notable for their move away from the documentary/war genre are *Caramel* (2007), which saw the directorial debut of Lebanese actress Nadine Labaki and which had its premiere at the 2007 Cannes Film Festival. It tells the stories of five women in a beauty salon and explores issues such as ageing, lesbianism, religious tradition and other universal human issues. Jocelyne Saab, veteran of some 20 documentary films, ventures into the realm of the surreal with *What's Going On?* (2010), exploring issues of women, identity and equality against the background of the complexities of life in modern-day Beirut.

There are many more films about Lebanon (and the wider Middle East region) and several of these are available via mail or online order from the **Arab Film Foundation** (*Suite 514, 3131 Western Av, Seattle WA 98121, USA;* \ *206 322 0882;* e *info@arabfilm.com; www.arabfilm.com*).

WEBSITES
Blogs

www.plus961.com Interesting and humorous musings about Lebanon from citizen journalist, Rami.

www.beirutspring.com/blog All manner of society and political topics are discussed here from Hezbollah to *hummus* by Tripoli resident Mustapha.

www.bloggingbeirut.com Eclectic blog covering serious and not so serious Lebanese issues and affairs.

www.mayazankoul.com Maya, a young Lebanese designer, uses a series of cathartic cartoons as release for the 'daily hassles' she experiences living in Lebanon.

www.shankaboot.com This Emmy Award-winning docu-drama, first broadcast in March 2010 and in its fourth series at the time of writing, is enlivened with humour and is the first Arabic based web series in the world offering a slice of Beiruti life through the eyes and experiences of its young protagonists.

www.shoofimafi.com Loosely translated, ShooFiMaFi means 'wassup'. This blog is a cornucopia of information on a wide range of topics and has good background information on Lebanon. The quirky 'Only in Lebanon' page makes this a must-read blog.

Newspapers and magazines

www.agendaculturel.com Bi-weekly magazine and website, in French, giving details of the capital's arts and cultural events.

www.annahar.com *An-Nahar* is Lebanon's largest circulation daily newspaper in Arabic.

www.dailystar.com.lb Lebanon's sole English language daily newspaper, with good coverage of local, national and international current affairs.

www.femmemag.com.lb Women's lifestyle magazine serving the usual journalistic diet of lifestyle, hair and beauty, together with profiles of local and international personalities and celebrities.

www.lorientlejour.com The French equivalent of *The Daily Star*.

www.mmorning.com *Monday Morning* is a weekly glossy digest of national and international news together with sections on Lebanese lifestyle. *Time* meets *Hello!* magazine.

www.opportunities.com.lb *Lebanon Opportunities* is a monthly magazine covering real estate, finance, business and general economic issues.

www.prestigemag.com Monthly lifestyle magazine for well-heeled socialite women concentrating on parties, weddings, health and beauty.

www.rdl.com.lb *La Revue du Liban* is the French equivalent to *Monday Morning* above.

www.timeoutbeirut.com Lebanon's version of London's long-established what's on, where and when listings magazine. A very useful resource.

www.yalibnan.com An online-only news resource from Lebanese journalists offering a less partisan view than many of Lebanon's other newspapers.

Useful travel information

www.cia.gov *World Fact Book* providing a range of country data across economic, political and social indicators.

www.destinationlebanon.gov.lb Excellent and comprehensive website from Lebanon's official Ministry of Tourism.

www.discoverlebanon.com Everything Lebanon.

www.fco.gov.uk Website of the British Foreign and Commonwealth Office offering up-to-date advice on travel safety and security in Lebanon and around the world.

www.lebanon.com A range of information including shopping, tours, weather, entertainment and online discussion forum of all things Lebanon.

www.lebrecord.com An excellent online only art magazine featuring artist interviews, trends and a calendar of events covering the whole gamut of the visual arts around the country.

www.lebanonroad.blogspot.com A good and well-organised site with useful background and practical information on the country together with a decent overview of where to eat and stay, what to do and useful suggestions for tours around Lebanon.

www.nowlebanon.com Acronym for New Opinion Workshop. Nowlebanon is an independent forum established in the wake of the 2005 Cedar Revolution to champion the cause for an independent Lebanon through debate of the key economic, political and social issues.

www.skileb.com Contains a wealth of detail on winter sports and outdoor activities in the country. An excellent cornucopia of information.

www.state.gov Website of the US Department of State with useful information on Lebanese history, its people, government, economy and much more. Less statistically based than the CIA site above.

www.travel-to-lebanon.com Excellent website for planning your visit to Lebanon with many useful links.

www.worldbank.org World Bank entry on Lebanon, giving statistics and information across economic, social and a range of other indices.

www.xe.com World currency converter.

Index

Page numbers in **bold** refer to major entries; those in *italics* indicate maps